MW00583689

PEOPLING THE CONSTITUTION

CONSTITUTIONAL THINKING

Jeffrey K. Tulis and Sanford Levinson
Editors

PEOPLING THE CONSTITUTION

John E. Finn

University Press of Kansas

© 2014 by the University Press of Kansas
All rights reserved

Published by the University Press of Kansas (Lawrence, Kansas 66045),
which was organized by the Kansas Board of Regents and is operated
and funded by Emporia State University, Fort Hays State University,
Kansas State University, Pittsburg State University, the University of
Kansas, and Wichita State University

Library of Congress Cataloging-in-Publication Data

Finn, John E., author.
Peopling the constitution / John E. Finn.
pages cm. — (Constitutional thinking)
Includes bibliographical references and index.
ISBN 978-0-7006-1962-7
1. Constitutional law—United States. I. Title.
KF4550.F55 2014
342.73'0011—DC23
2013045168

British Library Cataloguing-in-Publication Data is available.

Printed in the United States of America

10 8 6 4 2 1 3 5 7

The paper used in this publication is recycled and contains 30
percent postconsumer waste. It is acid free and meets the minimum
requirements of the American National Standard for Permanence of
Paper for Printed Library Materials z39.48-1992.

FOR ALEX AND ELLERY

Reality leaves a lot to the imagination.

—John Lennon

CONTENTS

FOREWORD

"There is hardly a political question in the United States which does not sooner or later turn into a judicial one." This famous observation is one of the most profound insights in *Democracy in America,* and it allowed Alexis de Tocqueville to show the world that modern democracies could overcome their natural tendency to succumb to majority tyranny. Democracies, he argued, tend to neglect forms and formalities and thereby gave free rein to the brute preferences of overbearing majorities. Majority tyranny could be precluded or ameliorated by democratic practices and institutions modeled on admirable aspects of aristocracy. A well-designed democracy could learn from aristocracy without becoming an actual aristocracy based on inherited social classes. These lessons from aristocracy could enable democracies to avoid their worst tendencies while enhancing the best attributes of democratic rule. The American institution he held in highest esteem—his surrogate for an aristocracy within a democracy—was the legal system, lawyers and judges.

Tocqueville's prediction that political reasoning would be supplanted by legal discourse and practice in American historical development could not have been more right. His prescience was truly stunning. Lawyers dominate the American political world today, and constitutional thinking is understood to be legal reasoning by nearly all citizens in the United States. However, Tocqueville's argument that this development would mark the maturation of a healthy democracy could not have been more wrong.

In the wide-ranging and probing book that you have before you, John Finn shows that the reliance on law, on the specialized language of lawyers, and on the assumption that constitutional questions require legal answers—which Finn labels the "Juridic Constitution"—is the very source of America's most serious political pathologies. Because the Juridic Constitution supplanted "the Civic Constitution"—an idea Finn first wrote about and a term he coined in an article published in 2001—American citizens are now distanced from, and often ignorant about, politics, and American politicians are incapable of even discussing and identifying, let alone solving, the nation's most serious political challenges. Features of legal reasoning that Tocqueville found so attractive, such as its reliance on specialized experts and on a technical language, depoliticized the American regime. Ordinary citizens retreated into their private worlds and left the practice of politics to lawyers or to politicians who deferred to lawyers and judges.

Ironically, the Juridic Constitution destroyed the constitutional vitality of another feature of American political life that both Tocqueville and John Finn agree is essential to the health of any well-designed democracy—voluntary associations and local political practices. Finn shows that these Tocquevillian practices are better understood as necessary features of the Constitution itself than as the cultural conditions for a Constitution understood as a "legal" instrument above and outside of society and the private sphere. It is in the associative life that Tocqueville so admired that constitutional thinking is best taught, learned, and practiced. Tocqueville failed to see how his ersatz aristocracy would sap democratic vitality and diminish the meaning and practice of citizenship.

John Finn makes the case for a civic understanding of constitutional theory and for a constitutional understanding of civic education. He returns constitutional theory to its political roots, and he develops a constitutional capacity for civic education. Although the Juridic Constitution has been very harmful to American political health, Finn does not argue that it should be eliminated. Rather he offers a capacious view of the Constitution and of constitutional theory in which both the Civic and Juridic Constitutions have their rightful places. Because the Juridic Constitution looms so large in contemporary America, Finn devotes most of his attention in this book to developing the civic alternative.

In developing a systematic account of the Civic Constitution, Finn draws upon much work by others who share a view of the Constitution as a political design containing a legal order within it. Some have labeled this political orientation the "Princeton School" of constitutional theory because many scholars working in this tradition were colleagues or students of Walter Murphy, a very influential Princeton professor with whom Finn himself studied. The Princeton School sought to develop an extrajudicial constitutional point of view, and it drew upon work in political science, political theory, and other disciplines. In addition to his own clear and original argument, one of the wonderful merits of John Finn's book is that it offers the best synthesis of this larger ambit of work and it brings the fruits of the Princeton School into conversation with leading "juridical" constitutional theorists in the legal academy. Finn prosecutes his thesis in a way that serves as a superb introduction to the entire field of constitutional theory and to the writings of political and social theorists of education and civic life.

The book is divided into three large sections that would reflect the principal concerns of a political architect: the founding, maintenance, and potential failure of political regimes. One could describe this orientation as Aristotelian because Finn looks at American politics as a whole, as a regime. Modern liberal democracies, and the scholars within them, tend to view and interpret politics from some part of the whole—such as the economy, legal system, or culture—because one of the hallmarks of modern politics is the separation of the private sphere from public life. Even though we rightly value privacy and individual liberty, Finn shows that the Constitution and public life necessarily superintend or configure the so-called private sphere. Thus, a perspective on the whole regime is as necessary in modern America as it was in ancient Athens. John Finn's articulation of the "Civic Constitution" offers a cogent regime perspective for our time.

Jeffrey Tulis
Coeditor

ACKNOWLEDGMENTS

I am in cheerful debt to the many friends and colleagues who helped me with this project. Among them are Bobbi Adams, Beau Breslin, Corey Brett-schneider, Bradley Hays, Gary Jacobsohn, Donald Kommers, Brett Marston, Walter Murphy, Robert Nagel, Miguel Schor, George Thomas, Keith Whittington, and at the University Press of Kansas, Sanford Levinson, Jeffrey Tulis, Michael Briggs, and Fred Woodward, and their staffs. I want also to thank my colleagues at Wesleyan University, and especially Richie Adelstein, Logan Dancey, Marc Eisner, and Elvin Lim. Eric Stephen provided invaluable research assistance.

My principal and happiest obligation, however, runs to my family. Thank you.

PEOPLING THE
CONSTITUTION

INTRODUCTION

In this book, I develop an understanding of the constitutional enterprise that illumines the Civic Constitution. The Civic Constitution, I have argued previously, is an approach to the Constitution of the United States that emphasizes its status as a constitutive political act.[1] It constitutes, literally, we the people, and in so doing transforms us into a singular political entity, We the People; it makes persons, citizens. The chief purpose of the Civic Constitution is to ordain a particular kind of community,[2] first by calling into being the collective We and second by articulating what We believe and that to which We aspire; it is, put another way, a public affirmation of the shared principles of national self-identity.[3] The Civic Constitution commits us to a constitutional order dedicated to a way of life defined and lived by our fidelity to the fundamental norms and precepts that make up liberal constitutionalism, as well as a vital and robust civic life informed by an ethos and practice of civility, in which citizens assume responsibility for tending to the constitutional project.

I call it the Civic Constitution for two reasons. First, it is the Civic Constitution because its principal ambition is to constitute a political community in which citizens shoulder a significant part of the responsibility for achieving and maintaining a constitutional way of life,[4] in which the most important questions of political life, concerning the meaning and application of constitutional principles to public life, are a shared public responsibility.[5] The Civic Constitution locates its essentia in the common life of the community.

Second, I call it the Civic Constitution to highlight how this understanding differs from another, more commonly held approach to the Constitution, which I have called the Juridic Constitution.[6] The main outlines of the Juridic Constitution are immediately familiar to most scholars. In contrast to the Civic Constitution, the Juridic Constitution finds its identity in law. I call it the Juridic Constitution, and not the legal constitution (as have some others),[7] because the word "juridic" highlights issues of ownership and exclusivity. The Juridic Constitution begins but is not coextensive with the proposition that the Constitution is fundamental (and fundamentally) law,[8] a claim voiced most prominently in the supremacy clause of Article 6. The Juridic Constitution did not emerge fully developed from Article 6, however,

1

or even from the more familiar claims of law advanced in *Federalist* #78 or in *Marbury v. Madison* (1803). Instead, judicialization of the Constitution took place over a long time and is intricately bound up with the development of law itself as a profession.[9] It continues to wax and wane.[10] Nevertheless, the basic logic of the Juridic Constitution traces to *Marbury*, where Marshall referenced the Constitution's status as a legal instrument in several places and then used that characterization to license judicial review.[11]

The Juridic Constitution is not just law; it is the property of judges and lawyers, who have assumed primary institutional responsibility for maintaining the constitution and for protecting it (us) from failure. Its relationship to the people is correspondingly remote. The Juridic Constitution constitutes the people in a legal sense and invests them with formal sovereignty, but it does not charge them with responsibility for attending to the Constitution. Part of my argument here will rest upon the (once common) proposition that nothing about the Constitution makes its meaning inaccessible except to the few schooled in the mysteries of law and legal logic. In contrast to the Juridic Constitution, whose meaning is private in the sense that it is restricted to legal and professional elites, the Civic Constitution is public, its meaning accessible, and knowledge of it broadly democratic. Indeed, to discharge its function, to work as a creed or as a statement of national identity, the Civic Constitution must not reduce to a private knowledge, for "knowledge cannot be at one and the same time accessible to the few and yet serve as the vital bond holding the entire community together."[12]

The Civic Constitution anticipates a community in which constitutional questions are not only questions of law, but are also publicly debatable civic aspirations. Its purposes are to establish a community, a civic culture, that prizes questions about the fundamental principles and purposes of constitutional life, principles that include, among others, the meaning of liberty, equality, and justice. The Civic Constitution thus offers a different understanding about what kind of an activity the constitutional enterprise is and, no less important, about whether and how citizens should take part in that enterprise. It assigns a broader, more expansive purpose to the text than simply subjecting the state to higher law, and consequently asks more of citizens in realizing that purpose. It requires that we rethink the proposition that the Constitution should be understood chiefly as a legal instrument as incomplete[13] or insufficient to the achievement of an authentically constitutional way of life.

The Juridic Constitution is synecdochic; it is a profound mistake to think that because the Constitution is the supreme law, it is *only* law, or that lawyers and judges alone can discern its meaning or have any special responsibility for maintaining it.[14] It is, moreover, a mistake to think that all or even the most significant problems in constitutional theory are questions about constitutional interpretation or require judicial exegesis of the text.[15] (Constitutional interpretation is only a small part of the constitutional enterprise.[16]) Part of my effort in this book will be to show how the Juridic Constitution impoverishes our understanding of the constitutional enterprise by neglecting other objects of constitutional concern, such as citizenship, civic education, and fidelity,[17] which are central to the creation, maintenance, and failure of constitutional orders writ large.

A conclusion that the Constitution is both Juridic and Civic, although at odds with many academic and most popular understandings of the Constitution, does not take us very far along to understanding precisely where and how it is one or the other, or to whether the two can be reconciled. My claim that it is both opens up significant questions about whether and how the Juridic and Civic Constitutions can coexist. In the three essays that follow, we will see that although there are areas where the Juridic and Civic conceptions are complementary, there are also areas of constitutional life where they pull in different directions. This has two important implications. First, it means that our constitutional identity, precisely because it must navigate the most fundamental sorts of political (constituting) questions, is never fixed but is instead continually contested and renegotiated.[18] As Gary Jacobsohn has observed, the disparate strands of constitutional identities may be harmonic or disharmonic, and are likely to be both: "to apprehend constitutional identity is to see its dynamic quality."[19] The relationship between the Juridic and Civic Constitutions is necessarily protean. Second, and related, my call for renewed attention to the Civic Constitution is not a quixotic quest to change who We are, or to remake (or reconstitute) our collective identity anew. It is, instead, a work of recollection and restoration. I might describe it as a work of constitutional imagination: "Imagination," writes Kahn, "constructs the political identity of the citizen."[20]

The disharmonic elements of the Juridic and Civic Constitutions reach at least as far back as the founding, and likely find their origins in political and philosophical conflicts that predate 1789. An intellectual genealogy of the two constitutions, which I do not pursue here, would certainly find elements of the Juridic Constitution in the political thought of the Federalists, and of the Civic Constitution in some anti-Federalist thinking. Even so, it is a mistake simply to equate Juridic with Federalist, or Civic with anti-Federalist, because neither denomination is intellectually homogenous, and because neither leads inexorably to a single preferred constitutional vision or design. We can find evidence for this in some of the important new scholarship that addresses Madison's understanding of constitutional design, especially in the work of George Thomas,[21] Colleen Sheehan,[22] and Stephen Elkin,[23] all of whom argue that much of the received scholarship on Madison's constitutional design substantially understates the role he envisioned for public engagement. The more complicated picture of Madison they proffer "invites struggle over constitutional meaning and identity"[24] and leaves room for finding elements of both the Juridic and the Civic Constitutions both at the founding and in the present; who we were informs who we are.

The Juridic and Civic Constitutions thus exist in a state of uneasy interdependence; a full account of the American Constitution must accommodate both. If a complete understanding of the American constitutional order must incorporate both the Juridic and the Civic constitutions, however, then it must also admit the important differences between them. Each conception implies a characteristic way of understanding what kind of a people we are and of the community in which we claim citizenship. Selecting between them, or, better, choosing to embrace elements of both, means making fundamental choices about the distribution of political power and self-rule and is itself an act invested with constitutional meaning.[25]

CIVIC ASPIRATIONS AS CONSTITUTIONAL COMMITMENTS

Following Pitkin, a constitution "is a characteristic way of life" for a community, "the national character of a people, their ethos or fundamental nature as a people. . . . In this sense, a constitution is less something we have than something we are."[26] The Civic Constitution anticipates a constitutional way of life in this richer historical, if not Aristotelian, sense,[27] as invoking a kind of political community that is both broadly deliberative and committed to the pursuit and development of virtue.[28] But it is not enough simply to declare that the Civic Constitution commits us to a way of life. We must further describe what a constitutional way of life looks like. Implicit in the Civic Constitution is a claim about the identity of the Constitution as well as what it means to say we know or have knowledge of it. To know the Civic Constitution, we must know the beliefs and aspirations around which We constitute and to which we commit ourselves, or, as Pitkin might put it—we must know who we are.[29] What are these aspirations and beliefs?

By a constitutional way of life, I mean the Civic Constitution envisions constitutional maintenance as embracing and preserving a particular kind of constitutional culture and a particular kind of constitutional citizenship, both of which differ in important ways from their juridic analogues. The Juridic Constitution establishes a thin conception of civic life, marked by occasional and small contributions on the part of citizens, and then usually only in their capacity as individuals (i.e., the citizen votes as an individual, whether in elections or on juries, and pays taxes as an individual). In a civic constitutional order, the Constitution seeks to create and sustain the kind of community in which the people can carry forward the constitutional project, by giving meaning to and assuming responsibility for honoring constitutional values. The Civic Constitution seeks a vibrant, thick conception of civic life, in which the activity of citizens as citizens extends to daily life and comprehends both rights and obligations, chief of which is the responsibility to tend to our constitutional ideals.[30]

A principal trait of the Civic Constitution, therefore, is its commitment to self-governance realized through civic participation. This requirement of robust civic engagement derives without difficulty from several of our aspirations and constitutional principles, some of which inhere in our commitment to constitutionalism itself, and some of which are particular to the Civic Constitution. The former include aspirations to self-governance, limited government, liberty, human dignity and equal moral worth, and public reason. The latter, as summarized only partly and imperfectly by the Preamble (the Preamble calls us to a *more* perfect union),[31] include establishing justice, insuring domestic tranquility, providing for the common defense, promoting the general welfare, and securing the blessings of liberty to ourselves and our posterity.[32] (I further discuss the provenance of civic commitments in the essays to follow.) The Preamble "sets forth in 'majestic generalities' what we believe in as a political community and what we hope to secure for ourselves and our posterity."[33] Our commitment to self-governance also follows from a belief in the equal moral worth and dignity of all persons. Self-governance is an expression of the equality principle because it presumes that all persons are equally capable of participating in public affairs (and possess an equal right to do so), and concomitantly that legitimate public authority must be predicated upon their free, informed, and voluntary consent.

CIVIC AND CONSTITUTIONAL

Maintaining a constitutional way of life requires us to think about the nature of the Constitution, and in particular about the character of its authority. The Constitution I have sketched so far is an admixture of constitutional and civic components. At the core of the Civic Constitution reside two irreduc-

ible commitments. The first is a commitment to constitutional norms, principles, and values—or a commitment to the commitments that inhere in the
Constitution itself.[34] A constitutional way of life therefore includes fidelity
to the fundamental norms and broad normative precepts historically associated with Western constitutionalism, as well as to those that are particular
to our own constitutional identity.[35] How do we know what these precepts
are? They are adumbrated, among other places, in the Preamble to the constitutional text and in other parts of the constitutional document, whether
explicitly, in the Fourteenth Amendment's commitment to equality and the
First Amendment's commitment to freedom of expression, or implicitly, in
the Thirteenth Amendment's concern for equality and human dignity, or in
the commitment to reason and deliberation that undergirds the due process
clauses.[36] They find expression also in other constitutive documents, including the Declaration of Independence, the Gettysburg Address, "Letter from
a Birmingham Jail," and others.[37]

The precise meaning and import of our constitutional commitments cannot be fully described, for a principal feature of the Civic Constitution is
precisely that contests about its meaning and application in the political life
of the community are the essence of what it means to live a constitutional
way of life. The identity and the meaning of the Civic Constitution is in
large measure found in these contests, in which citizens consider the purport
and application of fundamental constitutional norms and concepts, such as
equality, liberty, citizenship, and rights. Those arguments, about the meaning
of constitutional principles and their application in the life of the community, are the word-stock of the Civic Constitution.

Hence, the second component of the Civic Constitution is a commitment
to a vital and vibrant civic life, or to *civilis*. The Civic Constitution envisions
a community that aspires to live by constitutional ideals and to realize those
ideals in the life of the community. It envisions a *deliberative* community
knowledgeable of its constitutional commitments, and an *engaged* community, alive with civic concern and actively occupied in the work of self-
government. The Civic Constitution places a high value on the concept of
participation in the public and deliberative life of the polity. It thus requires a
political order with a robust conception of civic space, in which citizens tend
to constitutional concerns and act with an ethic of civility (I discuss tending
and the ethic of civility below and in Essays One and Two).

Like some recent interpretations of American constitutional practice that
reconsider the role of citizens in making constitutional meaning, among them
Larry Kramer's work on popular constitutionalism[38] and Bruce Ackerman's
We the People,[39] the Civic Constitution takes the people seriously. I discuss

both Kramer and Ackerman as we proceed, but for now I note simply that neither the literature on popular constitutionalism nor that on constitutional moments provides a satisfactory account of our civic responsibility for maintaining the Constitution.[40] Kramer, for example, has argued that civic attention to the Constitution is an essential element of our constitutional past, evident in periodic conflict and challenges to the judicialization of the Constitution.[41] For most popular constitutionalists, such histories become inquiries into the nature, possibilities, and limits of the people's interpretive capabilities and responsibilities.[42] (I speak at a very high level of generality here. There is no canonical understanding of what popular constitutionalism is or what it requires regarding the allocation of interpretive authority.[43] Some versions, such as those by Jeremy Waldron and Mark Tushnet, allocate little or no authority to judges to interpret the Constitution.[44] Sager rejects judicial supremacy, but not judicial review.[45]) For Ackerman, civic contributions to constitutional meaning are exceptional moments, not ordinary practice, and consequently do not provide a weighty account of civic responsibility for realizing our constitutional ideals. Instead, in the course of normal politics, the Court "speaks for" citizens in a "preservationist" function. Neither approach peoples the Constitution fully.

The Civic Constitution, in contrast, envisages citizens engaged in constitutional practice on a regular, recurrent basis and in a wide variety of civic spaces. Engaged citizens are citizens who practice their commitment to constitutional ideals. This is a conception of citizenship as work, or as practice[46] (and not simply as deliberation),[47] and it occurs as an ordinary and routine part of public life.[48] The Civic Constitution envisions a constitutional order in which responsibility for determining the meaning and the requirements of our constitutional obligations, although shared with other actors, is a civic no less than a judicial undertaking; the meaning of the Civic Constitution is the people's responsibility. The Civic Constitution thus combines a commitment to the values and principles of constitutionalism with a commitment to civic life in which citizens are the chief custodians of those constitutional values.

For some readers this conjunction of "civic" and "constitutional" might seem odd. As I will explain later, some of this unease is a consequence of the rise of the Juridic Constitution itself, and the resultant sense, prominent among many academics and citizens alike, that constitutional matters are well beyond the understanding of most citizens as well as unsafe in their hands.[49] Another reason the conjunction of civic and constitutional may appear incongruous relates to potential differences in the conception of authority that rests behind them. The constitutional component of the Civic Constitution references a conception of authority superior in rank to, or which trumps decisions made by, the democratic process. It thus seems ill suited to a conception of the Constitution that stresses the civic dimensions of political life, which seems by way of contrast to assign a very high measure of authority to decisions made by the democratic process. It is a mistake to overstate the tension between our commitments to constitutional ideals and to self-governance, but neither should we deny the tension between them—each invokes a somewhat different understanding of the constitutional order. We should also resist the sense that we must find a way to reconcile our constitutionalist commitments with our civic ones completely. Such an effort neglects the ways in which all healthy identities include diverse and often disharmonious elements.[50]

Is the Civic Constitution a Justice-Seeking Constitution?

Justice-seeking accounts of the Constitution stress the Constitution's centrality to an overarching theory of justice. A justice-seeking account of the Constitution sees it as "a document that takes establishing justice as a goal for legislation and as a guide to the document's own interpretation. Their position makes the Constitution and justice coincident, so that an inquiry into the Constitution's meaning is simultaneously, and indistinguishably, an inquiry into justice."[51] Prominent among justice-seeking accounts of the Constitution are the works of Christopher Eisgruber[52] and Lawrence Sager, both of whom have argued that our best understanding of the Constitution is to regard it as a commitment to securing fundamental principles of political justice. Thus, as Sager notes, "To make sense of our constitutional practice, we have to see it as justice-seeking—that is, as serving the end of making our political community more just."[53]

At first appearances it is difficult to imagine how the Civic Constitution could be a justice-seeking constitution, chiefly because most of us incline to the view that whatever its other virtues, self-government is an unreliable mechanism for securing justice. Indeed, Sager concludes, "the justice-seeking view of our constitutional institutions depends upon the belief that the judiciary—guided only broadly by the text of the Constitution—is a reasonably good guide to the most critical requirements of political justice."[54] As is well known, Sager treats judges as active partners in the enterprise of securing the fundamentals of political justice. What is perhaps less clear is that such a partnership is demanded, in part, because we harbor some doubt about the prospect of achieving justice without the assistance of judges as partners.

However, Sager also acknowledges that the domain of constitutional justice is more limited than the pursuit of political justice broadly. As a consequence, "justice-seeking theorists have the burden of explaining why the Constitution seems to fall so short of its target."[55] Without fully recounting the argument here, part of Sager's explanation for why constitutional justice stops so far short of political justice hinges on the distinction "between the Constitution proper and the adjudicated Constitution."[56] Sager's under-enforcement thesis holds that some principles of political justice, to which the Constitution is committed in abstract, "are wrapped in complex choices of strategy and responsibility that are properly the responsibility of popular political institutions."[57] Our commitment "to popular political institutions and our durable understanding [means] that these institutions have broad leeway in managing our political affairs."[58] Note too that these principles of justice "may impose affirmative obligations outside the courts on legislatures, executives, and citizens generally to realize them more fully."[59]

Consequently, a justice-seeking account of the Constitution is not necessarily incompatible with the Civic Constitution, insofar as it appears to commit the enforcement of some principles of constitutional justice to legislatures and executives, and to the people (this is what Sager calls the "partnership model," in contrast to the "agency model"). If we take the liberty of conflating "justice-seeking" with "moral readings" of the text (there are good reasons to distinguish between "justice-seeking" and "moral," especially in institutional terms, but at a higher level of abstraction the differences are not so important), then there is little reason not to conclude that the Civic Constitution is also a justice-seeking Constitution.[60]

On the other hand, some readings of Sager detect suspicion on his part that the people will take up that responsibility. As Fleming has noted, for example, "Sager's account is too court-loving and too skeptical about legislatures, executives, and the people themselves for its own good."[61] For somewhat more generous and sunnier accounts of the capacity of other institutions to address constitutional questions, consider the work of Tushnet, who writes of an "incentive-compatible" or self-enforcing Constitution,[62] and Sunstein, who argues that legislatures no less than courts can be forums of principle.[63]

Is the Civic Constitution a Deliberative Constitution?

In contrast to justice-seeking interpretations of the Constitution, deliberative accounts of the Constitution stress its centrality to creating a political order that facilitates authentic and extensive public deliberation.[64] In these narratives, "constitutions [are] mainly . . . instruments for facilitating a mode of political discourse in which the good is sought in collective decision-making and political association."[65] Deliberative theorists, as represented by Jürgen Habermas, Cass Sunstein, and others, emphasize a public sphere that is communicative and deliberative in character, and in which citizens exercise a significant measure of political responsibility.[66]

Democratic deliberation is a constitutive part of all constitutional orders because constitutional orders are committed to the necessity of reason in public affairs.[67] In Kahn's words, "Politics begins with deliberation."[68] The requirement of reason in public affairs inheres in the twin concepts of respect and justification. To put it simply, public deliberation on the basis of giving reasons is required by the principle of respect for others because democratic self-governance, to the extent it embraces a principle of majoritarian decision making, must justify results that necessarily produce winners and losers. The process of deliberation teaches citizens that they have a role in public decision making and are not simply the objects of it. Deliberation, in other words, is a process we use to distinguish citizens from subjects; citizens are entitled to deliberate with others, to be included in the process of decision making; subjects are not. The alternative to governing based on reason, as Madison foresaw, is rule by passion and irrationality[69]—an affront to efforts to govern wisely and well, but just as importantly an affront to the conception of human dignity that constitutional government invokes.[70]

I have argued elsewhere that the deliberative function of reason in a constitutional democracy also goes some way to telling us what kinds of reasons properly count as public reasons and what kinds of reasons should not.[71] Public reasons must advance arguments that invite exchange and deliberation instead of closing it down. Public reasons "should be accepted by free and equal persons seeking fair terms of cooperation."[72] In addition, public reasons must be framed as accounts of the public good or as arguments about the public good, as Rawls concludes.[73] Reasons that appeal to claims of faith, or that end ultimately in appeals to authority, must be rejected as claims of reason because they deny the utility and necessity of reason itself. In other words, constitutional reasons must be reasons that every and all citizens of the polity could recognize as a claim of reason, thus disqualifying claims grounded in my religious faith (God commands it)[74] or in my superior authority (Because I say so). A reason that depends for its ability to persuade solely on the authority of the speaker falls outside the pale of good reasons, because in such cases the speaker's position amounts to a claim that no justification is necessary.[75] Such claims are fundamentally undemocratic and uncivil in character because a failure to explain frustrates political dialogue.[76] Moreover, if reasons are to justify and not merely to rationalize or explain an exercise of power, they must be reasons that admit of and invite a response from others. Good reasons, in other words, make possible genuine exchange and deliberation. Reasons advanced on claims of superior expertise or exclusive knowledge shutter deliberation and exchange. The former reason is a private reason, not a public one, and the latter is no reason at all, or one that denies the democratic practice of reason giving as a preferred way of organizing political life.

My arguments for the Civic Constitution bear a deep similarity to these deliberative accounts of the constitutional order, especially insofar as both identify public deliberation as a critical component of constitutional governance. Indeed, the two cardinal elements of the Civic Constitution—its commitment to a robust civic life and its constitutionalist commitments, which include reason and deliberation in public affairs—tell us that it is partly deliberative in character. A full account of the Civic Constitution thus dictates some consideration not only of how the constitutional order can be designed to promote public deliberation (and some discussion about what deliberation means, or what it means to deliberate), but also of the mechanisms necessary to carry the burden forward.

We should be cautious, however, about concluding that the Civic Constitution establishes a deliberative constitutional order. Deliberation is an ambition of the Civic Constitution, but it is not our only aspiration. A constitutional way of life requires significant deliberative capacity in citizens, but just as importantly, it supplies the object of our deliberation and constrains it as well. To the extent citizens are responsible for maintaining the constitutional order, then, we are committed to more than just deliberation as a constitutional ideal. We are committed additionally to certain constitutional norms and precepts that we cannot, consistently with our aspiration to be a constitutional people, forswear or abjure. To put it another way, there are places where the public's deliberation cannot go without sacrificing other constitutional ideals. Deliberation is therefore a core element of the Civic Constitution, but it is subject to certain constitutional (or justice-seeking) restraints. This does not mean that deliberative and justice-seeking accounts of the constitution are incompatible in toto. Recently some scholars have sought to combine "constitutional and deliberative principles by developing an account of deliberative democracy within the context of a liberal constitutional framework. On first consideration the deliberative constitutionalist project would not appear to be a promising one, for the theoretical commitments of constitutionalism and of deliberative democracy seem to be in tension, if not utterly incompatible, with one another."[77] The incompatibility, if it is one, results from the suspicion that the deliberative, or civic, elements of deliberative constitutionalism will undermine (or rather, overwhelm) its constitutionalist restraints.[78]

These constraints matter because considerations of power and position will necessarily play a role in the process of deliberation, as will bargaining, negotiation, and even compromise. It is important not to romanticize or idealize what civic deliberation looks like in practice, or to imagine that it will always reflect our best constitutional selves. Nor will civic deliberation always reflect the considered judgment of an authentically "public" voice that incorporates or respects the voices of minorities, women, and other liminal groups. As Mary Ryan and other critics have noted of Habermas, for example, his deliberative sphere ignores the extent to which there is not one public, but several smaller ones, and how the terms and occasions of their interaction are grounded in struggle and power.[79] Conceptions of deliberative democracy, unadorned, may sentimentalize citizenship by referencing an idealized world of deliberation and reasoned exchange, divorced from the messy and raucous realities of public discussion.[80] Under the Civic Constitution, the justice-seeking, or constitutionalist, elements of the civic constitutional order seek to inhibit the excesses and inequalities that otherwise inhere in unconstrained public deliberation. Moreover, the virtues of civility and tending that the Civic Constitution cultivates will also work to mitigate incivilities in the public sphere. But we should not pretend that public deliberation will always elicit our best constitutional selves.[81]

Constitutional Maintenance and Civic Work

The Civic Constitution includes elements of both justice-seeking and deliberative constitutional designs, but even together, these two components yield an account of civic life unequal to the Civic Constitution. Constitutional maintenance, or the burden of carrying the Constitution forward, requires more than simply a revitalized public sphere in which citizens can talk about, or find their voice, on constitutional matters. Voice *is* important "because it empowers citizens."[82] But restoring "[D]eliberative democracy is not enough. . . . By uprooting citizenship from the everyday world of power, interests, and work, deliberative democracy sentimentalizes citizenship. To bring back a fuller account of public life it is useful to recall a third version of citizenship, aimed at developing the capacities of citizens for public work."[83]

As Boyte notes, we must distinguish between deliberation and civic work.[84] What the Civic Constitution requires are not citizen-philosophers, well tutored in the practices of deliberation, but rather citizens schooled in practical citizenship, "focused on the development of people's capacities for work together through civic-problem solving."[85] The Civic Constitution demands a conception of citizenship as work, and not simply as deliberation, because it is through civic work that citizens learn to act civically. And it is through civic work that citizens learn to (at)tend to concrete differences in power, resources, and status that may be masked by or papered over in purely deliberative accounts of the constitutional order.[86]

The project of civic maintenance therefore, cannot be immured to debates over the meanings of inspirational texts.[87] Maintaining the Civic Constitution means translating constitutional concerns and ideals into a way of life. A way of life requires that we commit to the performance of constitutional precepts and not simply pledge an allegiance to them. To paraphrase Hadot, a constitutional way of life is not only a way of seeing the world, it is a way of being in the world.[88] Civic maintenance thus finds expression wherever citizens take up matters that address the lives we lead in common. It occurs in those activities and places where citizens consider the meaning and application of constitutional norms and ideals. If "life in the polis is an education," as Dahl insisted,[89] then life in the Civic Constitution manifests in public conversation and controversies over matters that go to the centrality of the Constitution's vision for public life.

For this reason, when we look for the Civic Constitution, we must look beyond deliberation to engagement, and beyond seminal texts to lived practices. Our experience of these practices is not confined to the earliest period of our constitutional history or to such obvious examples as popular agitation concerning the Alien and Sedition Acts and abolitionism.[90] As Kramer and other have noted, they persisted through the Jacksonian era and later.[91] The populists of the 1880s and 1890s were centrally concerned with defending "a positive constitutional order,"[92] and the Progressives were likewise engaged in a self-conscious program of constitutional critique and reform.[93] The suffrage campaigns of the nineteenth and twentieth centuries, and civil rights struggles of the 1940s, '50s, and '60s,[94] are all instances of civic engagement with matters that define what it means to practice a constitutional way of life.[95] Recent examples of the Civic Constitution in practice include citizen campaigns surrounding the issues of same-sex marriage and health care, both of which involve disagreements about the meaning and import of first principles, over the commitments that comprise our identity.[96] (In Essay Two I shall argue that civic education must extend not only to teaching first principles, but also to teaching when and where citizens have participated in disputes about their meaning and application.[97])

Civic Space

Because the Civic Constitution requires us to conserve a constitutional way of life, first among its aims must be the establishment of civic spaces in which citizens can practice constitutional politics and not simply observe them at a distance. Civic space requires a substantial element of what Villa calls "public freedom," whose purpose is "to make concrete—to actualize—the 'active and constant surveillance' of the people's representatives,"[98] but it also requires a site where citizens can take up the meaning of the public good themselves. In other words, under the Civic Constitution, maintaining a constitutional way of life requires that we do more than profess fidelity to constitutional values; we must care for them and practice them, and this necessitates an expansive civic space where citizens can participate in a constitutional way of life.[99] Civic space is not simply physical or geographic. Nor is it confined to the spaces assigned to the formal practice or discharge of civic duties. Instead, it extends more broadly to include experiential space.[100] Experiential space refers to the kinds of experiences and activities that occur in the places where citizens actually talk about and practice political life. Civic space thus includes the obvious physical locations where we act out the familiar rituals of civic life, such as voting booths, town halls, and jury boxes,[101] but it also encompasses letters to the editor, farmers' markets,[102] coffee houses, barbershops, supermarkets, and a nearly endless variety of so-called third spaces,[103] in which citizens practice civility and engage in constitutional conversation.[104] In this space, populated by a wide variety of civic groups, fraternal organizations, churches and charitable societies, private and public foundations, and NGOs, persons learn how to become citizens by acting like citizens.

As Barber argues, civic space requires a model of public life that extends beyond the familiar two cells of public and private to a third cell, a civic cell. This third cell (Barber calls it variously the civil domain, civil society, and civic space)[105] "occupies the middle ground between government and the private sector." [106] It is "public without being coercive, voluntary without being privatized"; as Barber concludes, "Civil society is the domain of citizens."[107] Barber's conception of civic space is identified principally by noting which actors occupy the space and what they do in it—defined chiefly in terms of speaking in a public voice. This public voice "entails a lateral conversation among citizens rather than between them and their 'leaders.'"[108] Lateral conversations occur in the space of civil society. In contrast to certain other democratic practices, such as voting, conversation can be imaginative, in the sense that it may promote the imaginative faculties of participants,[109] as well as transformative, in the sense that it can expand one's view of the world by engaging with others.[110] Conversation itself, including and especially constitutional conversation, is a democratic skill,[111] in the sense that it must be learned and it must be practiced.[112]

The civic space required by the Civic Constitution is thus both deliberative and experiential, or one in which citizens possess civic agency. In Boyte's definition, appropriate here, civic agency refers to the "capacities, powers, and skills that the citizen needs to acquire . . . to become a serious and accountable actor and creator in public affairs."[113] In other words, the sort of civic space contemplated by the Civic Constitution is not simply liberal or deliberative. Nor does it require us to choose between thin liberal accounts of public life or thick deliberative accounts. It requires, instead, that we embrace and shoulder responsibility for achieving a constitutional way of life—a way of choosing, doing, and being.[114]

Some readers may wonder if the Civic Constitution's reliance on a robust notion of civic life and civic space is unrealistic, especially in light of work by such scholars as Cornell West, Michael Sandel, and Jürgen Habermas.[115] Habermas is especially relevant to my discussion of civic space as comprised of both spatial and experiential elements. He argues that the advent of a deliberative public sphere was tied closely to the development of urban culture and had an obvious spatial component, comprised in part of physical places, such as coffee shops, opera houses, lecture halls, museums, and other third spaces, that flourished with the burgeoning of urban culture. Moreover, "in such public spaces, patterns of communication emerged that were characterized by norms of inclusivity, the give and take of argument, and a relatively horizontal experience of power."[116]

The vitality of these public spaces is greatly diminished. We have, argues Habermas, lost the experience of public space characterized by "uncoercive interaction on the basis of communication free from domination."[117] Barber similarly concludes that one clear sign of the eclipse of civil society "has been the disappearance of those non-governmental spaces where citizens can talk to one another."[118] In my view, Habermas and Barber understate how much civic space actually exists in the United States, largely because their definition of what qualifies as civic talk is too narrow, but the larger point they make is central to the Civic Constitution: civic life can thrive only in a robust public sphere.

Habermas proffers a number of explanations for the diminishment of this public sphere, including the substitution for public deliberation of the disaggregation of the public interest into competing specialized interests, and a societal preoccupation with instrumental rationality. Barber also identifies a number of reasons for the precipitous decline of civil society (or more accurately, its envelopment by the cell of private action, so that groups, organizations, and associations are now cast "as exemplars of a . . . private interest association pursuing one more private good"[119]). Whatever the causes, the decline of civic space leaves citizens with neither "home for their civic institutions nor voice with which to speak."[120]

I would add that the Juridic Constitution further privatizes the public voice by framing politics in the language of law, a language that necessarily excludes the great majority of citizens. To talk about the Juridic Constitution one must be able to understand it as law—one must, in other words, know what the law is and how to read and speak it. If we accept the claim that talk about the Juridic Constitution is legal in nature, then in a certain sense the Constitution is, as Levinson has suggested, "a linguistic system, what some among us might call a discourse."[121] It is, moreover, an extremely exclusionary discourse, a point acknowledged, indeed celebrated, in *Federalist* 78, but routinely overlooked by the many academic lawyers who have stressed the ways in which the Constitution structures public conversation.[122] Attended to and protected by the bar, the Juridic Constitution ordains for the constitutional order an inherent inequality located in the unequal distribution of professional skills.

A diminished civic space is a matter of serious consequence for the Civic Constitution; its revitalization must be a primary object of a genuinely civic constitutional order. I have said twice now that the Civic Constitution requires civic space. By "requires" I mean more than that it needs such space or finds it useful. I mean literally that it compels such space and that under the Civic Constitution, we should regard civic space as a public good. As a public good, the creation and maintenance of civic space is properly a matter of public interest. The Civic Constitution thus regards public efforts to manufacture civic space, including the use of public resources to do so, as well within the proper aims of constitutional authority. Conceiving of civic space as a public good, moreover, tells us that the organization of the state, and especially the organization of state structures and institutions, ought to be concluded in ways that develop and nourish civic space (see the discussion in Essays One and Two on separation of powers and federalism).

Civility

There are two components to the conception of citizenship inherent in the Civic Constitution. One is *civility*, which speaks to the importance of reason and deliberation as key components of a civic constitutional order. The second component is *tending*, which speaks to the importance of public work, of the active practice of a constitutional way of life, to the constitutional order. Civility is a description of how we want citizens to behave in civil society. Tending describes how citizens should attend to their constitutional responsibilities. Civility is what makes a deliberative community possible, and tending is the quotidian manifestation of civic engagement, or in Boyte's language, of citizenship as civic work.

There is an intimate connection between civic life and civility. Civility encompasses both a disposition toward and possession of a set of skills necessary to sustain a robust public-spiritedness, or civic-mindedness, on the part of citizens. Civility represents an attitudinal predisposition on the part of citizens to act in ways that take seriously our commitment to a constitutional way of life. It is vital to a reinvigorated concept of citizenship. Thus conceived, civility is an important (and inescapably public[123]) virtue and a predicate of democratic life, a position easily ascribed to the civic republican tradition in American politics, but not confined to it.[124] "One prominent early meaning of civility was fitness for a civil, post-feudal society. Defining marks of that fitness included obeying authoritative law, refraining from violence, and having the literacy and education necessary for public service."[125]

Calhoun has remarked that "Contemporary political philosophers . . . take civility to be a mark of the good citizen."[126] If civility is a mark of the good citizen, then what civility means is tied to the definition of good citizenship. The good citizen of the Civic Constitution differs considerably from the good citizen of the Juridic Constitution. Under the Civic Constitution, "Constitutional discourse . . . is the public language of the civic community,"[127] and the good citizen must be prepared to engage in a shared civic conversation. As Barber argues, "Giving a civic and public voice legitimate civic articulation is a priority for all who want to invest that once sublime title citizen with renewed meaning."[128] To engage in civic life means to participate in common community with others, and "[i]rrespective of the appearance of the exchange, the hallmark of civility is the degree of engagement required of the interactants."[129] A key component of civility approached in this way is that it facilitates deliberation and the exchange of reason in public affairs. Accordingly, if "[t]he public voice of civility is deliberative,"[130] then the Civic Constitution demands that we find ways to encourage deliberation in civic life.

To act civilly is to think critically. I define constitutional civility, therefore, as a predisposition to reflect upon the meaning of the Constitution as a way of constituting the good life and as what we can constitutionally defend as the good society.[131] Civility in this sense includes but goes somewhat further than the duty of civility proposed by Rawls, which he defines as a duty to treat other citizens with respect by offering others reasons for the positions we advance in deliberations about the public good.[132] Thus, for Rawls, civility is a duty to "be able to explain to one another on . . . fundamental questions how the principles and policies they advocate and vote for can be supported by the political values of public reason. This duty also involves a willingness to listen to others and a fair-mindedness in deciding when accommodations to their view should reasonably be made."[133]

The Rawlsian conception of civility, because it hinges on the necessity to give reasons, incorporates the principles of dignity and equal worth that are at the heart of constitutionalism. My conception of civility, however, goes further than Rawls's, in that it requires citizens to act with civility in both public and private life.[134] (I shall elaborate on this point in my discussion of the relationship between the Civic Constitution and civil society in Essays One and Two.) My understanding of civility as a constitutional virtue recalls Virginia Sapiro's description of civility as "constructive engagement with others through argument, deliberation, and discourse"[135] about the constitution of public life. Thus, following Heller, civility is connected up with and requires civic engagement because "it requires a manner of looking at society in ways that evaluate how well the society works vis-à-vis its own articulated ideals, such as those of justice, equality, freedom of speech and so on."[136] Civility is a prerequisite for reasoned exchange, and in this sense "democracy rest[s] on a foundation of civil society."[137] Calhoun thus concludes, "Tolerant self-restraint . . . is only part of what fits citizens for life in a liberal democracy. In addition, citizens must seek accommodation and compromise through reasoned dialogue. As the virtue that fits citizens for life in a participatory democracy, civility thus gets equated with respectful dialogue—keeping a civil tongue."[138]

Civility is a precondition of deliberation.[139] Flammang likewise describes civility as a requirement of a healthy democracy, noting that reason and civility are mutually reinforcing. Rules of courtesy and civility require "a respect and willingness to consider things from another conversant's position . . . they are the conventions that make conversation possible."[140] Civility is an indispensable civic virtue because democratic societies must find peaceful and productive ways to entertain and navigate conflict about the public weal. The "generosity of spirit" that characterizes civility in democratic societies is important precisely because it establishes and promotes norms of diplomatic and thoughtful, if spirited, exchange. Generosity of spirit suggests yet another important component of civility—that of reciprocity. Reciprocity means not only that we must advance reasons *to* others—we must listen to the reasons advanced *by* others.[141] Barber thus notes that listening is a critical part of democratic deliberation. Herbst similarly concludes, "Listening is as vital to civility as respectful talk."[142]

To deliberate, therefore, is to exchange reasons with and to listen to others, who are themselves obligated both to listen and to advance reasons in support of their preferences. I wrote in *Constitutions in Crisis* that a reasons requirement is a constitutive principle of all authentic forms of constitutional life.[143] Under the Civic Constitution, reason and civility are mutually reinforcing. Because giving reasons is instrumental to the achievement of a constitutional way of life under the Civic Constitution, the requirement of reason giving applies to all exercises of public power, as well as to constitutional conversation generally. Echoing my discussion of the constitutive principle of reason as a prerequisite of constitutional life, Flammang concludes similarly that "democratic" equates to "give reasons."[144]

A reasons requirement is a structural imperative for the kind of public life the Civic Constitution envisions. Public engagement with constitutional life requires a civil discourse committed to reflection and to the production of reasons in support of policy positions. True dialogue is premised on claims of equality and respect, not on claims of superiority; consequently, arguments must depend for their cogency on their logic, coherence, and fidelity to larger constitutional imperatives.[145] In addition, this requirement places a set of limitations on civic discourse in a constitutional democracy by providing that constitutionally legitimate (and superior) arguments, no matter who makes them, including citizens, must be grounded in reason and must respect norms of civility.[146]

Civility is thus a necessary companion to the constitutive principle of reason and deliberation, but it is also a reflection of constitutionalism's commitment to the basic norms of human dignity and equal moral worth.[147] Civility depends upon the principle of respect for others and their status as persons both capable of and entitled to reasoned exchange. In the words of Edward Shils, civility is "respect for the dignity and the desire for dignity of other persons."[148] Civility also traces to constitutionalism's insistence upon the equal moral worth of all persons because "[t]he practice of civility generates a sense of inclusivity and moral equality, both in ourselves and for others."[149]

Implicit in the notion of engagement and deliberation is the related concept of conversation. Civility makes conversation possible. "Unless people think that they owe one another the courtesy of a conversation, there can be no civility or democracy."[150] This raises important issues about the nature and meaning of conversation as a civic virtue. Some scholars, for example, distinguish between two conversational models. The sociable model of conversation treats it as a source of pleasure and entertainment, or "as a means of cultivating sensibilities."[151] Problem-solving modes of conversation, by way of contrast, are governed by instrumentality and the exchange of reasons.[152] Schudson likewise distinguishes between homogeneous and heterogeneous conversations—the former emphasize shared or commonly held values; the latter are more likely to focus on areas of disagreement and uncertainty.[153] Schudson argues that heterogeneous conversational models are better suited to contemporary democratic life and to communities that are pluralistic (presumably the same logic argues in favor of the problem-solving model), but both are necessary to sustain the Civic Constitution. Our fidelity to the Civic Constitution commits us to a constitutional order that embraces the normative precepts that are central to constitutionalism (commonly held values) and to civic engagement (the exchange of reasons), and thus to a model of public conversation that incorporates both the heterogeneous and homogeneous models. The Civic Constitution envisions a model of discourse that approximates the concept of civic magnanimity proposed by Amy Gutmann and Dennis Thompson. The model of magnanimity requires that we acknowledge the moral status of the arguments of others, cultivate open-mindedness in civic conversation, and finally, embrace an "economy of moral disagreement" that seeks to minimize conflict without compromising deeply held convictions.[154]

Criticisms of Civility

By civility, I do not mean good manners. We must distinguish between what Calhoun calls polite civility and political civility,[155] although the two are obviously related, as Alexis de Tocqueville observed in *Democracy in America*.[156] Boyd offers a similar distinction between formal and substantive civility, the latter defined as "a sense of standing or membership in the political community with its attendant rights and responsibility. This sense of the term civility is most evident in formulations like "civil rights" or "civil disobedience," where the modifier "civil" refers to the condition of being a member of a political community."[157]

There are two principal reasons why we might reject political or substantive civility as a civic virtue. As several critics have observed, mores of civility sometimes seem to have a disciplinary character to them. Far from being instrumentally democratic or an expression of fundamental constitutional ideals like human dignity and equal moral worth, on this understanding civility is a weapon of class warfare or of exclusion, a way of distinguishing the civilized/superior "us" from the uncivilized/inferior "them."[158] Nancy Rosenblum, for example, concludes, "across time and cultures, most forms of civility have been patently undemocratic in their attention to rank, class, office, affiliation, or social standing."[159] As a consequence, "Insofar as being civil is identified with complying with class-distinguishing etiquette rules, civility appears not to be a moral virtue, but a badge of class distinction."[160] Nor are such concerns limited to historical accounts of the rise of courtly manners in Europe. They are also caught up with the development of the middle class in the United States, as noted by Margaret Visser, John Kasson, and others, who have noted that class differentiation through etiquette was related to the politics of immigration. Thus, "as new immigrants arrived, the middle class wanted to improve the manners of the working class as an attempt 'to establish order and authority in a restless, highly mobile, rapidly urbanizing and industrializing democracy.'"[161] As Boyd puts it succinctly, "civility has a chequered past. The notion that certain populations— immigrants, ethnic minorities, the poor, etc.—need to be 'civilised' in order to make them into responsible liberal citizens is an exclusionary trope running throughout modern social and political thought."[162] Thus, critics argue that civility is an artifice or, worse, a tool of exclusion rather than inclusion.[163]

One variation of the exclusionary argument asks us to rethink the claim that civility is especially well suited to heterogeneous and pluralistic societies. Demands for civility may assume, wrongly, that all groups in society will have an equal opportunity to be heard. As Sparks and others have noted, however, the burden of civility falls disproportionately on the liminal, especially if we abandon the assumption of equal access to civic space. Hence, we might object that the otherwise laudable requirement to treat others civilly places a disproportionate burden on those who have to shout or behave in ways we deem uncivil for us to hear them at all. Life in a political community brings together individuals and groups with different identities, dissimilar degrees of access to power and other civic resources, and different standing in the eyes of others. By virtue of the sameness and uniformity it imposes on difference, the claim is that civility excludes or dilutes those voices already most likely to be silenced in civic conversation.[164] A second and related criticism of civility charges that it is a device for the suppression of disagreement and conflict, both of which are a vital part of a healthy democratic community.

I do not deny that civic conversation can be elitist and exclusionary, though it is considerably less so than the language of law that attaches to the Juridic Constitution.[165] As I indicated above, some of the criticisms advanced against the Habermasian model of public deliberation, especially those that see in it a model that mutes conflict and systematically silences certain voices, are difficult to dismiss. However, critics of civility mischaracterize it as suppression of conflict. It is important to recognize that constitutional civility is not inherently a device for the suppression of conflict or of strong disagreement, not a mask designed to cover differences of class, gender, religion, or political persuasion. "To the contrary, civility is necessary precisely because there is conflict."[166] Civility can be a mechanism for recognizing and acknowledging difference; we can imagine, in other words, a "pluralistic, democratic and inclusive understanding of civility that differs from other more exclusionary permutations."[167] Manners of civility can be democratic because they promote and enable frank and honest exchange with others with whom we may disagree.[168] Flammang argues similarly that "true conversations are democratic insofar as conversants are tuned into differences."[169] Approached in this latter and not in the colloquial sense of politeness and gentility, civility is not a device for the suppression of conflict or of strong disagreement. Instead, civility is a mechanism for recognizing and acknowledging difference: "Civility . . . is a virtue that is called into play precisely when there are differences, especially among strangers."[170]

Civility also has an important connection with another principle commonly ascribed to Madisonian constitutionalism—the principle of pluralism. The respect and civility that make genuine conversation possible are especially necessary to pluralistic, or to heterogeneous, societies. "What is necessary for civil life is less some fundamental moral consensus about the rightness or wrongness of abortion, cloning, stem cell research, etc. than a way for different groups to minimise the conflicts and maximise the cooperation that this project of collective life entails."[171]

Hence, civility is necessary in a constitutional democracy precisely because there will be conflict about the good and because sentiment and passion will always have a role in deliberative decision making, as Krause and others have observed.[172] The resolution of conflict, especially over things that are important or fundamental, can occur in only a few ways. One way is through the imposition of one's will over another, or with superior force. In a constitutional democracy, however, conflict must be resolved through democratic means. Civility means that "[r]eason is not relied on in place of, or in opposition to, strong feelings or self-interest; rather, reason is used to deliberate about alternative courses of action, in settings with emotional import . . . and strongly held views."[173] The better view, therefore, is that civility is a constitutional virtue because it empowers rather than silences and because it reinforces the fundamental constitutional precepts of equal moral worth and the right of self-governance. The constitutional virtue of civility is not a high-minded, genteel version of comportment, but a practical, democratic virtue, designed to facilitate civic engagement.

Incivility

"The word incivility is derived from the Latin *incivilis*, meaning 'not of a citizen.'"[174] Incivility thus conceived is a failure to act as a citizen should act. Under the Civic Constitution, incivility is a failure to abide by the basic predicates of constitutional life, or to take up constitutional deliberations as an ordinary and recurrent part of our responsibilities as citizens. Failure to engage or to reflect upon constitutional precepts, and whether we have achieved them, to say nothing of forfeiting any genuine responsibility for their realization, amounts to a kind of incivility, or civic privation. We might describe occasional incivility as a constitutional lapse, or as an ordinary manifestation of human (and constitutional) imperfection. Epidemic incivility, I shall argue in Essay Three, amounts to a unique kind of constitutional failure insofar as it is a failure to achieve a constitutional way of life premised upon public reasonableness.[175]

Incivility also represents a failure to abide by several other fundamental constitutional principles, including respect for human dignity and the equal moral worth of all persons. "If . . . the good manners of civility serve to locate two otherwise different human beings as equal members of the same inclusive collectivity or public, then maybe the most harmful aspect of incivility is that it serves as a device of hierarchy, difference and exclusion."[176] To say that someone is not worthy of civil treatment in public life "is to say, *ipso facto*, that they are neither our equals, entitled to moral dignity, nor full-fledged members of the same moral universe."[177] "Failure to respect these rules by behaviours such as rudeness, condescension, mockery and other forms of incivility serves to locate others outside a common moral community."[178] Incivility slights our aspirations to public reason, equal moral worth, and human dignity.

In light of our discussion of civility and its capacity to suppress conflict, it is important to note that incivility is not simply the presence of disagreement, even strongly held disagreement, about the meaning or the desirability of our constitutional aspirations. In a polity truly committed to civic engagement, the precise meaning of our constitutional aspirations, and what they demand of states and citizens alike, must always be contingent in the sense that their definition is an ongoing object of discussion and debate. Although our commitment to constitutional principles cannot be compromised so long as we aspire to live as a constitutional community, their meaning must always be subject to negotiation and contestation.

The more difficult question is whether constitutionalists must admit into public conversation those who advocate public policy positions, or even the adoption of regimes, that reject the necessity of reason itself as a precondition of political life.[179] Sotirios Barber argues persuasively that we must, because the Constitution demands that we consider under what conditions "it would be rational to reaffirm the Constitution's authority."[180] The necessity of reaffirmation requires that we consider arguments that would lead us to reject the Constitution's authority. The underlying necessity of consent to notions of legitimacy (and authority, in contradistinction to power[181]) must mean that consent can be withheld or withdrawn. Hence, public discourse that rejects the moral or political force of our shared commitments, and not just the meaning or content of those aspirations, must also be counted as protected under the Civic Constitution, because communities founded on appeals to reason must treat such commitments as subject to reasoned disagreement themselves, or as provisional and contingent. To paraphrase Tulis, conclusions of reason invite challenges of reason.[182]

The Civic Constitution, therefore, admits if not welcomes challenges to constitutionalism as a preferred means of organizing political community. Consequently, when we look for the Civic Constitution as a lived practice, and not simply as a theoretical prospect, we must look for it not only in civic practices that celebrate or conform to constitutional norms and ideals, but also where civic practices challenge or reject those same norms. David Ray Papke, for example, has written extensively about episodes in our constitutional history marked by individuals and movements that have rejected our shared "legal faith . . . in a public, coherent, and aggressive way."[183] Among them, Papke points to William Lloyd Garrison, Elizabeth Cady Stanton, Eugene V. Debs, the Black Panthers, and others, all of whom Papke describes as "heretics" who appropriated constitutional ideals, and sometimes constitutional language, even as they rejected prevailing understandings of constitutionality and constitutional norms. The Civic Constitution, understanding civic practice to include rejections of constitutional faith,[184] invites us to see these episodes as further instances of the Civic Constitution made live.[185] I would add, as I have argued before, that insofar as such arguments embrace commitments that cannot be reconciled with the normative premises of constitutionalism itself (such as the commitment to equality and human dignity), they should be rejected by the community.[186] If the community does embrace them, in the sense that we choose to forswear our commitment to constitutional democracy, then we are in a state of constitutional failure (see Essay Three).

In Essays One and Two I shall consider common complaints about the incivility of our political culture. Robert Putnam, for instance, argues that for many years our civic life has been in substantial decline. "In America, at least, there is reason to suspect that this democratic disarray may be linked to a broad and continuing erosion of civic engagement that began a quarter-century ago."[187] There are several other well-known criticisms of our civic culture, including claims that its vision of economic life as aggressively individualistic and capitalist has led to an "acquisitive society" defined largely by the ideals and norms of the marketplace,[188] at the expense of a civic community concerned with the public good and social welfare. Similarly, critics argue that it has resulted in a public culture dominated by an individualistic "rights-talk,"[189] and a false preoccupation with "process" over "substance."[190] What is lost in this constricted public space, such critics allege, is the rich fabric of community and a commitment to *civilitas*.

The procedural republic and rights-talk said by these and other critics to subvert the "seedbeds of civic and personal virtue" are partly a by-product and consequence of the Juridic Constitution itself. The political culture of the Juridic Constitution is characterized by civic inattention to public affairs and by an impoverished conception of what the arena of public affairs encompasses. The Juridic Constitution restricts civic space to the few areas, such as elections and voting, that it assigns specifically to citizens. The demands of juridic citizenship, such as voting/accountability moments, are simply and only mimetic, or "devices employed to induce the individual to feel in certain circumstances and at certain times, in accordance with the conventions and manners of the epoch."[191] Public space under the Juridic Constitution is correspondingly constrained to discussion of what we might call second-order politics,[192] to questions of policy and even more of partisanship,[193] and not to first-order or constitutional questions about how to construct the well-ordered polity or to achieve the blessings of liberty.[194] Civic life under the Juridic Constitution does not extend to or prize a political culture that concerns itself with pursuing a constitutional way of life or with realizing constitutional aspirations. Consequently, objections to the Civic Constitution that rest on a dim appraisal of the types of citizens we have now miss the larger point: because its ambitions for civic life are so modest, the Juridic Constitution creates citizens who act incivilly, in the sense that they do not ordinarily engage in the self-reflective manner the Civic Constitution requires.

Tending

So far, I have argued that the Civic Constitution requires citizens who are committed, deliberative, and more than intermittently engaged in a shared responsibility to bring the constitutional project forward. I want to note again that this should not be described as promoting a kind of citizenship as concerned with civic virtue, in contrast, say, with notions of citizenship that abjure any such concern. Citizenship under the Juridic Constitution, no less than under the Civic Constitution, requires an element of civic virtue.[195] Instead, the differences, which are substantial and important, inhere in how we describe what it means to be virtuous. The virtuous citizen under the Civic Constitution differs from her counterpart under the Juridic Constitution not because she is virtuous, but rather in respect of what virtuous citizenship requires.

One element of virtue under the Civic Constitution is the ethic of civility. Another is a practice of care, or of tending, to constitutional life. The language of tending conveys a set of predispositions about the character and purposes of civic life. Wolin writes:

> [Tending] implies active care of things close at hand, not mere solicitude. . . . [T]he crucial point is that tendment is tempered by the feeling of concern for objects whose nature requires that they be treated as historical beings. . . . The idea of tending is one that centers politics around practices, that is, around the habits of competence or skill that are routinely required if things are to be taken care of. . . . [Alexis de Tocqueville presented the politics of tendment as] the product of the intimate political experience which Americans acquired in everyday existence.[196]

To tend, both colloquially and in the particular sense Wolin describes, is to show solicitude for the object of our attention.

Three points are critical for understanding tending as a civic virtue. First, tending requires an active, ongoing commitment, and consequently a citizenry that must bear some sizable responsibility for constitutional flourishing. In contrast with the political culture associated with the Juridic Constitution, in which citizens are only occasional actors, tending (like gardening) requires constant attention.[197] Second, tending implies a civic culture centered more on everyday practices of care and less on the periodic discharge of specific duties, such as voting. Third, tending requires and depends upon a specific and kind of knowledge, one grounded in the practice of politics and practical experience. As I indicated earlier, these activities and practices include the third spaces and associational life that we sometimes dismiss as constitutive and characteristic of the private sphere alone, when in fact they are public. As a consequence, civic culture is richer and more inclusive under the Civic Constitution, and finds expression in a much larger variety of practices and forums, than under the Juridic Constitution.

Readers familiar with Wolin's work may find some aspects of my usage a little peculiar. His original distinction, between "intendment" and "tend-ment," overlaps imperfectly with familiar distinctions between liberal and republican, and between Federalist and anti-Federalist. My distinction be-tween the Juridic and the Civic Constitutions, and their respective political cultures, invokes many of the same polarities, but I do not mean to suggest that the Civic Constitution is itself republican, or anti-federalist. I mean only that in contrast to the Juridic Constitution, it underscores and highlights the ways in which the Constitution is of, in, and about politics as well as law. I appropriate the language of tending as in "tending to" or as looking after another person, or to an activity, such as gardening, because it emphasizes the sense of the Constitution as a shared political enterprise, an ongoing political practice, that we must tend to if it is to flourish.[198] Citizens must be prepared to assume public stewardship in the sense that they must be *able*, possessed of both the skills and the resources necessary to practice it. But to tend has another meaning as well—one equally appropriate to the Civic Constitution. In this other usage, to tend means to be inclined to or disposed to doing something, and that is precisely the kind of constitutional culture the Civic Constitution seeks to promote—a culture in which citizens must also be disposed attitudinally, or *willing*, to assume this responsibility. Both senses are required if the Civic Constitution is to be the everyday work of citizens.

THE ESSAYS

There are two principal ways of comprehending the Constitution. One sees the Constitution primarily as a legal document, as the supreme law of the land. The other emphasizes its political character, its status not as supreme law but as political creed. Each conception implies a distinctive way of un-derstanding what kind of a people we are and the community in which we claim citizenship. Each constitutes "We the People" in a particular fashion. These diverse conceptions of the Constitution lead to very different under-standings about what the commutual activities of constitutional *founding* and constitutional *maintenance* demand of governments and citizens, and even of what founding and maintaining the Constitution means. They also encourage us to think in very different ways about what constitutional *fail-ure* means, and about what steps we should take to forestall or remedy it.

My understanding of the constitutional enterprise as temporal and se-quential (though not strictly linear) is not unique to the Constitution of the United States, or indeed to any particular constitution at all. It is, as I and others have argued,[199] an understanding of constitutional development broadly, or an analytical framework that applies to all efforts to build and sustain a constitutional polity.[200] The balance of the book thus unfolds as three essays, each of which addresses a distinct (but connate) part of the constitutional enterprise, and all of which are central to an overarching theory of what the Constitution is and what it does, as well as how it achieves (or fails to achieve) those purposes.

Why do I adopt the form of essays rather than chapters? In each of the essays, I discuss the constitutional order writ large at a particular moment in the constitutional enterprise, instead of a single topic in detail (like the separation of powers, or judicial review, or citizenship). Each essay aims to provide a comprehensive portrait of the constitutional order at a specific moment in its development, from founding to failure. And because each essay circles back on the others, essays better fit my premise that constitutional development is nonlinear and asynchronous. (For the same reason, I considered beginning the book with Essay Three, on constitutional failure, but I'm no James Joyce.[201]) The essay form also better fits the kind of inquiry I want to advance—one organized around questions, not answers, and one in which "nothing is ever really left behind, only put aside temporarily until [the] digressive mind summons it up again, turning it this way and that in a different light, seeing what sense it makes."[202] Finally, "the iron law of the essay is heresy,"[203] and an argument that champions the Civic Constitution and contests the Juridic has at least a small element of heresy built into its very fabric.

Essay One: Constituting

The first moment in the constitutional enterprise is a founding, or the literal act of constituting the (new) polity.[204] In Essay One, I shall consider how the Civic Constitution understands and approaches this initial moment, or what the Civic Constitution imagines the activity of founding to comprehend. Constituting includes the drafting of a foundational text or texts,[205] the creation (and limitation of) a new sovereign government, the delineation of the sources and objects of state power, and the design of constitutional structures and architecture, as well as the configuration of a constitutional culture and citizens. Hence, a constitutional founding—*constituting*—encompasses far more than just the creation of a constitutional text or a supreme law, contentious and complicated as that process may be.[206] It extends to the configuration of a constitutional order writ large, or a text *and* a polity.[207]

At a certain level of abstraction, then, constituting embraces four interrelated projects—the creation of texts, institutions, citizens, and cultures. These four projects are the objects of all constitutional orders; they are not specific or unique to the Civic Constitution or to the Juridic, or to any other particular understanding of constitutional community. They inhere in the very idea of founding, or of constituting, as a political project. How we understand and approach these objects, however, is very much related to our approach to the Constitution more generally. Both the Juridic and the Civic Constitutions fashion institutions, citizens, and cultures, but they constitute them in profoundly different ways and in different images. They anticipate different kinds of citizens, charged with different responsibilities, and they envision different kinds of cultures, concerned with different matters.

The Juridic Constitution, conceived chiefly as law, constitutes the regime in the image of law. It ordains institutions, citizens, and cultures in ways that reinforce and sustain the proposition that the Constitution's authority and meaning is grounded in legality.[208] The Civic Constitution, in contrast, constitutes the regime in the image of political identity. In Essay One, I develop the implications of this approach for citizenship and constitutional culture. In particular, I shall argue that the Civic Constitution constitutes a constitutional order that imagines constitutional questions to be properly the prerogative of citizens and as central to civic dialogue,[209] and that does not reduce essentially to the specialized and localized practice of constitutional interpretation by judges. As we shall see in Essays Two and Three, this in turn presages a different account of what constitutional maintenance requires as well as what constitutional failure means.

Essay Two: Maintaining

In Essay Two, I shall consider how the Civic Constitution leads us to think in different ways about three questions essential to a comprehensive account of constitutional maintenance.[210] First, the Civic Constitution points to a particular conception of *what* citizens must conserve. The Civic Constitution envisions constitutional maintenance as embracing and preserving a particular kind of citizenship and a particular kind of constitutional culture, both of which differ in important and substantive ways from their juridic analogues.

Second, the Civic Constitution assumes a particular response to the question of *who* is responsible for the activity of constitutional maintenance. Civic maintenance locates responsibility for the Constitution not only or chiefly in lawyers and judges but in citizens. As a result, responsibility for and participation in the constitutional enterprise is correspondingly more diffuse. Its catholicism means that responsibility for constitutional governance is a broadly democratic affair, properly the trust of every citizen, and fundamentally an activity grounded in politics rather than law.[211] The Civic

Constitution thus offers a different understanding about who should attend
to constitutional maintenance and, no less important, about what kind of
project it is (one that *does* require our recurrent attention as citizens to first
principles).

The Civic Constitution also informs our understanding of how constitutional actors and institutions should function and of what responsibilities we
should assign to them, because "The way political structures are crafted is
critical to the long-run education of a people."[212] The difference in orientation is both reflected in and a consequence of institutional design and functioning. The Juridic Constitution is more hospitable to an understanding
of constitutional conflict and disagreement that emphasizes the settlement
rather than the so-called dialogic function of constitutional arrangements.[213]
The Civic Constitution, in contrast, is better served by an approach to constitutional disagreement that privileges dialogue and ongoing conversation
between and among coequal constitutional actors.[214] Hence, my focus will
be on ways of approaching separation of powers and federalism that emphasize their capacity to work as agents of constitutional instruction. I propose conceptions of separation of powers and federalism that promote the
autonomy of nonjudicial institutional actors because they are more likely
to result in institutional actors keen to address constitutional issues as a
significant part of their institutional trust.

The Civic Constitution also bears on how we understand the allocation
of interpretive authority in the practice of formal constitutional interpretation. Both the Juridic and the Civic Constitutions allocate some degree of
interpretative authority to judges. The Civic Constitution does not deny that
the Constitution is law or that judges have some authority to interpret and
enforce it—it is simply a way of understanding the breadth and limits of that
authority. The mechanisms for maintenance under the Civic Constitution
include constitutional review (although not as manifest in strong-form judicial review or judicial supremacy), because such discussions can contribute
to a larger dialogic process. The Civic Constitution prefers a weak form of
judicial review in constitutional cases, a preference premised less upon the
system's need for constitutional settlement and more upon the necessity of
constitutional dialogue.[215]

Third, the Civic Constitution embraces a number of different approaches
to the question of *how* it should be maintained. Civic maintenance encompasses a variety of activities that, broadly speaking, develop and cultivate
civic engagement and constitutional literacy. The Civic Constitution also
underscores the importance of civic education. Civic education includes not
only formal education, but also the experience and active practice of local

government and the encouragement of a wide variety of associational activities in civil society. Hence, civic education must include the development of citizens possessed of civic virtue and aptitude, or be capacious enough to include the fostering of "republican habits of mind."[216] The Civic Constitution therefore requires us to reexamine the relationship between state and civil society—to recognize that the state has an interest in the character and formulation of civil society itself.

Essay Three: Failing

In Essay Three, I consider how the Civic Constitution upsets our understanding of constitutional failure. How might the Civic Constitution fail? Are there specifically civic modes of failure? Failure can take two forms under the Civic Constitution. We might fail to honor or practice our commitment to constitutional norms (failures of fidelity), and we might fail our civic obligations to shoulder responsibility for sustaining the Constitution (failures of civility). Distinguishing between failures of fidelity and civility reminds us that in most cases constitutional success and constitutional failure are matters of judgment, in part because the terms are political constructs, not bright-line legal tests, and in part because success does not require perfection.[217]

Under the Juridic Constitution, the concept of constitutional failure is conceptualized in terms of legality and manifest chiefly as the failure of institutions and rights. In contrast, the Civic Constitution asks us to consider a type of constitutional failure that is different from and that transcends the failure of constitutional institutions and the protection of constitutional liberties. I shall argue in Essay Three that there is a specific kind of constitutional failure, which I shall call constitutional rot, that can occur even and only when constitutional institutions appear to be in good repair.[218] It occurs when questions of legality obscure questions of constitutionality and where the people are unwilling or unable to take up those questions as their own. Rot can occur, in other words, only when the people neglect to live a constitutional way of life.

I conclude Essay Three with a question: Do the constitutional, legal, and cultural changes occasioned by 9/11 amount to an example of constitutional failure? The answer depends upon the kind of constitutional order we think we want. Measured against the demands of the Civic Constitution, however, constitutional rot appears to have settled in. We have suffered, I shall argue, from simultaneous and interrelated failures of fidelity and civility. The cure is restoring our commitment to the Civic Constitution.

CONCLUSION

The Civic Constitution requires our attachment to principles that inhere in all constitutional states and to the fundamental principles that comprise our particular identity. These principles include the blessings of liberty, self-governance, human dignity, equality, limited government, national citizenship, and reason. Equally importantly, the Civic Constitution calls for public participation in the articulation, definition, and realization of each of these commitments, expressed through the civic virtues of civility and tending. The Civic Constitution approaches these ideals as aspirations no less than as rights—as constituting a polity in which all citizens assume an obligation to participate in a communal effort to transform aspirations into practices. As John Adams wrote, "A Constitution, founded on these principles, introduces knowledge among the People, and inspires them with conscious dignity, becoming Freemen."[219]

My aim is to revitalize our understanding of the Civic Constitution and to renew our commitment to it—not at the expense of the Juridic, but alongside it, while recognizing also that a complete reconciliation of the Juridic and Civic Constitutions is neither possible nor desirable. A full account of the American constitutional order includes both its legal and its civic elements, elements that are simultaneously complementary and antonymic in character. In arguing for the Civic Constitution, I argue for the reinvigoration of one strand of many that comprise American constitutionalism and in so doing, I seek to restore and strengthen our commitment to an authentically constitutional way of life.

The Juridic Constitution is not the sole or even the most significant cause of civic debilitation, nor is restoration of the Civic Constitution the primary means of combatting it. Hence, "Constitutional reform may not be a panacea; indeed, it may not be the very first place to start," but it is an important part of the process of restoring civic life.[220] Restoring the Civic Constitution may help to reinvigorate civic life by recalling a constitutional language that is public and publicly accessible—a language of constitutional ideals instead of a language of constitutional legality.

ESSAY ONE

Constituting

The first moment in the constitutional enterprise is the act of constituting, or the founding of the new polity. Constituting is the first step to distinguishing between regimes that have their origin in a deliberative and conscious decision to construct a polity, and regimes that find their origins in spontaneous orders.[1] Invoking Hayek, constituted orders result from human action *and* from human design.[2] Behind them rests enlightenment-era optimism that humans need not be hostages to accident or force.[3]

A constituting moment, however, does not make a *constituted* regime a *constitutional* regime. A constituting moment is a necessary first step in the life span of all constructed political orders, including those that result from social contracts or purport to be constitutional democracies. But the familiar coincidence of democratic states and social contract states (the latter are necessarily constructed political orders) does not mean that social contract regimes, even when contractually committed to principles of democratic governance, are by virtue of that circumstance alone *constitutional* states. The effort to found a constitutional state requires an affirmative commitment to making only certain kinds of choices and decisions about the new political order and to rejecting other choices and possibilities.

The particular commitments we make when constituting thus have implications for determining whether the political order we have constructed is in fact a constitutional order as well as for the later stages of constitutional development. Some of the commitments we make are required by virtue of our desire to act constitutionally. As I have indicated in other writings, a community's aspiration to become a constitutional polity means first that it must respect certain preconstitutional or constitutive principles that comprise the definition of constitutionalism proper.[4] These principles include the familiar commitment to limited government, as well as to principles of self-governance, human dignity, liberty, equal moral worth, and national citizenship (as expressed in the phrase "We the People" and later in the Fourteenth Amendment), as well as to a less familiar but equally important principle that I have called "articulated" or public reason.[5]

33

A polity's obligation to these principles inheres in its aspiration to live constitutionally and not (simply or only) by virtue of its ratification or inclusion in a constitutional text. Preconstitutional principles are therefore a necessary part of any effort to found a constitutional polity.[6] That commitment is nonnegotiable in the sense that constitutive principles are definitional or foundational in character, and not simply elective. Every constitutional order must embrace them; to fail to commit to them is to fail to act constitutionally. Indeed, a text that repudiates those constitutive principles is not, I have argued, a constitution in any meaningful sense of the term.[7] Such principles acquire their bindingness or authority not because they are included in or have been ratified in a constitutional document, but through our desire to act constitutionally; they inhere in our commitment to the constitutional enterprise itself.

Because preconstitutional principles are a part of the fabric of constitutional forms, they are a component of both the Juridic and the Civic Constitutions alike. They do not trace to or find their authority in the Juridic Constitution or in the Civic Constitution, but are instead independent of particular constitutional form or iterations. *How* we understand and realize these principles, however, will be significantly influenced by our decision to embrace one or the other of the Juridic and Civic Constitutions. The differences will be especially apparent in the various aspects of constitutional design that we discuss in this essay, including how we engineer constitutional institutions and how we configure the relationship between state and civil society.

Other aspects of our constitutional identity are volitional. This electivity expresses itself in two ways. First, our understanding of what constitutive principles require of us, and of how they might be secured through constitutional design, leaves substantial room for variation. Although a system of separated power is constitutive of constitutionalism, for example, we might separate power in a great variety of ways. Our commitment to constitutional government does not bind us to a single understanding of what the separation of powers means or to one and only one architectural blueprint. Thus, we see considerable variation among constitutional democracies about how to effectuate (or operationalize) the separation of powers, and "[i]n most constitutional democracies . . . the structure of executive-legislative relations differs notably from the American" design.[8] Indeed, the exact nature of the system of separated powers in the United States is itself subject to considerable debate. Significant controversy arose in Philadelphia over how to separate power, with some advocates urging adoption of the so-called watertight model that existed in some of the colonies (notably Massachusetts), and others calling for mixed or blended models.[9] These disagreements continue to influence contemporary discussion about the meaning of separation of powers in the United States, as evidenced, for example, by ongoing debates concerning the extent of presidential power to commit American troops to conflicts in the Middle East,[10] or by questions concerning congressional power to superintend judicial sentencing in federal courts.[11]

Second, the facultative particulars of constitutional identity appear in (some of) the choices we make (and are free to make) about what ends we want to pursue and in what order of priority, or in the specific aspirations we embrace and abjure. The choices we make, for example, about the relationship of the state to religion, about how to accommodate linguistic or ethnic minorities, about where to locate the boundary between state and civil society, or about civic education, all common objects of constitutional design in contemporary democracies,[12] contribute to a specific and unique constitutional personality.

Every constitutional identity, then, is partly a function of our commitment to constitutional norms in general[13] and partly a function of other commitments that are particularistic and contingent. Together, in general and in fine, they comprise our unique constitutional identity.[14] Moreover, many of the cardinal components of a constitutional identity are established at the founding, but any constitutional identity is necessarily protean. Indeed, as we will see in this essay, the idea that there is a founding confined to a single, identifiable moment in time, and developmentally distinct from other constitutional moments, is predicated upon an understanding of the Constitution that undercuts its civic aspirations.

CONSTITUTING AND THE CIVIC CONSTITUTION

How does the Civic Constitution help us to understand the act of constituting as part of the constitutional enterprise? The civic part of the Civic Constitution points to a familiar if not ancient understanding of constitutionalism itself,[15] an understanding frequently described as Aristotelian in nature, because it envisions a constitution "as a way of life" or as "constituting the soul of the polis."[16] As Eskridge notes of the Aristotelian notion of a constitution, "Rather than a formal document, the constitution is the soul of a city. More than either its territory or even its inhabitants, a city's constitution accounted for its civic identity across time."[17] The linking of community and constitution across time, key to Aristotelian constitutionalism, is also a central element of the Civic Constitution; both take *civilitas* seriously, and both assume that constituting the *civilas* is an ongoing process that is not confined to a single moment in time. (There are additional points of comparison. Aristotle's constitutionalism, for example, had little interest in formal documents.[18])

This understanding of the Constitution—as constituting an intertemporal community in which citizens take the Constitution seriously—imposes certain imperatives on the project of founding. It requires that we write a certain kind of text, which is accessible to citizens and which does not speak to them in an "alien tongue," as Learned Hand once observed.[19] It requires also that we design institutions in ways that promote rather than stunt civic engagement and participation, that we fashion a critical and engaged citizenry, committed to the polity through bonds of reason (first) and affection (secondarily),[20] and that we configure a particular kind of constitutional culture, characterized by civility and an ethic of tending. A focus on the Civic Constitution, in other words, influences how we should write texts, design institutions, constitute citizens, and configure political culture. I take each up in turn.

The Civic Constitution and the Text

A conception of the constitutional enterprise as an effort to create an enduring constitutional order takes the constitutional text seriously, but it does not assume that constitutional text and constitutional order are coincident. In *From Words to Worlds*, Breslin makes the important point that my work, and the work of some other scholars (many associated with the so-called Princeton school), insofar as it asks citizens to think more capaciously about what a constitution is, what it includes, and what it hopes to accomplish, may relegate the text itself to "secondary" status.[21] It is true that in some ways my constitutional theory subordinates the text to the larger constitutional order in which it resides (and which it helps to ordain).

The differences, however, may lie more in emphasis than in any strong disagreement about the importance of constitutional scripts as instruments of governance or of identity. Any and every constitutional order includes texts, institutions, values, and citizens. *How* it includes them—how much weight and significance it gives to texts, how it designs institutions, and what it expects of citizens—depends in part upon the identity or personality of the regime in question, and identity is in some share a function of the text proper.[22] But it is in the interaction between text and the larger political order, over time past and present,[23] where constitutional meaning finally resides.[24]

So if a constitutional text and a constitutional order are not the same, they are interdependent—each influences and is influenced by the other. A text may seek to install, challenge, or complement civil society and political culture, as Jacobsohn has noted.[25] The nature of the constitutional order created in turn also influences how we understand the constitutional text. What we think the Constitution *is* governs how, and in the case of the Juridic Constitution whether, we read it.

The Civic Constitution invites us to approach the constitutional text from three perspectives. First, it asks us to think about how we should *write* the document in light of our purposes and aspirations. Second, it encourages us to *read* the text in particular ways, or to adopt particular interpretive postures and strategies. In other words, we must write and read the Constitution in ways that advance the civic project and help us to realize our civic aspirations. And third, it requires us to think more capaciously about *which* texts qualify as a part of the "Constitution."[26]

In the abstract, the difference between writing and reading a text may seem to be clear or at least to reference distinct and sequenced activities (that correspond to the serial projects of constituting and maintaining). In practice, the differences between writing a text and reading a text are not so stark. How we write a text, especially a constitutional text, is greatly influenced by who we think its readers will be. When we call a text into being we simultaneously call into being its readers. Recall Eco's observation in this respect that every text constructs (or constitutes) a model reader (citizen).[27] It is not simply the case that constitutions attract or even imagine a certain kind of reader—they actively *construct* those readers as citizens. Constitutions, like all texts, envision a particular sort of relationship between author and reader, one in which the text interacts with, "instructs," "directs," or "controls" the reader in certain sorts of ways and on specific terms.[28] Moreover, this process is ongoing, and not confined to a singular moment of constituting, because the writing is never complete. We continuously add to, subtract from, and rewrite the text, both formally, through Article 5, and informally, through the processes of constitutional interpretation and constitutional construction.[29] Writing and rewriting are especially prominent parts of the Civic Constitution.

The meaning of a constitutional text depends upon, and must finally reside in, the community it creates and presumes to govern.[30] I say "presumes" to govern because a constitution's claim to govern subsequent generations is, especially at first appearances, a presumptuous conceit, as Jefferson and Noah Webster both intimated.[31] The conceit is less problematic than first appears, however, once we recognize that subsequent generations ("to our posterity"—the text itself anticipates this issue) are not simply the passive recipients or subjects of a text that makes certain political commitments (at T^1) and then asks only, or at most, for our tacit agreement at T^2.[32] And just as there is no clear temporal distinction under the Civic Constitution between T^1 and T^2, there is no clear distinction between the corporate We the People (P^1) at the founding moment and We the People now (P^2); we are all part of a single people that has a "past (what I was), [a] present (what I am), [and] a future (what I aspire to be)."[33]

This ongoing interaction between text and reader, between constitutional script and citizen, complicates the distinction between writing and reading the text. Subsequent generations, at least under the Civic Constitution, are not passive beneficiaries of political decisions taken by a revered generation of founders (a point of especial importance in understanding the differences between the Juridic and Civic Constitutions), but are instead active participants in the making of constitutional meaning. If, according to Stanley Fish, the "efforts of readers are always efforts to discern and therefore to realize . . . an author's intention,"[34] then the process is complicated by realizing that the reader is, in some critical respect, also the author.[35] This understanding of the Constitution's authority implicitly undermines the distinction between writing and reading, as well as the distinction between constituting and maintaining.

Writing the Civic Text

The Civic Constitution requires us to write a constitutional document that encourages and gives life to the civic project. To facilitate civic life, we must write the constitution in terms that are not obscure or that do not have a technical meaning that eludes most readers.[36] Constitutional language must not intimidate or exclude but instead must welcome citizens.[37] The Civic Constitution must communicate in the inclusive political language of shared aspirations and ideals, of *civilitas,* identity,[38] and common fortune. To know the Civic Constitution we must speak a broadly common or civic tongue.[39] As I indicate below, the civic tongue is a language citizens must learn. This has important implications for the role and meaning of civic education in a constitutional democracy.

Where possible, therefore, constitutional language should avoid legalisms and other terms of art that require professional expertise or learning to comprehend.[40] The Constitution's status as supreme law, however, means that at times it must use the language of law. Although my purpose in this book is to explain and to advance the Civic Constitution, the Constitution is not only a profession of who we aspire to become—it is also a set of rules and regulations that organize, empower, and limit governmental authority. Consequently, it sometimes uses the language of law (Article 1, Section 7, is one example) and sometimes of politics (as in the Preamble).

Because the American Constitution is both Civic and Juridic, it uses two languages—the languages of law and of politics. Our task is to recognize, if not always to reconcile, this polyglossia.[41] As a corollary proposition, when we choose to privilege the Juridic or the Civic Constitution, we simultaneously choose to privilege one kind of constitutional language over another. These language choices are inescapably political in character and in effect, or a "political choice," as Weinstein argues.[42] Moreover, the "distribution of languages and their variations can have important consequences by affecting the distribution of a whole range of other burdens and benefits of political life."[43] The choices we make in writing the constitutional text (decisions that appear most prominently but that are not confined to a single moment of constituting), must therefore be attentive to their implications for civic life and engagement.

The chief characteristic of legal language is not its precision, as its defenders claim, or its obfuscatory denseness, as its many detractors charge,[44] but rather its exclusivity and privacy, a privacy that results from its inaccessibility to inexpert, ordinary citizens. As Jonathan Swift implied when he described lawyers as a society with a "peculiar Cant and Jargon of their own, that no other Mortal can understand," legal language is inescapably a language of power and social control. Law cannot function as a civic language or serve as the civic tongue precisely because it excludes most citizens. Its exclusivity is fundamentally incompatible with the structural prerequisites of constitutional civility and civic conversation.

What the Juridic Constitution does not itself make obscure, judicial exegesis does, so much so that it prompted the famous advice from Harvard Law Professor Thomas Reed Powell to his students not to read the Constitution, for it would only confuse them. The confusion, of course, lay in the lack of correspondence between the document and judicial constructions of it. As Powell intimates, the meaning of the Constitution (especially for its legal guardians) resides not in the document, but in judicial commentary on its meaning.[45] Accordingly, to know the Juridic Constitution we must know how judges overwrite the text with precedent, obscure formulisms and doctrinalisms, and other interpretive constructs[46] that are inaccessible and incomprehensible except to the specially trained.

Reading the Civic Text

At the present moment in the constitutional enterprise, our task is not to write a new constitutional document that gives life to the Civic Constitution. Instead, we are in the position of reading (or constructing, or interpreting)[47] a received text. *How* we read the text (as well as whether we read it, and what parts of it we read), is informed by the purposes we assign to it.[48] If we think the text means to advance the Juridic Constitution, then we will read it, as Marshall did in *Marbury*, in ways that both legitimate and advance our conception of it as a legal instrument.[49] Indeed, the rise of the Juridic Constitution leads us to read both the constitutional text and the founding itself as pregnant with juridic commitments and to overlook or diminish the significance of its civic ones.

The Juridic Constitution consecrates the text as law. If the text is law, then it speaks first and most fully to those of us who are fluent in the law; that fluency is a key element in the appropriation of the text by judges. The Juridic Constitution thus envisions a community of readers that is expert in the law. Better, it envisions several concentric communities of readers, each of which has a different relationship to the text. Implicit in this understanding of the Constitution as law is its juridicality—or the sense that because the Constitution is law, judges have some special responsibility for determining the meaning of the Constitution. But that responsibility can be justified only because and to the extent that the Constitution can plausibly be read as a set of legal rules and proscriptions. The Juridic Constitution thus sees the text chiefly as a set of judicially enforceable rules (Articles 1 through 3 are prime examples) and rights (Amendments 1 through 8). Part of the reason the text is so significant for the Juridic Constitution is because we *can* fairly read parts of the text to support the claim that the Constitution is fundamentally legal in character. Article 6 figures prominently in this claim because it provides the analytical edifice for emphasizing the Constitution's status as supreme law. (I would add, however, that we should also read Article 6 as embodying principles central to the Civic Constitution. Insofar as Article 6 asks citizens to affirm or reject the Constitution's claim to superiority, it envisions citizens capable of reason and deliberation.[50]) But the claim that the Constitution is law does not derive from Article 6 alone. The privileges and immunities clause of the Fourteenth Amendment, for example, seems to imply that the clause has the force of law by virtue of its supremacy over state laws that would "abridge the privileges and immunities of citizens of the United States."[51]

Under the Juridic Constitution, parts of the constitutional text (to say nothing of those parts of the Constitution that are not in the text at all) that do not reduce to rules susceptible of judicial application through constitutional litigation are simply ignored or of no significance (at least to courts). As a consequence, some parts of the text (the civic parts) form no part of the "real" or enforceable Juridic Constitution. These include the Preamble, the guarantee clause of Article 4, and the Ninth Amendment, and potentially several other parts of the text, all of which implicate "questions in their nature political," to borrow a phrase. Just as importantly, however, it means that other potential sources of constitutional meaning, including other important or foundational texts, likewise form no part of the Juridic Constitution, precisely because they have no status as law. Their significance, and their authority, is political and not legal. Thus, a juridic approach to the text systematically disqualifies parts of the text, and other texts altogether, from (judicial) consideration of the Constitution's meaning. As I shall indicate below, this is an area where there is significant divergence between the Juridic and Civic Constitutions.

Just as importantly, a juridic approach to the Constitution not only debases parts of the text (and other texts altogether), it influences how we read the rest of the document. Consequently, as we shall see when we take up constitutional interpretation as an instrument of constitutional maintenance in Essay Two, the insistence that the constitution is law has had a profound effect on both the purposes and the practice of constitutional interpretation. Approaching the text as law means "our conception of the Constitution has been shaped by [lawyers'] instincts and intellectual habits."[52] Consider, for instance, how debates over whether particular interpretive methodologies sufficiently cabin judicial discretion are predicated essentially on the premise that to move too far from the text is to invite judicial decision making grounded not in law but in politics.[53]

As a result, those elements of the text (such as the Preamble or the Ninth Amendment) not immediately accessible or meaningful as law shrivel in their capacity to influence constitutional development. Put simply, if they cannot support litigation, they do not matter. We then sometimes labor to (mis)read parts of the text as legal rules (the Tenth Amendment is a good example[54]), or as rights-bearing provisions that may be enforced against the state by judges through constitutional litigation, even in cases where it is clear that the text cannot easily support such an interpretation.[55]

It is worth noting that this compartmentalization of the text traces at least as far back as *Marbury*, where Marshall observed that judges cannot entertain "questions in their nature political." (Again, *Marbury* did not give rise to the Juridic Constitution in full bloom.) Presumably, the political parts of the text, because they cannot be enforced as law, have heuristic or rhetorical value only; if they are of any practical import, it is only because political actors (not judges) have given them sanction (and this is made less likely by strong-form judicial review and the resulting concept of judicial overhang,[56] one of the chief features of the Juridic Constitution, as I discuss in Essay Two). The coexistence of constitutional provisions that manifest as judicially enforceable rules of law and nonjusticiable questions of politics in a single text again demonstrates that the Constitution is both civic and juridic.

Wherever possible, we should adopt strategies for reading the text that enable civic life to flourish. If we confine our reading to the text (a point I dispute; see pp. 47–53), then we should pay especial attention to those parts of it that speak in majestic generalities about our promises to ourselves and to posterity, such as the Preamble, the Guarantee Clause, the Bill of Rights, and the Ninth, Tenth, and Reconstruction Amendments. Each of these provisions embodies aspirations to a certain kind of civic life, one that finds value in public spiritedness and public engagement with constitutional questions. The Preamble, for example, speaks of our aspiration to secure a more perfect union and to establish justice, as well as to secure the common welfare, domestic tranquility, and the blessings of liberty. It speaks, as Barber has noted, to the "substantive constitutional ends" we seek to realize.[57] These ends, rich with "substantive significance,"[58] commit us to a constitutional project dedicated to achieving a certain kind of political community.

The Fourteenth Amendment speaks in a similarly aspirational voice, protecting life, liberty, and property, as well as equality. It makes these ideals possible to achieve in practice by incorporating principles, such as a reasons requirement, that are the preconditions of their realization. A reasons requirement inheres in the due process clauses of the Fifth and Fourteenth Amendments because, reduced to its essentials, a due process requirement is simply a demand that authority produce reasons in support of public policies that touch important liberty claims.[59] The production of reasons is a precondition for the kind of constitutional conversations the Civic Constitution requires.

For an example of how a civic reading of the text might yield a different understanding of what the text means than a juridic reading, consider Section 5 of the Fourteenth Amendment. Section 5 provides that "The Congress shall have power to enforce, by appropriate legislation, the provisions of this article."[60] The precise dimensions of congressional authority under Section 5 have always been unclear. In *Katzenbach v. Morgan* (1966), the Court held that Section 5 of the Fourteenth Amendment is "a positive grant of legislative power authorizing Congress to exercise its discretion in determining the need for and nature of legislation to secure Fourteenth Amendment guarantees." *Katzenbach* is well known for its so-called ratchet theory of congressional power under Section 5, in which Congress may expand upon judicially recognized protections, but may not shrink them. The ratchet theory thus recognizes some room for congressional interpretation of the Fourteenth Amendment (or a limited form of coordinate construction), but it remains a system in which the interpretive primacy of the Court is largely unchallenged. On the other hand, writing in dissent, Justice Harlan argued that even the limited grant of interpretive authority to Congress recognized by the majority posed a threat to judicial power and hence to the separation of powers more generally, an aggressively juridic reading of the text.

The Court reasserted its interpretive primacy in *Boerne v. Flores* (1997). In *Boerne*, the Court considered the constitutionality of the Religious Freedom Restoration Act of 1993 (RFRA), a congressional response to the Court's decision in *Employment Division v. Smith* (1990). In *Smith*, Justice Scalia, writing for the majority, concluded that some free-exercise challenges to governmental action ought to be assessed using the familiar rational-basis test, rather than the considerably more demanding strict-scrutiny test that had seemed to govern such challenges since the Court's decision in *Sherbert v. Verner* (1963). Congress announced its preference for the *Sherbert* strict-scrutiny standard by providing that the RFRA's purpose was "(1) to restore the compelling interest test as set forth in *Sherbert v. Verner*, 374 U.S. 398 (1963) and *Wisconsin v. Yoder*, 406 U.S. 205 (1972) and to guarantee its application in all cases where free exercise of religion is substantially burdened."

The Court rejected Congress's claim of coequal interpretive authority to determine the meaning of the Fourteenth Amendment. Writing for the Court, Justice Kennedy held:

> In assessing the breadth of § 5's enforcement power, we begin with its text. Congress has been given the power "to enforce" the "provisions of this article." We agree with respondent, of course, that Congress can enact legislation under § 5 enforcing the constitutional right to the free exercise of religion. . . .
>
> Congress' power under § 5, however, extends only to "enforcing" the provisions of the Fourteenth Amendment. The Court has described this power as "remedial." The design of the Amendment and the text of § 5 are inconsistent with the suggestion that Congress has the power to decree the substance of the Fourteenth Amendment's restrictions on the States. Legislation which alters the meaning of the Free Exercise Clause cannot be said to be enforcing the Clause. Congress does not enforce

a constitutional right by changing what the right is. It has been given the power "to enforce," not the power to determine what constitutes a constitutional violation. Were it not so, what Congress would be enforcing would no longer be, in any meaningful sense, the "provisions of [the Fourteenth Amendment]."

The Court's holding in *Boerne* reflects a particular understanding of the separation of powers doctrine, in which the Court's authority to interpret the text, grounded in its status as law, necessarily trumps the interpretive powers possessed by the other branches. (This is a claim of judicial supremacy, though not of judicial exclusivity, as Harlan made clear in his dissent in *Katzenbach*.) *Boerne* thus depends upon two of the main elements of the Juridic Constitution—that the Constitution is first and primarily a legal instrument, and its final meaning the prerogative of judges.

A civic reading of congressional authority under Section 5, by contrast, would afford more interpretive authority to Congress and thus help to advance the ideals of the Fourteenth Amendment as civic commitments. As I shall demonstrate in greater length in Essay Two, a civic reading of congressional authority under Section 5 of the Fourteenth Amendment contributes to constitutional conversation by increasing the number of voices and points of view represented in that conversation. Put another way, the Civic Constitution's preference for interpretive pluralism, grounded in its capacity to contribute to constitutional dialogue and civic deliberation, would require a different result in both *Katzenbach* and *Boerne*. A civic reading of Section 5 of the Fourteenth Amendment would advance the purposes of the Civic Constitution by encouraging Congress, and by extension citizens, to embrace its responsibility to tend to constitutional precepts. A civic reading of the Fourteenth Amendment sees in it both an opportunity and a responsibility for Congress (and thereby citizens) to pursue a constitutional way of life. (The civic reading thus informs our understanding of *who* should read Section 5 and *how* it should be read.[61])

The Civic Constitution likewise tells us something about how *not* to read the text: Readings that emphasize the jural character of the document, and that simultaneously disqualify or disable nonjudicial voices in constitutional dialogue (like those in *Boerne*), should be disfavored. In silencing those voices, the *Boerne* Court teaches Congress and citizens that their responsibility for the Constitution is narrow and, because not to be trusted, of limited reach and consequence. The irony, of course, is that the RFRA shows a Congress far more solicitous of religious freedom than the *Smith* Court.

The Civic Constitution thus influences how we should read specific constitutional provisions, such as the Fourteenth Amendment, but it also influences our reading of the text in a more comprehensive fashion as well. The Bill of Rights, in the Juridic Constitution, becomes a laundry list of negative liberties that citizens can sometimes enforce against state action.[62] This contrasts with the civic understanding, which sees the Constitution generally, and the Bill of Rights in particular, as positive incentives to the achievement of a particular kind of community and not simply as a set of legal immunities from state action.[63] (Here I agree with George Thomas that the Bill of Rights, insofar as it embraces the Aristotelian understanding of constitutionalism as "a way of life," shapes civil society by "giving us more than a 'negative' charter of liberties."[64])

I want to make clear that the juridic reading of the Bill of Rights as a list of negative liberties enforceable against the state with the aid of courts is not a *mis*reading of the text. It is, however, an incomplete or inadequate reading, and hence, not the best reading of the text.[65] A civic reading of the Bill of Rights sees it as a set of civic ideals and as a means for securing the blessings of liberty. On this reading, the chief value of the Bill of Rights is found not in its justiciability but in its recitation of "solemn political truths" that express "fundamental maxims of a free Government," in the words of Madison.[66] So we may read the Bill of Rights as a text of civil instruction, or as "political law," not "ordinary law," and "As such it must be interpreted by the various political organs that call it into being, not just courts."[67] From the perspective of the Civic Constitution, the Bill of Rights "acts as a kind of republican schoolmaster, serving as a civic lexicon by which the people teach themselves the grammar and meaning of freedom."[68] The text itself becomes a part of our civic education. Again, this does not mean that its proscriptions are *not* legal rights, just that they are not *only* legal rights. A civic reading reveals them as a fundamental part of a larger constitutional project, a project whose responsibility falls not only or even chiefly on judges.

It is not unusual for constitutional documents to include positive policy prescriptions, in the sense that the state is committed to their realization, but that are not judicially enforceable. The Irish Constitution includes a set of Directive Principles of Social Policy that commits the Irish Republic to a number of ascriptive principles and policies, among them directives that "justice and charity" must "inform all the institutions of the national life," that everyone has the right to an adequate occupation, and that the free market and private property must be regulated in the interests of the common good. Similarly, Article 4 of the Indian Constitution contains several Directives of State Policy, including directives that commit the state to social, economic, and political justice, that guarantee the rights to work, education, and several others. As in Ireland, these directives are not enforceable by law, but they do have constitutional importance.[69] I am not suggesting that we should consider key provisions in the Bill of Rights to be social directives, but neither does their significance reside solely in their status as judicially enforceable rights.

My reference to the civic educative purpose of the Bill of Rights may trouble some scholars. Without reviewing the full range of survey data available on the question,[70] it seems clear that most of our fellow citizens know little about the Bill of Rights or the Constitution. Obviously such ignorance must be a matter of concern for the Civic Constitution—it is difficult to see how a constitutional way of life can be realized in the face of such ignorance—but it is not clear why it should bother us under the Juridic Constitution. As I will argue in Essay Two, the Juridic Constitution entrusts to the people no significant responsibility for maintaining or protecting constitutional principles. It *does* ask citizens to venerate the Constitution, largely for its importance as a national artifact, much as we venerate the founders, the flag, and the Liberty Bell. Its slogan might be: "The Constitution—Fuck Yeah!"[71] But it does not require us to *know* anything about the Constitution. Genuine concern about constitutionally illiterate citizens makes sense only if we think citizens really do or should have some responsibility for the Constitution. (In Essay Three, I shall consider whether a polity whose citizens do not understand or accept their responsibility for helping us to achieve a constitutional way of life should be considered an instance of constitutional failure.)

Hence, in addition to telling us how to read the text, the Civic Constitution also tells us who should read the text. In contrast to the Juridic Constitution, read and interpreted by interpretive communities comprised of lawyers, judges, professors, and others possessed of expert training, the readers of the Civic Constitution must be all citizens. Platitudes aside, why should citizens bother to read the Constitution? Under the Juridic Constitution, at least, their status as readers implies no responsibility for giving the Constitution meaning. The Juridic Constitution disqualifies most of We the People from discussion. From the perspective of the Civic Constitution, this is self-defeating, first because it does not actually constitute us, but also because it makes it unlikely that we will achieve and maintain a constitutional way of life.

In sum, the Civic and Juridic Constitutions require different kinds of texts. They also demand that we read them in different ways and with different kinds of strategies.[72] The Civic Constitution anticipates a reader and a reading that (unlike the Juridic Constitution) welcomes the autonomy and criticality of the nonexpert citizen reader.[73] The reader/citizen stands in a different relationship to the text, not as the passive recipient of received meaning, but rather as a maker of meaning. The citizen approaches the text from the vantage of choice, or rather, the power to make choices. Finally, we must remember that we are not simply giving the text a "civic" reading, or looking to advance its civic meaning, so much as we are trying to integrate the civic with the juridic text. The full constitution is polyglossic (or disharmonic, to use Jacobsohn's terminology), or both and simultaneously Juridic and Civic. Recognizing this disharmony, and finding ways to live with it, is one of the objects of a civic constitutionalism.

One Constitution, Many Texts

The broad principles and normative commitments that comprise the Civic Constitution may be absent from or only imperfectly realized in a foundational constitutional document[74] (the text admits as much in its search for a more perfect union). Our understanding of what those principles are and what they mean might well appear in other texts and in other forms and civic practices, especially as the constitutional order develops over time and as our understanding is shaped by recurrent contests concerning their meaning and applicability to public life. This means we must also address another question: *where* precisely should we look for evidence about the content and meaning of our civic aspirations and normative commitments? The obvious answer—look to the Constitution itself—is the least satisfactory of the several options that present themselves.[75] In addition to overlooking important questions about what parts of the text matter and which ones do not, this answer assumes implicitly that the text locates its identity in law and that the law is confined chiefly if not exclusively to the interpretation of legal texts.

By comparison, our inquiry into the meaning of the Civic Constitution requires that we consult a wide variety of sources in addition to the formal constitutional document.[76] Our civic identity is partly constituted by a number of other foundational documents. These additional sources of constitutional meaning include the Declaration of Independence, the Articles of Confederation and Perpetual Union, and the *Federalist Papers*, as well as several other texts that contribute to, celebrate, and contest[77] our civic identity, such as some of the works of the anti-Federalists, the Gettysburg Address, Lincoln's First Inaugural, and Martin Luther King's "Letter from a Birmingham Jail."[78] These texts contribute independently to our understanding of what our shared aspirations are and what they mean, but they also influence how we read the text of 1789, by functioning as prefatory statements of purpose[79] or as a moral prism,[80] or by facilitating interpretive appeals to purpose and history. Each contributes to a kind of constitutional bricolage.[81]

This list is not exhaustive. Obvious additional candidates for inclusion in the constitutional canon might include William Lloyd Garrison's "covenant with hell" and Roosevelt's "Economic Bill of Rights" speeches, as well as several others. Less obvious, but perhaps still canonical, might be the May-flower Compact, Paine's *Rights of Man*, the Virginia Declaration of Rights, Washington's Farewell Address, the Northwest Ordinances, John Brown's Provisional Constitution and Ordinances, the Seneca Falls Declaration of Sentiments, and *Message to the Blackman in America* by Elijah Muhammad (Malcolm X). I cite these as examples not because they resonate in popular culture (some do, some don't), but rather because each sheds light on some important aspect of our civic aspirations; each is part of a continuing public conversation about the meaning of our constitutional aspirations.[82]

I want to be clear that these documents are not simply aids or supplements to constitutional meaning, or devices we can use to use to assist us in discerning the meaning of the "constitution." They are, in contrast, a part of the very thing we should call the Constitution. To get a clearer sense of what I mean, consider the recent work by Akhil Reed Amar, who argues in *America's Unwritten Constitution* that there is an unwritten constitution that exists in dialogue with the written constitution.[83] The unwritten constitution, at a minimum, "encompasses various principles implicit in the written document as a whole and/or present in the historical background, forming part of the context against which we must construe the entire text."[84] Amar argues that neither constitution, "standing alone," offers a satisfactory account of the American constitutional order; the written constitution, standing alone, is inadequate to the task of actually ordering political practice, because parts of it are indeterminate and "even perverse when measured against the larger purposes of the document itself." On the other hand, the unwritten constitution, standing alone, "would appear to be illegitimate," especially insofar as it may degenerate into an "assortment of 'constitutional rules' conjured up out of thin air."[85]

Amar posits a relationship between the written text and the unwritten in which the written text must have what I will call presumptive authority. Indeed, it is the presumptive authority of the text itself that authorizes occasional recourse to the unwritten constitution. As Amar writes, "the written text presupposes and invites certain forms of interpretation that go beyond clause-bound literalism."[86] Amar's sense that appeals to the unwritten constitution "must understand not only where to start but also when to stop, and why," leads him to conclude that "[t]he unwritten Constitution should never contradict the plain meaning and central purpose . . . of an express and basic element of the written Constitution."[87]

So in the relationship between the written constitution and the unwritten constitution, the written has presumptive authority.[88] The written consti-tution deserves a strong form of judicial fidelity, Amar concludes, "both because it is law and because, for all its flaws, it has usually been more just than the justices."[89] This is an interesting claim—or better, two claims. The first is that the written constitution has some claim on judicial fidelity be-cause it is law. But what is the point of describing the unwritten principles and practices of the constitutional order as the unwritten "constitution" if not also to claim for them the status and superiority of law to politics? If both constitutions are law, then claiming judges must be faithful to the law does not tell us why the written text trumps the unwritten one. Secondly, if the written text deserves our fidelity because it comes nearer to justice (are we to understand the written constitution first as justice-seeking and second-arily as populist?), what should we do in those cases (surely there will be some, perhaps many!) when it is the unwritten text that is nearer to justice? I wonder if Amar might imagine a few cases where the unwritten constitution does indeed trump the written text—perhaps because it comes closer to the vision of constitutional justice that inheres in the text, or perhaps because that principle has been ratified by the people themselves.[90] Amar seems to suggest the latter possibility in his discussion of erroneous judicial prec-edents. "An erroneous precedent that improperly deviates from the written Constitution may in some circumstances stand . . . if the precedent is later championed not merely by the court, but also by the people. . . . When the citizenry has widely and enthusiastically embraced an erroneous precedent," a court "may view this precedent as sufficiently ratified by the American people."[91] Putting aside the question of whether it is possible to reconcile this populist understanding of constitutional rightness with a justice-seeking account, this seems to admit there are times when the unwritten constitution supersedes the written one.

It is important to be clear about whether the unwritten parts of the Con-stitution are "in" the constitution or simply aids to meaning. Calling the unwritten parts of the American Constitution a "constitution" is more than just a verbal trick, because it ascribes to them a very strong element of constitutional authority, more than they get if we simply call them aids to interpretation. To be clear, I have no objection to this result.[92] Indeed, I think the Civic Constitution requires us to regard some unwritten practices and other texts (see above) as part of the Constitution proper, or as part of the canon, and not just as interpretive aids.

Unlike Amar, who refers to the written Constitution of 1789 and its Article 5 amendments as the canonical constitution, my use of the word "canonical" in the previous paragraphs is intentionally ironic.[93] Which texts (and civic practices) qualify as a source of meaning about the nature and content of our shared civic aspirations must always be an open question. The document ratified in 1789 and its formal amendments are self-evidently canonical (Amar is right to call them canonical in this limited sense) in that any discussion of our national identity and civic aspirations must begin with them.[94] Beyond the Constitution so defined, however, we must regard any canonical list of texts as contestable and subject to ongoing civic debate, or (to be flippant) as noncanonical.[95]

Consider the Declaration of Independence. Few readers would contest its importance as a contribution to our civic identity and as an important source of our civic aspirations. (As Tulis has observed, the Declaration references a people who "create themselves by articulating and subscribing to a set of principles that define their collective identity."[96]) Appeals to the Declaration of Independence are a common and recurrent feature of constitutional discourse, especially if, as the Civic Constitution requires, we expand the arena of discourse beyond courts to include citizens and social movements.[97] Its ringing rhetoric and insistence upon the principle of equality greatly influenced, for instance, the civil rights movements of the 1950s and 1960s, as well as the abolitionist movement and the Seneca Falls Declaration of Sentiments and Resolutions in the previous century.

Arguments that the Declaration, if not part of the Constitution, is a key to understanding it, are commonplace.[98] President Lincoln famously argued that the Declaration of Independence was a founding document of the United States, and that this had important implications for interpreting the Constitution.[99] Gary Wills argues that Lincoln's insistence that the Declaration must guide our interpretation of the Constitution, vigorously contested at the time, is now widely shared: "For most people now, the Declaration means what Lincoln told us it means, as a way of correcting the Constitution itself without overthrowing it."[100] In similar fashion, Mortimer Adler suggests that we consider the Declaration as a "preface" to the Constitution.[101] (As the Court has recently reminded us, prefatory clauses are an important guide to the meaning of the constitutional text proper, and thus are sometimes a significant aid in constitutional interpretation.[102]) Sounding a similar theme before he was appointed to the Court, Clarence Thomas wrote, "The Constitution is a logical extension of the Declaration of Independence."[103]

But there have also been periods in our constitutional history where the self-evident truths of the Declaration have been rejected by significant

members of both the constitutional elite and the constitutional public. Of
the many examples one could cite, perhaps the best known are associated
with mid-nineteenth-century defenses of slavery. In response to the claims
of some abolitionists that the Constitution prohibited slavery,[104] Senator
Macon of North Carolina simply observed that the Declaration, because it
was not part of the Constitution, was not relevant to the discussion. Others argued that Lincoln's inclusion of the principles of the Declaration in
the Constitution distorted the latter by improperly expanding the reach of
federal authority.[105] John C. Calhoun argued that the equality claim was
factually false,[106] and Senator John Pettit of Indiana went further, declaring
it a "self-evident lie."[107]

A juridic reading of the Constitution has little use for the Declaration. Its
grandiloquent claims, the Court tells us, are political truths, not justiciable
rights.[108] Wills's insistence that Lincoln's understanding of the Declaration
is widely shared is not, in fact, widely shared by federal courts. According
to one study,

> there are at least 100 United States Supreme Court cases that mention
> the words 'Declaration of Independence' somewhere in the dicta of that
> opinion. Yet, not one single case can be found where the authority for
> the holding in that case was the Declaration of independence. There
> is not a single case that was 'specifically decided on the Declaration of
> Independence or its provisions.' No decision has turned or can turn on
> the Declaration of Independence itself.[109]

Instead, for most constitutional lawyers, the Declaration has no legal force
and no legal meaning.[110] The issue came up, if only obliquely, during the
recent confirmations hearings for Elena Kagan. Senator Tom Coburn asked
Kagan "if she disagreed with the Declaration of Independence that there are
inalienable rights given by God. Kagan answered, 'Sen. Coburn, I believe that
the Constitution is an extraordinary document, and I'm not saying I do not
believe that there are rights preexistent [to] the Constitution and the laws. But
my job as a justice is to enforce the Constitution and the laws . . . I think you
should want me to act on the basis of law.'"[111] Implicit in Kagan's response
is the proposition that the Constitution is law, but the Declaration is not.

If I am correct that the Civic Constitution requires us to expand the margins of the Constitution to include other foundational documents, then there
remains the question of how we know which texts qualify and which do not,
as the debates over the Declaration make clear. Generally, however, national
treasures like the Declaration and the Gettysburg Address are easy cases.[112]

What should we make of the Kentucky and Virginia Resolutions,[113] or of Calhoun's *Disquisition on Government*? An answer that courts have rejected the arguments advanced in such works misses their very real significance in contributing to the meaning and practice of American constitutionalism, as well as their ongoing relevance in both scholarly and popular constitutional discourse. The Resolutions, for example, have featured prominently in recent scholarly debates concerning nonjudicial interpretation of the Constitution[114] (and indeed have done so throughout American history). The doctrines of interposition and nullification similarly resurface periodically in American constitutional history, most recently in civic discourse on racial desegregation in public elementary schools,[115] illegal immigration,[116] healthcare,[117] and even light bulbs.[118]

We might argue the same about the Articles of Confederation and Perpetual Union. Plainly the Articles have no force of law, but it is less clear that they have no influence on how we understand and interpret certain parts of the Constitution of 1789 (the necessary and proper clause is one prominent example, the Tenth Amendment another). It is even less clear that they have no contemporary significance as a part of our rich and complex constitutional identity.[119]

My claim that the Civic Constitution includes documents that have no force of law may sound odd: imagine an attorney arguing that a national health care law is an unconstitutional exercise of federal authority because it violates the Articles of Confederation. The claim is not odd because it makes an argument that is *incorrect*, but rather because it makes a claim that seems to most of us not *relevant* to an inquiry into its constitutional legality. It sounds odd, then, because we are preoccupied with the Constitution's claim that it is *law*. Because the Articles of Confederation are not (or are no longer) part of our public law, they play no meaningful part in debates over what the law permits or prohibits. If instead we see the Constitution as a set of civic aspirations and as designed to promote civic engagement about the meaning and realization of those aspirations, then it should seem strange *not* to include other texts (and especially texts that styled themselves as constitutions) that contribute to discussions about the meaning and desirability of those aspirations. Similarly, my argument that the Civic Constitution includes documents unknown or obscure to most Americans may seem equally odd. If the argument seems improbable, however, it is chiefly because the Civic Constitution—or rather, the kind of citizenry it envisions—has fallen into disrepair under the onslaught of the Juridic Constitution.

In sum, a large part of civic debate concerning our deepest aspirations and the meaning of particular constitutional guarantees occurs and is revealed in other texts, and these texts are properly a part of the Civic Constitution itself. But the meaning of the Civic Constitution is not confined to the texts that make up the constitutional library.[120] The meaning of the Civic Constitution is located even more prominently in the political life and practices it calls into being.[121] The forums in which these activities take place are multifold and constantly changing; they include formal and organized civic activity,[122] as well as the innumerable informal locations where citizens talk about and practice politics.

Constitutions as Civic Practices

A constitutional order is never entirely coincident with a founding text or texts.[123] The text matters, because it helps to call the constitutional order into being and in doing so contributes significantly to its particular character,[124] but constitutional orders in turn influence how we approach the text. And more broadly, a constitutional order is not constructed solely by the foundational text—it is constituted by discourses and practices that are external to it. The text alone does not begin to capture the full range of our civic aspirations or shed much light on what those aspirations mean and why they have significance. Instead, their meaning is in the practices they constitute.

The Civic Constitution is practiced on those occasions when citizens take up conversation and political activity about the meaning and significance of civic life. It extends to conversations about values and norms that have wider expanse than legal rules amenable to judicial interpretation and to practices that encompass far more than the ritualistic activities of voting and pledges of allegiance. To hear this civic voice, we must consult sources that reach well beyond court cases and law review articles. We find evidence of the Civic Constitution in the great variety of places and activities, many unconventional in a strictly legal sense, where citizens address issues of constitutional significance. Obviously there are times when this quotidian public voice is louder than others, but it is not confined to extraordinary constitutional moments.[125] Beaumont suggests, for example, that such civic activity was especially prominent not only during the founding period, but also surrounding the abolition movement, the women's suffrage movement, and the campaign for national civil rights legislation.[126] Notable historical examples of the Civic Constitution in practice would also include popular opposition to the Alien and Sedition Acts, to conscription in the Civil War and World War I, the labor movements of the nineteenth and early twentieth centuries, and the Progressive era, as well as several others.[127]

We also find the Civic Constitution manifest in contemporary civic debate concerning the meaning of equality and same-sex marriage, health care, gun control, legislative redistricting, campaign finance, birthright citizenship, and abortion. In each of these instances, citizens address themselves to controversies about the public weal that implicate constitutional norms of the most fundamental sort. When fully realized, we would find the Civic Constitution practiced in the locations that constitute the varied landscape of civic engagement, including in families, schools, churches, sports leagues, civic associations, farmers' markets, and many others.[128] From a design/constituting perspective, then, our aim must be to construct a constitutional order in which such organizations and practices can thrive. We must find ways to promote civic space and arrange incentives in ways that encourage citizens to tend to constitutional precepts.

THE CIVIC CONSTITUTION
AND INSTITUTIONS

Institutional design is a critical part of the process of constituting new governments. How we structure institutions, the powers we entrust to them, the limitations we impose upon them, and how we expect them to function are all components of the process of constitution making. Fixing the particulars of institutional design has long seemed to many scholars to be the paradigmatic function of constitutions. Indeed, Giovanni Sartori's classic *Comparative Constitutional Engineering*[129] masterfully reviews the many design decisions that confront founders. Whether about presidentialism or parliamentarianism, proportional or direct representation, separated institutions or separated power, unitary or federal, to include or omit a bill of rights, the choices we must make about institutional design when constituting are complicated and momentous.[130]

Just as importantly, every decision about structures and institutions is also a decision, if only implicitly, about politics and values. Even if the institutional framework of constitutional democracy is meant to be a machine that will go of itself,[131] its architecture is necessarily caught up with larger ends. Walter Murphy captured this sense when he wrote that no constitutional document is concerned with "solely ordering offices."[132] This is why the process of designing institutions is typically so contentious and contested in founding moments: decisions about institutions are "self-conscious choices"[133] about aspirations and identities, about who We want to be as a people and how to become that people.

Like Publius, I begin with the assumption that the sort of citizenry anticipated by the constitutional enterprise is more likely to prosper under some types of institutional arrangements than others. The Civic Constitution also informs our understanding of how constitutional actors and institutions should function and of what responsibilities we should assign to them, because "[t]he way political structures are crafted is critical to the long-run education of a people."[134] Discussion regarding institutional design figured prominently in Philadelphia. Civics classes still ask students to learn to distinguish between the Virginia and New Jersey Plans and the Connecticut Compromise, as well as to identify the basic outlines of the separation of powers and federalism.[135] Although nominally about the allocation and distribution of power,[136] these discussions were not far removed from concerns about what kind of people we were and who we might become. James Savage has argued, based on a content analysis of Madison's *Notes*, that although the founders did not attempt directly to promote civic virtue through institutional design, they did see institutional design as centrally related to the promotion of (classical) regime values.[137] Similarly, Grofman and Wittman remark, "The Founding Fathers set out deliberately to design the form of government that would be most likely to bring about the long-range goals that they envisaged for the Republic. What is most unusual about Madison, in contrast to the other delegates, is the degree to which he thought about the principles behind the institutions he preferred."[138] Others have noted of Madison's institutional design that "[p]rior to such structural devices, however, are Madison's principles of government, grounded in morality and prudence. And prior to those is his basic moral vision, from which the political principles and the constitutional structure ultimately flow."[139]

Once we acknowledge the close relationship between institutional design and the promotion of regime values, we will see that the Civic Constitution is more likely to flourish under some types of institutional arrangements than others. Macedo's argument about the constitutive character of liberal constitutional institutions captures some of the Civic Constitution's approach to the importance and purpose of institutional design for civic life. "Successful constitutional institutions," he writes, "must do more than help order the freedom of individuals prefabricated for life in a liberal political order; they must shape the way that people use their freedom, and shape people to ensure that freedom is what they want."[140] In addressing how texts constitute institutions, we sometimes forget that institutions in turn constitute citizens.[141] The Civic Constitution asks us to think about whether there are ways to construct institutions that promote a constitutional way of life that has meaning for and is the responsibility of citizens. We must arrange institutions to promote rather than stunt civic engagement. This imperative influences institutional design in several ways.

It is a staple of constitutional scholarship that the institutional architecture the founders devised, far from advancing civic engagement, instead sought to depress or minimize it. According to these accounts, the Federalists crafted institutions designed to depress civic engagement by redirecting energy into the private pursuit of happiness, measured chiefly in capital.[142] The reasons advanced for this redirection are various—some are almost crassly materialistic,[143] others rest more on a deep skepticism about either the capabilities or the virtue of ordinary citizens.[144] Similar if less strident accounts are a commonplace of the large scholarly literature that considers whether and to what extent the founding rested on liberal skepticism about the possibilities of republican virtue.[145] I discuss the founders' assessments of citizens more fully in the next section, when I take up the question of what kind of citizens the Civic Constitution envisions. I will note there that some recent scholarship significantly qualifies the proposition that the Federalists, or at least Madison, were intent on curtailing routine public engagement with constitutional principles.[146] The important point here is that the founders *did* devise to construct institutions based on the assumption that institutional design will have an impact upon civic engagement, whether salutary or suppressive.[147]

Hence, the logic of the claim that the Civic Constitution requires certain kinds of institutions should sound familiar to most students of constitutional engineering. Is it possible to design institutions in ways that promote civic engagement and deliberative competence in citizens? From the perspective of constituting, we face two questions.[148] First, how can we design institutions to promote civic engagement? Second, since the act of constituting is in a literal sense in our past,[149] how should a commitment to the Civic Constitution influence our understanding of existing institutions and institutional practices? Is it possible to recalibrate our institutions in ways that advance the ends of the Civic Constitution? The categories of constituting, maintaining, and failing are not strictly sequential or linear. Hence, to realize the Civic Constitution, we need not only to understand the design choices we made at the founding, but also to revisit our understanding of extant institutions.

The institutions of the Civic Constitution must be broadly democratic in character, in the sense that they must provide incentives for public participation in both the articulation and the practice of constitutional ideals. To do this, institutional design must engender civic space. Civic space is not simply physical, but also refers to the kinds of experiences and activities that occur *in* the spaces where citizens actually talk about and practice political life.[150]

Institutional arrangements that channel responsibility for constitutional matters into a single institution choke civic space. They leave little room for others (citizens) to take up such questions, and just as importantly, give them little incentive to do so. The Juridic Constitution in particular minimizes experiential space by directing constitutional dialogue into a few select institutions (and to courts in particular) and by transforming talk about the constitution from the language of civics to the language of law. The Civic Constitution is better served by an approach to constitutional disagreement that privileges dialogue and ongoing conversation between and among co-equal constitutional actors, and between those actors and citizens.

Separation of Powers

Although the separation of power is an essential property of constitutional orders,[151] there are a great many ways in which the separation of power might be secured; no particular design is required.[152] When we give the principle effect under the Civic Constitution, we must recall that institutional design constitutes not only institutions, but also citizens and cultures. Some measure of learning to be public-spirited, or of learning what constitutional norms are and what they mean, as well as how to give them life through engagement with others, comes from watching political actors.[153] As Murphy reminds us, borrowing from Justice Brandeis, "A regime also teaches . . . through its decision-making processes."[154] Citizens will learn norms about constitutional civility by observing whether and how their representatives take up their own responsibility for the Constitution. A civic approach to the separation of powers therefore requires an architectonic that increases the spaces and places where citizens can engage the Constitution and participate in constitutional conversation.

Increasing the number of arenas in which discussion occurs promotes civic engagement by encouraging institutions to engage in constitutional dialogue between and among themselves. On this understanding, the separation of powers is essentially a dialogic device, or a means of establishing constitutional conversation among the branches. Institutional designs that reduce the number of sites where constitutional dialogue occurs thus defeat the purposes of the Civic Constitution in at least two ways. First, they constrict public space directly, and second, they teach citizens that their own responsibility for securing a constitutional way of life is inconsequential.[155] Both are substantial disincentives to civic engagement.

The Civic Constitution prefers models of the separation of powers (and of federalism, see below) that promote constitutional dialogue and in which each of the branches functions as an important participant in the effort to promote a constitutional way of life. Thus, under the Civic Constitution the separation of powers doctrine is intended "not only to prevent faction but also to promote public deliberation."[156] Consequently, when we draft the Civic Constitution, we should favor designs for the separation of powers that entrust all institutions with some measure of responsibility for interpreting and enforcing the Constitution. Moreover, we should design institutions that have some incentive to participate in constitutional conversation. The Civic Constitution favors a model of the separation of powers that is sometimes called the "mixed" model, or a model in which, to use Neustadt's famous phrase, separate institutions share power.[157] In this model, the separation of powers is a system in which each branch must engage the others to exert power. This is the underlying logic of *Federalist #51*:

> But the great security against a gradual concentration of the several powers in the same department, consists in giving to those who administer each department the necessary constitutional means and personal motives to resist encroachments of the others. The provision for defense must in this, as in all other cases, be made commensurate to the danger of attack. Ambition must be made to counteract ambition. The interest of the man must be connected with the constitutional rights of the place.[158]

Behind this concept of checks and balances is the proposition that no branch should be insulated from the others by virtue of a grant of autonomous power, whether legislative, executive, or judicial. Instead, these three categories of powers are shared across their institutional counterparts. The separation of powers, on this understanding, is neither neat nor tidy—it is, in Corwin's famous phrase, an invitation to struggle, a phrase that invokes a political meaning rather than a legal principle.[159] The conceptualization of the separation of powers as a political imperative, rather than as a set of judicially enforceable legal commands, betters suits the Civic than the Juridic Constitution.[160]

It is especially important for nonjudicial branches to participate in constitutional discourse because the resources, analytical tools, and vocabularies they bring to such dialogue are deeply and broadly democratic in nature. Legal language, in contrast, chokes the civic enterprise. A conception of the separation of powers that welcomes nonjudicial interpretation of the Constitution is better suited to constitute a genuinely civic discourse, thus recalling my earlier discussion of the kind of constitutional language best suited to drafting the Civic Constitution. A good example is the Gettysburg Address, which educates citizens about the meaning of constitutional ideals by using language that is broadly inclusive and accessible.[161] Additional examples would include George Washington's Farewell Address and Franklin D. Roosevelt's State of the Union address in 1944, in which he famously proposed a "Second Bill of Rights." Recent congressional contributions to constitutional dialogue might include Senator Rand Paul's filibuster regarding President Obama's use of drones on American soil, or the many Senate hearings on campaign finance, some of which were prompted by citizen action—or by the Civic Constitution in practice. In February 2012, fifty different organizations presented letters to the House and Senate Judiciary Committees requesting congressional hearings to consider amending the Constitution to overturn *Citizens United v. Federal Elections Commission*.[162]

This democratic discourse stands in sharp contrast to the exclusionary vocabulary and tools of analysis utilized by courts. As I wrote earlier, the chief characteristic of legal language is precisely its exclusivity. Law is a private language, reserved to those who possess the specialized training and educational background necessary to learn it.[163] The language of law is spoken not only by lawyers and judges, but also by an interpretive community that extends to academics and others who possess the requisite professional skills and vocabulary. Some scholars have suggested the existence of interpretive communities softens the antidemocratic criticisms typically advanced against judicial review,[164] but membership in these interpretive communities is limited—to be a member, one must possess certain skills and resources. As Ira Strauber has argued, "to be a member of the interpretive community is to question, clarify, formulate, categorize, and analyze the way lawyers do."[165] And as Cotterrell and others have concluded, "it is . . . profoundly unrealistic to consider non-lawyer citizens, on the one hand, and lawyers or judges, on the other, as part of the same community of legal interpreters."[166] The very existence of an interpretive community organized around ownership of a (legal) text raises rather than settles important issues concerning the distribution of political power.

I do not argue that courts cannot play an important role in civic conversation. Indeed, many scholars have taken for granted that the Supreme Court, in particular, can serve an important pedagogical function in a constitutional democracy.[167] As Dean Rostow famously observed, the "Supreme Court is, among other things, an educational body, and the Justices are inevitably teachers in a vital national seminar."[168] Rostow's observation is widely quoted, if little examined. Christopher Eisgruber notes, for example, that scholars and justices of nearly every persuasion, including "liberals, con-

servatives, communitarians, republicans, and feminists,"[169] have embraced
the sentiment. But what it means to call the Court an educative institution
is less clear, and we lack a fully developed account of how courts teach,
when they teach, or what they teach. In Eisgruber's view, the Supreme Court
discharges its educational function primarily on those infrequent occasions
when, instead of taking up scholarly analysis of the Constitution, it conveys
"the meaning of arguments that people have considered—and perhaps accepted—but not taken to heart. The point of such explanations is to recall
values, commitments, or ideals which people have somehow neglected, and
to cause people to honor these values in their actions."[170] Notable examples
of such instruction would include cases such as *West Virginia v. Barnette*
(1943), *Cohen v. California* (1971), and *Brown v. Board of Education*
(1954), but there are several additional cases we could list, as well as individual concurring and dissenting opinions, not all of them salutary.[171]

Eisgruber's treatment is important for our understanding of institutional
design and the Civic Constitution for several reasons. If Eisgruber is correct, then the Court best advances its pedagogic function when it under-
takes to teach lessons that have less to do with the law, or with scholarly
analysis of the Constitution, than when it tells us "something about [our]
own identities."[172] The Civic Constitution invites the Court to contribute
to civic dialogue about the meaning of constitutional ideals, but the Court
must do more than lecture—it must converse with other institutions and
with citizens. Recalling our discussion of conversational models in the Introduction,[173] conversation is facilitated by schemes of interpretive pluralism
in particular, and of the separation of powers more broadly, in which the
branches must interact on a plane of horizontal equality. Conversely, strong-
form judicial review impedes conversation by making authority claims that
are essentially hierarchical.[174]

Whether the Court is institutionally suited to discharge this educative
function, especially given that it is, as Rostow wrote, simply one of many
functions it performs, is an important question. Eisgruber concludes, for example, that other constitutional purposes—"in particular the need for conclusive and competent adjudication—limit the Court's capacity to teach."[175]
Among these constraints is the possible corruption of other important constitutional norms, as well as certain structural features of the constitutional
order that appear to counsel against excesses of public spirit. Eisgruber identifies two potential complications. The first is that the Court may need to
"bring its message down to the level of the people," which "risks corrupting
the Court (or, at least, the Court's message.)"[176] Behind such an assumption is the juridic/Hamiltonian belief that the law is too complicated for

ordinary, inexpert citizens. The second compromise Eisgruber fears is the "republic might be vulnerable to pernicious teachings."[177] Again, such fear assumes a public with a profoundly limited capacity to deliberate, but it also presupposes, as I shall argue in Essay Three, a particular, and limited understanding of what constitutes constitutional success and failure. Both concerns presume a constitution that is first juridic, and only secondarily, if at all, civic in character.

Federalism

The prescription that counsels a robust (dialogical) separation of powers tells us also that the Civic Constitution favors an approach to federalism in which states and local governments can make significant contributions to the construction of constitutional meaning.[178] A robust doctrine of civic federalism is especially important to the Civic Constitution because it provides for an immediately accessible public space in which citizens can be active in the political and constitutional life of the community. Associational and communal life thrives in small, local communities. The Civic Constitution therefore requires that we find ways to encourage the development of local civic work by making it rewarding and consequential.

One argument in favor of departmentalism is that institutions teach or educate citizens by example. This learning is more likely when citizens have local opportunities to watch and to act in their own communities, and when they can have some confidence that their participation will be meaningful. In contrast, constitutional blueprints that disable these immediate and direct opportunities for civic experience (or that constrict civic space) undermine the richness and importance of civic life. The argument is even more salient when considering state and local governments. The states are especially important sites for engagement because, as Jefferson and other civic republicans insisted, they are near to citizens and more likely to promote civic virtue in their citizens.[179]

Strong-form, or civic, federalism thus extends the model of constitutional dialogue on a vertical plane. There are good reasons why we might expect state and local governments to make significant contributions to constitutional conversation. First, as Bradley Hays suggests, dialogue on a vertical plane may provide more and different voices an opportunity to participate in constitutional conversation, especially in those cases where other factors (such as one-party control of federal institutions, or instances where the federal government's collective self-interest overcomes party or ideological differences) mitigate against departmentalism's promise of interpretive pluralism. In these cases, states and local governments may be an especially important complement to constitutional dialogue.[180] Second, absent in much of this literature is a sustained account of how, structurally or institutionally, citizens can make their voices heard.[181] Hays's attention to the role of state legislatures in contributing to constitutional dialogue may supply one such mechanism by contributing to the creation of civic space.

There are two obvious concerns one might raise about this sort of civic federalism. First, we all know the states have sometimes been laboratories for experiments that have not served the causes of liberty, equality, civic virtue, or civility. I consider in Essay Two the important concern that civic federalism increases opportunities for local communities to subvert our constitutional ideals, in particular through an examination of the doctrines of interposition and nullification.[182] Here I note only that our commitment to and practice of federalism is constrained by the terms of Article 6 and the supremacy clause, as well as by the constitutive principles of constitutionalism more broadly. The Civic Constitution welcomes, indeed requires, citizens to participate in the making of constitutional choices, but the choices we may make are constrained by our desire to act constitutionally and by the particular constitutional aspirations that define our identity. The Civic Constitution includes constitutional and civic components; civic engagement, alone, is not constitutional self-governance and may threaten constitutional failure, a possibility I explore in Essay Three.

Second, constitutional formulations that invest the states and citizen participation in state politics with real importance may exist in some tension with the national citizenship contemplated by the Constitution, especially when they result in politics and policies that undermine our collective constitutional aspirations. Sotirios Barber, for example, notes that states' rights versions of federalism (in contrast to what Barber calls Marshallian and process federalism) are difficult to reconcile with an understanding of the constitutional order that commits us to "desirable social states of affairs," or to ends rather than institutions or means. (The difficulty is twofold. First, it is impossible to overlook the historical association of states' rights claims with principles and practices, such as slavery, that are utterly incompatible with fundamental constitutional precepts. Second, arguments defending states' rights federalism are "a self-defeating enterprise," because they deny "what any effort to justify their position assumes: that there is one best conception of the good society; that good-faith participants in the debate aspire to approximate it; and that exchanging reason is the way to do that.")[183]

This is not a necessary consequence of federalism in itself, but rather a consequence of a particular form of federalism, or a particular constellation of arguments concerning the meaning and purpose of federal arrangements.[184] Thus, Barber writes, "the mere maintenance of constitutional institutions, including federalism, is not an end for which the Constitution was established. . . . Citizens value the separation of powers and other institutional forms . . . but they do so assuming they will secure goods like liberty, fairness, security, and plenty."[185] Following a similar logic (though not necessarily one Barber would countenance), the Civic Constitution values strong-form federalism not as an end in itself, but rather because of its capacity to promote the civic virtues of deliberation and engagement and to expand civic space.[186]

In sum, the Civic Constitution asks us to approach the separation of powers doctrine and federalism in ways that emphasize their capacity to work as agents of constitutional instruction. I propose conceptions of separation of powers and federalism that promote the constitutional autonomy of nonjudicial institutional actors because they are more likely to result in actors keen to address constitutional issues on their own. This in turn makes an important contribution to constitutional maintenance because, as Elkin and several others have argued, "public struggle and debate among the branches will be educative."[187]

Other Design Decisions

There are many other decisions founders must make about constitutional design. These include whether to install a presidential or parliamentary system, whether to adopt a single transferable or proportional voting system, whether or not to draft a bill of rights, and how to design a mechanism for constitutional review. The Civic Constitution has important implications for how we approach each of these design decisions. For reasons of economy, and to accentuate the distinctions between the Juridic and Civic Constitutions, I take up just one—constitutional review.

Constitutional Review and the Civic Constitution
The differences between the Juridic and Civic Constitutions weigh importantly on how we should design a system of constitutional review. Some mechanism for constitutional review is a constitutive element of true constitutional regimes.[188] Constitutional review may take any number of institutional forms, including review by courts, but judicial review is only one of several possible institutional manifestations of the larger principle.[189] Unlike constitutional review, judicial review is not strictly necessary to constitutional government. There may be good reasons why constitutional review *ought*

to include some form of judicial review, but those reasons are contingent in the sense that they trace to the particulars of individual constitutional regimes, and not to constitutionalism itself. Equally important, constitutional self-governance, in itself, tells us nothing about whether adopting a system of judicial review commits us to judicial supremacy (strong-form judicial review), to interpretive pluralism, to departmentalism, or to any other particular exemplar of judicial review.

Both the Juridic and the Civic Constitutions allocate some degree of interpretative authority to judges, and Article 3 is sufficiently elastic to support a juridic reading or a civic reading. A civic reading of Article 3 sees it as installing a form of coordinate construction. One advantage to the civic reading of Article 3 is that it more easily accommodates the reservation of congressional power under Section 2, which affords Congress some voice in determining constitutional meaning by allowing it to alter the appellate jurisdiction of federal courts. A judiciary that consistently ignores congressional decisions about constitutional meaning risks its own ability to contribute to constitutional dialogue in certain kinds of cases. Similarly, as I indicated above, a civic reading of Article 3, or a reading that adopts the departmentalist account of judicial review, would reconfigure our understanding of congressional power under Section 5 to enforce the Fourteenth Amendment. It would likewise suggest that cases such as *Katzenbach v. Morgan* (1966) and *Boerne v. Flores* (1997), insofar as they advance judicial supremacy, are wrongly decided.[190]

A juridic reading of Article 3 has equally little difficulty concluding that it establishes, if only implicitly, a system of judicial supremacy. A primary purpose of the Juridic Constitution is to insulate the Constitution from recurrent popular comment and controversy by removing such conflict from public arenas and directing it into narrow and highly circumscribed forums. It transforms talk about the constitution from the language of civics to the language of law. Following this logic, the allocation of interpretive authority to courts is a rational (though not an inevitable) design choice. Courts do possess a significant degree of specialized knowledge and institutional expertise, and there are institutional advantages to channeling disputes about the meaning and application of law into these specialized forums. Notwithstanding obvious objections grounded in claims of elitism or some other democratic sentiment, most forms of democratic theory do find ways to reconcile popular governance with claims of judicial expertise.[191]

However, judicial supremacy is supremely ill suited to the Civic Constitution. The Juridic Constitution substantially constricts civic space. Strong-form judicial review reduces the number of forums in which constitutional dialogue occurs, in large measure by creating disincentives for other actors to address the Constitution. It leaves little room for nonjudicial actors to take up constitutional questions, and just as importantly, gives them little reason to do so. A judicial monopoly over constitutional interpretation,[192] as Jefferson cautioned, teaches other constitutional actors and citizens that their own powers of constitutional interpretation are irrelevant, if not vaguely threatening to the constitutional project.

Second, judicial supremacy creates significant disincentives (why bother?) and imposes hurdles (of specialized knowledge and educational background) for citizens to participate as well. The exclusion of citizens is twofold. First, citizens are excluded because they lack the training and expertise necessary to hold the office, and second because that office, and only that office, possesses interpretive authority. Of course, even strong-form judicial review under the juridic constitution does not entirely disqualify citizens from engaging in the interpretive enterprise, but it does reduce both the number of opportunities and the incentives for citizens to participate in the process, as well as diminishes the weight and significance of their participation.[193] The civic objection to this allocation of interpretive authority is not simply or even chiefly the familiar claim that it is counter-majoritarian, and consequently undemocratic,[194] but rather that it undermines the object of constitutional maintenance more broadly by discouraging a sense of civic responsibility. The problem is far more significant because it threatens the constitutional project directly. As Nagel has observed, the predominance of the judiciary in giving the Constitution meaning undermines "both fidelity to constitutional principles and the general health of the political culture."[195]

We can advance the civic approach to constitutional design by finding ways to democratize constitutional interpretation or by institutionalizing some sort of interpretive pluralism.[196] According to one definition, "interpretive pluralism (or pluralist interpretation) means nothing more than the absence of a single binding or authoritative interpretation. That is, it simply refers to openness to multiple interpretations . . . of law."[197] Insofar as it references only openness to multiple interpretations (and interpreters?), this is a weak form of interpretive pluralism. A stronger form of interpretive pluralism, required by the Civic Constitution, not only demands openness to multiple interpretations but must admit instances where those other interpretations will not be inferior in station to judicial interpretations of the Constitution. The difference between weak and strong forms of interpretive pluralism is tied directly to the relative strength of these alternative claims to interpretive authority.

Strong forms of interpretive pluralism create incentives for other actors to take the Constitution seriously by attaching weight and significance to their contributions.[198] Just as significantly, strong or civic interpretive pluralism creates a system of incentives for courts as well, in particular by leading them to see constitutional interpretation as an exercise in reason and persuasion, and less one of command and announcement. As Stith observes, interpretive pluralism establishes structural incentives for judges "to persuade others of the correctness of their legal decisions."[199] Pluralism fosters a constitutional model that is dialogic, or that parallels the conversational model of discourse I described as central to the concept of civility. This in turn may yield judicial opinions that, now in contest for persuasive authority, must adopt a voice that speaks inclusively, or that comes closer to a model of civic discourse as conversation and deliberation.[200] Interpretive pluralism is thus better suited to a way of constitutional life conceived in terms of civility and tending.

Departmentalism also rearranges incentives to share in constitutional conversation by requiring institutions to engage with one another. As Benjamin A. Kleinerman writes, under a system of departmentalism, the other branches are less likely to assume that "the Court will clean up" their constitutional missteps.[201] Just as important, under a system of departmentalism, other constitutional actors are more likely to take care to avoid such missteps in the first instance, and in cases of disagreement, to advance arguments that support their interpretations of the constitution. Following the missteps argument, departmentalist accounts of interpretive authority engender constitutional responsibility and maturity; strong-form judicial review, in contrast, encourages irresponsibility. Departmentalism increases both the frequency and the quality of constitutional conversation.

We must be careful to note that there is no single model of departmentalism. I have already suggested that we should distinguish between strong/civic and weak/juridic models of interpretive pluralism. Some scholars have suggested we should distinguish between a model of separation and a model of coordination.[202] The separation variant of departmentalism denies to courts authority to review the constitutional decisions of coordinate constitutional actors. The coordination model, in contrast, envisions a system in which all departments possess authority to review each other. Both models of departmentalism are compatible with the Civic Constitution; the question is whether we have good reason to think one model will go further to establishing an understanding of constitutional life that welcomes the voices of citizens or quiets them. The coordination model of departmentalism is the better choice because it does more to encourage the branches to converse with each other and hence does more to promote the exchange of reason on a conversational or heterogeneous model of dialogue. (And because it includes judicial review, it accommodates both the juridic and the civic components of the Constitution.) The separation model, in contrast, allows the branches to withdraw from engagement—it allows them to be "self-contained," and to make pronouncements instead of speaking in dialogue with the other branches.

Two additional variations of departmentalism promise to make space for citizen voices. The first of these considers interpretive pluralism on a vertical, as opposed to a horizontal, plane. Thus, as we saw earlier and as I shall explore more fully in Essay Two on constitutional maintenance, Bradley Hays, Robert Schapiro, and some other scholars press a form of federalist interpretive pluralism, in which states and local actors are also invited to participate in the construction of constitutional meaning.[203] Sanford Levinson has proposed another variant of departmentalism, in which constitutional review sometimes takes the form of "citizen review."[204] Under this approach, individual citizens have some responsibility for determining the constitutionality of official action for themselves.[205] Under the Civic Constitution, citizen review, broadly conceived as an inquiry into the meaning of the Constitution as a political charter and not simply as a set of legal rules, is a condition of citizenship itself.

Some scholars argue that departmentalism subverts a primary constitutional function: the settlement of constitutional controversies.[206] In brief, the settlement argument is that constitutional regimes must incorporate some mechanism by which we can resolve (settle) disputes, or through which we can achieve some measure of finality. If left unsettled, constitutional disputes disrupt and disturb civic tranquility, as well as subvert the important constitutional function of providing order and finality. (I shall argue in Essay Three that we have more faith in the durability of juridic settlements than is warranted by experience.) This proposition makes sense if we start from the assumption that contested constitutional meaning is a dispute about what the *law* requires (or if the Constitution is Juridic), but not if these contests are fundamentally about politics writ large. In particular, the settlement function rests on the premise that settlement is a legal and not a political concern. Its primary institutional manifestation thus occurs through constitutional interpretation, a professional practice grounded in claims of professional expertise and necessarily outside the competence of ordinary citizens. Perhaps less obvious, under the Juridic Constitution, the settlement function is also a way of determining who can participate in and who is excluded from constitutional deliberations. It is precisely the fear of public engagement that leads some to prioritize the settlement function in accounts of constitutional maintenance. The settlement function is, at bottom, a way of choking debate. Conceived in this way, where we rank order the settlement function as higher in priority than the dialogic function, and where we assume it is best performed by judges, the settlement function is difficult to square with the Civic Constitution. So where the Juridic Constitution rank orders the settlement function higher than the dialogic function, or of civic dialogue about what a proper settlement should look like, a civic account requires us to find a way to hold the dialogic and settlement elements in balance.

Second, critics argue that given what we know about how other institutional actors regard constitutional values, as well as what citizens actually know about the Constitution, we are more likely to achieve the "best" constitutional resolution of controversies by entrusting such controversies to a "forum of principle."[207] If the end we desire is a constitutional way of life, then we should design institutions and assign them powers that promote the "best" settlements of constitutional disputes. Even admitting that judges will not always reach the best or even better settlements (*Dred Scott* comes to mind, along with several other examples),[208] the argument goes, there remain institutional imperatives and constraints that make better outcomes more likely if settled by courts than if left to the people: we might well fear for the civil liberties of unpopular minorities if their protection is left to the people, especially given what we seem to know about citizens' knowledge of the Constitution generally.[209] I take up these objections in several places in later essays, but in brief, it is not at all clear that courts are more reliable guardians of civil liberty than the people and their elected representatives, as our earlier discussion of the Religious Freedom Restoration Act and *Boerne v. Flores* (1997) suggested.[210]

Alternatively, we could argue that assigning *any* interpretive responsibility to courts undermines the Civic Constitution because it removes some element of the Constitution from the civic to the judicial arena. In light of the overhang problem and its deleterious effects upon civic maintenance (see Essay Two), why not eliminate judicial review of the Constitution altogether?[211] Jeremy Waldron, for instance, has claimed that judicial supremacy is deeply troublesome in part because it goes a long way to silencing citizens.[212] There are, however, two reasons for preserving a weak form of judicial review even under the Civic Constitution. First, some measure of review might help to preserve constitutional liberties, at least in the short run,[213] and thus help to preserve the components of the Constitution that *are* cast in terms of legality. As a practical matter, our task as guardians of the Constitution means that we must find ways to reinvigorate its civic elements, elements that have atrophied as the juridic has swelled, while not denying that there is a role for courts to play in enforcing certain constitutional rules.

Secondly, the Civic Constitution's preference for departmentalist accounts of judicial review does not displace the Juridic Constitution or judicial review; instead, it forces us to adopt a different understanding of judicial review, or to alter its practice to conform to other constitutional imperatives. It forces the Court, in other words, to engage in conversation with other political actors and not to superintend them. A weak form of judicial review, in which courts cannot command but must instead persuade other actors, may encourage courts to speak (or converse) in a language that is more accessible and inclusive, or more democratic. As Balkin has observed, courts work best in "dialogue with other institutions."[214] This does not mean that the Court does not or cannot ever discharge the settlement function, but it restricts it to cases in which there are genuine disputes about what the law requires, and then only to the case at hand (more like a system of *inter partes* than *erga omnes*).[215] Some models of judicial review, in other words, advance the ends of the Civic Constitution, first by helping to ensure our fidelity to constitutional values, and second by promoting constitutional conversation instead of quieting it.

In sum, we cannot achieve a constitutional way of life from the top down. An important part of what a constitutional way of life requires is civic engagement, and civic engagement must be nurtured by institutional design. The kinds of institutions we engineer determine the kinds of citizens we get.

THE CIVIC CONSTITUTION AND CITIZENS

The Constitution and citizenship are intimately connected, and in ways we do not always fully appreciate. As Adler has noted, "These two things come into existence together: constitutional government and citizenship."[216] They are constituted together, simultaneously and in the same (constituting) act. In creating a new American polity, the founders had

> to create a new citizenship that would incorporate, but not completely eliminate, many of the local allegiances of the past, allow for the entrance of strangers into the new community, decide what few "loved things held in common" were to be revered by all, and then create institutions which would at the same time allow for individual participation . . . and focus the attention of men who now might live a thousand miles apart upon matters of common interest touching a common welfare.[217]

Constituting citizens is in the first instance a question of determining the *who* more than the *what* of political membership, of creating community by determining who is in and who is out. The process is one of inclusion and exclusion. It is an elemental, primitive act of politics—the very first political act, according to Schmitt,[218] and not coincidentally, an act of identity.

Schmitt's conception of political identity located personality at the intersection of them and us.[219] Identity, in other words, looks both inward and outward. The Civic Constitution constitutes the "us" as intergenerational, as looking forward and backward as well as inward and outward, and in so doing, it makes the moment of constituting an ongoing project of constituting and reconstituting from generation to generation. It evokes a vision of citizenship in which "past, present, and future are represented . . . as part of an educational program and of an inspiring moral tradition in which each generation acknowledges a connection to all others and a responsibility to them for the maintenance of community and . . . traditions."[220] We the People are always constituting and reconstituting ourselves.

I noted in the Introduction that the categories of constituting, maintaining, and failing are not strictly sequential or linear. The point is made especially clear when we consider how questions concerning citizenship, far from settled at the founding, recur throughout American constitutional history. The Constitution of 1789 did little to address the question of citizenship directly. Indeed, Ackerman notes, "When it came to citizenship, the founders were full of paradox."[221] Unresolved questions about constituting the We at the founding arguably led both to constitutional failure (in the Civil War) and to a re- or a new constituting through the Reconstruction Amendments (in creating a national citizenship and reallocating power along the vertical axis of federalism).[222] Moreover, the category of national citizenship created by the Civil War Amendments, then a matter of intense controversy (see, for instance, the *SlaughterHouse Cases* [1873]), remains a politically volatile question, as evidenced by periodic concern in the body politic about immigration, and by contemporary proposals to eliminate or restrict the birthright citizenship created by the Fourteenth Amendment.[223] These controversies, past and present, are fundamentally constitutional in character precisely because they turn on the definition of who We the People are—and, no less importantly, about who is entitled to share in the blessings of liberty.[224] Indeed, the distinction between the privileges and immunities and the due process and equal protection clauses in the first section of the Fourteenth Amendment incorporates (bad pun!) the basic premise that *personhood* entitles one to certain basic human rights, but only *citizenship* entitles one to the full register of constitutional freedoms and protections.[225]

Just as the categories of constituting/maintaining/failing are not water-tight, the distinction between citizen and noncitizen is also fuzzy, or noncat-egorical. Wayne Moore makes this point clear in his discussion of Frederick Douglass. Although by virtue of *Dred Scott v. Sandford* (1857), Douglass was not a citizen in a formal, jural sense, he acted like and claimed to be a citizen. Moore notes that even at the cost of a certain degree of constitu-tional coherence, "the Constitution neither fully supported nor completely undercut" these claims.[226] We cannot dismiss Douglass's claim to citizenship as constitutionally wrong *except* as a narrow claim of legality. Douglass complicates our understanding of what it means to be a citizen of the Con-stitution, and of what (and whom) citizenship consists, especially by demon-strating the ongoing contestability and nonunitary nature of these concepts.

Moore's analysis has two important implications for my argument. First, Moore traces the evolution of Frederick Douglass's constitutional thought from denouncing the Constitution as "a most foul and bloody conspiracy" in favor of a "radical reinterpretation" that was "fundamentally preserva-tive"[227] of the larger Constitution. Moore argues persuasively that "nor-mal and ongoing processes of constitutional criticism and affirmation" by citizens is an important part of the process of "creating and re-creating constitutional norms."[228] This is an important example of the Civic Con-stitution in practice, of the quotidian construction of constitutional mean-ing by citizens by contesting the meaning of citizenship itself. Nor is it an example confined to the nineteenth century. Consider, for instance, the example of several undocumented immigrants who revealed their identities and their undocumented statuses in a 2010 march to Washington, D.C., to urge Congress to pass the DREAM Act, or the Rally for Citizenship in the spring of 2013.[229]

Second, Moore concludes that "[a]llowing for degrees or variations of constitutional coherence is suitable for analyzing problems of political mem-bership because the concepts of membership and participation are them-selves variable and not simply dichotomous."[230] Moore makes an important point about constitutional analysis and its implicit reliance on the desir-ability of dichotomous results. The juxtaposed categories of constitutional/unconstitutional both re-create and are the result of an approach to the con-stitution as law. Conflicts of law necessitate a dichotomous result (a particu-lar form of settlement);[231] the law has the character of either/or, categories that are too blunt to serve as the basis for civic dialogue about the mean-ing of constitutional norms and values, as Moore's discussion of Douglass's citizenship claims illustrates. Those sorts of claims are perfectly consonant with the Civic Constitution, however, which conceptualizes citizenship in political and not legal terms, as a compound state of being/becoming, not as a dichotomous either/or, as settled/unsettled.[232]

Part of the reason for ongoing uncertainties in the definition of citizen and in the meaning of citizenship is that that the Constitution is notably silent on both questions. Its silence pertains first to the question of who we are, about who *constitutes* and who is *constituted* by the Constitution itself.[233] One of the obvious explanations for this silence is the institution of slavery. Whether one thinks the founders' failure to end the practice was a necessary if unfortunate accommodation to politics[234] or a moral (and constitutional) failure of the highest order,[235] provisions such as Article 1, Section 9, and Article 4, Section 2, are clear evidence of the kinds of compromises they made concerning slavery.[236] Moreover, they indicate the founders were well aware that constituting cannot be confined to a specific point in sequential time, and that decisions made when constituting may have important (and perhaps dire) implications for constitutional maintenance and constitutional failure. As Madison is reputed to have remarked on a proposed twenty-year window for the import of slaves, "Twenty years will produce all the mischief that can be apprehended from the liberty to import slaves. So long a term will be more dishonorable to the National character than to say nothing about it in the Constitution."[237]

Second, the silence of the text extends to the equally important matter of the *kind* of citizens the Constitution envisions. The Constitution has little to say about the duties or responsibilities of citizens of the United States, about what it means to be a citizen, or about the burdens that attach to this status. The unamended text mentions citizenship in just four places, and in three of those (Article 1, Section 2; Article 1, Section 3; and Article 2, Section 1) references it only as a precondition for holding an elected office in the national government. Article 1, Section 8, also assigns the power of naturalization to Congress, which further underscores the centrality of citizenship as membership in We the People, especially in contrast to the Articles of Confederation, which was notably silent on the matter of naturalization. The comparison further illuminates a central difference between the two texts. The Articles did not create a new body politic, did not in any meaningful sense constitute a We the People, and hence had no need to control or regulate entry into the new corporate We. (Instead, such decisions were left to the individual states.)

At first appearances, the silence of the Constitution concerning the what (as opposed to the who) of citizenship might seem odd. The construct (as an analytical concept and in the active sense of *construc*tion) of citizenship is central to constitutional government. Citizenship is an artificial political category. It invests the fact and status of political membership with an elevated dignity that transcends the status of mere subjects, who are possessed of a lesser degree of power, agency, and autonomy. Adler argues that the distinction between subject and citizen hinges on the (Aristotelian?) distinction between being ruled and participating in rule, and that it is only in constitutional governments, where legitimate authority rests upon the consent of the governed, that we find the latter. Adler too easily conflates consent, citizenship, and participation, but the larger point he makes—that constituting creates both a constitution and citizens of that constitution—is well taken. Consent transforms the relationship between *subject* and *power* into a relationship between *citizen* and *authority*.[238] The importance of this transformation is critical to understanding citizenship under the Civic Constitution.

The Constitution's silence in respect of the duties and demands of citizenship might indicate that there are no such responsibilities, or very few of them. It is not difficult to pull together an account of the founding, we might call it a Federalist narrative, in which the founders' dim perception of human nature and consequent apprehension of the people ("that great beast," in Hamilton's unflattering characterization[239]) yields a thin understanding of citizenship. On this view, the Constitution asks little of citizens because it looks upon them with disdain or even suspicion. Wolin captured this sense of thin citizenship in *The Presence of the Past*.[240] Accepting the premise that the Constitution marked a counterrevolutionary departure from the democratic impulse of the Declaration of Independence, Wolin notes that the Constitution "had to create a new type of citizen"[241] that could be reconciled to a heavily circumscribed role in public governance. In Wolin's account, these new citizens of the Constitution would be directed to the private pursuit of happiness and discouraged from frequent participation in public affairs.[242]

We can find some obvious support for this account in *Federalist* #49, where Madison warned of "[t]he danger of disturbing the public tranquillity by interesting too strongly the public passions." Madison's remarks were an objection to the "frequent reference of constitutional questions to the decision of the whole society."[243] Public discussion of first principles, he warned, was as likely to be inflamed by "passion" as informed by "enlightened reason." Similarly, in *Federalist* #55, Madison observed, "In all very numerous assemblies, of whatever character composed, passion never fails to wrest the sceptre from reason. Had every Athenian citizen been a Socrates, every Athenian assembly would still have been a mob."

I observed earlier that how we characterize a text determines how we read it. Part of the reason we read *Federalists* #49 and #55 as cautions against involving too frequently the people in the project of maintenance is because we read them through the lens of the Juridic Constitution, just as we read judicial review into the text and have come to regard as inescapable the conclusion that the Constitution was conceived in and should be regarded as law first. How we read crucial elements of Madisonian constitutional engineering is profoundly influenced by our understanding of whether the Constitution should be seen as a legal or as a political project.

It is also possible to see in the Madisonian conception of constitutional maintenance a vision of the Civic Constitution, in which the Constitution requires citizens who are both enlightened and engaged, or who have substantial public as well as private selves. The constitutional design is significantly more nuanced than the foregoing narrative lets on, as Colleen Sheehan and others have argued. Sheehan argues that contemporary scholars grossly underestimate the extent to which Madison's constitutional thought "calls for the active role of an enlightened citizenry in republican self-government."[244] According to Sheehan, what Madison envisioned was "a 'dialogical community,' based not on possessive individualism or market liberalism, but on a 'marketplace of ideas operating in a system premised on shared principles. . . .' While Madison's conception of the rule of reason does not require philosophic wisdom in the populace, it does call for a participatory, enlightened, and responsible citizenry."[245] Thus, Sheehan writes that a full account of Madison's thought must address not only its "foundational elements, that is, the extended republic, representation, separation of powers, checks and balances, and federalism . . . [but also] the importance of civic education and the need to form republican habits of mind."[246] (Indeed, Sheehan has argued that civic education was central to Madison's solution to the problem of "regime degeneration," and a stark point of difference between Madison's understanding of constitutional maintenance and John Adams's.[247]) Elkin makes a similar point, arguing that Madison's constitutional design required both a "capable" citizenry (invested with "sufficient virtue and intelligence") and one that was "public-spirited."[248] Unfortunately, as Elkin also notes, Madison was ambivalent about the capabilities of citizens, and the "absence of a considered discussion of public-spiritedness leaves a substantial hole at the center of Madison's constitutional theory."[249]

Wolin's argument, if not a fully accurate ledger of Madison's design, nonetheless expresses the essence of citizenship under the Juridic Constitution. The Juridic Constitution envisions citizens who have few responsibilities to care for the Constitution, and whose fidelity to it is built chiefly on affection and veneration instead of reason and critical engagement. We might read the Constitution's silence respecting the obligations of citizenship, then, as an indication that the founders did not expect much of citizens and so entrusted them with little responsibility for achieving a constitutional way of life.[250]

Indeed, read juridically, the text assigns no duties at all to citizens, not even to participate in the already narrowly proscribed venue of electoral politics.

We Americans are frequently reminded that it is our solemn civic obligation to vote. As Alexander Hamilton noted, "A share in the sovereignty of the state, which is exercised by the citizens at large, in voting at elections is one of the most important rights of the subject, and in a republic ought to stand foremost in the estimation of the law."[251] But it is easy not to appreciate just how solemn the act of voting is, especially since it so often seems meaningless, or "little more than an 'accountability moment' that occurs once every four years."[252] The founders, however, spoke reverentially of voting in terms of duty and obligation. Samuel Adams, for example, wrote, "Let each citizen remember at the moment he is offering his vote that he is not making a present or a compliment to please an individual—or at least that he ought not so to do; but that he is executing one of the most solemn trusts in human society for which he is accountable to God and his country."[253] John Jay likewise invoked the language of divine duty, writing, "Providence has given to our people the choice of their rulers, and it is the duty, as well as the privilege and interest of our Christian nation, to select and prefer Christians for their rulers."[254] No matter how solemn the responsibility, though, the founders made voting a choice, not a duty. The obligation (better, responsibility) it carries is political, not legal in character.

It is not uncommon for constitutional democracies to require voting by statute or by constitutional command.[255] The failure of the Juridic Constitution to do so is further evidence of the limited demands it makes of citizens. The failure makes sense if we assume citizens are not naturally disposed to reason or to virtue, or can be trusted only so far to govern responsibly. The unspoken assumption is that voting, the *sine qua non* of democratic participation, may be too important to require of all citizens.[256] (Indeed, a similar rationale underlay the functional nonvoting literature in political science in the 1950s.[257]) The demands of citizenship are discharged only through the limited, periodic, and voluntary sacrament of voting, where the political engagement of citizens is routed, in large part by the mechanisms of political parties, into electoral contests. Under the Juridic Constitution, the public life of citizens encompasses these accountability moments, but extends no further. Citizenship under the Juridic Constitution, reduced to voting/accountability moments, is mimetic rather than real.[258]

On the other hand, the Juridic Constitution does not entirely ignore the concept of civic duty. If it does not require citizens to vote, it nonetheless requires electoral contests as a part of its commitment to a republican form of government. The text also seems to reference the idea of civic obligation in two other places. First, the constitutional provisions that mention militias (Article 1, Section 8, clauses 15 and 16; and the Second Amendment) should be understood in the context of a larger conversation about civic duty. As Hemberger notes, "For the Antifederalists . . . much more was at stake in debates over the militia than the question of who would go to war. Militia musters, even more than elections, were the occasions on which white men experienced their status as republican citizens. . . . Thus, when the Federalists held out the possibility of relief from this admittedly burdensome obligation, the Antifederalists foresaw the destruction of a vital civic institution."[259]

Secondly, the concept of civic duty is also related to the institution of the jury, which is referenced in Article 3, Section 2, and in the Sixth and Seventh Amendments. Like militias, juries were an occasion for civic duty: "both were institutions in which ordinary citizens would exercise power, and both provided opportunities for local knowledge to be brought to bear in the implementation of national policies."[260]

These are not insignificant incidents of citizenship,[261] and they had (at the founding) and continue to have both practical and symbolic importance.[262] Many of the controversies that have dogged the definition of citizenship in the United States, such as who qualifies for citizenship, who is excluded, and why, have occasioned similar controversies concerning who is eligible to serve on juries, both grand and petit.[263] The points of similarity testify to the significance of civic duty as a part of the definition of citizenship and identity. Nevertheless, although significant, jury service, like the act of voting, is episodic in character and duration.[264] It is not an ongoing burden or one that requires a citizen's constant or even recurrent attention to civic affairs.

Constituting Citizens

Our understanding of citizenship, "the name for public life,"[265] is directly related to our sense of what public life demands of us. In some accounts, citizenship is a moral code that provides the basis for national identity and community,[266] and in others it is "a demand for active participation in civic life."[267] Citizenship under the Civic Constitution incorporates these traditions, recalling a conception of citizenship that recognizes rights but also imposes obligations.[268] The Civic Constitution can flourish or thrive only in certain kinds of conditions, and like all constitutions, it seeks to create those very conditions. If an engaged and committed citizenry is a precondition of the Civic Constitution, then it must create, or literally constitute, that citizenry.

There are points of constitutional design where the Juridic and Civic Constitutions push in the same direction, but here they diverge. The Juridic Constitution calls for an occasional citizenship, one in which the participation of citizens is limited to periodic electoral contests and in which they are relieved of any burden for giving the constitution meaning or for maintaining it. In so doing, it counsels citizens that their political engagement is desirable only periodically, and should be directed to constitutional first principles only on occasion.[269] It asks for citizens who venerate the Constitution, but it does not require or even desire citizens who know the Constitution in any meaningful sense.[270]

In contrast, the Civic Constitution calls upon a tradition in which citizenship, far from a synonym for the pursuit of private interest, is a "path to virtue" and "a means well suited to draw out the best in people."[271] It is a conception of citizenship that is broadly public, in contrast to the private account of citizenship anticipated by the Juridic Constitution. By public,[272] I mean that citizens of the Civic Constitution must be oriented to public affairs in ordinary as well as (and not only in) extraordinary moments.[273] Under the Civic Constitution, public life "has to do with active participation in debates and decisions concerning our collective fate and . . . the fate of our public institutions."[274] It captures some of the sense of Aristotelian citizenship: "Unlike modern citizens . . . Aristotle's citizen is a constant actual performer of civic duties."[275]

The Civic Constitution's need of an engaged, committed citizenry is not simply more ambitious than the Juridic Constitution, it is incompatible with the underlying tenets of the Juridic Constitution. The Juridic Constitution purposefully drives citizens into the private. Its vision of citizenship has no obvious connection to the promotion of virtue, private or civic, and the demands it makes of citizens free them of responsibility for attending to civic life. The Juridic Constitution expects citizens to expend resources in private rather than public concerns.[276] It is important to recall here that juridic citizenship is not simply a concession to the insistent press and pull of private life. The Juridic Constitution actively encourages citizens to pursue the private interest first and their shared civic interests only secondarily; it does so, in part, because it conceptualizes the constitutional enterprise as an activity best entrusted to elites.[277]

Constant actual performance of the Aristotelian sort is plainly too onerous a requirement of public life in the modern constitutional state. The demands of economic competition and the attraction of a private sphere that frees citizens to pursue personal notions of the good mean that many citizens will pursue virtue, or happiness, liberty, and property, in activities and pursuits that are located chiefly in civil society or that have little to do with the public weal. Moreover, because time is a limited resource, attention devoted to the responsibilities of citizenship is a considerable expenditure (cast typically in the unpalatable language of civic duty—a tough sell) and one that appears to have little immediate or material benefit.

Here it may be useful to recall Murphy's distinction between ideal and adequate citizens. Ideal citizens are "politically aware, active in trying to persuade fellow citizens about desirable public policies, knowledgeable about how to communicate opinions to officials, how to hold them accountable through electoral, administrative, and/or judicial processes, and also ready to fulfill their own political obligations."[278] In comparison, adequate citizens are "occasionally if not constantly attentive to politics" and have political preferences that "are not necessarily irrational."[279] Citizens of the Civic Constitution are not Aristotle's ideal citizens, but they must be nearer to the ideal than to the adequate. Indeed, Murphy's adequate citizens are adequate only when assessed against the perfunctory requirements of the Juridic Constitution. The "not necessarily irrational" political preferences of adequate citizens need not reference constitutional values, norms, and aspirations or even, it seems, be grounded in reason or rational calculation. It is difficult to see a genuine conception of public-spiritedness in the simply adequate citizen. Her attention to civic matters is at best desultory; she assumes no significant responsibility for the civic or public life of her community. Such citizens might better be called absentee citizens. Absentee citizens act incivilly insofar as they do not ordinarily engage in the self-reflective manner required by the Civic Constitution.

How to Create Civic Citizens

Among the primary objects of constitutional design must be the creation and education of citizens with the civic virtues necessary to sustain the constitutional order. Every constitutional order shapes or makes its citizens in certain ways, in part by providing incentives and disincentives for citizens to behave in particular kinds of ways. It is thus inaccurate to say that the Civic Constitution differs from the Juridic in its concern for shaping citizens—both the Juridic and the Civic Constitutions share this concern. Where they differ is in how, why, and to what extent they take on the project of creating citizens and the kinds of citizens that result from their efforts.

How does the Civic Constitution create the kinds of citizens it needs to flourish? As Macedo puts it, the question is "how do our institutions . . . provide or fail to provide for the virtues that facilitate the success of this project"?[280] Constituting the public citizenship necessary to sustain the Civic

Constitution requires the creation of space for civic engagement, as well as a constitutional order that generates incentives for such engagement. If citizens are to devote themselves to public life, especially when other communities (family, faith, work, fraternity) also demand their devotion, then they must be confident their participation will have meaning and is a judicious use of their resources. Thus, as I wrote earlier, constitutional engineers must design institutions in ways that do not discourage citizens from exercising their civic duties. "The way political structures are crafted is critical to the long-run education of a people."[281]

It is not enough, however, simply to expand the public realm to accommodate and empower citizens. Realization of the Civic Constitution also requires citizens who are attitudinally disposed to public life, or who are possessed of the right "habits of the heart," in Tocqueville's famous phrase. Habits of the heart, moreover, must be learned; they require a "very complex and structured schooling."[282] What we need, in Thomas's words, are citizens of a particular constitutional mindset.[283] This in turn requires that citizens possess civic knowledge and civic capability, or the capacity to engage in the exchange of reasoned argument with other citizens and public officials.

How do we instill in citizens the civic virtues and civic capacity that sustain a constitutional way of life? The answer lies in considering how the Civic Constitution approaches the relationship between personhood and citizenship. My understanding of the relationship between persons and citizens is captured in the idea of self-government. Self-government has an immediate, obvious meaning in democratic theory, and a less immediate one. The obvious meaning invokes self-government as a means of democratic governance, neatly captured in the phrase "government by the people." Its less obvious meaning, at least to most political theorists, concerns the government (control) of one's self.[284] We think of governing ourselves most commonly in the sense of reining in our worst impulses and tendencies, or in resisting temptation, sin, or vice. Self-government of this sort references the government/control/disciplining of oneself, not simply as an analogue to the sorts of difficulties of governance that communities confront,[285] but instead in the literal sense of how to constitute one's self to live a preferred way of life. To speak in the latter sense, of governing one's self, is plainly to invoke the language of virtue. I reference self-governance in this second sense, as a way to constitute/govern persons as well as communities, as a mission that implicates civic virtue and vice. But the concept of self-government, of government of the self, has also a political component,[286] for it involves the exercise of power and control in matters of self-identity, in the narrow sense, and questions about how to constitute one's self to pursue one's commitments,[287] in a wider sense.

A civic concept of constitutional self-governance incorporates both the collective and the individual notion of self-governance—a constitutional way of life must be an ambition not only of states or communities but also of persons. To discharge their civic responsibility, citizens of the Civic Constitution must possess certain political skills and certain attributes of character. Developing in citizens those skills (the capacity and disposition to reason and deliberation, as well as an appreciation of what a constitutional way of life comprehends) and attributes of character (civility, an ethic of tending) is properly a concern of the community. Under the Civic Constitution, "Government should pursue a formative project to foster the capabilities for self-government, both in the sense of democratic self-government and personal self-government."[288] The state should be invested in projects that create good citizens and good persons.[289]

The Civic Constitution thus leads us to revisit the neglected relationship in constitutional theory between persons and citizens. At the risk of oversimplification, it is fair to say that most constitutional theories—and certainly juridic ones—posit a sharp distinction between persons and citizens. The former is largely outside the parameter of constitutional design, confined to what is the private sphere or to civil society. The person is nearly a natural fact, a condition of being both more complete and comprehensive, as well as prior in time, to the more limited and artificially constructed concept of citizen. Moreover, persons, insofar as they represent identities informed by a lifelong series of choices about who we are, what we believe, and what aims we pursue and abjure, are private in a classically liberal sense. Put another way, in liberal constitutional theory the person is off-limits. Our identities as persons, as far as possible, must be a set of private choices and decisions. Liberal constitutional regimes are liberal precisely and partly to the extent they recognize and respect the liberties and rights of their citizens to organize and direct their lives as persons without the superintending or even the intervening direction of the state. *Federalist* #10 casts a long shadow.

One of the attractions of the Juridic Constitution, following this line of thought, is that its thin understanding of the burdens and claims of citizenship impinges only incidentally on the lives of persons. The Juridic Constitution leaves persons relatively unburdened by a responsibility or ethic of care for the public weal. It not only frees up space and time to pursue the private, it creates incentives to do so nearly exclusively. The Civic Constitution reminds us that the pursuit of the private comes at considerable cost to other of our constitutional ambitions.

Civic Skills and Competencies

Citizens of the Civic Constitution must have the skills and competencies necessary for meaningful participation in the public life of the community. Because these skills and competencies must be learned, the Civic Constitution requires instruction in civics. It should be clear that the purposes we assign to formal civic education will differ under the Civic and the Juridic Constitutions. At the highest level of abstraction, however, both the Juridic and the Civic Constitutions require such education to be both factual and fraternal.[290] The differences are of degree. The Civic Constitution, because it demands a far stronger commitment on the part of citizens to carry the deliberative burden of the regime—or to advance our constitutional aspirations—plainly anticipates a sophisticated citizenry with a high degree of civic competence.

The Juridic Constitution makes no substantial demands for the actual practice of citizenship. Civic service is restricted to voting and even more infrequent participation in a select few other rituals and practices. Some of these rituals, such as voting, do require a level of civic competence and knowledge, but it is also very easy to overestimate how much civic knowledge should be a prerequisite for casting one's vote. Unlike the practice of civility—of direct engagement with others and the use of reason to facilitate public responsibility for the attainment of constitutional ideals—voting requires very little civic knowledge.[291]

Under the Juridic Constitution, consequently, the project of civic education is important but shallow and uncomplicated. What juridic citizens must learn is a feeling, a predisposition, facilitated by the teaching of stories, myths, and a litany of simple facts that help to solidify an emotional attachment to the constitutional order.[292] The essentially affective bonds necessary for the Juridic Constitution are best forged in the learning and recitation of widely shared civic myths and practiced in public ceremonies and fetes.[293] Ritualistic forms of participation, such as the Pledge of Allegiance, the national anthem, and other emotive ceremonials are all that are needed to inculcate the devotion required by the Juridic Constitution. The strength of the juridic bond does not require or depend upon extensive or intimate civic knowledge or experience; indeed, as Madison intimated, civic ignorance of our many failures to realize our constitutional ideals may make the heart grow fonder.[294]

Fidelity to the Civic Constitution, however, requires more than affection. The Civic Constitution's requirement of citizens fully engaged in a collective political bond presupposes "a citizenry with a sound grasp of the distinctive ideals that inspire its political practice."[295] The Civic Constitution thus requires the public-spiritedness that Madison envisioned, and public-spiritedness (unlike patriotism) must be informed by civic knowledge and engagement. Consequently, civic knowledge is not confined to a precise set of facts about the constitutional order or of the founders, but rather consists of deliberative competence and an understanding of the normative commitments that inhere in constitutional self-government.[296] It must extend "to the understandings presupposed by the Constitution that must be thought and lived by."[297]

George Thomas reminds us that several of the founders understood the intrinsic connection between citizenship and civic education. Thomas notes that every president from Washington to John Quincy Adams proposed a national university because "an educated public was essential to maintaining a constitutional government."[298] In this instance, the constitution's identity influences our impression not only of how we should design institutions and allocate power among them, but also of what institutions are necessary in the first place. Some of the opponents of a national university argued that it exceeded even the far reaches of congressional authority under Article 1, Section 8.[299] (I do not mean to suggest that opposition to the national university was grounded in a juridic reading of the Constitution, but clearly some of the opposition to it did center on a particular way of reading certain key provisions in the text, notably the necessary and proper clause. A civic reading of the necessary and proper clause, especially if read in conjunction with the Preamble and the general welfare clause, would have little difficulty reaching the conclusion that a national university was directly related to promoting civic participation and consequently to creating a citizenry equal to the task of achieving a constitutional way of life.) Proponents of the national university, in contrast, saw it as "a necessary supplement to the formal institutions of government; it would help 'constitute' the American mind in a manner that carried forward the constitutional enterprise."[300]

Implicit in debates concerning the establishment of a national university is an important question: does the Civic Constitution make civic education mandatory? The Civic Constitution seeks citizens who can carry forward the constitutional enterprise, and to this end, citizens must be equipped with the intellectual and pragmatic skills equal to the burden of a constitutional way of life. It thus requires the state to provide free, universal public education as an instrumental necessity, or as a condition of its very realization. The operative assumption behind this requirement is that civic habits and *moeurs* must be cultivated. By cultivation, I mean that the state must act in ways that help to create citizens with a civic predisposition. Unpalatable as such a prospect may be to some, we already subscribe to the general proposition that possession of civic knowledge should inform citizenship decisions in our naturalization processes. We do so because we assume that the affective bonds of naturalized citizens, even if fully matured, are insufficient to make a good citizen, and because we assume that natural citizens will have acquired some measure of such knowledge through formal schooling.[301]

Compulsory civic education may seem paternalistic, or at least deeply illiberal and in some tension with other constitutional ideals, such as liberty, self-definition, and a commitment to pluralism. The potentially illiberal aspects of civic education are immediately obvious in *Minersville v. Gobitis* (1940), as well as in several other cases.[302]

Minersville is a more difficult case than it seems. As described later in *West Virginia v. Barnette* (1943), flag salute laws had as their purpose "teaching, fostering and perpetuating the ideals, principles and spirit of Americanism, and increasing the knowledge of the organization and machinery of the government." A fair reading of Justice Frankfurter's majority opinion for the Court must confront his observation that the state has a legitimate interest in promoting "national cohesion": "We are dealing with an interest inferior to none in the hierarchy of legal values. National unity is the basis of national security. To deny the legislature the right to select appropriate means for its attainment presents a totally different order of problem from that of the propriety of subordinating the possible ugliness of littered streets to the free expression of opinion through distribution of handbills."

Back of Frankfurter's rank ordering of the interest in national cohesion is the undoubted concern every constitutional regime has in the creation of citizens. Our discomfort with the holding in *Minersville* should stem not from a rejection of that interest, but instead from our knowledge that overly aggressive efforts to promote it may do damage to other bedrock constitutional ideals, as Justice Jackson observed in *Barnette*:

> We can have intellectual individualism and the rich cultural diversities that we owe to exceptional minds only at the price of occasional eccentricity and abnormal attitudes. When they are so harmless to others or to the State as those we deal with here, the price is not too great. But freedom to differ is not limited to things that do not matter much. That would be a mere shadow of freedom. The test of its substance is the right to differ as to things that touch the heart of the existing order.

At issue in *Minersville* and *Barnette* is precisely the tension between our interest in creating good citizens, equal to the task of citizenship in a constitutional community, and the compatibility of that interest with other constitutional aspirations. The potential illiberality (if not the offensiveness) of the former is exacerbated by the terrible repercussions of *Minersville*,[303] but those are not an argument against mandatory civic education. Instead, they are an argument against the worst kinds of jingoistic civic education that can result when we conceive of such education as geared to veneration and to creating an emotional attachment between citizen and state.[304] What happened after *Minersville*, an incivility of the most profound and disturbing sort, happened in part because we have failed to develop an account of civic education appropriate to the Civic Constitution.

As I indicated earlier, the fundamental issue here is the relationship between personhood and citizenship. We must seek a balance between the state's undoubted interest in the creation and education of good *citizens*, and parents' equally compelling interest in the creation and education of good *persons* (while admitting that neither interest is or can be exclusive, as I shall argue immediately below). The former interest is sufficiently strong to authorize the state to exercise some degree of curricular control over private and parochial schools, even though such requirements might otherwise impinge on the religious freedom of parents and children, as well as on parental liberty. On the other hand, civic education can be a powerful tool for the creation of civic homogeneity, which itself poses dangers for constitutional democracy, as Tocqueville warned.[305] The purposes we assign to civic education—to teach civility and criticality or to promote public reasonableness—will blunt the worst forms of this despotism, but all forms of civic instruction are illiberal in the sense that they are inherently transformative. A *civic* account of civic education, however, although not neutral regarding the desirability and normative superiority of our aspirations, at least allows opportunity for citizens to challenge those aspirations.[306]

Put another way, what the Civic Constitution requires of civic education is that we devise institutions that teach citizens how to practice civility. Constitutional civility is a predisposition to reflect upon the meaning of the Constitution as a way of constituting the good life and as what can be constitutionally defended as the good society.[307] Recall too that incivility is not simply disagreement, even strongly held disagreement, about the meaning or even the desirability of our constitutional aspirations. Our conception of civility must be expansive enough to admit challenges to the desirability of constitutionalism as a way of organizing public life.

THE CIVIC CONSTITUTION AND CULTURE:
CONFIGURING A CIVIC CULTURE

The act of constituting comprehends far more than just putting a plan to paper. A constitution must constitute a political culture as well, and it must do so in ways that support its claim to authority. We might dismiss the main principles of constitutional architecture, such as the principle of checks and balances, as mere parchment barriers but for their grounding in a civic culture that regards them as valuable and insists upon some measure of fidelity to them by political actors and citizens.[308] Every constitution rests upon, and indeed helps to create, a boundary between the spheres of public and private life, or between state and society. These categories are not just empirical political facts to which founders must conform. They are themselves *objects* of constitutional design. In the words of George Thomas, "The resultant 'civil society' created by a constitution will inexorably shape the lives of the citizens who inhabit that order: 'private' life is a result of constitutional design (including economic and commercial life)."[309] Every constitution demands a political culture that supports its claim to authority; every "modern liberal democracy needs the right sort of civic culture."[310] And as we shall see when we take up constitutional maintenance and failure in Essays Two and Three, the relationship between constitution and culture must be mutually reinforcing. To endure and to thrive, a constitution must constitute a political culture in ways that support, or at least that do not undermine, the constitutional enterprise.[311]

We must seek a certain degree of congruence between constitutional norms and civil society.[312] A civic reading of the Constitution will therefore influence our sense of where we ought to draw the distinction between state and civil society (or if one prefers, between public and private, or between citizen and person). This prompts two specific questions concerning the Civic Constitution and political culture. First, what *kind* of a civic culture is necessary to sustain the Civic Constitution? And, second, *how* do we engineer that culture? What elements or features of constitutional design are instrumentally necessary to achieve the kind of civic culture necessary to sustain the Civic Constitution? I start from the premise that a wide variety of institutions in civil society, including families, schools, churches, and youth sports leagues, as well as civic and charitable associations, plays an important, if not critical, role in the promotion of civic virtue. Because they do, these institutions are properly a subject of constitutional interest. Macedo makes the same point, writing, "If a constitutional regime is to succeed and thrive, it must constitute the private realm in its image, and it must form citizens willing to observe its limits and able to pursue its aspirations."[313]

Making persons into citizens is a familiar project in political (though not constitutional) theory,[314] as well as a contemporary one, represented not only by Macedo, but also by Robert Putnam and other social capital theorists.[315] The basic features of arguments about the declination of social capital in advanced industrial democracies are well known. It is important, however, to recall that social capital arguments have at least two dimensions. The first dimension concerns the empirical question of whether there has been a decline in social capital, of what may cause it, and how we may avert or remedy it. The second and more important dimension is the implicit suggestion in Putnam's work (and others) that our understanding of social capital depends, as Macedo writes, upon a "substantive social ideal—one containing resources that advance a specifically liberal democratic project."[316]

My argument makes a structurally similar claim: our understanding of civic capital must be influenced or tied to a substantive social ideal that "contains resources that advance a specific conception" of the constitution and the constitutional order. A vibrant civic order, committed to an ethos of civility and the practice of tending, cannot simply hope that the attributes and characteristics that comprise good citizenship, engagement, civility, and an ethic of tending, will flourish without being cultivated in civil society. The Civic Constitution requires us to reexamine the relationship between state and civil society—to recognize that the state has an interest in the character and formulation of civil society itself. It subscribes to the view that "civil society institutions play a crucial role in fostering civic virtue, and that this recognition justifies a variety of political interventions in civil society, including those implicit in the establishment of the constitutional order itself."[317]

To some extent, then, the Civic Constitution should play a formative role in inculcating civic virtue in its citizens.[318] Those elements of civil society that promote an ethic of tending, of civility, and of civic engagement are proper objects of governmental promotion and favor. Equally, the state should facilitate objects, institutions, and associations in civil society that promote civic values. Putnam's distinction between "bridging" and "bonding" associations, in which the latter look inward "and tend to reinforce exclusive identities," and in which the former are "outward looking" and "encompass people across diverse social cleavages,"[319] is relevant here, but not because the Civic Constitution requires one and excludes the other. Instead, the distinction is relevant because it reminds us that the constitution of civil society is relevant to the political constitution of the state.[320]

The Civic Constitution therefore teaches us that the institutions of civil society are proper objects of constitutional concern. But it does not collapse the distinction between state and civil society. Its concern for the development of virtuous citizens does not always trump the choices of the people (such as parents), or of the institutions (such as churches), we routinely trust to develop persons into good citizens, to pursue other ways of life. There are many ways to live virtuous lives and to develop the habits and to learn the skills that help us to live a constitutional way of life. The concept of civic virtue is sufficiently expansive to tolerate great diversity in how citizens perceive and pursue it in their lives as individuals and as private persons. The Civic Constitution is not Rousseau's constitution for the government of Poland.[321] But neither can the Civic Constitution completely ignore or disregard the constitution of civil society, in part because civil society is itself partly the product of that order, and in part because state and civil society are deeply intertwined and interdependent. There can be no sharp distinction between civic virtue and private virtue.

A civic political culture is defined by its concern and care for a politics that is other- or community-directed, a culture in which we all share an obligation to tend to and care for the public weal. A civic culture encourages citizens to tend to first-order political concerns and to do so as an ordinary and not as an occasional part of their public life.[322] It invests civic space, and concern for it, with weight and dignity. It rejects the premise—shared "by politicians and business leaders, but also by average citizens, educators, and even legal theorists—that the *raison d'etre* of American constitutional government is to facilitate economic activity."[323]

This kind of culture is not an inevitable by-product of constitutionalism itself; it must be carefully cultivated. "[T]he cultivation of public spirit [depends] on a real constitutional or institutional presence, a 'public space' that [is] both durable and accessible to ordinary people."[324] Foremost among the aims of the Civic Constitution, therefore, must be a civic culture in which citizens can tend to the constitutional enterprise. Tending requires a civic culture centered more on everyday practices of care and less on the periodic discharge of specific civic duties (such as voting). Tending also requires and depends upon a specific kind of civic knowledge, one grounded in the practice of politics and practical experience. It requires that we learn how to be *civil* in the larger sense I identified in the Introduction and earlier in this essay. Civility encompasses both a disposition toward and possession of a set of skills necessary to sustain a robust public-spiritedness, or civic-mindedness, on the part of citizens.

In contrast, civic space under the Juridic Constitution is constrained to discussion of what we might call second-order politics,[325] to questions of policy and even more of partisanship,[326] and not to first-order or constitutional questions about how to construct the well-ordered polity or to achieve the blessings of liberty.[327] It is a sparse and intermittent space, characterized by competition and horse-race concerns; it occupies our attention only occasionally and then for a very short period.

It is important to remember that the anemic political culture we have under the Juridic Constitution is partially a consequence of deliberate design. As some of the *Federalist Papers* make clear (notably ##9, 10, 49, 55, and 78), Publius did not value a political culture that would routinely engage constitutional questions. Moreover, if we think the Constitution should be understood as a counterrevolutionary instrument, designed chiefly to blunt the democratic impulses of the Declaration and the Revolution,[328] then we might read the *Federalists* #9 and #10 as descriptions of how the new constitutional order sought to remake political culture by redirecting civic energy from public affairs to the private pursuit of capital and property. As I indicated above, this represents a juridic reading of the founding, or a way of understanding who we *were* that is deeply influenced by who we think we are *now*.

Such thinking recalls the argument by Norbert Elias and others that a key development of the modern state is how conspicuous economic consumption generally yields the depoliticization and consequent incivility of society.[329] Here incivility references the inability or unwillingness of citizens to reason or to think critically about public affairs, in favor of a retreat into things private. Incivility in this argument evokes my earlier discussion of civility as a key component of the Civic Constitution. Under the Civic Constitution, incivility is a failure of citizens to take up constitutional deliberations as an ordinary and recurrent part of their responsibilities as citizens.

CONCLUSION

Constituting, the first moment in the constitutional enterprise, requires that we draft a document, design institutions, create citizens, and configure a political culture in ways that advance a constitutional way of life. These imperatives inhere in all efforts to constitute a constitutional polity. They are not unique or peculiar to the Juridic or to the Civic Constitution, or indeed to any specific constitutional identity. Our approach to the Constitution, however, does greatly influence *how* we conceive of these functions and equally how much importance we attach to them. The Civic Constitution approaches these questions from a position that assigns primary responsibility for attaining a constitutional way of life to citizens. In so doing, it favors decisions at the founding that constitute institutions and citizens in ways that both enable and encourage them to take up that responsibility.

An approach to the founding that emphasizes its civic ambitions is important to constitutional life because ownership of the founding narrative has political effect. Casting the founding in one light or another——as fatally flawed, as some have argued,[330] or as divinely inspired, according to others[331]—teaches us something about ourselves and about what we believe. If we think the founding locates the Constitution chiefly in law, then fidelity to that moment requires that we believe in certain kinds of things and behave in certain kinds of ways (none of them, coincidentally, especially auspicious for serious civic engagement). If we see that the founding included a commitment to a shared way of life, or a common commitment to normative principles that help to constitute a more perfect union, then we can start to reclaim the Civic Constitution.

ESSAY TWO

Maintaining

The decisions we make in the act of constituting (founding) have profoundly important implications for establishing the constitutional identity of a new political community, but they rarely conclude or are fully determinative of identity.[1] Identity is necessarily and always inchoate at any single moment; it develops over and through time, occasionally in sharply discontinuous ways.[2] It is informed and influenced by the decisions we make at foundings, but a founding starts rather than settles the process of forming a more perfect union.[3] Our constitutional personality is positioned in a series of choices and choosing that pervades the present and the past.

Discerning our constitutional identity, therefore, determining who We the People are constitutionally, is not simply a set of deliberative choices confined to the founding.[4] Instead, determining who we are and what we believe is a part of an intertemporal constitutional enterprise; maintaining the constitution is no less a work of constituting it than was the founding. Conceived in this way, maintaining the constitutional order requires that the commitments we made at the founding remain in some way our commitments now and in the future, a part of our constitutional imagination.[5] I say "in some way" because maintaining the Civic Constitution imposes on us the burden to choose what those commitments mean and how to hold their diverse elements in balance. As a consequence, constitutional maintenance is not simply a project of maintaining what or who we have chosen to be; it resides also in the activity of *choosing* what to maintain, what to change, and what to reject.

Many of us take for granted that the work of constitutional maintenance is fundamentally juridic in nature, a project in law, a responsibility entrusted chiefly to judges, and most evident in the practice of constitutional interpretation. (Indeed, for some writers, constitutional maintenance and constitutional interpretation are the same thing, indistinguishable in purpose and in practice.[6]) That most of us equate juridic maintenance with constitutional maintenance more broadly, however, is not simply a path-dependent consequence of choices we made at the founding. Like any good prophecy, the

Juridic Constitution affects what we see when we look to our past as much
as the future—it influences our perception of the choices We made at the
founding and why we made them. The rise of the Juridic Constitution leads
us to see both the founding and the constitutional text as pregnant with
juridic commitments and to overlook or discount its civic ones. We read the
evidence backward.[7]

In emphasizing its juridic components, we fail to recognize how the
founding and the constitutional order it fashioned included civic as well
as juridic elements, and how our subsequent constitutional development
likewise includes both civic and juridic features.[8] Our search for constitutional unity distorts the constitutional enterprise,[9] not only by misleading us
about what the founding *means* (in contradistinction to what it *meant*—the
distinction is a key to understanding the Civic Constitution), but also by
misleading us about what sort of occupation constitutional maintenance is
and what kinds of projects it comprehends.

The Civic and Juridic Constitutions lead us to think in different ways
about three questions essential to a comprehensive account of constitutional
maintenance.

- First, w*hat* do we seek to maintain? The Civic Constitution commits us
  to maintaining a constitutional order dedicated to the achievement of a
  shared political life defined and lived by our fidelity to certain norms,
  principles, and values. These include a commitment to fundamental
  principles of constitutional government: to reason and deliberation in
  public affairs, the separation of powers, a principle of constitutional
  review, equal moral worth, and human dignity. The way of life contemplated by the Civic Constitution is also deliberative in character;
  decisions about the public welfare must be objects of civic deliberation and concern. The Civic Constitution is further committed to self-
  governance and to a conception of civic engagement as civic work,
  practiced in the activities of tending and dedicated to the civic virtue
  of civility.
- Our discussion of the object of constitutional maintenance, of the
  what, takes us to the second question of *who* is responsible for maintaining the constitutional order. Whereas the Juridic Constitution entrusts responsibility for constitutional maintenance chiefly to judges,
  the Civic Constitution asks other institutions and citizens to take up
  that burden. A central object of the Civic Constitution, therefore, must
  be equipping citizens with the knowledge, skills, and virtues necessary
  for civic life. This requires an ambitious project of civic education.

- Third, *how* do we maintain the Civic Constitution?[10] The Civic Constitution embraces a number of different approaches to the question of how it should be maintained. A full account of constitutional maintenance requires us to address issues of institutional design, especially concerning the separation of power (horizontally and vertically), the practice of constitutional interpretation, and the dynamics of constitutional amendment. Unlike the Juridic Constitution, which reduces constitutional maintenance to interpretation by judges in cases and controversies, the Civic Constitution locates the activity of maintenance in places and practices that transcend interpretation by courts.[11] A civic approach to constitutional maintenance thus requires us to elaborate the ways in which citizens actually participate in and are excluded from the project of constitutional governance.

WHAT: MAINTAINING A CONSTITUTIONAL WAY OF LIFE

Maintaining the Civic Constitution requires us to consider the essence of the constitutional order it prescribes. What vision of constitutional life does the Civic Constitution ask us to conserve? The Civic Constitution "is a characteristic way of life" for a community, "the national character of a people, their ethos or fundamental nature as a people."[12] In a civic constitutional order, the Constitution seeks to create and sustain the kind of community in which the people carry forward the constitutional project by giving meaning to and assuming responsibility for honoring constitutional values. As I shall expand upon later in this essay, some of these commitments are pre-constitutional or foundational in pedigree; they reside in our commitment to constitutionalism itself. But the Civic Constitution is also committed to self-governance and to a conception of civic engagement as civic work, manifest in practices of tending and dedicated to the civic virtue of civility. Unlike the Juridic Constitution, then, the Civic Constitution ordains a community in which questions of constitutional significance are not (only) questions of law but are (also) questions about the meaning and application of constitutional principles in the everyday life of the polity.

Following this logic, civic maintenance is not simply the enforcement of specific constitutional rules by judges, but rather the preservation of a shared political community founded upon and committed to the realization of certain fundamental constitutional norms and civic commitments. Making good on those commitments, giving them life and meaning, is the essence of civic obligation. The Civic Constitution thus comprehends maintenance as a different *sort* of activity than does the Juridic Constitution. Instead of promoting and safeguarding the formalities of constitutional legality through judicial review and constitutional interpretation, the Civic Constitution requires that we maintain a civic constitutional culture comprised of constitutional and civic elements.

It is worth restating how this understanding of constitutional maintenance differs from the one we typically associate with the Juridic Constitution. Where the Civic Constitution values passionate, even hoarse public debate about the meaning and significance of first principles, the juridic account sees in such debate a threat to constitutional tranquility. Recurrent public deliberation about constitutional principles, a cornerstone of the Civic Constitution, compromises constitutional maintenance because, as Madison argued, it might unsettle the public's reverence for things constitutional. On this reading, the *Federalist Papers* conceive of constitutional maintenance as an enterprise largely remote from and unsuitable for citizens. In Madison's view, the constitutional enterprise is better served by a citizenry whose affection for the Constitution is not burdened by responsibility, because "every appeal to the people would carry an implication of some defect in the government, [and] frequent appeals would . . . deprive the government of that veneration which time bestows on everything, and without which perhaps the wisest and freest governments would not possess the requisite stability."[13] The juridic constitutional order is "far more concerned with insuring domestic tranquillity and securing the blessings of liberty than it is with building cathedrals, spreading imperial domains, or grooming excellence in virtuous citizens."[14]

One way to understand Madison's argument (recall from Essay One that there are less juridic ways to comprehend Madison's constitutional design) is to see it as a partial solution to the Jeffersonian intergenerational problem. Developing public reverence for the Constitution secures the consent of later generations, and hence the Constitution itself, by forestalling serious public engagement into the question of constitutional legitimacy. There are good reasons for adopting this approach. One might wonder, for instance, what sorts of public and private goods will be sacrificed if we require each new generation of We the People to reexamine the legitimacy and desirability of constitutional first principles. Moreover, we might doubt the ultimate success of the constitutional order if it is subject to a recurrent, public form of strict scrutiny, perhaps fearing that citizens might choose to reject constitutional norms as a desirable way of constituting political life. I consider both possibilities as we go forward, especially under the rubric of constitutional failure in Essay Three.

Another approach to the reverence argument goes further. Madison's fears might be less about the incapacity of citizens to deliberate reasonably concerning matters of great public or constitutional import, and more about the unsuitability of reason itself as a mechanism for securing the Constitution.[15] There are two questions here. First, is this really the basis of the Madisonian objection to public engagement with first principles? And second, perhaps more importantly, is the objection a sound one? Regarding the first question, the weight of recent scholarship on Madison's constitutional thought, although far from conclusive, should persuade us that Madison anticipated a citizenry that was more engaged, or possessed greater civic capacity, than *Federalists* #49 and #55, standing alone, might indicate (see Essay One). Part of the reason we read *Federalists* #49 and #55 as cautions about involving too frequently the people in constitutional maintenance is because we read them through the lens of the Juridic Constitution, just as we read judicial review into the text and have come to regard as inescapable the conclusion that the Constitution was conceived in and should be regarded as law first. How we read Madison's constitutional blueprint is profoundly influenced by our understanding of whether the Constitution should be seen as a legal or as a political project. The second question—regarding the implausibility of reason as a way of constituting a constitutional order—goes to the prospect of the Civic Constitution itself. I address this concern throughout, but I note here that insofar as this doubt rests upon an assessment of contemporary citizenship as shallow and irresponsible, or at least as inattentive to constitutional concerns, it fails to appreciate that we have precisely the sort of citizens we should expect under the Juridic Constitution.

WHO: ASSIGNING RESPONSIBILITY FOR MAINTAINING THE CONSTITUTION

Civic maintenance locates the Constitution in citizens. As a result, responsibility for constitutional governance is a broadly democratic affair, properly the province of every citizen, and fundamentally an activity grounded in politics (deliberation and engagement) rather than law (interpretation).[16] The Civic Constitution imposes burdens on citizens in the sense that they bear the obligation of civic duties. Of course, this is true no less of the Juridic Constitution than the Civic: both constitutions invest citizens with some measure of civic obligation. The difference lies in the breadth and weight of those burdens and what they portend for maintaining the Constitution.

Implicit in every constitution is a claim about the properties of its authority, as well as what it means to say we know or have knowledge of it. To know the Juridic Constitution we must know law.[17] To know the Civic Constitution, we must know ourselves. The Civic Constitution consequently requires a particular kind of citizenry, with a particular kind of competence, and a particular kind of knowledge—a civic knowledge, or knowledge of what a *civis* is and of what *civitas* means.[18] In practice, then, the Juridic and Civic Constitutions attach very different meanings and responsibilities to the concept and practice of citizenship. I want to stress that these different conceptions of citizenship are not simply analogues to conceptions that contrast citizenship as rights and citizenship as obligations, between thin and thick conceptions of citizenship, or between liberal and communitarian approaches to citizenship. Instead, the conception of citizenship I propose subsumes rights and obligations, and it does not suppose they are easily combined or can always be made to coexist harmoniously.[19]

The Juridic Constitution imagines a particular kind of citizen.[20] The new science of politics sought a citizen who would be less inclined to act in concert on public affairs than to concentrate on the private pursuit of happiness. The framers transformed a citizenry "into a pluralistic population pursuing its multitude of private concerns. They remade 'the people' into a plural noun" and devised mechanisms to forestall "perpetual public discussion of first principles."[21] There is, therefore, little cause to consider to what extent citizens bear any substantial responsibility for maintaining the Juridic Constitution. Their burden for maintaining the constitutional order, although meaningful as far as it goes, does not go very far. Under the Juridic Constitution, the virtuous citizen has only three responsibilities—a citizen must pay taxes, must report for jury service, and must (should is a better description) vote. In extraordinary moments, the virtuous citizen (or some of them) may even be asked to defend the country, but such calls are extraordinary precisely because they are so far beyond the conventional claims made of the good citizen. So, under the Juridic Constitution, citizenship is an occasional, part-time practice, restricted chiefly to the roles of taxpayer, juror, and voter.[22] Juridic citizens are bound to the Juridic Constitution through reverence and ritual. Their identity as citizens is subordinate to their status as subjects.

Unlike subjects, citizens participate directly in constitutional maintenance. Their burden for maintaining the constitutional order, although conditional (in the sense that their commitment may be withdrawn through the exercise of reason, as I discuss below), is weighty. What the Civic Constitution requires is a conception of citizenship in which the office of citizen is more than episodic and ceremonial. Unlike the Juridic Constitution, the Civic Constitution seeks an active transformation of persons into citizens, or of personhood into citizenship.[23] In addition, the Civic Constitution, because it requires a certain kind of citizen, also requires a certain kind of person. To put it simply, under the Civic Constitution the concepts of personhood and citizenship are entwined if not indivisible. It cannot draw a sharp, impregnable distinction between what is public, or of public concern, and what is private, or beyond public concern. As Aristotle wrote in *The Ethics,* "the main concern of politics is to engender a certain character in the citizens and to make them good and disposed to perform noble actions."[24] Without pushing the similarity too far, we might describe the main concern of the Civic Constitution as to make citizens "good and disposed" attitudinally to perform constitutional actions, or to pursue constitutional ideals in political community with other citizens.

In Essay One I considered how we can construct the virtuous citizenry the Civic Constitution demands. I stress here that this is not a venture confined to the founding moment, but is instead a continuing concern of constitutional maintenance. We must also consider that it may not be possible to make such citizens. Some scholars argue that "It is a mistake to hope that legal reform, constitutional design, or constitutional interpretation can bring about a rich, deliberative civic life in a large-scale modern democracy"[25] because "there are features basic to any democratic constitution that are likely to provide citizens with incentives of exactly the wrong kind—incentives that lead them to be selfish and lazy rather than public-spirited and active."[26] Among these features are the electoral institutions often associated with large-scale democracies. Elections reduce citizens "to alienated spectators,"[27] and voting reduces our civic impulses to the pursuit of self-interest or partisanship. Some voting rules, such as the guarantee of anonymity, further create an "incentive to act on the basis of self-interest" precisely because voters need not defend or account for their decision as an exercise of deliberation about the public good. (I am not suggesting the Civic Constitution requires voters to give a public account of the reasons for their decision—I simply observe that design decisions create incentives and disincentives to vigorous citizenship.) A related concern holds that disengaged citizens, or a thin view of civic life, is a necessary consequence of our desire for liberty. As Eisgruber puts the problem, modern liberal polities must afford citizens the "liberty to be bad," or to elevate private interest above public obligation. (The objection should sound familiar to students of *Federalist* #10.)

There are two claims here, one normative and one empirical. The empirical claim is that large-scale, modern democracies make a rich deliberative politics difficult to achieve. In some ways, it recalls the Habermasian critique of deliberative democracy,[28] that a genuine culture of civic deliberation cannot be realized in contemporary democratic states. Unlike the Habermasian critique, this objection appears to assume constitutional design can create an incentive structure that discourages citizenship (such as certain voting rules), but cannot use institutional design to promote the civic. It understates the capacity of constitutional design to create incentives for citizens to act virtuously, in part by denying the civic elements of the constitution itself.[29]

The normative claim is that citizens must be free to be bad, or to act on self-interest, or in ways that are not virtuous. The force of this objection, whether grounded in some version of liberal theory, liberty, or privacy, is not self-evident. Its persuasiveness rests on inexplicit assumptions about the kinds of lives and citizens the Constitution should prefer. It assumes, in other words, that the thin citizenship contemplated by the Juridic Constitution is normatively superior, or reflects a better (read: liberal) understanding of the proper relationship between the state and citizens. It likewise assumes that this preference is an irreducible part of the constitutional structure, instead of recognizing that the structure to which it is attached—the Juridic Constitution—reflects a particular and contestable understanding of the constitutional order.

The meager demands of citizenship in the modern state have been a long-standing matter of concern for political and constitutional theorists.[30] As Aleinikoff observes, "American constitutional law has an implicit and powerful narrative that portrays citizenship as a core concept in a liberal democratic state. The narrative begins with the opening words of the Constitution, 'We the People.'"[31] In Aleinikoff's view, widely shared among scholars, our constitutional order reifies the *idea* of citizenship but gives it little weight or effect. Instead, its significance is chiefly symbolic. There are, of course, recent treatments of citizenship that do take citizenship seriously. But even these richer and more exacting conceptions of citizenship leave the polity with citizens whose duty for tending to the care and maintenance of the polity is episodic at best. Bruce Ackerman, to take the most notable example, asks us "to behold . . . a pretty picture: an America in which a rediscovered Constitution is the subject of an ongoing dialogue amongst scholars, professionals, and the people at large."[32] As a way of revitalizing citizenship, the approach Ackerman asks us to consider is unsatisfactory. Ackerman's citizens look after the constitutional project only at certain moments; in all others, in the many ordinary, unexceptional, nonconstitutional moments (that is to say, in *most* moments), citizenship is an empty, honorific category.

The most serious burdens of Ackerman's citizenship were discharged long ago or await us. In most moments, however, citizens have little obligation to tend to the Constitution or even to public life more broadly. And even in the infrequent constitutional moment, most citizens are absent or quiet.[33] Instead, constitutional moments call upon an engaged citizenry comprised chiefly of politicians and other political actors.[34] Hence, in assessing whether constitutional change has occurred outside the confines of Article 5 (a topic I take up later in this essay), Ackerman "turns to the documentary record of the debates, speeches, and actions of the political actors and engaged citizens, whom Ackerman dubs 'public citizens,' involved in the constitutional struggle."[35] Public citizens, for Ackerman, view citizenship "as a higher calling, the source of the deepest values to which men and women can ordinarily aspire."[36] Public citizens of this sort are in short supply, as are "perfect privatist" citizens, or citizens who equate self-interest with public interest. Between the two extremes of public and private citizens are *private* citizens—who evince some concern for the public good but deliberate infrequently—and private *citizens*—who often and carefully deliberate about the public good.[37] Most citizens fall into the former category of *private* citizens; they have little occasion to deliberate or to act on the public good, and little incentive to do so.

Similarly, Ackerman does not provide an account of what vigorous civic life would look like or how we might promote it. The omission is not a flaw, for there is no need for such an account except in the rare constitutional moment. Indeed, we might say, as Fleming has astutely noted, that in this and similar approaches the citizen has "two selves"—their ordinary selves and their constitutional selves.[38] Fleming goes on to note, in ways equally applicable to most other accounts of citizenship,[39] that these narratives do not offer up an analytically robust account of the constitutional self, or of how our constitutional selves can acquire or exercise any authority for bringing forward the constitutional project.

From the perspective of the Civic Constitution, however, we should resist the distinction between our two selves because it invariably privileges the private self over the public self. (Moreover, the relationship between these two selves, while ordinarily quiet, can occasionally be a source of conflict, especially between what the present, ordinary self desires and what our constitutional selves might prefer.[40]) The concept of constitutional self-governance incorporates both the collective and the individual notions of self-governance because a constitutional way of life must be an ambition not only of states or communities but also of persons.

Civic Virtue and Civil Society

To discharge their civic responsibility, citizens of the Civic Constitution must possess certain political skills (the capacity to reason and deliberate), and certain attributes of character (civility and an ethic of tending). We cannot assume these attributes and skills will simply appear in citizens unprompted, or that civic virtue will flourish in communities where the promotion and development of virtue is left to chance. In Essay One I therefore concluded that the development of civic virtue, or more broadly of virtuous persons, is properly a concern of the Civic Constitution. Similarly, a civic approach to constitutional maintenance requires us to think anew about the state's relationship to civil society. At the founding, we must ask if there are ways to facilitate, through constitutional engineering, the growth and vitality of civic space. The same project, conceived through the lens of constitutional maintenance, must be about the restoration and revitalization of the institutions and places we have now, many of which have withered under the hegemony of the Juridic Constitution. In Barber's words, "to recreate civil society on this prescription does not necessarily entail a novel civic architecture; rather, it means a reconceptualizing and repositioning of institutions already in place."[41] Institutions already in place include "restaurants, schools, jails, community gardens, and farmer's markets," as well as civic foundations, NGOs, community movements, and other civil associations.[42] All of these institutions are locations where citizens learn how to be civic. In them, citizens acquire and practice important civic virtues, among them the virtues of tending and civility.

Rehabilitating civic institutions to promote civic life requires us to consider in more detail the relationship between civic life and civil society. Following Linda McClain, we might conceptualize the relationship between civic and private virtue in three ways. First, we might start from the standpoint that there is little or no overlap between civic and personal virtue. McClain cites as an example John Rawls, who advances a conception of political justice that includes certain virtues, such as "civility and tolerance . . . reasonableness and the sense of fairness."[43] Rawls further imagines the state does have an interest in the cultivation of virtue, even personal virtue, insofar as some private institutions, like families, contribute to a "fund of implicitly shared ideas and principles"[44] that makes civic life possible. Indeed, writing of families, Rawls notes they will play an important role as "seedbeds of virtue," and in cultivating the "sense of justice and the political virtues that support political and social institutions."[45] Nevertheless, Rawls does not advance a comprehensive account of a good person. His political liberalism starts, rather, from a "position of discontinuity,"[46] or from a clear distinction between civic and personal virtue.

A second position, which some find implicit in *Federalist* #55,[47] holds instead that there is an important but limited element of continuity between the virtues necessary for self-government in both its meanings. This element of continuity, which McClain calls the "civil society thesis," assumes that "the institutions of civil society [will] be the primary 'seedbeds of civic virtue,'" or "foundational sources of competence, character, and citizenship."[48] In these seedbeds of virtue, "the cradle of citizenship," children learn "the essential qualities necessary for governing the self: honesty, trust, loyalty, cooperation, self-restraint, civility, compassion, personal responsibility, and respect for others."[49] Perhaps more importantly, in these same places children acquire virtues that are undeniably civic—"deliberation, compromise, consensus building, and reason-giving."[50] Partly because sites like families and elementary schools are so significant as cultivators of civic virtue, the second position holds that "both government and civil society play a role" in helping these civil institutions prepare us to "become good people and good citizens."[51]

A third position likewise considers that there is an important area of overlap between personal and civic self-government, but the influence runs in both directions: the civic virtues necessary to sustain democratic self-government "are also those that make possible—and should inform—governing of the self."[52] A prominent argument for this understanding of civic virtue is Macedo's *Diversity and Distrust*, in which Macedo concludes that the virtues of "civic liberalism" should run to private life generally. Thus, he argues, "[l]iberal citizens should be committed to honoring the public demands of liberal justice in all departments of their lives. . . . A basic aim of civic education should be to impart to all children the ability to reflect critically on their personal and public commitments for the sake of honoring our shared principles of liberal justice and equal rights for all."[53]

In all three positions, there runs a common proposition: the constitution of civil society is of central interest and importance to the preservation of the constitutional order. What distinguishes them is the degree of the state's investment in the institutions of civil society and how far the state may intervene in civil society to promote the inculcation of civic virtues. The Civic Constitution is best advanced by something akin to the third conception of civic liberalism, in which the Constitution envisions a civil society constituted in its own image. The project of developing virtuous citizens is equally about developing virtuous persons—we need to connect up self-government with government of the self. My argument, that the development of virtuous citizens requires some attention to the development of virtuous persons, does not assume that citizens will never act on the basis of self-interest, or selfishness, or without public regard, but it does reject the claim that because citizens must have a liberty to do so, they should not be encouraged to act otherwise. Instead, the Civic Constitution starts from the assumption that the community has a collective interest in encouraging individual citizens to act with regard for the collective interest and that the virtues necessary to achieve and to sustain a constitutional way of life are neither strictly public nor private, but are both, or lie at the intersection of public and private. On this understanding, "one cannot readily separate matters of personal morality from political morality, or civic renewal from moral renewal."[54] Under the Civic Constitution, then, the project of creating and educating citizens must extend to include a wide variety of institutions, organizations, and associations in civil society.[55] The Civic Constitution warrants the state to offer resources and support for organizations, such as families, private associations, schools, and civic and fraternal groups, which seek to develop the civic virtues of civility and tending.

To be precise, my argument is not simply that organizations and associations we typically assign to the private sphere are important to constitutional maintenance because they are sites where civic virtues are inculcated. I do not, in other words, mean simply to rehash familiar claims that significant developments in the private lives of citizens have important implications for our public life (for example, the long-standing claim that the decreasing incidence of family meals has contributed to increases in social alienation. My reason for using the family meal as an example will be apparent shortly). Instead, my argument is that constitutional maintenance, properly conceived, both occurs and is learned in these places. It is in such places where we must look for the Civic Constitution; its absence there, if it is absent, is cause for concern.[56] These associations, organizations, and institutions are not outside of politics, "they are constitutive of politics."[57] As a result, our larger constitutional commitments ought to govern them.

Consider the example of the family. (I take up public schools in my discussion of civic education, below.) We have long regarded the family as an important barometer of civic health and a matter of profound public concern. Writing in the *American Sociological Review*, James H. S. Bossard observed that it is at the family table where we are "inducted into the life of society.... The family not only introduces the child to its own particular culture, but also to that of the larger society. In this latter capacity, it not only interprets this larger culture, but creates also attitudes toward it. Much of this happens as a by-product of family table talk."[58] Bossard wrote in 1943.

The snapshot of the family table he provides seems almost quaint, inattentive to contemporary understandings of how gender and, to a lesser extent, class might have influenced the analysis or the conclusions. But although the world is greatly changed, the sense that family meals are of great social and civic significance remains a staple of popular culture and some fields of academic scholarship.[59]

As Linda McClain observes, "the health of families is thought to bear a close relationship to the overall moral and civic health of our nation, just as a weakening of families is thought to reflect and to lead to moral and civic decline."[60] Theda Skocpol has also concluded that if we are to renew democratic life, we must begin "by mixing politics and civic activity with family life and socializing."[61] Janet Flammang has likewise argued at length that families and the household are important sites for the cultivation of civic virtue, and in particular the democratic virtue of civility: "For democracy and civility to thrive, people need frequent, everyday occasions to share pleasures, fears, and opinions with others. . . . Sharing a meal at a table is temporary, yet frequent, locus of civilizing and democratic practice."[62] Flammang's reference to everyday occasions points to still another reason why the Civic Constitution must concern itself with the constitution of civil society: the citizenship the Civic Constitution envisions is an everyday, quotidian responsibility.[63]

I am not sure the institution of the family meal is the best or even a very good meter of civic health, but few would dispute that families play an important role in the development of personal virtue. Indeed, the notion that the Constitution protects a parental liberty to direct the upbringing of a child is predicated on the notion that parental decisions about the education and upbringing of children are important and consequential to both parent and child.[64] The same decisions, however, reflect another widely held assumption: families are important as objects of community concern precisely because they teach virtues and vices that have important implications for public life.

Simply establishing that families play an important role in teaching and transmitting the civic virtues of self-government (in the two senses I referenced earlier) is not enough to advance the argument that the Civic Constitution authorizes a "formative project"[65] of citizenship building, much less that such a project invests the state with authority to superintend that process. The authority of the Civic Constitution comes, instead, from a somewhat stronger claim, namely that the cultivation of civic virtues cannot take place unless we assume that a constitutional way of life may be materially assisted or impeded by the congruence or incongruence of the two forms of self-government. Private institutions, such as families, that inculcate virtues incongruent with the civic virtues contemplated by the Civic Constitution undercut the possibility of a constitutional way of life. Or to put it affirmatively, civic virtues are more likely to thrive when they go some way toward constituting the institutions of civil society.

We can find some consideration of the concept of congruence in the work of Nancy Rosenblum. In *Membership and Morals*, Rosenblum considered the proposition that "the membership and internal organization of associations should be congruent with larger liberal values," a conclusion she largely rejects not only as inconsistent with political liberalism, but as destructive of it.[66] Rosenblum makes a compelling argument against a strong version of vertical congruence, noting in particular that there is a liberal virtue in pluralism itself. I shall argue below that the Civic Constitution likewise contemplates room for plurality and civic disagreement, even regarding fundamental constitutional precepts,[67] but the congruence argument *is* sufficiently robust to support a different claim: the state has a sufficient interest in creating the conditions of its own realization to support forms of civic education that may impinge on private choices. We can find some empirical support for the proposition that congruence tends to fortify democratic stability in the work of Harry Eckstein.[68] Eckstein's congruence theory holds that "patterns of authority" exist in all varieties of social institutions (or civic culture), and that greater or lesser degrees of congruence between these patterns of authority contribute significantly to stable democracy. Eckstein argues that congruence is of greater importance in social units and aspects of civic culture that are "more adjacent" to "governmental performance," while simultaneously suggesting, probably incorrectly, that "family life probably is less important for congruence in advanced industrial societies than in others." Still, "it is inconceivable that a democracy could be highly stable and effective if authority relations in families . . . are despotic." If Eckstein is correct, then the kinds of political authority that obtain in spheres of conduct and relationships we dismiss as private and nonpolitical have great significance for civic life and democratic maintenance more generally.[69] The connection between the organization and character of civil society and the state is captured not only in the relationship between person and citizen, but also by examination of continuity or discontinuity in vertical patterns of authority. (I will take this point up again in my discussion of federalism, below.)

To summarize, the Civic Constitution envisions a citizenry committed to a constitutional way of life. Essential to maintaining that way of life are the civic virtues of civility and tending, virtues that citizens learn, cultivate, and practice in civil society. Cultivating those virtues is thus properly a concern of the constitutional order, and that concern means the state must help to develop those virtues in its citizens. A civic reading of the Constitution will therefore have a substantial influence on our sense of where we should draw the distinction between state and civil society.

Citizenship and Civic Education

What does the Civic Constitution tell us about civic education? A full account of constitutional maintenance must be attentive to the purpose and content of civic education because it is through civic education that citizens learn what they must *know* to maintain the Constitution and what they must *do* to maintain it.

There is, therefore, an intimate connection between the state, citizens, and civic education. This logic explains founding era proposals to establish a national university: the founders (or some of them) believed "an educated public was essential to maintaining a constitutional government."[70] If not persuaded of either the constitutionality or the wisdom of a national university, anti-Federalists nevertheless saw the republic itself "as a school for citizenship as much as a scheme of government."[71] Many anti-Federalist arguments for a bill of rights, to take one example, referenced "the effect of education, a series of notions impressed upon the minds of the people by examples, precepts and declarations."[72] This is the reading of the Bill of Rights suggested by Jefferson, who argued we should see it as a "text for civil instruction."[73] For the anti-Federalists, the Bill of Rights was instructional, or had a civic purpose, in another way as well. As described by Suzette Hemberger, the anti-Federalists' support for the bill of rights "involved a recognition of the need to organize popular opinion on a national basis outside of government. Anti-federalists demanded a bill of rights because they wanted Americans to have a shared understanding of the appropriate limits on governmental power."[74] These understandings of the Bill of Rights stress its civic educative function—the Bill of Rights constitutes not only the state but citizens by teaching them about what the Constitution requires of us all. In contrast, the juridic understanding of the Bill of Rights emphasizes its enforcement by judges in constitutional litigation. It stresses that the meaning and enforcement of the Bill of Rights is a task best left to judges, and in so doing undermines the civic understanding of the Bill of Rights.

The constitutional text provides for civic instruction in other ways as well, as in its provisions for jury service, and in the Second Amendment's provisions regarding the militia, both of which demand (or were once thought to demand) a significant measure of civic engagement.[75] The civic inclinations of the constitutional text are readily apparent in the Sixth and Seventh Amendments. Many democratic theorists have identified the jury as an important instrument of civic education.[76] As Toqueville observed, "the jury is both the most effective way of establishing the people's rule and the most effective way of teaching them how to rule."[77] Especially for the anti-Federalists, service on local juries was a vital occasion for civic engagement and learning.[78] Conceived as instruments of reason and deliberation, juries are a critically important device for civic education, not simply because they teach, but also because they can have a "profoundly transformative effect" in converting "private individuals into public citizens, private interests into public judgments. . . . Simply put, deliberation promises to change how people act as citizens."[79] Juries as institutions depend upon the civic virtue of civility, and equally promote the fundamental constitutional norms of reason, deliberation, and conversation. They model a pattern of civility and conversation for the body politic more broadly. Moreover, because service on a jury often involves a considerable expenditure of time and resources, in sharp contrast to ritualistic exercises of citizenship like voting and saluting, jury service affords citizens an opportunity (albeit an infrequent one) to practice the civic virtue of tending.[80]

The Civic Constitution consequently embraces the constitution itself as an instrument of civic education that helps to inculcate civic virtues.[81] But the Civic Constitution does more than simply recognize the importance of civic education: it *requires* civic education as a condition of its own realization. The Civic Constitution, in other words, requires the state to assist in developing the civic agency of its people. The Civic Constitution demands a "formative project" of civic education in which the government has an obligation to develop in citizens the civic virtues—of civility and tending—upon which it rests. It assumes the skills, education, and virtue necessary for excellence in citizenship cannot be confined to a category of citizenship/ public life sharply segregated from a category of personhood/private life; instead, there is a close relationship between self-government, in the public sense, and government of the self, in the private sense. Virtuous citizenship, on this account, requires virtuous persons.[82]

Civic education helps us to make the transition from private to public, from person to citizen. The notion of civic education as transformative has a long lineage—elements of it certainly trace, if not to Aristotle, then to Rousseau, who writes how the voice of duty must replace or overcome the voice of appetite.[83] As Jane Mansbridge observes, for Rousseau this transformation will be effected through good laws and a "civil religion that will promote social unity and make each citizen love his duty," but not, necessarily, through any exercise of civic deliberation.[84] The transformative dimension of civic deliberation is, in contrast, a key part in *Democracy in America*, where Tocqueville concluded that town meetings "are to liberty what primary schools are to science; they bring it within people's reach, they teach men how to use and how to enjoy it."[85] Or as Carole Pateman argued in *Participation and Democratic Theory*, participation helps to develop the faculties necessary for democratic life.[86]

The Civic Constitution and Civic Knowledge

According to one formulation, civic education in schools should focus upon "developing the skills necessary for competent and responsible citizenship in our constitutional democracy."[87] Unfortunately, this formulation does not tell us what those skills are or how they are best acquired.[88] Insofar as different understandings of the constitutional project conjure different kinds of citizens, they inspire different kinds of civic education. Different understandings of the character or identity of our constitutional selves ask citizens to learn different things, if not to learn differently. The Juridic Constitution will teach citizens that to act like a citizen is to salute the flag, vote, pay taxes, and profess one's fidelity to the Miracle at Philadelphia; its understanding of what constitutional democracy is tells us what citizens must know about it. Schoolbooks in the nineteenth century, Papke tells us, routinely spoke of the Constitution as divinely inspired.[89]

The Civic Constitution requires an account of civic education that prepares citizens for the deliberative and the tending aspects of constitutional maintenance, or for the prospect of citizenship as a kind of civic work. The purpose of civic education is not to inculcate reverence for the (juridic) constitution but rather to prepare citizens to participate in governance, in the civic life of the community. A program of civic education under the Civic Constitution must be concerned with helping citizens to achieve a constitutional way of life.[90] What is needed to carry forward the Civic Constitution, therefore, is a conception of civic education that "should . . . impart to all children the ability to reflect critically on their personal and public commitments for the sake of honoring our shared principles of liberal justice and equal rights for all."[91] It requires citizens whose knowledge resides less in recitation than in understanding the "central and political traditions of the nation." Hence, civic education requires not simply literacy but engagement, defined as "a kind of public problem solving . . . that develops . . . the civic skills of critical thinking, democratic deliberation, collective action, and social ethics."[92]

In short, the Civic Constitution requires an education in civic knowledge. How does civic knowledge differ from legal knowledge? Different kinds of knowledge tend to take on reasonably distinct vocabularies. There is an important sense in which to know something is to know how to talk about it—a point that should be evident to anyone trained in any of the professions. The Juridic Constitution is part of a set of discursive practices with a distinct community of practitioners. The common tongue of that community is law. Only a fraction of the broader civic community can talk about or know the Juridic Constitution in any meaningful sense because few of us have the language skills necessary to participate in discussions about it. The language of civics, by contrast, is inclusive. To know what it means to be a citizen is to know something about a public identity we share with others. A language about *civis* must thus be a broadly shared language, a broadly common tongue.[93]

In another sense, to know something is not only to know how to talk about it, it is to know how to do it. (Some of this is captured when we talk about the *practice* of law as a profession.) Civic maintenance, the burden of tending to the Constitution and carrying it forward, requires more than simply a revitalized public sphere in which citizens can talk about, or find their voice on, matters constitutional. Maintaining the Civic Constitution means translating constitutional concerns and ideals into a way of life. It is for this reason that when we look for the Civic Constitution, we must look beyond civic texts to civic practices, and it is for the same reason that constitutional literacy demands more than knowledge of constitutional facts and the exercise of reason. So civic education must also equip the citizens it makes with the deliberative and practical skills necessary to carry out their obligations—in other words, it must create civic agency. What civic maintenance requires is not citizen-philosophers, but rather citizens well-schooled in "practical citizenship."[94] It is through civic work that citizens learn to act civically.

Civic education occurs in three places and takes three forms. The first consists of pedagogy, or formal schooling in civics, history, and government. A second kind of civic education comes from participating in the organized political life of the community, by serving on juries or by participating in state and local politics. Third, following Tocqueville, there is a kind of civic education consisting of associational life in institutions and organizations that we typically assign to the private domain, such as in families, in churches, and in a great variety of fraternal and voluntary organizations.

Formal Pedagogy

The first form of civic education consists of pedagogy, or formal schooling in civics, history, and government, in which citizens acquire basic regime knowledge. This prescribed instruction is deeply and inescapably political in character. It is political in the immediate sense that such instruction has an explicitly political purpose—or better, political purposes. One such purpose is to instill in citizens a degree of civic competence. This requires some basic regime-specific and factual knowledge, as well as the development of critical faculties that enable citizens to participate in public life, such as the capacity to reason, to assess arguments and to weigh evidence, and a capacity for discernment. Another purpose is to arouse an emotional bond in the citizen. Formal civic instruction helps to cement attachment and stimulate loyalty.

What should be the content of this program of civic education? In addition to including basic factual knowledge, focused "mainly on the relations of the student to the central agencies of government," it must include "an overview of fundamental values, practices, and interpersonal relations in a democratic society."[95] At the risk of tautology, its content must be critical, because citizens must learn to reason, to engage, and to be percipient,[96] and it must be constitutional, in that it must instruct citizens about the genealogy and meaning of constitutional values and precepts. As Murphy argues, "Its goal should be to move citizens to think in informed and critically analytical ways about politics."[97] More precisely, its goal should be to move citizens to think in ways that advance our commitment to a constitutional way of life. This means that civic education must teach citizens about the concepts that are fundamental to that way of life and equip them with the knowledge, skills, habits, and traits of character that are central to it.

Civic Curricula

A discussion of civic education must include some consideration of curricular design and content, or of what comprises civic knowledge. We should first recognize, however, that decisions about the content and nature of civic knowledge are themselves frequently subjects of fervent public debate, as evidenced not only by the intense controversy that surrounds textbook adoption in some states (Texas is a notable example),[98] but also by recurrent episodes of enforced rites of patriotism and Americanism in public schools (the flag salute cases[99] are obvious examples, but there are many others). Discussions about what students should learn are decisions about what kinds of knowledge we think are important, as well as about who we are. They are the sort of deliberation the Civic Constitution prizes. Such discussions lie at the very heart of civic education under the Civic Constitution, in which "past, present, and future are represented . . . as part of an educational program and of an inspiring moral tradition in which each generation acknowledges a connection to all others and a responsibility to them for the maintenance of community and . . . traditions."[100]

Formal programs of civic education will therefore have to reach further and be more ambitious under the Civic Constitution than under the Juridic. Obviously, a civics curriculum must include, especially in the lower grades, basic factual and historical information about the structure of the American constitutional order and American history more broadly.[101] As students progress into higher grades, the emphasis on factual learning must be replaced with a curriculum that instructs students in the skills that make up civility—the ability to engage with others through the use of reason, to marshal evidence and to parse arguments with critical reasoning, and to connect up such arguments with our deepest constitutional aspirations. These are the broad goals established by the National Standards for Civics and Government, which "are intended to help schools develop competent and responsible citizens who possess a reasoned commitment to the fundamental values and principles that are essential to the preservation and improvement of American constitutional democracy."[102] The standards proposed for high school students, for example, generally take the form of open-ended inquiries, such as:

What are Civic Life, Politics, and Government?

A. What is civic life? What is politics? What is government? Why are government and politics necessary? What purposes should government serve?
B. What are the essential characteristics of limited and unlimited government?
C. What are the nature and purposes of constitutions?
D. What are alternative ways of organizing constitutional governments?[103]

These are precisely the kinds of inquiries that contribute to civic literacy.

The second aspect of the APSA's description of civic education is equally important to learning the Civic Constitution. The report calls for teaching "our traditions." Teaching our traditions means teaching about our successes and our failures (the latter is less of an imperative under the Juridic Constitution), as well as acknowledging that many if not all of our constitutional ideals admit of several meanings. It means that a full program of civic education must teach students about the contested meanings of such basic constitutional commitments as equality, justice, and fairness, and it means that citizens must be equipped to address their meaning directly.[104] In other words, we must approach constitutional maintenance as an activity that is both irreducibly and expansively political in character, an activity represented, for instance, by citizen engagement in controversies concerning abolition, women's suffrage, and national civil rights legislation.[105] To borrow from our earlier discussion, civic education requires us to know more than just the simple facts of these campaigns. We must understand how they implicated our commitment to fundamental constitutional values, how the struggle to realize them was carried on by citizens, and not just by courts, and appreciate that the results of those struggles were not inevitable or foreordained. As an example, consider how we might teach *Korematsu v. United States* (1944). I know instructors in high schools who have been advised not to teach it all, presumably because it casts doubt upon some of the celebratory tropes of American constitutional history in general and of the Supreme Court in particular. But of course it is perfectly possible to teach *Korematsu* in ways that reaffirm our sense of patriotic pride.

One way to do so, for example, is to assure students that everyone knows *Korematsu* was wrongly decided.[106] (A patent but convenient untruth.[107]) Another approach is to highlight the Court's formal commitment to the use of strict scrutiny for racial classifications. More sophisticated variations on this silver lining strategy point students to *Korematsu v. United States*, 584 F. Supp. 1406 (N.D. Cal. 1984), in which Judge Marilyn Hall Patel held that "there is substantial support in the record that the government deliberately omitted relevant information and provided misleading information in papers before the court" and thus set aside Korematsu's conviction. On this telling, the constitutional order makes mistakes, sometimes grave ones, but is also reassuringly (and judicially) self-correcting.

An education in the Japanese internment cases attentive to the Civic Constitution would stress, by way of contrast, the critical role of citizen activists both in challenging the original orders and in making the District Court's decision possible.[108] "Beginning in the 1960s, a younger generation of Japanese Americans who felt energized by the Civil Rights movement began what is known as the 'Redress Movement'—an effort to obtain an official apology and reparations (compensation) from the federal government for interning their parents and grandparents during the war."[109] Similarly, a different kind of civic education would highlight the role of other constitutional actors in confronting the legacy of *Korematsu*. In 1980, President Carter directed the Commission on Wartime Relocation and Internment of Civilians to review

Executive Order 9066 and "to recommend appropriate remedies."[110] The commission's final report, "Personal Justice Denied," concluded that "the decision in *Korematsu* lies overruled in the court of history." President Reagan subsequently signed the Civil Liberties Act of 1988, which provided redress of $20,000 for each surviving detainee, totaling $1.2 billion dollars. These too were the result of a long campaign of civic work by citizens themselves.

Holloway Sparks argues that in these and similar campaigns we see an important kind of "dissident citizenship," or a citizenship that "encompasses the often creative oppositional practices of citizens who, either by choice or (much more commonly) by forced exclusion from the institutionalized means of opposition, contest current arrangements of power from the margins of the polity."[111] Just as a narrative concerning the expansion of constitutional rights and liberties cannot be complete without hearing the voices of the citizens who waged those campaigns, a complete account of constitutional maintenance must include the creative and sometimes oppositional practices of citizens.[112] Recall, for example, our discussion of Frederick Douglass in Essay One. Other examples might include William Lloyd Garrison, Elizabeth Cady Stanton, Eugene Debs, the Black Panthers, and aspects of the anti-abortion movement, all identified by David Papke as "legal heretics" who have challenged our faith in the law itself.[113]

To some readers this ambitious vision of civic education must seem fanciful, if not utopian. It is common practice to bemoan what appear to be unpardonably low levels of civic knowledge in the American public,[114] and often to then rely on such ignorance to further argue that constitutional maintenance cannot safely be entrusted to citizens. Without questioning the accuracy of these surveys, it is fair to ask if they really speak to the public's aptitude for constitutional maintenance. Citizens may well recognize the terrible denials of human dignity and equality represented by racial segregation, or in denying the right to vote to others, as constitutional failures of the first sort without knowing how many justices sit on the Supreme Court, their names and which President appointed them, or even whether our constitutional commitment to equal protection locates in the Declaration, the First Amendment, the Fourteenth Amendment, *Brown v. Board of Education*, or somewhere else. There is no necessary connection, in other words, between knowledge of constitutional facts and knowledge of constitutional ideals. Or to put it another way, it is not obvious that a greater knowledge of constitutional facts inspires greater fidelity to constitutional ideals. What is required is some appreciation of what those ideals are, what they mean and have meant, and how they are a part of us insofar as they constitute our constitutional identity. Knowledge of these ideals, unlike knowledge of facts and formulas, is difficult to measure. A program of formal civic education must teach both.

Civic education in schools, therefore, must extend well beyond the teaching of constitutional facts to include constitutional historiography. It must also, as the American Political Science Association Task Force on Civic Education concluded, "teach tolerance; teach collaboration; teach analysis; [and] teach our traditions."[115] Two aspects of the APSA Report are especially important to the Civic Constitution. First, the report calls for civic education to teach the concept of tolerance. Tolerance is closely related to the civic virtue of civility. In *Mozert v. Hawkins* (1986), involving a challenge by Christian Fundamentalist parents to the use of certain textbooks in local schools, the District Court noted

> The Supreme Court has recently affirmed that public schools serve the purpose of teaching fundamental values "essential to a democratic society." These values "include tolerance of divergent political and religious views" while taking into account "consideration of the sensibilities of others." The Court has noted with apparent approval the view of some educators who see public schools as an "assimilative force" that brings together "diverse and conflicting elements" in our society "on a broad but common ground." . . . The "tolerance of divergent . . . religious views" referred to by the Supreme Court is a civil tolerance, not a religious one. . . . It merely requires a recognition that in a pluralistic society we must "live and let live."[116]

The district court's reference to secular tolerance is a key element of a conception of civility. But it also raises an issue we have considered before: the concept of secular tolerance, as a constitutional virtue, represents simply one way to organize a body politic. How are we to respond to claims of those who, like the parents in *Mozert*, reject secular tolerance as a virtue, or who would prefer to instruct their children into other value systems? Consider, for example, the argument by William Galston that public institutions should not promote values that are "at odds with the deep beliefs of many of . . . loyal citizens."[117] Civic education may present a substantial challenge to the parental interest in instructing their children into their preferred values.[118]

In contrast, Macedo argues that "If a constitutional regime is to succeed and thrive, it must constitute the private realm in its image, and it must form citizens willing to observe its limits and able to pursue its aspirations."[119] Macedo's justification for the "moderate hegemony" of liberal education resides in its transformative purpose: because liberal constitutional democracy seeks the active creation or transformation of persons into liberal citizens, he is willing both to grant and to accept that there is a coercive element in this transformative enterprise.

The question is how much coercion we are willing to tolerate and for what purposes.[120] Here it would be wise to distinguish, as Murphy reminds us, between compulsory civics education and compulsory attendance at public schools. Arguments in favor of mandatory attendance in public schools hold that it promotes civic engagement by forcing students to confront dissimilar others and in so doing promotes the kinds of civil exchange and tolerance that constitutional democracies prize. But no matter how important the purpose or how ecumenical the curriculum, compulsory attendance at public schools has an illiberal, paternalistic feel to it. Every act of constituting is simultaneously creative and destructive in character. In constituting the ideal citizen, committed to civility and public reasonableness, the state may destroy or injure other (illiberal and particularistic) attachments. Additionally, compulsory attendance at public schools wrestles with another fundamental principle of constitutionalism—the liberty to make some choices about one's self, independent of the majority and of the state, or literally, the right to constitute one's self as a person. As the Court said in *Pierce v. Society of Sisters* (1925), "the child is not the mere creature of the state." Similarly, in *Meyer v. Nebraska* (1923), the Court referenced and rejected the communal child-rearing practices of Plato's Republic and of Sparta, in which children were separated from their parents and raised by the state. "Such restrictions" on family life, the Court said, would "do . . . violence to both letter and spirit of the Constitution."[121]

Moreover, and perhaps counterintuitively, mandatory education in public schools may deprive citizens of another opportunity to exercise the skills necessary for citizenship, because decisions about whether and when to pursue private educational opportunities, and about how to educate children, may themselves be an occasion for civic discourse. Finally, these associations are necessary because, insofar as they contribute to civil diversity, private educational opportunities help to guard against faction and homogeneity. They increase opportunities and venues for civic engagement; in some ways, such associations and communities expand civic space even as they withdraw from it.

The better argument, then, is that although formal civic education under the Civic Constitution is a necessary part of our commitment to constitutionalism itself, we should not require students to attend public schools. It is true that in some cases, private schools may embrace pedagogies and philosophies that are deeply inconsistent with constitutional values and precepts (see the discussion above about the importance of dissident citizenship and "counter publics"[122]). Education that rejects the moral or political force of our shared commitments, and not just the meaning or content of those aspirations, must also be protected under the Civic Constitution, because communities founded on appeals to reason must treat such commitments as provisional and contingent, subject to reasoned disagreement. The Civic Constitution does not require citizens to accept the content and character of public aspirations uncritically.

The state may insist, however, upon certain formal curricular requirements in private schools to ensure that students in these schools can fulfill the demands of citizenship. These requirements are not simply about producing competent adults or workers—they are about producing citizens equal to the task of a constitutional way of life. The Civic Constitution requires a program of civic education in private schools that teaches citizens about the value of civility and, equally, how to be civil. This requires some education for all students into the civic norms and commitments of the regime, and the provision of the basic intellectual and rhetorical skills necessary to civic participation in it. In light of my earlier discussion of this problem, the preferable resolution is to equip students, even in private schools, with the critical skills necessary to deliberate rationally about competing conceptions of what it means to live a virtuous life. The Supreme Court ruled similarly in *Pierce*, stating explicitly "no question is raised concerning the power of the state reasonably to regulate all schools . . . [or] to require that all children of proper age attend some school." Indeed, the Court underlined this principle by emphasizing the necessity that schools teach skills for "good citizenship" but nothing "manifestly inimical to the public welfare."

There is undeniably a coercive element even to this thinner account of compulsory civic education, especially for communities and citizens who might reject reason itself as a component of the good or a just way of life. In defense of this coercive element, we should note that the Civic Constitution, like all political orders, envisions and promotes the conditions that ensure its establishment, while simultaneously carving out substantial public space for challenges to its presumed normative superiority.[123] Moreover, in comparison to the civic education we associate with nonliberal states, or even with the Juridic Constitution, the illiberal character of civic education is muted insofar as it provides citizens with a set of skills that enables them to converse with and possibly to persuade fellow citizens that their vision of a constitutional way of life is less desirable than some other (nonconstitutional) way of organizing political life.

Formal instruction in civics does not take place only in schools. It transpires in other institutions as well, including, for instance, in political parties and through service on juries. Formal programs also accompany the process of naturalization, and there are other, less obvious (and perhaps less significant) occasions for civic instruction. One of the more interesting of these other occasions is Constitution Day (previously known as Citizenship Day). Federal law provides that all publicly funded educational institutions must celebrate the history of the American Constitution on September 17 by offering some sort of educational program. (The act does not determine the precise content of the educational materials.) Several organizations, such as the National Constitution Center[124] and the Bill of Rights Institute,[125] offer a wide variety of materials to help schools and institutions develop such programming.

Perhaps ironically, some commentators have suggested Constitution Day might be unconstitutional as an unwarranted exertion of federal power, not fairly traceable to Article 1, and perhaps also a violation of the First Amendment.[126] The Article 1 argument is especially relevant for understanding the constitutional enterprise—it recalls founding-era arguments about whether the new government ought to establish a national university.[127] Putting aside its doubtful wisdom (such rituals, rather than increasing our understanding, likely exacerbate the Constitution-worship we have under the Juridic Constitution), Constitution Day is constitutionally permissible as an exercise of the Civic Constitution's interest in creating its own citizenry. The same interest counsels that Constitution Day programs should educate citizens about the contested meaning of our constitutional norms and aspirations, while simultaneously leaving open the possibility that citizens might reject them, as well as the Constitution (and Constitution Day) itself.[128]

Political Participation

A second type of civic education consists of participation in politics. In addition to holding or running for office in state, county, and municipal governments, or contributing to the work of various political parties (in many communities there are more than two political parties and party organizations), opportunities for civic participation include service on school boards, PTAs, zoning and planning commissions, water districts, and innumerable other governmental or quasi-governmental organizations.

Participation in state and local politics is an essential mechanism of civic instruction under the Civic Constitution because, as I indicated above, civic agency requires civic engagement. Formal instruction in civics enables us to speak the language of civic life; it equips us with the skills and learning necessary to reason and deliberate. But there is also a kind of knowledge that consists not only of knowing how to *talk/deliberate* about something, but also of how to *do/practice* something. Participation in local politics is an education in how to do what civic engagement requires. In Murphy's words, citizens "can begin to learn to be citizens of a constitutional democracy by acting like citizens of a constitutional democracy."[129]

What is essential under the Civic Constitution is a political landscape that provides citizens with both opportunities and incentives to participate in public life. We must eschew institutional arrangements that create monopolies on constitutional dialogue and instead seek to configure a culture in which citizens can be confident their participation will be meaningful and effectual. Citizens must have some genuine power of influence if not of decision in the public life of the community. As a consequence, the Civic Constitution favors constitutional designs and public policies that enhance the importance and autonomy of local actors; this in turn increases opportunities for citizens to govern as well as to be governed. As we concluded earlier, this requires a commitment to a kind of federalism in which state and local governments have enough responsibility for governance to convince citizens their participation matters.

As Stephen Elkin writes, "Two of the most influential students of democracy, Tocqueville and Mill, pointed to local political life as the only place where the concerns are broad enough to invite discussion of the public interest and where it is possible for large numbers of people to take part in such discussions."[130] It is no longer clear, however, that state and local political life is well suited to advancing a civic education in constitutional democracy. In Elkin's view, local politics is principally about "rearranging local land use" and "trying to retain and attract mobile capital."[131] As a result, it no longer affords citizens the opportunity to deliberate about broader interests: "Instead of regular deliberation about the concrete meaning of the public interest, there is complex bargaining around land use allocation."[132]

There are two immediate questions suggested by Elkin's remarks. First, we might wonder why decisions about land use allocation and capital are not instances of deliberation about broader interests and thus in fact schools for citizenship. It does not seem obvious that decisions about land use do *not* involve concrete bargaining about the public interest. Indeed, because such questions often directly implicate the financial and aesthetic well-being of the community, and thus touch matters of common and immediate interest to most citizens, they seem to be precisely the kinds of issues that invite and reward public participation. Elkin's response is that while citizens do get an education "in the value of these elements of the public interest," the education they get "is lopsided."[133] The lesson is simply that they, or their communities, must "accommodate themselves to public forces."[134] What is absent is the opportunity to determine if inducements to capital are too generous: "There is, therefore, little room to engage in the kind of deliberative weighing of the elements of the public interest that a public-spirited citizenry must have if it is to judge whether its lawmakers have any inclination to do the same."[135] In many instances, however, these are precisely the sorts of questions that animate political conversations in state and especially in local politics. Examples include the development of charrettes in facilitating local decision making, especially in land-use and zoning controversies,[136] and the proliferation of so-called big-box protests. In many of these cases, public discussion centers precisely on whether inducements to capital are too generous, and in all of them questions about the character and identity of local communities (of who we want to be) loom large.

Elkin argues that we should expand the authority of local officials and municipalities to govern themselves. He proposes, for example, reconsideration of legal doctrines like Dillon's Rule,[137] which substantially restricts the legal authority of municipalities, and a consequent revitalization of the contrasting Cooley Rule.[138] The Civic Constitution, precisely because it anticipates a political order in which citizens must be afforded significant opportunities to practice a constitutional way of life, would counsel similar changes in constitutional doctrine regarding the authority of local governments.

Second, Elkin's understanding of local political life is too narrowly focused in its definition of politics and in its understanding of where local politics is practiced. At least implicit in Elkin's description of local political life is an institutionally directed conception of politics, one that calls to mind zoning boards, city councils, and town managers. The image does not include the wide variety of practices, activities, and places where citizens engage and address matters of shared and common concern. Much of local political life occurs in the purlieu of formal institutions, in PTA meetings, on school boards, on inland wetlands commissions, on charrettes, in ad hoc citizen's groups, and in many other civic organizations that straddle state and civil society.

Associational Life

Following Tocqueville, civic learning also occurs in a wide variety of associational organizations and activities in civil society. Associational learning helps to bridge the distinction between civic knowledge as defined by the what and by the how. This kind of civic education, like participation in politics, locates civic knowledge in the practice of citizenship. In the words of John Dewey, democracy is a learned behavior, and it is "best learned in the associational life of the community."[139]

"In a world where people's primary energies are (necessarily) devoted to the pursuit of private interest,"[140] active associational life is possible only by making sure there are "ample opportunities for the gradual education and generalization of interests" through experience.[141] Are there elements of constitutional design and structure that can increase or decrease opportunities for associational life? Certain sorts of textual guarantees can help: a constitutional regime that wants to promote associational life, for instance, demands something very much like the association, speech, and religion guarantees of the First Amendment. We value these guarantees not simply because the resulting pluralism in civil society may guard against the tyranny of faction, but because they provide a legal and structural framework in which citizens have opportunities to form associations and, in them, to learn the art and virtues of self-government.

Understanding First Amendment freedoms as structural mechanisms that allow associational life to prosper, and thus as facilitating the learning of civic skills and habits, gives us some guidance about how we ought to interpret them. We ought to favor readings of the First Amendment that facilitate the flourishing of a wide variety of associations and communities of faith. Our interpretation of First Amendment guarantees ought to enhance social, cultural, and religious pluralism by creating opportunities for citizens to associate with others in civil society. In other words, we should favor interpretations of the First Amendment that open up civic space and help to populate it. This tells us, in particular, that cases like *Wisconsin v. Yoder* are correctly decided because they promote the autonomy and flourishing of a great variety of religious associations, in which citizens can pursue commitments and lives of their own choosing.[142] *Yoder* advances a pluralistic understanding of civil society by offering refuge to communities of faith; in so doing, *Yoder* generates and expands civic space.

What distinguishes *Mozert* and *Yoder*, or why the interest of the state in inculcating civic virtue overcomes competing conceptions of virtue in *Mozert* but not in *Yoder*, is that the school and education in *Mozert* are public instrumentalities, entrusted with a deeply public function and responsibility. They are a shared and commonly held resource with a broad and diverse clientele. In *Yoder*, by contrast, the schooling and education is inclusive and private, indeed, discriminatory in the sense that a private group controls access to the resource based on purely local and self-selected criteria. This does not mean that the state has no interest in how the Amish educate their children. The state *does* have an interest in ensuring that Amish children possess the minimum set of skills and civic virtues necessary for them to function as potential members of society.[143] We sometimes overlook the Court's conclusion in *Yoder* that the state's interest in developing citizens did support a measure of mandatory education, a measure satisfied, in the Court's judgment, by requiring Amish attendance at elementary and middle schools. The same interest would also support, as I noted above, the state's insistence upon a formal program of state-approved civics instruction in Amish schools. The state's interest is significant but limited, not nearly as expansive as it must be in the tenor and character of public schools. Similarly, decisions like *Employment Division v. Smith* are inconsistent with this approach to the First Amendment. In *Smith*, the Court's preference for the rational-basis rule yields an approach to the Free Exercise clause that, insofar as it makes no accommodation for associational diversity, is fundamentally hostile to the pluralistic purposes of religious and associational freedoms. *Yoder* is correctly decided because its accommodation, insofar as it offers refuge for communities of faith, enhances religious pluralism and diversity. *Smith* does just the opposite.[144]

We might object, however, that simply opening up opportunities for associational life misunderstands the utility of associational life to maintaining the Civic Constitution. Associational freedom does not guarantee that citizens will learn the ways of constitutional life or that associations will necessarily promote constitutional values. Why should the state accommodate groups and associations, religious or not, that subscribe to articles of faith (and understandings of civic virtue) that are inconsistent with the normative premises of a constitutional way of life?[145] Is there a value in pluralism itself, or should we value pluralism only insofar as it yields communities and associations that are in harmony with our constitutional commitments and values? As I indicated in our discussion of civic education in public schools, the question is about how best to maintain our commitment to a constitutional way of life. It is tempting to adopt a position that gives preference only to associations that are consonant with our most fundamental of constitutional commitments: our earlier discussion of the relationship of the Civic Constitution to civil society made clear that the state does have a substantial interest in the constitution of civil society. The presuppositions of the Civic Constitution seem therefore to tell us that the state need not be neutral in its treatment of associations and organizations that promote values and virtues that undermine constitutional principles.

This position takes too narrow a view of what it means to live a constitutional way of life. Our commitment to a constitutional way of life does not require us to silence organizations that ask their members to subscribe to principles that question the desirability of civic virtues or a constitutional way of life; there must be room under the Civic Constitution for dissension, or for dissident citizenship.[146] As we discussed earlier, the constitutional principles of reason and deliberation, embedded in the understanding of the Constitution's authority as revealed in Article 6, require room for reasoned disagreement and even for the rejection of shared constitutional ideals.[147] The question of whether we should give our allegiance to the Constitution must be a central component of any account of constitutional authority.[148] Maintaining the Civic Constitution, and its approach to the question of legitimacy and temporality, requires citizens to be open to questioning their constitutional faith.[149] This in turn means we must provide citizens with the space and opportunities to question their faith.

Unlike the Juridic Constitution, which requires our reverence, the Civic Constitution welcomes citizens who think critically about the desirability of the constitution and even of constitutionalism. In that sense, it embodies an understanding of the Constitution's authority premised upon its ability to persuade us that its vision of who we are, and who we should be, is one we should embrace.[150] The Civic Constitution must therefore accommodate associations and organizations that reject the normative premises of the constitutional order itself. An added advantage to this understanding is that it makes unnecessary a systemic inquiry into the actual beliefs of various organizations and an assessment of their compatibility with constitutional norms.[151]

To conclude, the Civic Constitution thrives only when the mechanisms and means of civic education, broadly defined, are in good working order. Because it envisions virtuous citizenship as requiring an active commitment to public work, or to the practice of tending, the Civic Constitution "places special value on the kind of experiential learning" that characterizes informal civic education.[152] It is in these other areas of civic life that we learn the traits and habits necessary to sustain the Civic Constitution. Participation in the political and associational life of the community is a civic education in the virtues of civility and tending.

HOW TO MAINTAIN THE CIVIC CONSTITUTION

To this point I have discussed the what and the who of constitutional maintenance, or what it is we seek to maintain and who bears responsibility for maintaining it. There remains an equally important question: How do we maintain and preserve a constitutional way of life? A full account of constitutional maintenance requires us to address issues of institutional design, especially concerning the separation of power (horizontally and vertically), the practice of constitutional interpretation, and the dynamics of constitutional amendment.

Separations of Power: Horizontal and Vertical

Our discussion of constitutional interpretation in Essay One has already revealed that the Civic Constitution requires an approach to the horizontal separation of power that promotes the capacity of other institutions to address constitutional questions. I use the phrase "to address constitutional questions" instead of "questions of constitutionality" because the latter seems to ask whether some policy or prescription is constitutional from a juridical perspective. To "address constitutional questions," in contrast, intimates a range of issues and questions that reach more broadly than questions about constitutional legality. The Civic Constitution prefers the more expansive meaning.

Interpretive pluralism contributes to constitutional maintenance by institutionalizing the idea that the construction of constitutional meaning is best served by a multiplicity of voices contributing to constitutional deliberation. The same logic—multiplying the number of voices that participate in constitutional conversation—requires an understanding of the separation of powers doctrine in which each of the branches has some responsibility to care for the Constitution. The Civic Constitution envisions an approach to the separation of powers that encourages the development of these institutional centers, chiefly Congress and the presidency, to address constitutional concerns as a routine and significant part of their institutional responsibilities. In so doing, these institutions engage in the practice of constitutional maintenance both directly and indirectly. They are engaged directly insofar as they contribute to the making of constitutional meaning and thereby facilitate the dialogic function of constitutional self-governance. To borrow a phrase from Corwin, the separation of powers is an invitation to struggle over the meaning of the Constitution,[153] and that struggle necessitates deliberation between and among institutions that share power.

It may be, however, that the separation of powers doctrine, understood in ways that promote the interpretive capacities of all three branches, is more important for its indirect contributions to constitutional maintenance. When all of the branches engage the Constitution, they teach citizens that the responsibility to maintain our constitutional way of life cannot be delegated to others more expert or responsible than ourselves. They teach citizens that constitutional questions, and especially questions about how to preserve our commitment to constitutional ideals, do not reduce to questions of legality, technicality, or judicial interpretation, but are instead questions about who we are and to what we are committed; they are questions of identity, not of legality.

This will have important consequences for civic education, because some measure of learning how to be a citizen comes from the experience of watching how political representatives address political issues. How the other branches respond to claims of judicial authority, and especially to assertions of judicial supremacy, teaches citizens something about what it means to live a constitutional way of life. Congressional representatives who choose not to engage issues of constitutionality, for example, especially when they believe such issues are committed elsewhere, teach citizens that their own responsibility for the Constitution is slight.[154] Moreover, courts speak in a language inaccessible and remote to most citizens. It is of profound significance for the Civic Constitution that the elected branches speak the more familiar language of politics. Their ability to speak to the people, and in a common language, gives elected officials a unique capacity to communicate with citizens about the meaning of the Constitution.

As I indicated in Essay One, at a certain level of abstraction, the separation of powers has both a horizontal and a vertical plane. Following a similar logic, the project of civic maintenance prefers a form of federalism in which the states are an important contributor to constitutional dialogue, or which promotes constitutional conversation on a vertical plane.[155] The argument that institutions educate by example is even more salient when considering state and local governments. Strong federalism is especially important to the Civic Constitution because citizens learn by watching and by doing. This learning is more likely when citizens have opportunities to watch and to act in their own communities, and when they can have some confidence that their participation will be of consequence.

A robust doctrine of federalism is especially important because it provides for an immediately accessible public space in which citizens can participate in the political and constitutional life of the community. The states are singularly important sites for this engagement in part because, as Jefferson and other civic republicans insisted, they are near to citizens and more likely to promote civic virtue in their citizens.[156] Understanding how to preserve and maintain the constitutional order therefore requires that we promote a constitutional way of life that gives meaning, significance, and dignity to local politics, that we find ways to encourage the development of local civic work by making it consequential. Constitutional blueprints that disable municipal opportunities for civic experience, in contrast, undermine the richness and importance of civic life.

Most of the current scholarship on popular constitutionalism has concentrated on a model of political dialogue that occurs chiefly on a horizontal axis, or between coordinate constitutional actors. Arguments in praise of weak-form judicial review (see Tushnet, for example[157]) or departmentalism typically assume a model of constitutional dialogue in which the chief conversants (the Court; Congress; the president) might all be said to occupy the same plane of constitutional authority. As Robert Nagel notes, most discussions of the Constitution outside the courts "assign little or no role to state institutions."[158] Instead, they either discount the significance of federalism explicitly, or, like Ackerman and Tushnet, simply envision the people "as an undifferentiated national entity."[159] Nagel makes two useful points about this assumption. First, he describes it as "puzzling," given the "occasionally low quality of national political discourse."[160] (In Nagel's view, many deficiencies of discourse are likely "inherent in modern circumstances."[161]) The puzzle is explained, I think, by the widely held view among legal academics that there is not much civic virtue to be found in state and local politics. Second, and more importantly for our purposes, Nagel suggests that "decentralized discourse" will have "certain clear advantages over nationalized debate," though these advantages "only make admirable dialogue possible, not inevitable."[162] What makes local political conversation superior to national debate? "Participants would be more likely to have some personal contact with one another," and could "draw more on common experience. . . . Debate might be less personalized, less extreme, and less threatening."[163] Absent local forums for public dialogue, Nagel warns, it might be that expanded national conversation about a constitutional way of life will be "just as cheap and demeaning as much of the rest of our national political life."[164]

There is another reason why we might expect state and local governments to make significant contributions to constitutional conversation. As Bradley Hays suggests, vertical dialogue may open up opportunities for different voices to participate in constitutional conversation, especially in those instances where other factors (such as one-party control of national institutions, or instances where the federal government's collective self-interest overcomes party or ideological differences) mitigate against departmentalism's promise of interpretive pluralism. In these cases, states and local governments might be an especially valuable complement to constitutional dialogue.[165]

Hays and Nagel argue persuasively that federalism is an important resource for helping citizens to live a constitutional way of life. In contrast, many discussions of federalism seem predicated on the implicit assumption that strong accounts of federalism put our most basic constitutional ideals at risk.[166] Federalism might threaten our constitutional ideals in two ways. First, there is the danger that strong accounts of federalism will encourage (or at least enable) citizens to pursue ends that are hostile to our basic constitutional ideals, as they have sometimes in the past. There is no guarantee, in other words, that strengthening the states as participants in constitutional conversations will further our sense of obligation to the Constitution or that the resulting conversation will be undertaken in a spirit of fidelity to the Constitution.[167]

We must consider, then, the concern that strong-form or civic federalism increases opportunities for local communities to subvert our constitutional ideals, in particular through the doctrines of interposition and nullification. Both doctrines have sorry histories as instruments for the subversion of constitutional ideals and for the protection of slavery. Many antebellum uses of interposition involved states' resisting federal efforts to guarantee the civil liberties of slaves, African Americans, and other minorities. That is not their only history, however. In several instances, nullification and interposition have been mechanisms for the protection of constitutional principles and practices far more consonant with our highest constitutional aspirations and our best constitutional selves. Examples include the Kentucky and Virginia Resolutions, directed in large part against the Alien and Sedition Acts, as well as the efforts of some Northern states to resist the Fugitive Slave Acts of 1793 and 1850. Moreover, somewhat modified versions of these doctrines might still provide citizens with the constitutional forums and resources necessary to contribute to the realization of our highest constitutional ideals. Hays, for example, has proposed a "thin account" of interposition, which he argues affords citizens "constitutional resources that can enhance democratic practices and provide greater civil libertarian protection from executive authority."[168] Hays suggests that contemporary threats to civil liberties often originate from national actors (especially the president), which should lead us to rethink the benefits of interposition as a mechanism for protecting liberties.[169] Thin interposition, like theories of departmentalism, "spurs constitutional deliberation."[170] In a similar fashion, revitalized conceptions of federalism, rather than posing a threat to liberties, may actually advance the protection of fundamental rights. Robert Schapiro, for instance, has proffered a theory of "polyphonic federalism," in which the states are meaningful contributors to the protection of civil liberties through a system of "plurality, dialogue, and redundancy."[171] Both proposals may help to open up the civic space necessary for citizens to participate in discussion about what those principles mean.

One might object secondly that civic federalism demeans a national identity centered on a shared understanding of constitutional commitments with legal superiority over countervailing local opinions (by virtue of the supremacy clause of Article 6). But strong-form federalism of the sort necessitated by the Civic Constitution does not undermine the supremacy clause. Instead, civic federalism is necessary to make good on Article 6 itself. The supremacy of the Constitution is a claim about the importance of constitutional maintenance as an undertaking, or a way of insisting that the Constitution must in fact *be* maintained, both temporally and as against countervailing (local) claims of political authority. Moreover, as Barber has argued, Article 6's claim to superiority must be one that citizens can, through the exercise of reason and deliberation, accept or reject.[172] Implicit in this approach is a citizen who can make informed choices about whether to accept or reject the Constitution's claim to authority. The instrumental mechanisms for creating that kind of citizen, for creating the kind of citizen Article 6 requires (citizens who can make reasoned decisions to accept or reject the Constitution's claim to authority), should include the development of state and local forums in which citizens can learn to be those kinds of citizens. Robust states, states that have a role in the construction of the Constitution's meaning, are thus compatible with if not required by the supremacy claim, though admittedly sometimes in tension with it as well.[173]

Constitutional Interpretation as Constitutional Maintenance

What role does constitutional interpretation play in constitutional maintenance? Maintaining the Constitution requires We the People to look both backward and forward—to elucidate what the Constitution has meant,[174] to consider what it means now, and to imagine what it might mean in the future. Insofar as the Constitution purports to extend through time (if not in perpetuity), there must be some way of connecting the past (an act of will) to the present (an act of understanding).[175] The interpretive exercise thus conceived is itself an act of constitutional fidelity, for it takes seriously our commitment to honor our commitments. In the words of Sotirios Barber, "The ends of constitutional interpretation require that we view the constitutional text as adumbrating an ideal way of life that defines the nation's aspirations."[176]

Apprehending a constitution through an act of interpretation is a key component to understanding how constitutions can survive time—and enduring time, although not the sole or even the primary object of constitutional maintenance, is still a part of what maintenance presupposes as an end. But constitutional interpretation is not strictly necessary for a Constitution to endure. A Constitution can persist as a revered symbol, without significant popular understanding, for a very long time;[177] such a Constitution need not be interpreted by anyone, and there need not be any institutional mechanism in place for routinized interpretation of it. Such a Constitution exists as a sacred artifact; it needs our faith,[178] not our understanding: "Faith establishes the sacred quality of the text, interpretation gives a narrative shape to the appearance of the sacred."[179]

A Constitution that purports to govern political affairs in more than purely symbolic ways, however, needs our faith *and* understanding.[180] And because no text can be completely self-executing or prescient, its meaning and application must be a question of judgment and discernment; *understanding* a text requires that we *interpret* it. Under the Civic Constitution, however, understanding encompasses more than formal or institutionalized interpretation, for we cannot fully know its meaning (or better, its meaning is not fully established) except through text and practice.

The necessity of interpretation traces additionally to the nature of constitution making as an activity compromised by language and human incapacity. A constitutional text requires interpretation for three reasons. First, the limits of language to ordain human affairs mean that constitutional language is sometimes imprecise and inexact.[181] Second, and related, the politics of constitution making and draftsmanship, a politics that ordinarily asks the drafters of constitutions to paper over uncertainties, inconsistencies, and disagreements,[182] typically yields a language of compromise. And third, interpretation is compelled by the temporality involved in constitutional maintenance, or in the necessity of applying constitutional commands over time. (Papering over likewise has a temporal element, insofar as it leaves certain issues to the judgment and resolution of a set of constitutional actors [our prospective selves] in the future.[183]) For all of these reasons, every account of constitutional maintenance must address the practice of constitutional interpretation.[184] That the two are related tells us the activity of constitutional interpretation—what we imagine it to be, how we conceptualize it, and how we organize and practice it—must be in service of maintaining our commitment to a constitutional way of life.

Establishing that a constitution requires interpretation does not settle the question of who should interpret it or how to interpret it.[185] The more perplexing questions are how to carve up interpretive authority, or how to determine where, institutionally, to assign it, and how to describe what kind of practice it is. Our understanding of the Constitution as Juridic, Civic, or both will have a profound effect upon how we address such questions.

The Juridic Constitution and Constitutional Interpretation

The Juridic Constitution reduces constitutional maintenance to constitutional interpretation. Constitutional interpretation in turn consists of judicial determination of the meaning of and enforcement of indeterminate constitutional rules that constrain governmental officials and the state. The enforcement aspect of this juridic conception of maintenance is sometimes not fully explored in juridic accounts of constitutional interpretation, chiefly because they typically focus on another difficulty that is logically prior to the issue of enforcement. The difficulty is well-known: before constitutional rules can be enforced, they must be known and characterized by a degree of specificity that makes them capable of being enforced by judges at all. To the extent that constitutional provisions cannot bear or be made to possess that degree of specificity, they are unenforceable (at least by judges); we sometimes choose to call these unenforceable provisions nonjusticiable, or norms rather than rules. We explain (excuse?) their presence in the constitutional text by distinguishing between the thick and the thin constitution, or between the judicially enforceable and political constitution, or some similar classificatory schema.[186] In a larger sense, we exclude them from the province of constitutional interpretation altogether.[187]

The text itself makes no distinctions of this sort, but they have great importance for how we conceive the relationship between constitutional maintenance and interpretation. First, they constrict what maintenance is by confining it to certain provisions in the document—to those that are judicially enforceable. Second, they assign maintenance to Article 3 courts. The two work hand in hand. Constitutional maintenance reduces to judicial interpretation of those parts of the Constitution that are capable of enforcement by judges. The *what* and the *who* of maintenance shrink to a single activity, constitutional interpretation, and become the responsibility of a discrete set of actors—judges and, to a lesser extent, other legal authorities and members of various interpretive communities—with professional expertise.

Therefore, a theory of constitutional interpretation under the Juridic Constitution cannot be a theory about how to maintain the Constitution in its entirety. Insofar as the interpretive authority of judges is hitched to the claim that the Constitution is law, those claims must be confined to the parts of the Constitution that look like law and are capable of being treated as legal commands. Several scholars, myself included, have explored the implications of this for understanding the Constitution writ large.[188] Recently, for example, Lawrence Sager and others have tried to distinguish between the thick and thin constitutions, or between judicial supremacy and popular constitutionalism, in an effort to give weight to those parts of the Constitution that are judicially unenforceable.[189] All of these efforts have behind them a lingering sense that there is something deeply undemocratic and unsatisfying about apprehending the Constitution only as a legal instrument. This is an implicit recognition that the Juridic Constitution cannot be a full account of the Constitution. Some of the same concerns animate the long-standing fascination with the counter-majoritarian difficulty, a staple of constitutional scholarship at least since Bickel[190] (and in earlier formulations, at least since Thayer[191]). The counter-majoritarian difficulty is ostensibly a question of institutional legitimacy: how can democracies justify assigning any significant measure of political authority to unelected judges? Most efforts to solve the counter-majoritarian difficulty predictably center on ways to deflate the claim that judges are antidemocratic, or, similarly, that the process of constitutional interpretation is not democratically accountable.[192] These attempts to solve the counter-majoritarian difficulty typically rely in part on a strategy that cabins judicial authority to only certain parts of the Constitution.[193] None of these efforts amounts to an argument that judges have authority or responsibility to interpret (maintain) the Constitution writ whole. None of them, in other words, challenges the claim that constitutional maintenance is fundamentally about judicial interpretation of *part(s)* of the text.

Thus, as Sager has written, "Even proponents of robust, wide-bodied judicial review do not regard most of the elements of a good society as something that is within the grasp of the judiciary."[194] For Sager, there is an important distinction between the "scope of the Constitution itself . . . and the distinctly narrower scope of the judicially enforced Constitution."[195] In terms of constitutional maintenance, the distinction between the "Constitution itself" and the judicially enforceable constitution results in a "division of labor between the judiciary and other governmental actors."[196] Broadly speaking, courts entertain responsibility for those parts of the Constitution that do not elude judicial enforcement; those that do are someone else's purview. The resulting (judicially enforced) Constitution is thin in that "it falls so far short of addressing unduckable elements of fundamental political justice."[197] Sager concedes that responsibility for addressing those unduckable elements of justice rests with other actors, but at bottom, he appears to have little confidence that the thick Constitution can be preserved or enforced in any significant measure. This skepticism is evident in Sager's comments about another approach to the concept of a thin Constitution, developed by Tushnet.

In *Taking the Constitution Away from the Courts*, Tushnet advances a broad argument against judicial review, claiming that it discourages and disables citizens and other constitutional actors from taking responsibility for protecting fundamental constitutional liberties.[198] The reach of Tushnet's Constitution is limited in ways that make it possible to think the people will honor it and abide by it. Such a Constitution is defined by the normative commitments that inhere in the Declaration and in the Preamble, or in "values that we all salute."[199] Other elements of the Constitution, such as the emolument clause, and most other provisions of the "body" of the Constitution, would be discarded, at least in the sense of their enforcement by judges—hence the title, *Taking the Constitution Away from the Courts*. Tushnet's Constitution is the responsibility of the people, but it is thin because it excludes a range of commitments and provisions that we often think comprise the Constitution's architectural design for the operation of government. In another sense, Tushnet's Constitution demands much from its citizens, who now possess primary authority for making good on its substantive commitments (these commitments, in comparison to those of the Civic Constitution, are themselves thin).

In Sager's view, Tushnet's constitution results in a constitutional order that cannot make claims to certain kinds of social rights, such as minimum welfare, because it understands constitutional conversation as limited "only to exclude certain dark impulses"—"no substantive rights to material outcomes can be invoked in the name of the Constitution."[200] (In this sense, Tushnet's constitution is thin both in its normative base and in its substantive reach.) In contrast, Sager concludes that the Constitution should include "some normative premises, albeit judicially unenforceable, that are categorical, non-negotiable, and demanding of priority."[201] By Sager's own admission, such principles are for others to secure. And in the end, Sager's insistence that these constitutional norms are a part of the realm of constitutional justice, though not judicially enforceable, leads him not, as it does Tushnet, to forswear judicial review, but instead to argue for a partnership between courts and other constitutional actors (in contrast to an agency model). But if this is a thick Constitution, it is also unlikely to be realized, even on Sager's terms, and he seems fairly skeptical about the chances of its enforcement by nonjudicial actors.[202]

Tushnet's Constitution is thin, therefore, because it reduces to a commitment to a limited number of basic or fundamental principles, identified in the Preamble and the Declaration, which are entrusted to the people for their realization. (The Civic Constitution, in contrast, extends to a much larger constellation of texts and civic practices.) Indeed, Sager describes the Tushnet constitution as a palimpsest, or as reducing to what is "so uncontroversial for the American people as to be reliably respected by them; it doesn't actually constrain or even inspire."[203] Sager therefore concludes that "there surely is no good reason to be confident that it will be widely accepted and well-served by popular politics."[204]

For reasons I have discussed, the objection that Tushnet's constitution is thin because it offers little evidence in support of the claim that the Constitution, if taken away from the courts, will have any discernible effect on how the people act, ignores how the Juridic Constitution functions to depress civic engagement. But "thin" here has another, related sense: we might wonder, as we noted earlier, whether there is anything seriously "constitutional" in these and other accounts of popular constitutionalism.[205] Sager describes Tushnet's Constitution as thin because it is spare in the kinds of claims it makes for political justice, or in its normative reach. Fleming describes the problem in similar but broader fashion, asking us to think about what "the domain of popular constitutionalism" includes.[206] The question has two components. First, it asks us to think about whether popular talk about the constitution "differs from people's discourse about . . . their wants and interests and . . . their conceptions of justice and morality."[207] In response, we should note that the relevance of the distinction, and its location, relate back to a prior understanding of how thick or thin we imagine the Constitution itself to be—thin versions of the Constitution raise the question of differentiation more insistently than do thick versions. Second, Fleming notes also that "it is not clear that the Constitution, or constitutionalism, is doing much of the work in popular constitutionalism. . . . [I]t is not clear that the people themselves, when they triumph over judicial supremacy, are ultimately interpreting the Constitution, as distinguished from it simply being the case that public opinion about wants, interests, or justice has prevailed as a fact of political power."[208] In some ways this second objection trades on the first—both reference a more or less clear distinction between (thin) constitutional claims and other sorts of claims, which in turn presuppose some understanding about which texts and civic practices count as part of the constitutional canon. But more significantly, as I indicated in Essay One, my understanding of the Constitution is thicker than that advanced by Tushnet (or Kramer) precisely in its insistence that the constitutional commitments constrain the populist elements of the constitutional order, and precisely because those normative commitments have a provenance and an expanse that reach wider than the (canonical) document itself.

Implicit in Sager's work is suspicion that any part of the Constitution not enforceable by judges is a poor candidate to be maintained, at least insofar as maintenance is the peoples' responsibility. This confuses constitutional maintenance with the realization of constitutional norms and practices. It excludes as "constitutional" public debate and discussion not only about what these norms actually mean or require, but also and more importantly, public discussion about whether and why such norms and principles ought to be respected or preserved. Sager's reservation sounds familiar because it resonates with the widespread assumption that the people are fickle. Leaving the Constitution (defined thickly or thinly) to them is a risky if not foolhardy maneuver, and one that judges must superintend. Sager seeks to carve out a role for courts in two ways. First, he argues that judicial review contributes to the realization of some constitutional rights by providing a forum in which they can be heard and (presumably) safeguarded against majoritarian tyranny. Second, participation by a constitutional judiciary can provide an "opportunity to provoke dialogue and goad the conscience of the community"[209] and thus assists the people in the exercise of their deliberative function. Both points start from an assumption of civic incapacity or ill-disposition, an incapacity that can be offset at least partially by a Court that serves as backstop and conscience. From this assumption, it is an easy if not inevitable assumption that the Court ought to assume primary responsibility for tending to the Constitution. In contrast, the Civic Constitution assumes the people are genuinely capable of civic responsibility and that constitutional maintenance includes maintaining a constitutional order, and not just a constitutional document.

The Civic Constitution and Constitutional Interpretation

The Civic Constitution takes judicially unenforceable commitments seriously by expanding the object of constitutional maintenance to include them. Civic maintenance thus extends to those parts of the constitutional text, and more generally to those parts of the Constitution writ large, that cannot be made to conform to the requirements of justiciability. (This does not concede that civic maintenance excludes the justiciable parts of the Constitution.) One way to conceptualize the Civic Constitution, then, is to see it as an argument in favor of a robust conception of constitutional maintenance that exists alongside and in companion to the Juridic Constitution—as assuming, in other words, that there exists a reasonably neat and compartmentalized division of labor between the Juridic and Civic Constitutions.

But over the long run (part of what an inquiry into maintenance requires us to investigate), this simple compartmentalization is likely to yield a constitution whose civic parts become anemic. This is especially so to the extent our understanding of the Juridic Constitution yields, over time, a theory of interpretive authority that approaches judicial supremacy. Judicial supremacy does not simply diminish the constitutional responsibilities of other actors with respect to the judicially enforceable constitution—its logic necessarily infects the entire constitutional order, in part by creating a system of disincentives for other constitutional actors to take up their constitutional responsibilities.[210] It causes a type of civic and interpretive aphanisis, or what Tushnet calls a problem of "overhang."[211] This is not simply a consequence of a system of judicial supremacy, though supremacy exacerbates it—it is a condition of the Juridic Constitution itself. Nevertheless, the overhang problem is particularly pronounced in systems that adopt judicial supremacy. The most significant component of judicial supremacy is its hierarchical conception of interpretive authority, in which the authority of courts is superior in rank to other claims to interpretive authority. Judicial supremacy expels other institutional actors, and citizens, from an expanse (indeterminate in its boundaries, but the boundaries themselves are set by judges, or self-regulated) of constitutional decision making.[212]

Judicial supremacy is adapted to the Juridic Constitution because it prizes settlement over dialogue. The settlement function is premised upon the claim that interpretation is a legal and not a political activity, and that what the law requires is clarity and finality, if not dichotomy, as a condition of its realization. This has important implications for constitutional maintenance. The settlement function is, at bottom, a way of choking debate. Perhaps less obvious, under the Juridic Constitution, the settlement function is also a way of determining who can participate in and who is excluded from constitutional deliberations.

The overhang argument demonstrates why the Juridic Constitution inhibits civic engagement. But Eisgruber (and others, including Sager) argues that judicial review does not significantly influence, much less inhibit, popular discussion of constitutional matters. Eisgruber sees little evidence that judicial review actually undermines or "stifles popular activity," or demotes citizens to spectators.[213] Moreover, he concludes that public debates surrounding cases like *Dred Scott* and *Roe* tell us that judicial review generates public deliberation as often as it suffocates it. Sager likewise argues that participation by a constitutional judiciary can provoke dialogue and assist the people in the exercise of their deliberative function.[214]

The Supreme Court does have a role to play in civic education. But we are mistaken to imagine the Court as engaged in an ongoing seminar or conversation with the nation or the people in any meaningful sense. It is naive to think that judicial opinions are anything like democratic conversation. The structure and complexity of judicial opinions precludes conversation.[215] Judicial talk about the Constitution transpires in a professional language that excludes most citizens. Moreover, I suspect those judicial opinions that do provoke public reaction produce less in the way of genuine deliberation and more in the way of impotent outrage. At best, these judicial decisions produce a public conversation that has no weight or significance because it has nowhere to go and no mechanism to give it influence. Under strong forms of judicial review, public conversation about the Constitution has no consequence.[216] On the other hand, although Eisgruber and Sager overestimate the capacity of courts in a system of strong-form judicial review to initiate public *conversation* about the Constitution, there are times when judicial decisions do spark civic *engagement*. The obvious examples are the cases Eisgruber cited, *Dred Scott* and *Roe*, and many others come to mind, such as *Brown*, the *School Prayer* decisions, and *Citizens' United*. The real contributions of these decisions to civic engagement, however, are not immediate, but instead consist of the organized and sustained campaigns they generated. In other words, these decisions had civic effect to the extent that they prompted sustained civic mobilization.[217]

Even granting the point about civic mobilization, however, it is notable that instances of popular deliberation following upon judicial decisions are not the norm but the exception, provoked not as an ordinary or routine element of constitutional life but instead only on those occasions when the Court missteps or grossly mistakes popular sentiment. The structural form is akin to Ackerman's argument about the exceptionality of constitutional moments—the key element in both accounts is that public deliberation about the Constitution is exceptional and episodic. It is unlikely to advance an authentically civic conception of a constitutional way of life.

To prosper, the Civic Constitution must do more than simply exist in companion to the Juridic Constitution; it must make claims upon it. Because the Juridic Constitution manifests most prominently in constitutional interpretation, the Civic Constitution must likewise influence how we approach constitutional interpretation as a part of the project of constitutional maintenance. Phrased differently, the Civic Constitution demands that we adopt an approach to constitutional interpretation that advances, rather than impedes or obstructs, the larger aim of civic maintenance. This approach to constitutional interpretation has two components—the who and the how, to follow Murphy's well-known heuristic. The first concerns the allocation of interpretive authority. The second concerns the methodology of constitutional interpretation.

Allocations of Interpretive Authority

Some mechanism for constitutional review is a constitutive element of all authentic constitutional regimes.[218] But a commitment to constitutional self-governance, in itself, tells us nothing about whether adopting a system of review by judges commits us to judicial supremacy (strong-form judicial review), or to departmentalism, or to any other particular structural iteration of judicial review.

The Civic Constitution prefers a weak form of judicial review. This preference is grounded less in the need for constitutional settlement (or the resolution of disagreements about the meaning and application of constitutional rules, especially as concerns the division and separation of powers), and more upon the necessity of constitutional dialogue, or ongoing consideration about the meaning and relevance of our largest constitutional commitments and norms.[219]

In Essay One I distinguished between weak and strong forms of interpretive pluralism. The difference between them is tied directly to the relative strength of their claims to interpretive authority. Weak forms of interpretive pluralism call simply for multiple interpreters and multiple interpretations. Strong forms of interpretive pluralism imagine that these other interpretations will not be inferior in authority to judicial interpretations of the Constitution. Just as importantly, strong-form pluralism promotes a constitutional model that is dialogic, or that parallels the conversational model of discourse I described as central to the concept of civility. This in turn may yield judicial opinions that, now in contest for persuasive authority, are more likely to adopt a voice that can speak inclusively, or that comes closer to a model of civic discourse as conversation and deliberation.[220] Strong interpretive pluralism, as a way of allocating interpretive authority, is thus better suited to a civic conception of constitutional maintenance precisely because it prizes dialogue over settlement.

Interpretive pluralism does not require that we silence courts. The Civic Constitution does not deny the Court some measure of interpretive authority under Article 3 to enforce the Constitution; it is simply a way of understanding (reading) the breadth and limits of that authority. Ordinarily a judicial decision "settles" the Constitution in the sense that it resolves questions

of both legality and constitutionality (especially under the Juridic Constitution), but there are instances in which the distinction between legality
and constitutionality must be acknowledged and preserved. (In some ways,
though not perfectly, the difference between legality and constitutionality
tracks the distinction between judicial opinions that bind *inter partes* as
opposed to *erga omnes*.[221]) The latter determination, of constitutionality, is
a larger, more delicate and significant question, and because it speaks more
directly to the project of constitutional maintenance, it must hear nonjudicial voices. Two examples of this sort of constitutional conversation immediately suggest themselves—President Lincoln's response to the decision in
Dred Scott v. Sandford (1857), and congressional passage of the Religious
Freedom Restoration Act following *Employment Division v. Smith* (1990).
In his First Inaugural Address, Lincoln answered the Court's decision in
Dred Scott by stating:

> I do not forget the position assumed by some that constitutional
> questions are to be decided by the Supreme Court, nor do I deny that
> such decisions must be binding in any case upon the parties to a suit as
> to the object of that suit, while they are also entitled to very high respect
> and consideration in all parallel cases by all other departments of the
> Government. . . . At the same time, the candid citizen must confess that
> if the policy of the Government upon vital questions affecting the whole
> people is to be irrevocably fixed by decisions of the Supreme Court, the
> instant they are made in ordinary litigation between parties in personal
> actions the people will have ceased to be their own rulers, having to
> that extent practically resigned their Government into the hands of that
> eminent tribunal.[222]

Lincoln's reference to the binding effect of the Court's decision "upon the
parties" invokes the distinction between *inter partes* and *erga omnes*, as well
as the distinction between legality and constitutionality. More broadly, it
democratizes constitutional maintenance.

In *Boerne*, the Court ruled that Congress's Section 5 enforcement power
under the Fourteenth Amendment does not extend beyond "enforcing" the
terms of the amendment itself. In so ruling, the Court set aside the Religious
Freedom Restoration Act (as applied against the states), in which Congress
had sought to reinstate the compelling-state-interest test from *Sherbert*. The
Court concluded that Congress had altered the meaning of the First Amendment:

The design of the Amendment and the text of § 5 are inconsistent with the suggestion that Congress has the power to decree the substance of the Fourteenth Amendment's restrictions on the States. Legislation which alters the meaning of the Free Exercise Clause cannot be said to be enforcing the Clause. Congress does not enforce a constitutional right by changing what the right is. It has been given the power "to enforce," not the power to determine what constitutes a constitutional violation. Were it not so, what Congress would be enforcing would no longer be, in any meaningful sense, the "provisions of [the Fourteenth Amendment]." (citations omitted)

Whereas Lincoln's response to the Court was intended to provoke civic conversation, the Court's decision in *Boerne* undermines the Civic Constitution by teaching Congress, and by extension, citizens, that their own powers of constitutional interpretation, and hence their responsibility to maintain and preserve the Constitution, are insubstantial. Ironically, parts of Justice Scalia's opinion for the Court in *Smith* can be read to encourage just the sort of civic engagement and responsibility for the constitutional project that the Civic Constitution anticipates and that Congress acted on in the RFRA. In *Smith*, Justice Scalia observed that

Values that are protected against government interference through enshrinement in the Bill of Rights are not thereby banished from the political process. Just as a society that believes in the negative protection accorded to the press by the First Amendment is likely to enact laws that affirmatively foster the dissemination of the printed word, so also a society that believes in the negative protection accorded to religious belief can be expected to be solicitous of that value in its legislation as well.

Scalia points to an important role in constitutional maintenance played by nonjudicial actors. One of the Court's errors in *Smith* was in assuming this constitutional role is inferior to and must complement its own power to determine what the Constitution means. The Court repeated the mistake in *Boerne*, when it again insisted that the role of other institutional actors and citizens in preserving constitutional norms and values is necessarily subordinate to its own, even when the text appears to assign considerable authority to Congress, as it does in Section 5 of the Fourteenth Amendment.[223] Consider this quote, where Justice Kennedy speaks directly to constitutional maintenance:

Our national experience teaches that the Constitution is preserved best
when each part of the government respects both the Constitution and
the proper actions and determinations of the other branches. When
the Court has interpreted the Constitution, it has acted within the
province of the Judicial Branch, which embraces the duty to say what
the law is. Marbury v. Madison. . . . When the political branches of the
Government act against the background of a judicial interpretation of
the Constitution already issued, it must be understood that in later cases
and controversies the Court will treat its precedents with the respect
due them under settled principles, including stare decisis, and contrary
expectations must be disappointed.

Kennedy's description of our national experience is unmistakably juridic
in its outlook; it equates the project of constitutional maintenance with judicial interpretation of the text, and in so doing discourages other officials
and citizens from attending to it. As I mentioned earlier, the flaw in *Boerne* is
precisely the Court's insistence that the dialogic model of conversation must
submit to the logic of command and finality (settlement).

How to Interpret?

The Civic Constitution alters how we should think about the allocation of
interpretive authority. It also influences how we should think about the ritu-
alisms of constitutional interpretation, or about what sort of a rite it is and
when and how it should be performed. If interpretation means determining
what a constitutional provision means in an Article 3 case and controversy,
then what we call interpretation will become a highly stylized practice, organized around a fairly stable set of canonical questions and professional
assumptions in the interpretive community.[224] This is not to say the assumptions are uncontested and the questions easily resolved. Rubenfeld, for example, has reached the "embarrassing conclusion" that constitutional law
"has no very good account of its own interpretive method."[225] It might be
better to say that constitutional law has too many accounts of its own interpretive method, some of them simplistic, others sophisticated and nuanced,
but none that approaches paradigmatic status.[226] Accordingly, students of
constitutional interpretation, or members of the interpretive community,
must be literate in a wide variety of hermeneutic approaches and concepts,
as well as conversant with the literary, philosophical, and sometimes theo-
logical traditions that undergird them.

Possessed with this understanding, we might well worry about whether
constitutional interpretation should be entrusted to citizen-unsophisticates

untrained in the requisite disciplinary arts. In Richard Posner's estimation, for instance, the idea that the people might embrace responsibility for the Constitution is "laughable," not only because most of us are fully preoccupied with our private pursuits, but also because "the law has become exceedingly complex and the legal profession and judiciary formidably professionalized."[227] This is an objection to popular responsibility for interpreting the Constitution solidly grounded in the Juridic Constitution. It assumes maintenance is secured through constitutional interpretation, and it assumes interpretation is a legal enterprise that requires the professional training of lawyers and competence in the law.

Under the Civic Constitution, in contrast, "theories of constitutional interpretation . . . start with interpretation by citizens as the standard case."[228] Balkin's understanding of constitutional interpretation by citizens as the standard case, and by judges as a special case, is premised on the claim that the Constitution must be understood as an ongoing project, one in which citizens must choose to assume responsibility for making the Constitution their own. This conception of constitutional authority bears a deep similarity to Barber's reading of Article 6, and to some (but not all) of the premises of the Civic Constitution. Understanding requires that we engage the Constitution critically, and in doing so we might sensibly lose our faith in it. (Balkin defines faith as "attachment to the constitutional project."[229]) Emphasizing the "citizen's perspective" in constitutional interpretation, Balkin matches up a theory of constitutional interpretation with a theory of constitutional fidelity. He is right to do so: as we have seen, our conception of what fidelity requires of citizens cannot be distinguished from our conception of the Constitution's authority.

A civic definition conceives of constitutional interpretation as a political enterprise. To put it another way, under the Civic Constitution, constitutional maintenance *is* constitutional interpretation, let loose from the institutional confines of cases and controversies and freed of the assumption that interpretation is a project in law. And because it is let loose from Article 3, concerns about the institutional and structural constraints of courts as institutions, concerns that might disqualify some interpretive methodologies and nod toward others, are inapt as well. As a result, some of the questions we typically ask about interpretive methods are not entirely on point (such as whether the method in question does enough to constrain judicial discretion or hedges sufficiently against the counter-majoritarian difficulty), because the institutional concerns and features that attach to judicial interpretation do not factor when we approach constitutional interpretation as a civic practice.[230]

Does the Civic Constitution have any bearing on the question of how the Court should interpret the Constitution or its choice of interpretive method? It is not always clear that different interpretive techniques are directly related to conceptions of the Constitution's authority. But they are. Constitutional theorists frequently defend one or another of various interpretive methodologies on grounds of institutional competence, as well as on what kind of claims the Constitution makes about its authority.[231] Joseph Raz provides one example: "Since the authority of long-established constitutions rests primarily on the desirability of securing continuity, the same desirability should inform constitutional interpretation as well."[232] Raz reminds us that constitutional interpretation is an act of constitutional maintenance, and at the core of "maintaining" lies the question of identity, or of what we seek to conserve.[233] The Civic Constitution, because it conceives of maintenance as conserving a constitutional way of life, privileges methods of constitutional interpretation that promote civic engagement and that do not disfranchise citizens or discourage their participation. As we have seen, this requires an allocation of interpretive authority that is departmentalist, or that embraces interpretive pluralism.

A similar kind of pluralism must govern our consideration of interpretive methodologies. I have in mind more than the simplistic claim that interpreters ought to use more than a single interpretive method (although even this claim has significance, especially, as I demonstrate below, for most varieties of originalism). I mean, instead, that the authority and meaning of the constitutional text/s exists simultaneously across a number of strata, some textual, some historical, some aspirational,[234] and that a constitutional way of life, because it asks citizens to give meaning to and to realize constitutional principles, must employ interpretive methodologies that recognize the Constitution as a work in progress, and not as a settled fact with a settled meaning.[235] Thus, as Balkin has noted in his recent discussion of living originalism, a comprehensive methodology of constitutional interpretation must accommodate both "text and principle." For Balkin, the legal (or juridic) aspects of the Constitution's authority require an approach to the text that is essentially originalist, a consequence of taking the Constitution seriously as law. In Balkin's view, constitutional interpretation must "preserve the meaning of the words that constitute the framework" of the Constitution as written law.[236] But the Constitution is not only law, or not only a set of legal constraints. It is also an "open-ended" set of standards and principles that delegate some power of constitutional authority and decision making to We the People, past, present, and future. Because it is both, Balkin concludes, we should adopt interpretive strategies that combine elements of both originalism and living constitutionalism. This is the approach, moreover, that is required if citizens are actually to live a constitutional way of life, because "[f]idelity to the Constitution should therefore be provisional and contingent on our ability continually to reaffirm it for what it expressly says it is: as an instrument of justice and the general welfare."[237]

So we might argue that originalism is best suited to the Civic Constitution because it connects up questions of fidelity with interpretive methodology. This claim does not originate with Balkin—it has been an important part of originalist arguments for some time. As Whittington puts it, the argument is that originalism is both required by and an act of fidelity because originalist interpretations of the Constitution connect up the We the People to our past in an act of faithfulness. On this logic, the project of constitutional maintenance requires an originalist interpretive methodology precisely because maintenance is partly about preserving our commitments to ourselves. Thus, "we should respect the substance of the constitutional choices of the founding not because the founders necessarily got it right, but because we take seriously the idea of constitutional deliberation and founding as conscious, real-time political events."[238] Implicit in this kind of rationale (though not necessarily in Whittington's account of originalism as an interpretive practice) is a particular understanding of what originalism is or requires. On some understandings, originalism asks interpreters (judges) to function as "agents" of the founders, as "duty bound to carry out their instructions."[239] This variant of originalism, closest to framers' intent models, is essentially preservationist in purpose, as Justice Scalia has often observed.[240]

Preservationist originalism is difficult to reconcile with the Civic Constitution, which requires the people to exercise reason and deliberation as an incident of their responsibility to care for the Constitution.[241] Such an understanding of originalism disfranchises citizens by denying them an ongoing responsibility for constitutional maintenance; it results in, if it does not encourage, the founder-worship characteristic of the Juridic Constitution. Originalism, narrowly conceived, holds us hostage to the past and silences the civic voice, or at least civic efforts to assume responsibility for tending to the Constitution. Strang likewise notes, "The common perception . . . that originalism and popular constitutionalism are incompatible," but suggests also that this perception rests implicitly on discrete understandings of what originalism entails as an interpretive methodology.[242] Cornell reaches more broadly, concluding that "[p]opular constitutionalism . . . is . . . ultimately incompatible with all forms of originalism."[243]

I have already referenced what some justices and scholars call preservationist originalism. There are, obviously, many kinds of originalism.[244]

"Originalism is . . . a family of theories of constitutional interpretation: it is not monolithic."[245] Less confining forms of originalism, in which original meaning is a guide to but does not exhaust the current meaning of the Constitution, are arguably more hospitable to the Civic Constitution because they afford more respect for the intertemporality of the constitutional enterprise and the inchoate nature of constitutional identity.[246] Thus, in *Living Constitutionalism*, Balkin emphasizes the responsibility of "[p]eople in each generation" to "figure out what the Constitution's promises mean for themselves" and to participate in a broad project of constitutional interpretation conceived as a political activity first and as a judicial responsibility second. This leads Balkin to conclude that our choice of interpretive methodologies should free us to adopt a wide variety of argumentative models, including arguments grounded in history, precedent, originalism (broadly conceived as "living originalism"), and appeals to purposes and principles. Balkin's conception of living originalism combines more traditional understandings with elements of the "living constitutionalism" tradition by encouraging appeals to "text, rule, standard, and principle."[247] Living originalism is therefore a theory of constitutional interpretation, but it is not a theory of judicial interpretation, or a theory "about what judges should do" precisely because a theory of judicial interpretation is at "odds with the very assumptions behind the living Constitution."[248]

I want to be careful here. A civic approach to constitutional interpretation does not preclude every use of originalism at every turn. What is disqualified is the strong claim that *only* an originalist interpretive methodology is appropriate. Additionally, I hesitate in making any claims at all about originalism as a method of interpretation, in large part because there are now so many versions of originalism that speaking about *an* originalist method is almost nonsensical.[249] If everyone—Dworkin and Balkin included—might plausibly be described as an originalist,[250] then we should conclude not that originalism has succeeded in establishing its paradigmatic status (or, as Justice Kagan has remarked, that we are all originalists),[251] but rather that the term has no useful meaning. Or maybe we should say pluralism has come to originalism, because it now admits of so many different meanings. In either event, claims about the compatibility or incompatibility of the various interpretative methodologies used by judges with the Civic Constitution require close inquiries into definition.

Another effort to connect up constitutional maintenance and interpretive methodology is by Jeb Rubenfeld. Like Whittington and Balkin, Rubenfeld sees maintenance as a project of fidelity, not simply to our past selves, but to our constitutional commitments. Rubenfeld advances what he calls a "paradigm-case" interpretive methodology, in which judges begin from the proposition that they must take the text seriously. The interpretive method that takes the text seriously (but is not textualism), and that honors the commitments we gave to ourselves originally (but is not originalism), is the "paradigm-case method," in which "the initial question . . . is always this: What are the core historical applications of this right? In particular, what were the abuses of power that those who fought for this right fought most fervently to abolish?"[252] In Rubenfeld's view, these "core historical applications" establish the "foundational paradigm cases," which are inviolable because "they define the provision."[253]

Rubenfeld's interpretive methodology, insofar as it privileges what might be called the original meaning of constitutional provisions (he describes these as questions of historical fact), is not the same, he argues, as originalism. The meaning of any constitutional provision beyond the paradigm case "remains a matter of interpretation."[254] And that interpretation cannot be originalist because "[a] commitment to a principle . . . is a commitment to see that principle through, even if it requires one to give up practices that seemed perfectly reasonable, perfectly natural, at the time one embarked upon the commitment."[255] Nevertheless, succeeding interpretations must take a form that is consistent with paradigm cases.

Joseph Raz proposes a somewhat different approach to constitutional interpretation. Raz denies there can be "specifically legal ways of interpretation."[256] "There is no general theory of constitutional interpretation," Raz concludes, "if that is meant to be a general recipe for the way such interpretation should be conducted that is set out in some detail in order to guide the interpreter every step of the way with practical advice. There is little more that one can say other than 'reason well' or 'interpret reasonably.'"[257] What we need is a "normative account of constitutional interpretation," an account of the reasoning involved in making sense of the constitution's provisions. Raz then concludes that constitutional interpretation cannot be a strictly legal enterprise, but instead must, in at least some cases, involve an element of moral choice. A key point of Raz's approach is that courts must be authorized to engage such questions, and in so doing they are engaged in "changing" the constitution or its meaning.[258] In some limited sense, he concedes, this is true, but he warns "against confusing change with loss of identity."[259]

My concern, similarly, is not to indicate which interpretive methodologies are better or worse suited to constitutional maintenance, but rather what considerations should inform our choice. Our choice of interpretive methodologies must be governed by the fundamental object of constitutional maintenance: interpretive methods that augment civic engagement should be preferred to methods that inhibit it. Just as there is an overhang effect to strong-form iterations of judicial review, some interpretative methodologies will welcome and others will alienate or discourage civic involvement or participation by nonlawyers. Originalist methodologies must generally be disfavored, because in most instances they require highly specialized and esoteric inquiries into inaccessible historical materials well beyond the reach of most citizens,[260] and equally because they go very far toward divesting the current We of the authority to govern ourselves and to determine the meaning of our constitutional commitments. On the other hand, some accounts of originalism, such as those proposed by Whittington or Balkin, are more hospitable to the Civic Constitution, chiefly because the questions in such cases are more general and include room for inquiries into the meaning of constitutional ideals and aspirations. Such approaches are expansive enough to accommodate investigation into the meaning of fundamental constitutional ideals and into the nature of our constitutional identity.

In short, how we allocate authority to interpret the Constitution is of greater import to the project of maintenance than the selection of interpretive method by judges in constitutional litigation, but civic maintenance should bear on those choices too. Just as a system of strong-form judicial review has an overhang effect, with significantly adverse consequences for civic constitutionalism, there may be an overhang effect that traces to some methods of judicial interpretation of the Constitution.[261]

CONSTITUTIONAL CHANGE AND CONSTITUTIONAL AMENDMENTS

Every account of constitutional maintenance includes, if only implicitly, an understanding of how constitutions change and of constitutional amendment. Indeed, in some ways, a theory of constitutional maintenance *is* a theory of constitutional change. But because it requires conserving a constitutional way of life, maintenance also embraces an element of preservation. As Pitkin writes, "our constitution is (what is relatively stable in) our activity."[262] Pitkin's formulation suggests that stability is an important part of constitutional maintenance.[263] Constitutional maintenance necessarily implies an element of preservation and continuity, and this in turn implies a set of limits to what we can change.[264]

A constitutional identity can change in at least two ways.[265] First, and most obviously, identity can change as the objects of our commitments change, are forgotten, or renounced. Consider a brief example. The several decisions we made at the founding about slavery greatly influenced subsequent ideas about what it meant to maintain the constitutional enterprise, and even whether it was desirable to do so. Did constitutional maintenance demand preservation of the institution of slavery, or of a conception of federalism that would enable it to subsist, as John C. Calhoun and others argued?[266] If so, then we might argue that the Reconstruction Amendments replaced our commitment to slavery, or to federalism, with a commitment to racial equality, and thereby worked a radical, and perhaps revolutionary, change in the constitutional order.[267]

Second, identity can change as our comprehension of what extant commitments mean or require of us changes over time. We might conclude instead that our commitment to federalism remained undisturbed by the Reconstruction Amendments, but that our understanding of what federalism meant was required to change as we embraced a commitment to human equality after the Civil War, perhaps in realization of constitutional aspirations that were manifest but only imperfectly realized at the founding. This might require us to excise practices, putatively constitutional in the sense that the text appeared to sanction them, that could not be reconciled with a commitment to our most fundamental of constitutional aspirations, as was argued by Frederick Douglass and Lysander Spooner.[268] Recalling my earlier observation about the permeability of the analytical categories of constituting/maintaining/failing, should we conceptualize this sort of change as constitutional maintenance or as a moment of reconstitution?[269]

Antebellum efforts at constitutional maintenance thus demanded inquiry into and raised conflict about the meaning of our constitutional commitments, about what kind of polity we aspired to become, about who "We the People" were, and about how (and for whom) we hoped to secure the blessings of liberty.[270] They teach us that a discussion of constitutional change requires us to *identify*, in the sense of ascribing or discerning *identity*, which principles are determinative of our constitutional identity, and to what extent, if any, those principles can be changed without changing who We are. Asking after the limits of constitutional change is to ask questions fundamental to constitutional identity.

It might seem strange to begin a discussion of constitutional amendment with a discussion of what we can change without changing who we are, but questions of identity are central to amending the Civic Constitution for two reasons. First, inquiries into constitutional change require us to settle on the baseline from which we can identify or recognize change.[271] Second, the concept of identity, in addition to raising questions about *what* we can and cannot change, also raises questions about *who* has the authority to set the conditions of amendment. In Michelman's words, "The charterers ('We the People of the United States') seem to stand . . . on a different plane of ruler-ship from the chartered ('our posterity'), as creators to creatures. Amending the Constitution therefore necessarily implicates tricky questions about both the reach and the locus of constitutional authority."[272] Or even more funda-mentally, as Paul Kahn has astutely noted, "Amendment is simply a point of contest between competing understandings of the political order."[273]

One point of contest concerns whether the constitutional order is first constitutional and secondarily civic, or first civic and secondarily constitu-tional. Implicit in this contest is the pull between the Constitution's consti-tutionalist elements and its civic elements, a tension that we explored in the Introduction and that is fundamental to constitutional identity. A related question is whether the American constitutional order is foundationalist (or rights-foundationalist) or is, in Ackerman's words, dualist-democracy.[274] The tension between the Constitution's civic and constitutional elements is even more pronounced if, as I intimated earlier, the Constitution includes entrenched or foundational commitments that cannot be abridged by the people.

The entrenched elements of the Civic Constitution imply substantial and significant limits to both the objects and the parameters of constitutional change and amendment. Put simply, an entrenched or a foundational com-ponent of a constitutional order is by design a hedge against change—an effort to immunize certain of our constitutional commitments against certain kinds of changes. Foundationalists typically hold that some constitutional guarantees locate their authority in a source other than a democratic act of will by the people.[275] Foundationalists, or rights-foundationalists (these are not quite the same thing, though there is an obvious familial resemblance),[276] trace the authority of at least some basic constitutional commitments to a source independent of the constitutional text or the social fact it represents. The authority of some constitutional principles is *pre*-constitutional, in the sense these commitments inhere not in texts but in the logic of the constitu-tional enterprise itself, or in a natural order, or human nature, or some other source.[277] I have argued, for example, that some principles are constitutive to constitutionalism, or inhere in the nature of the constitutional enterprise.[278]

The authority of foundational principles therefore does not follow from their democratic pedigree, but has some other provenance; their founda-tional status is independent of their s/election through democratic means. Indeed, the foundational elements of constitutional orders, precisely because they *are* immune to constitutional amendment, must set limits to the proper objects of democratic action. Foundational commitments are muscular limits on constitutional change, and hence on the authority of the people to reject or to replace constitutional principles.[279] Their foundational status, in other words, constrains the civic ambitions of the Civic Constitution.

Some constitutional texts make selected principles insusceptible to democratic invasion by entrenching them. The German Basic Law, for example, entrenches principles of federalism, human dignity, and the free democratic order.[280] An example in the American Constitution of an entrenched provision, immune from constitutional amendment because the people (acting as their constitutional selves) have so determined, is Article 5's stipulation that no state may be deprived of its equal suffrage in the Senate without its consent. An entrenched provision, like a foundational provision, is putatively immune from constitutional amendment. (I use the word "entrenched" in its strongest sense here; some scholars adopt a weaker sense, in which "entrenched" means simply that the principle in question has been constitutionalized and hence protected against normal mechanisms of political change.[281]) Its immunity, however, is grounded in a constituent decision of a sovereign people to grant it such status and is reflected in the constitution (defined in the catholic sense I described earlier, as comprising many texts and the civic practices that complement them) itself. Why might we do this? It is worth considering in some detail how entrenchment provisions relate to the dynamics of constitutional change and identity: the whole point of an entrenchment provision is to cabin constitutional change. Thus, the German entrenchment provisions limit change by ruling some kinds of changes, regarding the constitutional commitments regarding federalism, human dignity, and the free democratic order, out of bounds altogether. In other words, changes that would abrogate those commitments are illegitimate within the framework of extant constitutional principles. Of course, entrenchment provisions cannot literally prevent change if the people insist upon it—they are parchment barriers.

In such cases, entrenchment is a founding act, but it is also a strategy of constitutional maintenance, a way of conserving constitutional principles, compromises, or settlements we fear may be assailable. Some principles may be vulnerable because of the political circumstances of the founding. Founders routinely compromise principles in service of constitutional ends. Behind these compromises commonly are one or both of two fears—first, an apprehension that the act of constituting itself cannot proceed without such compromises, and second, a foreboding that what has been constituted may yet be undone by lingering conflict concerning some deeply contested matter. So we might explain Article 5's limits on the amendment process as a compromise to circumstances, or as a necessity of the Constitution's realization. Or we might see them as a compromise of our ideals: "Perhaps Article 5 entrenches provisions that reflect deep compromises with our Constitution's constitutive principles: the protection of the African slave trade with the principle that all persons are created equal."[282]

Implicit then and central to any constitutional order that utilizes entrenchment (or is foundationalist) is a sense that constitutionally orthodox change must fall within certain principled parameters. (In the American case, change must comport with the mandates of Article 5.) Change that falls outside the pale of entrenched principles is revolutionary by constitutional definition, whether or not it is revolutionary by any other measure. Consequently, the form a change assumes or the process it follows cannot be the sole standard of the constitutional legitimacy of that change.[283]

Without foundationalism or entrenchment of some sort, any substantive principle we embrace in the act of constituting must later be a fair target for constitutional change, including outright abolition or repeal.[284] Under such circumstances, all change is of the same character constitutionally, by which I mean there is no ordinal principle that enables us to distinguish between substantive change that is constitutionally permitted and change that is constitutionally proscribed. Likewise, there is no mechanism available to distinguish, constitutionally, between change that is nominal and change that is revolutionary; indeed, the terms have no sense constitutionally. We might use such language to refer to changes in their political, economic, social, or cultural dimensions, but those terms offer us no guidance in terms of constitutional or jurisprudential identity.

Some accounts of the American Constitution have concluded it is not a foundationalist or rights-foundationalist charter. Bruce Ackerman, for example, in *We the People*, concluded that the Constitution is not rights-foundationalist because it has no entrenched provisions. Instead, in Ackerman's view, the American Constitution should be described as a "dualist-democracy," in which our commitment is first to democratic rule, and secondarily to the protection of rights and liberties against legislative (i.e., democratic) encroachments. In contrast, he argues, rights-foundationalist regimes (Germany, for one) elevate the protection of (at least some) constitutional rights to first position. Ackerman underscores the difference through reference to practices of constitutional entrenchment. In *Foundations*, Ackerman finds significance in the absence of entrenched provisions protecting liberties in the American constitutional text. Their omission there, he concludes, suggests the American constitutional order cannot be "rights-foundationalist."[285]

I think Ackerman is wrong in characterizing the American constitutional order as dualist and not foundationalist.[286] Ackerman does not consider the possibility that principles might be entrenched even in the absence of a textual provision so indicating, a possibility that most foundationalists take seriously and that the Civic Constitution, comprised of many texts and practices, will have no difficulty comprehending. (This is especially surprising given his rejection of hypertextualism generally.) And Ackerman concedes, with more import than he acknowledges, that there are entrenched provisions in Article 5.

Jeb Rubenfeld has also argued that Constitution does not (and cannot) include entrenched claims, because "The very principle that gives the Constitution legitimate authority—the principle of self-government over time—requires that a nation be able to reject any part of a constitution whose commitments are no longer the people's own."[287] Consequently, a constitution cannot be entrenched; "nor can there even be a single permanently entrenched provision."[288] The core of Rubenfeld's argument is his conception of "constitutionalism as democracy," in which the principle of self-government as temporally extended requires that present iterations of We the People must have the authority to reject "any part of a constitution whose commitments are no longer" our own.[289] How then does Rubenfeld account for Article 5? There are two points to make here, because Article 5 has two significant components. First, Article 5 does erect significant barriers on the people's authority to rewrite the Constitution. Rubenfeld is willing to abide Article 5 limitations on the people's authority as a way of ensuring that the people are prepared to make a temporal (enduring) commitment to what We desire. He writes, "the function of the supermajoritarian process is temporal."[290] But Article 5 imposes a second limitation on the amendment process: It rules out some amendments altogether. Rubenfeld appears not to address the part of Article 5 that actually does entrench a constitutional commitment. I assume he must think that part of Article 5 is unconstitutional, or at least cannot and should not be enforced and so does not constrain our efforts to change the Constitution.

Entrenchment provisions are definitional markers. They enable us to understand what sorts of changes square with what I have called constitutive principles of the constitutional order, and which do not.[291] There are changes that may be effected without challenging the core legitimacy of the basic order or without forcing a change in constitutional identity. Changes of this sort may be subsumed within the larger definitional or predicate norms that constitute the constitutional order. They may, of course, work significant changes in that order, and thus effect transformations in it, to use Ackerman's word. But they do so in ways, again using Ackerman's language, that synthesize[292] those changes with the underlying commitment to first principles. Hence, to use an example, extensive changes in the practice of German federalism may result in a transformation of the Basic Law's understanding of what federalism is or requires, but a proposal to dismantle the federal order and replace it with a unitary state would repeal or obviate first principles.[293]

Changes of the latter sort do not maintain and consequently cannot be subsumed under first principles. (In specific cases, we may argue about whether particular changes fall into one or the other category. The disagreement is about whether the alteration challenges first principles, not over whether such principles exist or whether they constrain the process of constitutional revision.) Nor do they work a fundamental revision, or transformation, in them. Instead, they abrogate such principles or replace them with new ones. Change of this kind does not simply transform the constitutional order, but rather replaces it with something else.[294] It effects not a change in degree, but rather a change of constitutional identity.

Entrenched or foundational principles are thus rigorous constitutional limitations on the authority of the people to govern themselves. The apparent tension between entrenched constitutional provisions and the authority of the people to govern themselves is especially acute for the Civic Constitution, which takes the self-governance claims of constitutional democracy seriously. But its foundational elements mean also that the people are not free to make constitutional principles mean whatever they want them to mean. The ultimate criterion of "rightness in political arrangements," to borrow a phrase from Frank Michelman, is not the "entitlement of the people . . . to decide the country's fundamental laws," but rather the conformity of those decisions with the constitutive principles of constitutionalism. For this reason, the Civic Constitution cannot be described as a populist constitution, defined by Michelman as "the proposition that among the requirements of rightness in political arrangements the most basic is the entitlement of the people of a country . . . to decide the country's fundamental laws."[295] Popular constitutionalism elevates the principle of democratic participation in self-governance to a position of preeminence in constitutional decision making.[296]

In contrast to Ackerman and Rubenfeld, I argue that the American Constitution does establish a constitutional order defined by commitments that are foundational in station. I indicated in the Introduction that these foundational components, derived from the nature of constitutionalism itself, include commitments to the principles of limited government, separation of powers, accountability and constitutional review, reason and deliberation, human dignity, and equal moral worth.[297] These principles are constitutive of constitutionalism; we cannot deny them without sacrificing our commitment to constitutional government, even if we do so within the procedural confines of Article 5. Like the foundational components of the American constitutional order, the entrenched provisions in Article 5 of the constitutional text also tell us there are some issues for which the "requirements of rightness," include more than "the entitlement of the people . . . to decide."[298] Constitutional rightness also consists of fidelity to those basic principles, and the rightness of those principles is not simply a consequence of a decision made by the people to respect them. Instead, they inhere in the constitutional enterprise proper.[299]

Is it possible to reconcile foundationalism, or a commitment to foundationalist principles, with the civic component of the Civic Constitution? There are two approaches to resolving this difficulty. The first requires us to examine the relationship between the concepts of time and identity. The second approach requires us to understand how the terms "democratic" and "civic" differ in meaning.

Time and Identity

An entrenched constitutional provision, insofar as it allows the dead to govern the living, is necessarily an effort to govern across time. But it is not, as some critics mistakenly posit, fundamentally undemocratic in reach. Approached from this concern, the problem is one of authority—of whether and why actors at T^1 have authority to govern those at T^2. This is a longstanding problem in constitutional theory, highlighted by Jefferson's well-known remarks,[300] and even more directly in Noah Webster's observation that "the very attempt to make perpetual constitutions is the assumption of a right to control the opinions of future generations."[301]

Several scholars have exposed the flaws, both ontological and practical, that inhere in this Jeffersonian understanding of constitutional authority.[302] One difficulty is that on this objection the entire notion of constitutional restraints must collapse: every effort at self-government expires when the present runs into the future. To put it another way: any effort at self-governance must account for the passage of time; and, the problem of the dead governing the living is not different in kind than the problem of one moment in time governing any subsequent moment in time. Both require us to ask why the past has authority to bind the present, and why the present has authority to bind the future. Described in this way, the problem of generational authority is not peculiar to entrenched provisions, or to provisions, like Article 5, that might be said to rig the game in favor of past generations. It is instead an element of all efforts at constitutional governance precisely because all such efforts involve the past making a claim on the present.

It is true, though, that the problem of constitutional authority seems especially acute in dealing with entrenched provisions, and for foundationalists generally. Foundationalists do more than claim for the past/founders the authority to govern the present/us; they deny to the present/us the authority to make certain choices altogether.[303] Foundational provisions do more than rig the rules of the game or simply shift the power to control the agenda, though that in itself is a significant exercise of political power;[304] they foreordain, at least partially, the results of the game. The authority and the reach of the past over the present is a very substantial constraint on the present We to govern ourselves as we wish. As Rubenfeld observes, "a written constitution is a thing of the past; self-government belongs to the present."[305]

Every account of constitutional maintenance, because it presumes an authority on the part of the past to govern the present, must explain why we the living should respect that claim. The relationship between past and present is therefore an authority puzzle. Examining the relationship between past and present as an authority puzzle requires that we think systematically about the temporality of the constitutional enterprise, or about what Rubenfeld has called the "constitutional problem of time."[306]

Temporality is a component of any framework of governance that seeks to govern more than the moment.[307] Conceived in terms of the legitimacy of political authority, the temporal problem is endemic to all efforts at durable human governance, and not just to the Civic Constitution. Both the Juridic and Civic Constitutions assume intertemporality, but the temporal configurations they assume differ in important respects. The temporal structure implied by the Civic Constitution is less strictly linear and chronological than the Juridic Constitution. For the Civic Constitution, the authority puzzle is not just a problem concerning the authority claims of T^1 regarding T^2, or of T^2 regarding T^3. This formulation, and the conception of authority it embodies, presumes sharp analytical distinctions between the categories of creating, maintaining, and failing, as well as linearity in the progression from past to present to future.[308] Even accounts of constitutional authority that do attempt to account for the relationship between T^1 and T^2, or from past to present (Rubenfeld and Ackerman come to mind as notable efforts), typically conceptualize issues concerning constitutional authority as unidirectional and linear.

Embedded in that assumption is a specific understanding of constitutional identity. The authority puzzle implicitly assumes the claims of the past are claims made on us by someone other than ourselves—even if it is only an earlier version of ourselves.[309] Additionally, it posits that these claims of authority are different in kind, and more problematic, than a decision made by our current selves to govern our current selves. Consider the quote from Webster, earlier, in which he observed that the attempt to make perpetual constitutions "is the assumption of a right to control the opinions of future generations."[310] Implicit in Webster's claim is the supposition that *we* (the present) have no claim on *them* (the future). The absence of authority between two distinct (sovereign) entities is even more apparent in Jefferson, who sees no difference between the authority claims made by one generation over a subsequent generation and those from one nation to another, or between claims made across time and those made across space: "We seem not to have percieved [*sic*] that, by the law of nature, one generation is to another as one independant [*sic*] nation to another." [311]

Both claims make assumptions not only about *authority* but also about *identity*. They assume a locus of authority in a present "us" that is a different person or legal creature than a future "them"—as distinct from us as another sovereign nation state. Understanding the import of these assumptions requires an inquiry into who we and they the people are, or into our collective and intertemporal constitutional identity. The Civic Constitution takes identity as a project entrusted to the present and the future as much as to the past, and hence as a venture not settled by or determined by the founding.[312] It requires us to explore a conception of constitutional authority that runs in the opposite direction, from T^2 to T^1, from present to past, or future to present, and to do so while also acknowledging the simultaneous authority-claims that run in other directions.

Fully understanding the apparent tension between a foundationalist and a civic constitution therefore implicates the concept of constitutional identity, or identifying who "We" the people are. So we might instead characterize the temporal problem not as an authority puzzle but as an identity puzzle. We have an identity that resides in a specific conception of who we are and where we are in time. How we approach one concept influences how we see the other. Alexander and Schauer, for example, have argued that "[i]t is only the present (and not the past) that can constitute a legal order for its population, and the question of what (has and should have) the status of law can only be decided nonhistorically."[313] This position assumes our identity is fully in the present moment, that who we are now is not the We the People of the past or the future, because they (the past) have no authority to choose for us (the present)—a position deeply Jeffersonian and populist (in Michelman's terms) in nature.

A less obviously populist account is implicit in Ackerman's notion of constitutional moments. Michelman argues that Ackerman's fundamental object of analysis is the concept of the "generation," as in We the People constitute the Constitution through "a conversation between generations," and not the constitutional text or some theory of it (by which Michelman means a larger account of the Constitution's "rightness").[314] At bottom this generational approach is a kind of constitutional populism too because it assigns constitutional legitimacy to decisions made by the people (acting in the present, albeit in conversation with our past selves).

Michelman contends the authority claims made by the Constitution must always be contingent in the sense that We are bound to respect the constitutional voices of the past, not because they spoke constitutional truth, but because their voices are in some way our voices. As Michelman concludes, "Our task is nothing more or less than to listen to ourselves."[315] Implicit here is a conception of constitutional identity that exists in and through time, but also a conception of authority that is populist as well, for in listening to ourselves we locate the authority of the Constitution in ourselves (temporally extended), and not in its claims to truth or justice.[316] So insofar as conceptions of constitutional identity traverse time, they locate authority not in the past or in the present, but in a We that exists intertemporally. To this extent, the Civic Constitution must be a populist constitution. But as we saw, under the Civic Constitution, it is not the case that the ultimate criterion of constitutional rightness is simply that the decision in question was made by the people (defined temporally) our/themselves.[317]

Constitutional government cannot mean that We the People can do whatever we want and pretend that we are acting constitutionally. As Rubenfeld has argued, "for a people to be self-governing, there must be more than a politics permitting citizens to give voice to their will. There must be an inscriptive politics at the foundation of the legal order."[318] Rubenfeld makes two points here. First, the people are not an entity that exists only at a single moment in time. We the People exist in past, present, and future iterations, and our identity inheres in all three iterations simultaneously. Second, because it does, there must be an inscriptive set of commitments that informs the identity of the people—an inscriptive politics is a commitmentarian politics. In Rubenfeld's words, "self-government consists of living under self-given commitments laid down in the past to govern the future."[319] For Rubenfeld, these commitments are not foundational or entrenched, and cannot be, because the people must have the authority to reject "any part of a constitution whose commitments are no longer" our own.[320] Entrenched provisions cut too deeply into the democratic authority of a self-governing (and temporally extended) people.

We might conclude, then, that a foundationalist constitutional order is necessarily inscriptive, but not all inscriptive orders are foundationalist. In our case, I have argued, some of these inscriptive commitments *are* foundational, an entrenched part of our constitutional identity. This foundationalist constitution is not an undemocratic exercise of will by the past over the present/future (or as Schelling describes it, "a continual contest for control" between "two selves"[321]), but rather an ongoing commitment of a *single* self (our self) that has a past, present, and future. Imagining the "people" as a being that exists in time, as a living body politic that has a past, present, and future, takes some of the immediate sting out of the charge that foundational commitments are fiercely antidemocratic, or inconsistent with the civic elements of the Civic Constitution. I said "some" of the sting because even if we assign to the People a single or corporate identity, one that extends through time, we will not have solved entirely the problems of democratic political authority that inhere in these kinds of self-commands.[322]

We therefore can go some distance toward answering the democratic objections to self-commands by reconceptualizing them as commitments[323] We (identified in the temporally extended sense I discussed above) have made for ourselves. The move is not entirely satisfactory from the perspective of democratic theory, however, at least if our understanding of democratic theory does not reduce to the claim that the people, at any given moment, can do whatever they want. But few democratic theorists will embrace such a thin conception of democratic life. There are well-known difficulties with this position, not least that its underlying conception of what consent means— the capacity of morally autonomous persons to make rational decisions for themselves—must mean that we cannot consent to a political order that denies that very premise. Perhaps more importantly for an account of constitutional maintenance, as Murphy notes, "[a] current majority that decides to end self-government treats as less than equal not only their own future selves but also all other majorities that follow. . . . Democracy must mean more than one person, one vote, one time."[324] Most of us are willing to concede the need for some set of constraints on democratic choice, let's call them procedural, or instrumental, designed to make democratic choice feasible, not only at any single moment in time, but across time.[325] And behind these restraints are commitments to substantive conceptions of human and moral goods—of consent, rationality, and equal moral worth.[326]

On this logic, we might justify some foundational or entrenched constitutional provisions, even against populist conceptions of the constitutional order, as democracy-reinforcing. Some entrenched principles are not in tension with the Constitution's civic components but instead facilitate them.

Following the same logic, however, we might also conclude that we cannot defend some other foundational principles and provisions as strictly necessary or instrumentally important to the functioning of democratic self-governance.[327] I am generally reluctant to distinguish between procedural and substantive constitutional provisions in this way,[328] but to the extent the distinction works at all, it fails to provide a civic justification for most of the foundational commitments in the Constitution. Some of them, such as Article 5 and the constitutive principles of reason and deliberation, might be described as democracy-reinforcing, but others (such as the commitments to human dignity and equal moral worth) are less easy (though not impossible) to describe in this way. Consequently, the tension between a foundationalist understanding of the Constitution and the responsibility the Civic Constitution assigns to citizens to maintain the Constitution cannot be fully resolved by characterizing entrenched commitments as democracy-reinforcing or by insisting they find their authority in a democratic/populist decision by the people to adopt them.

Another approach might reconcile our commitment to fundamental constitutional principles and to civic engagement by immuring the former from the Civic Constitution altogether. This strategy begins by recalling what I argued in the Introduction, namely that the Civic Constitution is not the sum of the American Constitution—it exists alongside the Juridic Constitution. We might conclude, in consequence, that the responsibility of citizens to maintain the Constitution is shared with the maintenance responsibilities the Juridic Constitution assigns to courts, and moreover that the division of labor tracks more or less precisely the distinction between foundational/immunized provisions, assigned to judges and thus secure against popular mismanagement, and those entrusted to citizens.[329] (For a discussion of structurally similar arguments, in that they distinguish between parts of the Constitution that are judicially enforceable and parts assigned to other actors, see my treatment above of the under-enforcement thesis.) Part of the difficulty here will be to show that foundational commitments are justiciable (in the classic sense of the term)—to show, in other words, that such commitments match up well institutionally with courts, and also to justify the facile assumption that such principles are more secure if left to judges instead of citizens. Neither claim is self-evident, though we often take both, and especially the second, for granted.

There is a larger problem: If we assign responsibility for the preservation of foundational principles to the Juridic Constitution, and hence to judges, and insist also that they trump efforts by the people to violate them, then is it not the case that the Civic Constitution is necessarily inferior in rank to the

Juridic Constitution? I have already suggested that some of the civic components of the Civic Constitution are necessarily constrained by the entrenched components of the Constitution, so it might seem a short step to conclude that the Civic Constitution is subordinate to the Juridic Constitution in the same way. We should resist this conclusion. The Juridic Constitution, as I argued earlier, is territorial if not imperialistic in its character; it threatens to overwhelm the civic components of the constitutional order, in part by helping to create civic habits of deference and docility inimical to the engaged civic life that the Constitution demands.

One way to resist the subordination of the Constitution's civic elements to its juridic ones is to distinguish between judicial supremacy and judicial review of foundational principles, seeing in the latter a more modest claim by the Juridic Constitution to the territory of the Civic. Or we might attempt to distinguish, as have some scholars, between the interpretation of texts, assigned to courts, and of norms, assigned to other actors or to the people.[330] One advantage to these approaches is that they attempt to marry conceptions of the Constitution as justice-seeking and as deliberative, and so comport with my claim that the American Constitution is both Juridic and Civic. But they do so at a considerable cost to the civic element of the Constitution, reducing it in reach and importance. They teach citizens that their responsibility for maintaining the Constitution is largely ceremonious.

Civic Not Democratic

A second approach to resolving the strain between the Constitution's constitutionalist and civic elements builds on the distinction between democratic and civic. Although there is an obvious degree of overlap, "civic" is not simply a synonym for "democratic." The concepts of civic and democratic are not interchangeable; constraints on democracy are not also and equally constraints on civic life.

The term "democratic" refers to a specific way of grounding and organizing political authority, one in which individuals (citizens) have the right both to hold office and to determine officeholders through elections.[331] There are few limitations on either the objects or the organization of democratic authority, save for a small number necessary for any democratic society to function, such as freedom of expression and association, periodic elections, and the temporal limitations I discussed above.[332] Additional limitations on the exercise of democratic authority by the people must originate outside of democratic theory itself, say in conceptions of liberal democracy, or in constitutional democracy. In both cases, the additional limitations stem from the substantive, qualitative modifiers themselves or from values that originate from a set of concerns external to and independent of our commitment to democratic self-governance, such as our commitment to liberalism, or to constitutionalism.[333]

In contrast, the term "civic" references a particular way of thinking about our membership in a community we share in common with other members. It encompasses the sense of interconnectedness and duty, of responsibility and fraternity, that attends to political fellowship. Thus, according to one definition, "A morally and civically responsible individual recognizes himself or herself as a member of a larger social fabric and therefore considers social problems to be at least partly his or her own; such an individual is willing to see the moral and civic dimensions of issues, to make and justify informed moral and civic judgments, and to take action when appropriate."[334] Conceived in this way, a democratic form of government is simply a way of tallying preferences to produce a collective decision. A civic community, in contrast, is about establishing bonds of fellowship.[335] A strong civic culture likely has democratic elements, but not all democratic states have strong civic cultures, as is represented by the work of Putnam and others.[336] Civic engagement likewise encompasses a much wider expanse of activity than is captured by most understandings of contemporary democracy, in which civic activity consists chiefly of voting.

The constitutional components of the Civic Constitution are constraints upon democratic authority, or the authority of the people; they impose substantive restraints on the objects and the means of democratic action. They are also constraints upon civic life insofar as they supply the purpose of civic life and insofar as there must be some measure of congruence between the constitution of state and of civil society.[337] The same components, however, also inform, guide, and *enable* civic life. The commitments of our constitutional order provide the fabric within which civic action flourishes. They provide the objects and aspirations, or what we might call the grammar, of our shared public concern.[338] Constitutional commitments thus both limit and enhance our capacity and disposition to configure the common life of the community. Consequently, constitutional restraints, even to the extent they place significant limitations on the democratic authority of the people to govern themselves, are not necessarily encumbrances on the civic capacity of the people.

For the above reasons, grounded in how the Civic Constitution understands who We the People are, and in the differences between democratic and civic engagement, we should not overstate the tension between the Constitution's civic and constitutional components. We should also resist the sense that we must find a way to reconcile our foundational commitments with our civic ones completely. All identities, constitutional ones included, include diverse and indiscerptible elements.[339]

It should be clear, then, as we formulate an account of constitutional change under the Civic Constitution, that its civic elements are not so weighty that they override its constitutive constitutional elements. A discussion of constitutional change must first therefore account for the limits placed on the enterprise by the nature of the constitutional order that one seeks to change. This means we start from two fundamental premises. First, it means that we cannot accommodate as constitutionally authentic every change we make in the body politic, even if such changes have a broadly civic provenance. This has implications concerning what we can change and why, but also and just as importantly for the process of constitutional change. Second, the civic element of the Civic Constitution means our approach to constitutional change (and to amendments, as I shall elaborate below) must be one that accommodates, indeed invites, participation by an active and engaged citizenry.

Article 5 Amendments

On some readings, Article 5 is intensely inhospitable to the civic elements of the constitutional order.[340] First, Article 5 discourages civic attention to formal constitutional change by erecting significant structural impediments to success. The most obvious of these obstructions are the supermajority requirements that attach to both of the formal approaches to amendment specified in Article 5, but there are more subtle impediments as well, including the common practice of including time limits on the ratification process.[341] Second, the overall tenor and effect of Article 5 is to discourage formal constitutional change altogether or to preserve constitutional tranquility (in Madison's famous phrase). This in turn, like the Juridic Constitution generally, has the effect of teaching citizens to leave the constitutional enterprise to someone else. It may further intimate that the Constitution is perfect[342] or nearly so and as such needs our reverence, not critical appraisal. Levinson makes the point most forcefully about the bridling effects of reverence, noting the predilection of Americans to "venerate the Constitution and find the notion of seriously criticizing it almost sacrilegious."[343]

Although much of the foregoing discussion is common in Article 5 scholarship, Article 5 is not as disagreeable to the Civic Constitution as it might seem. First, the actual terms of Article 5 suppose that citizens can and should be trusted to take up amendments and thus have some ongoing responsibil-

ity for writing the Constitution. (This ongoing responsibility further complicates the founding/maintaining/failing heuristic.) The supermajority requirements place limits on the process, but the existence of the process itself, and
in particular the option that permits two-thirds of the states to call for a
convention, are premised crucially on a requirement of popular ratification.
In addition, tracking the distinction between democratic and civic, it may
be that Article 5's limitations function less as barriers to civic engagement
than as procedures designed to provide for it. Sager, for example, argues that
these requirements encourage citizens to deliberate about matters of constitutional change. It "causes popular constitutional decision-makers to take
account of their own future interests."[344] (Article 5 thus "fosters the partnership model" of judicial and popular responsibility for the Constitution
that Sager envisioned.[345]) Put yet another way, the apparent antidemocratic
features of Article 5 do not inhibit but in fact facilitate civic life.

This may be an overly generous reading of Article 5, especially given the
relative infrequency with which we amend the Constitution. But the vitality of the Civic Constitution should not be measured by the infrequency of
successful campaigns for amendment, in part just because the criteria for
success (defined as passage of an amendment) are so clearly freighted in
terms of stability.[346] Instead, the measure of success should be in terms of
civic mobilization, or how often citizens mount such campaigns, coupled
with some (admittedly imprecise) measure of public engagement in them.
Mobilization is a better metric because it incorporates the ethic of tending
as civic work and engagement.

Unlike constitutional amendments, *efforts* to amend the Constitution
are a common and notable feature of public life. Indeed, performing the
Civic Constitution is intricately caught up with the politics of constitutional
amendments. As Kramer and others have demonstrated, amendment campaigns are a rich source for finding the Civic Constitution alive and in practice.[347] There are many obvious historical examples, including the suffrage
movements of the late-nineteenth and twentieth centuries.[348] Even a narrow
reading of the object of the suffrage campaigns must recognize their centrality to and invocation of fundamental constitutional principles of representation, human dignity, and equality. (As I alluded to in my discussion of civic
education, their stories must be a part of our civic literacy.[349]) Contemporary
examples of civic mobilization include proposed constitutional amendments
concerning human life and abortion, same-sex marriage, balanced budgets,
school prayer, the Pledge of Allegiance, flag burning, term limits, birthright
citizenship, campaign finance,[350] and many others. Moreover, several of the
most profound modifications to the constitutional order in the past two cen-

turies, both in the form of Article 5 amendments (such as the Seventeenth, Nineteenth, Twenty-Third, and Twenty-Sixth) and statutory law (such as the abolition of literacy tests and poll taxes), are evidence of the Civic Constitution in practice as well as advances of the Civic Constitution itself, insofar as they facilitate civic participation.[351] These changes have augmented the civic elements of the constitutional order even as its juridic elements were consolidated through theories of judicial supremacy.

Extra–Article 5 Amendments

The Civic Constitution also bears on the much-discussed issue of constitutional amendment exterior to Article 5. As an initial matter, the Civic Constitution welcomes the idea, advocated by Ackerman, Amar, and others, of amendment outside the formalities of Article 5,[352] chiefly because it opens up space for civic engagement with constitutional politics—it affords citizens greater opportunity to act on constitutional matters. On this view, the constitutional activity described by Kramer and others as instances of genuine constitutional self-governance, or as instances of popular constitutionalism, might sometimes and on certain conditions amount to extraordinary constitutional moments of amendment.

The best known of these arguments is Ackerman's reference to exceptional constitutional moments, or points in time when the people, acting in concert, undertake profound, if not revolutionary, constitutional change through some other political process. Such moments include the robust changes in the American political order occasioned by Reconstruction and the New Deal.[353] In *Transformations*,[354] Ackerman rejects the hypertextualism of those who insist that constitutional change must be measured solely by Article 5. By hypertextualist, Ackerman means a reading of Article 5 that privileges it as the mechanism for legitimate legal change. Instead, we must get "beyond Article 5" and adopt what he calls a pluralist account of higher lawmaking. The reasons we must move beyond hypertextualism are centered chiefly upon the need to realize the promise of popular sovereignty. Realizing that promise means understanding how the polity can embrace and has embraced the process of constitutional reconstruction and higher lawmaking outside the parameters of Article 5.

Much of *Transformations*, therefore, is devoted to showing why a hypertextualist approach to Article 5 is an inadequate way of assessing constitutional change in the United States. The rejection of hypertextualism means, though, that Article 5 cannot be the only criterion we use to evaluate change. Of course, as Ackerman shows, it is not so clear even what the rules set out in Article 5 actually require. But the gravamen of Ackerman's point is not that Article 5 is vague. Rather, he disputes the claim by "most lawyers," who he thinks are positivists, that Article 5 is the sole mechanism for such change and that we are left always with a choice between the "legalistic perfection" of Article 5 and "lawless force" to assess change. That claim, he argues is "morally obtuse"[355] and wrong as a matter of history.

Once we are free of Article 5, what, if anything, constrains the processes of constitutional amendment? Are there limits on the amendment process? Are there substantive constraints that put some kinds of changes out of bounds? If so, the rejection of hypertextualism must mean those constraints cannot find their source in any written provision that speaks to entrenchment. This is not so much of a problem for foundationalists, or even for popular constitutionalists who take our constitutional commitments seriously, but it is a problem for Ackerman, who, as we saw earlier, insists there are no foundational or entrenched principles in the American constitutional order.

There are reasons, however, why the Civic Constitution might be less receptive to these forms of constitutional amendment, as Ackerman's own work demonstrates. The geniality of such approaches must be determined by an inquiry into the details of their own standards for determining the legitimacy of such change. A coherent account of constitutional amendment outside Article 5 must supply criteria to determine when we have crossed the threshold between change and amendment—and there is no reason why those criteria must be more accommodating of civic participation than is Article 5.

It is important to note, therefore, that both Article 5 and extra–Article 5 approaches to constitutional amendments must offer a way to distinguish between changes that are consonant with our fundamental constitutional commitments and those that are not. The discussion is complicated further when we consider the amendment process(es) and entrenched provisions. An approach we might consider, but should reject, would be to distinguish between Article 5 amendments and extra–Article 5 amendments by holding that some kinds of constitutional change must satisfy the terms of Article 5, whereas other kinds need not. We might argue that changes that impinge upon our most fundamental of commitments (whatever those are—a different discussion, but for now let's say the foundationalist or entrenched ones) must pass the (presumably?) more rigorous terms of Article 5, whereas amendments that do not can be left safely to other processes. We would argue that amendments that seek to alter a foundational or entrenched provision must overcome these higher burdens of process and procedure, and they warrant these tougher burdens precisely because they are foundational.

There are insurmountable difficulties with this approach. First, on this logic, entrenched provisions are not genuinely foundational, but only presumptively so. Conceived this way, foundational constitutional provisions are simply more important than other constitutional provisions—more important, that is, than those that are subject to amendment outside Article 5, but still subject to amending. But a provisional entrenchment is no entrenchment at all, literally a contradiction in terms. Moreover, determining which provisions are more important, and why, but are still subject to amendment, will be no easy task.

Second, why should we assign foundational principles and provisions to the Article 5 track instead of the extra–Article 5 amendment track? The presumption that Article 5's requirements are sterner or more burdensome and thus offer greater security for entrenched principles than those we attribute to the extra–Article 5 track depends upon what the actual requirements of the extra–Article 5 path are. Precisely because the path is defined by historical practice and the larger universe of constitutional meaning envisioned by the Civic Constitution, and not by the constitutional text, it will be difficult to determine in advance precisely what those requirements are or will be, or when they have been satisfied. (In Ackerman's model, the requirements are staged, or consist of a process that includes elements of signaling, proposal, mobilized deliberation, and legal consolidation.[356]) One approach to this question, although flawed in its own way, would be to consider the frequency of amendments under Article 5 and under Ackerman's alternative track. Using this approach—frequency of amendment—we are likely to find that the extra–Article 5 track is actually more rigorous, or difficult to satisfy, than the Article 5 track.[357] If this is true, then we must rethink the assumption that Article 5 should be reserved only for amendments that concern the foundational components of the constitutional order.

So, in the end, the Civic Constitution is sympathetic to the notion that there can be fundamental constitutional change, legitimate against some kind of rule of recognition, outside the parameters of Article 5. This is primarily because opening up the avenues for such changes provides citizens with direct and important opportunities not only to deliberate about the meaning and desirability of constitutional ideals, but also to take up active responsibility for, or to tend to, constitutional maintenance. Nevertheless, these extramural changes, like Article 5 amendments, must still comport with the constitutional (foundational) elements of the civic constitutional order.

CONCLUSION

Our obligation to maintain the Civic Constitution means preserving our commitment to a constitutional way of life, to maintaining a constitutional order more than a constitution. It is a charge entrusted to citizens as well as to institutions, and it comprehends far more than just constitutional interpretation by courts. It should lead us to reconfigure our understanding of constitutional institutions, offices, and processes, as well as what it means to be a citizen, in ways that move us away from the occasional and limited forms of citizenship that characterize the Juridic Constitution. We need a conception of citizenship that does not reduce to rights, but instead sees citizenship as including both rights-claims and civic obligations. Sturdy citizenship of this sort may be in decline, a victim in part of the Juridic Constitution, but we do not need to invent it. The vision of citizenship the Civic Constitution prizes is a living tradition.

ESSAY THREE

Failing

In this essay, I take up a topic I have dealt with before: constitutional failure. In an earlier work, I wrote, "Crises are especially important to the theory and practice of constitutional government precisely because they . . . challenge the claim that constitutions can govern."[1] I continue to think a comprehensive constitutional theory requires an account of constitutional failure, if only because failure is both the ordinary and the inevitable outcome of constitutional ventures. At a minimum, a general theory of constitutional failure must identify what we expect it to explain and what we expect it to accomplish. Is the purpose of such a theory to tell us how best to design constitutional orders? To predict when and under what circumstances constitutional failure will occur? To explain the dynamics of failure? To diagnose failure? To remedy it?

Nevertheless, my purpose in this essay is more modest: I consider what failure means as an incident of the Civic Constitution. I also discuss a particular kind of failure, what I will call "constitutional rot," as unique to and best comprehended through the lens of the Civic Constitution. I concentrate on this particular form of failure for an important reason: constitutional rot will be impalpable to those who approach the Constitution as a legal construct. Constitutional rot is not a problem of constitutional legality or a failure of constitutional law—it is a failure of constitutional politics, a specific genus of failure unique to the Civic Constitution, but facilitated by the Juridic Constitution.[2] The inability of the Juridic Constitution to comprehend this sort of failure testifies to its insufficiency as a way of understanding constitutional life. The Juridic Constitution alone, that is to say, is inadequate to a comprehensive or even a workable theory of the Constitution, in part because it does not allow us to make provision for a certain and especially insidious manner of constitutional failure and because it contributes to the likelihood of that failure. Finally, and of more immediate significance, I weigh whether we are in a state of constitutional rot now.

NOT A GRAND UNIFIED THEORY OF
CONSTITUTIONAL FAILURE

What is constitutional failure? That the varieties of possible failure are many
is axiomatic for students of constitutional governance. If, as Elkin observes,
"[t]he central concerns of constitutional theory . . . are the realization of
good regimes, [and] their maintenance once established,"[3] then the category
of failure must be equally comprehensive. As an abstract proposition, there
are many ways for constitutional democracies to fail. States break down
for many reasons—they may be overcome by a stronger external force or
by domestic violence, or succumb to economic collapse.[4] Speaking broadly,
and imprecisely, any failed state possessed of a constitution might be said to
have failed constitutionally. There is, in other words, an empirically trivial
sense in which any and every failure of a constitutional state is an instance
of constitutional failure.[5]

   Is there any stronger, nonobvious sense in which these sorts of failures
are meaningful as *specifically* constitutional failures?[6] As James Fleming has
observed, "[t]o be talking about distinctly constitutional failure, surely one
has to be talking about failures of the Constitution, failures caused by the
Constitution, failures stemming from a feature or defect of the Constitution,
or the like."[7] The difficulty, of course, is that tracing causality in this way
is simultaneously too difficult (how do we disaggregate and then measure
the impact of the relevant variables?) and too easy (the objects of constitutional engineering typically extend, at least in part, to important aspects of
economy and culture, as well as to politics). Any number of failures might
be "attributable to the Constitution in the sense that they are made more
likely by our constitutional design."[8] Collapsing them all under the rubric
of constitutional failure is likely to mislead us as to the reasons why states
fail, and just as likely to misdirect our efforts to forestall or remedy failure.[9]

   One place we might start is with typology. Following Brandon, we might
identify four kinds of failure, including a failure "to employ basic principles
of constitutionalism" that inhere in (written) constitutionalism, a failure of a
particular constitution (or of a constitutional text), of a constitutional order
(or of the political regime authorized by a constitution), and of constitutional
discourse (or when a "constitutional order is unable to speak coherently
or, more seriously, to sustain itself through constitutional interpretation").[10]
Whittington also identifies four possible kinds of constitutional failure: resistance; forgetting; neglect/ignoring; and contesting.[11] In contrast to the Brandon typology, which concentrates on what might fail, or the objects of failure,
Whittington's list tells us how things can fail, or the modes of failure.[12] The

schema are not mutually exclusive, and failure in either one need not be confined to a single category. More importantly, success in one category does not preclude failure in any other category.[13] Indeed, success in one category may make failure in another more rather than less likely, as we will see below when we discuss how civic deliberation might result in a repudiation of constitutionalism itself as a way of organizing political community.

These typologies are useful starting points, but insofar as they overlook substantive differences of meaning and content—for example, insofar as they mask over important differences in the Juridic and Civic Constitutions, or between different types of constitutional orders— they take us only to recognizing different kinds of things that might fail and how they might do so, and not so far along to recognizing or identifying actual instances of failure. This suggests our definition of failure must presuppose some understanding of constitutional success,[14] as is implied in the logic of Carl Schmitt's inquiry into the relationship between the norm and the exception (because the category of exception can be recognized as such only against a prevailing, superordinate norm).[15] Sotirios Barber has made a similar point, arguing that a theory of constitutional failure "depends in part on a successful theory of constitutional ends."[16] In Barber's terms, "a constitution is successful if the government it establishes maintains arguable fidelity to its terms and arguable progress . . . toward . . . publicly reasonable versions of constitutional ends."[17] I want to stress that success must be tied to identifiably *constitutional* ends.[18] We might disagree about what those ends are and their provenance, but they must be recognizable as commitments to a constitutional order as distinct from the organization of political community on the basis of some other set of principles. (This recalls the distinction between constituted and constitutional orders.)

The distinction between constitutional legality and constitutional politics, a principal point of divide between the Juridic and the Civic Constitutions, has an important bearing on our understanding of constitutional disappointment. Failure under the Juridic Constitution is typically approached as an inquiry into the threats posed by crises or emergencies, such as those posed by war or terrorism or civil insurrection. In addition, in such conceptions, failure typically assumes one of two primary forms. One is institutional inadequacy, or the inability of constitutional institutions to act (or to be capable of acting) in ways that resolve crisis and yet still conform to constitutional strictures, conceptualized more in terms of limitations on power than as fidelity to aspirations.

The second typically assumes the form of a failure of constitutional rights and civil liberties, or the inability to resolve crisis without effecting far-reaching compromises of liberty. Barber associates these two categories of crisis with two distinct schools of constitutional theory. Conceptions of constitutional failure as institutional failures, he argues, have behind them proceduralist constitutional theories, or theorists (such as John Hart Ely) that "emphasize democratic processes and associated values and conditions (political freedoms mostly) over goods like national security and prosperity."[19] Failures characterized by "chronic disregard" for constitutional liberties, Barber continues, are associated with negative libertarian constitutional theories, represented by theorists like Randy Barnett[20] and Michael Zuckert.[21] These theories "emphasize negative rights over constitutional processes and substantive ends like national security and the general welfare."[22] Barber's own conception of constitutional failure is informed instead by his commitment to a third kind of constitutional theory, which he describes as "welfarist." Welfarist constitutional theories (or "ends-oriented" theories) "place equal or greater emphasis on preambular ends like the common defense and the general welfare."[23] For welfarist theories, constitutional failure must be approached in terms of substantive constitutional ends and the conditions under which those ends may be secured or frustrated. At a less abstract level of analysis, the definition of constitutional failure must incorporate, or be tied to, the definition of constitutional ends themselves. Following Barber's classification, the Civic Constitution is a welfarist theory of the Constitution, largely because it defines a constitutional way of life both in terms of ends and as an end in itself.

THE CHRONOLOGY OF FAILURE

Because all constitutions are a project of We the People past, present, and future, constitutional failure, like the constitutional enterprise writ large, has a chronology. The Civic Constitution might fail at the moment of conception, by neglecting to establish the institutional and structural architecture necessary for its realization.[24] Additionally, the Civic Constitution might fail through inadequate constitutional maintenance, or by neglecting to re-create the architecture and the citizens necessary to sustain itself at every subsequent moment in the constitutional enterprise.[25] Establishing the temporal location of potential failure in a founding moment and in maintenance again reveals the artificial linearity of the founding/maintenance/failure heuristic; the categories, though chronologically sequential, are not insular. And because they are not, the categories of founding failures and maintenance failures are equally porous.

Founding Failures

The Civic Constitution might fail at the moment of conception by neglecting to establish the institutional and structural architecture necessary for its fulfillment or for attaining and practicing a constitutional way of life. In Essay One, I concluded that founding the Civic Constitution requires an effort to constitute the civic spaces where participation can take place. If a principal component of the Civic Constitution is its effort to constitute a particular kind of political order, one that prizes civic deliberation and engagement, then the most obvious and profound of failures would be a political order that creates neither space nor opportunity for civic agency. Similarly, failure might consist in the regime's incapability to constitute a constitutional order in which citizens have sufficient incentive to attend to their constitutional responsibilities, or lack sufficient opportunities and resources to do so. What might cause this? We might fail by constructing institutions in certain ways, or by assigning to them certain functions (such as strong-form judicial review), that discourage civic engagement and thus subvert our constitutional ambition. In both instances, the failure is not of law or legal commands, but rather a failure precipitated by unsound constitutional design.[26]

A constitution might also fail in the making by neglecting to constitute citizens equal to the demands it makes on them. Founding failures thus include the inability of the constitutional order to produce citizens sufficiently knowledgeable of constitutional principles and norms to discharge their civic responsibilities. (On the other hand, the weak form of contemporary citizenship is not just a potential marker of constitutional failure under the Civic Constitution; it might simultaneously signify the success of the Juridic.) The Civic Constitution might fail to constitute citizens (i.e., those who are unquestionably members of the relevant constitutional community[27]) with the skills and aptitudes necessary to sustain the constitutional order itself. As we saw in Essays One and Two, it is at least arguable that the founders envisioned an enlightened and engaged citizenry. Stephen Elkin concludes, however, that Madison neglected to provide for the cultivation of such citizens, and that this neglect represents a serious omission at the heart of Madison's constitutional design.[28] If he is correct, then the failure to constitute the kinds of citizens presupposed by the Constitution must be a kind of constitutional failure more broadly. And because the Constitution must continually constitute new citizens, it is also a failure that might manifest at later moments in the constitutional chronology.

Maintenance Failures

Inadequate maintenance references failures of the ordinary institutional, structural, and civic mechanisms of constitutional maintenance we discussed in Essay Two. Maintenance failures, for the most part, are not about our fidelity to commitments but lie in how we (fail to) pursue them. I first intimated that we can approach constitutional failure through the lens of inadequate constitutional maintenance in my piece on the Civic Constitution in a festschrift for Walter Murphy.[29] A few years later, in his last work, Murphy covered some of the same ground, explicitly noting, as I had, for example, that some schemes for the allocation of interpretive authority (such as departmentalism and coordinate construction) are more conducive of constitutional maintenance than others (such as judicial supremacy).[30] This is not the place for a full review (or critique) of Murphy's understanding of constitutional maintenance. I reference it to reinforce the claim that our understanding of constitutional failure must be centrally tied to our understanding of what constitutional orders are.[31]

Speaking at a high level of abstraction, maintenance failures can take two forms. First, we might fail to maintain constitutional institutions in ways that encourage civic responsibility through civility and tending. Constitutional maintenance might fail, for instance, if we adopt structural devices and mechanisms, such as judicial supremacy, that routinely disable and disfranchise citizens from constitutional decision making. Hence, as I argued in Essay Two, systems of judicial supremacy (and the preclusive presidency, as I will argue below in my discussion of constitutional rot after 9/11), contribute to maintenance failures by dampening or discouraging civic agency. Poor maintenance might manifest similarly in the selection of interpretive methodologies, such as some kinds of originalism, that confound maintenance with taxidermy.[32]

Secondly, inadequate constitutional maintenance might result in constitutional failure in cases where we do not do enough to nourish a conception of citizenship that gives citizens the disposition, the knowledge, and the skills necessary for civic life. So we should count as maintenance failures a system of civic education that does not equip citizens to act with the degree of civic agency necessary to discharge their responsibility for maintaining the Constitution. Similarly, we should count as potential maintenance failures conceptions of constitutional doctrine that restrict or diminish associational freedoms, for these reduce opportunities for citizens to learn and to practice the virtues we associate with civic life.

CONSTITUTIONAL FAILURE
AND THE JURIDIC CONSTITUTION

Under the Juridic Constitution, the expansive territory of constitutional failure is ordinarily confined to an examination of the conditions in which law itself might fail. This kind of failure has generated a well-known and sophisticated scholarly literature.[33] Perhaps the best known treatment is also one of the earliest—Clinton Rossiter's *Constitutional Dictatorship*.[34] Rossiter's work on the constitutional dictatorship was part of a larger scholarly literature that included work by Carl J. Friedrich, Frederick Watkins, Karl Loewenstein, Edward Corwin, and Carl Schmitt,[35] much of it prompted by the breakdown of several European constitutional democracies in the interwar years.

The central problem that animated this scholarship was this: how do we protect the rule of law and the Constitution from the corrupting politics of emergency? Put in the broadest possible terms, such treatments conceptualized crisis as a problem of constitutional legality. But not all theorists concluded that the problem could be solved within the framework of legality. Reaching back at least as far as Locke, some accounts of executive prerogative argued that there must be times when an executive may act outside of the law. In the *Second Treatise of Government*, Locke argued, as did Jefferson later, that "a strict and rigid observation of the laws [in some cases] may do harm." The executive must have a power—the prerogative—to act "according to discretion, for the public good, without the prescription of law, and sometimes even against it."[36] In Locke's formulation, the prerogative power exists outside the law, without its prescription, and may sometimes be used against law, if necessary (in the executive's view), to preserve the law itself against misfortune. Nevertheless, as Tulis has argued, there is an important respect in which Locke's sense of the prerogative, although it may be used against law, remains bounded by and emanates from law itself—chiefly because the prerogative is a supplemental corrective to the insufficiency of law as an ordering principle of political experience. Thus, as Tulis writes, "For Locke, prerogative power . . . grows out of law and remains in service to it, monitored by the people for whom it is exercised."[37]

Most if not all of these early studies conceptualized constitutional crisis as institutional failure or as a failure to respect constitutional liberties; constitutional fixes for these failures, to the extent they could be had, typically called for an involved set of procedural and institutional mechanisms designed to guard against the possibility that such failures would become permanent, or for more and more elaborate forms of constitutional engineering. Rossiter, for example, drawing heavily on the Cincinnatian/Roman model, developed an elaborate set of eleven conditions to govern the exercise of the constitutional dictatorship. (Following the same precedent, Friedrich reduced the Roman model to four requirements.)

Writing in the immediate aftermath of the Nixon presidency, Arthur M. Schlesinger Jr. devoted much of *The Imperial Presidency* to the problem of emergency government.[38] Schlesinger concluded that emergency government should be recognized "for what it is: an extra-constitutional resort to raw political power, necessary but not lawful." The alternative view, that the Constitution contemplates (if it does not authorize) extraordinary power, renders the document so meaningless that it fails to possess real authority even in normal conditions. Corwin reached a similar conclusion earlier in his pointed analysis of the effects of World War II and the New Deal upon American constitutional law,[39] and it is central to my discussion later in this essay of the concept of constitutional rot. The similarities between Schlesinger's argument and the Lockean defense of executive prerogative are substantial. The prerogative of the Crown, or some institution like it, suggested for Schlesinger that the American presidency "must be conceded reserve powers to meet authentic emergencies," albeit subject to a number of restraints, most but not all of which were directed toward establishing the authenticity of the emergency.

Typically these restraints did not find their source in the constitutional document; presumably their authority resides in political necessity and in their fidelity to the Roman principle that all exercises of emergency power must be directed to defense and restoration of the constitutional order. But we might well wonder why principles of this sort should bind in the absence of an obligation to respect limitations in the constitutional document itself.[40] As Madison counseled, "The restrictions however strongly marked on paper will never be regarded when opposed to the decided sense of the public, and after repeated violations in extraordinary cases they will lose even their ordinary efficacy."[41] It is not difficult to see why a crisis severe enough to overwhelm barriers consecrated in law will also overwhelm the extratextual restraints proposed by Rossiter, Schlesinger, and others.[42]

More than any other scholar, Carl Schmitt revealed that constitutional crises are not problems about constitutional legality, as first formulated by Locke's description of the prerogative, but are instead contests between law and politics. Where Locke saw the prerogative as a problem grounded in and bounded by the law itself, Schmitt saw crises as states of exception to governing norms, intimately caught up with sovereignty and politics. For Schmitt, the power to decide the exception is sovereignty itself: "Sovereign is he who decides on the exception."[43] The exception exists outside constitutional legality, outside the Constitution itself, and hence cannot be constitutionalized or constitutionally tamed. "So, in the state of exception, in the space outside the constitutional order, the statesman is sovereign because only his will governs."[44]

Where Locke, Rossiter, Schlesinger, and, more contemporaneously, Ackerman and others[45] have proposed schemes to discipline and constitutionalize the prerogative by attaching conditions to its use, Schmitt concluded that the executive's powers in the state of exception cannot be constrained by law. Schmitt accomplished this by making the fundamental point, too often overlooked, that a written constitution is no guarantee of political or democratic unity, much less a guarantee of constitutional democracy itself. In *Legality and Legitimacy*,[46] for example, Schmitt concluded, "the law cannot protect itself."[47] As Ellen Kennedy observes, this meant that the formal guarantees of a constitution cannot be independent of political circumstances.[48] Schmitt alone comprehended that a crisis was not a self-contained problem about law, but was instead a problem about the relationship of law to politics and thus could not be insulated from politics. Both the causes and the solutions to constitutional crisis are found in politics.

Kennedy reminds us that Schmitt's comments were not simply an indictment of Weimar, they were also part of a larger attack on liberalism as a governing political philosophy.[49] Hence, the failure of Weimar, to which most of Schmitt's work was directed, was not confined to specific constitutional provisions and practices but was instead a failure of the larger constitutional jurisprudence and the conception of deliberative democracy upon which it rested. The flaw was not in Article 48; not a failure of constitutional design or constitutional institutions. Rather, it was a failure of the "substance informing the constitution of political unity; the institutions of the text did not cease to function in a technical fashion—they were evacuated of all meaning and significance."[50] In considering the viability of Weimar's jurisprudence in the context of liberal thought, Schmitt moved far beyond the legalistic jurisprudence of contemporaries like Kelsen. Hence, following Schmitt's lead, I described the fall of Weimar as a failure not of the Weimar Constitution but as a failure of constitutional jurisprudence—a formalist, positivist jurisprudence unable to distinguish between legality and legitimacy, or between friend and foe, and unable to open questions about the legitimacy of the state or about a conception of justice relevant to the relationship of power and authority in the state.[51]

Understanding the differences between the Constitution as law and as politics can help us to resolve some of the problems that have long been a

staple of crisis scholarship.[52] Tulis has observed that "Schmitt's argument
was designed to contest an overly legalistic view of constitutionalism. The
American system is not as vulnerable to his critique as was the Weimar regime because the core of our arrangement is political, not legal. President
and Congress contest the context of their powers by negotiating the terrain
they cover. . . . Citizens and scholars concerned about the scope of executive
power in America today would do better to criticize Congress than to worry
so much about executive power, per se."[53] Tulis is correct that the core of the
American political order is political rather than legal, but he overestimates
the vibrancy of the political order and consequently the capacity of politics
or political contestation to restrain the exercise of extraordinary presidential
power. Or to put it another way, he does not recognize the extent to which
the Juridic Constitution undermines the health of the political order. Later
in this essay I shall argue that the Juridic Constitution disables civic conversation by facilitating the growth of the imperial, unitary, or preclusive
presidency, which poses a direct challenge to the concept of the separation
of powers Tulis describes, and by debilitating the culture of civic deliberation
that might enable us to contest extraordinary claims of power.

   Tulis presents his argument as a stylized account of constitutional aspiration more than as an empirically accurate description of contemporary
political practice. Indeed, he notes "there are good reasons to argue that two
features of our political condition erode, though they do not totally subvert,
the separation of powers design."[54] One such feature is the development of
political parties, and the second is the "legalization of inter-branch conflict,"
which means that both "the Congress and the president now routinely defer
to Courts over matters about which they had previously contested."[55] As
should be clear by now, the legalization problem Tulis references is larger
and more comprehensive than the way he describes it. Indeed, the post-9/11
jurisprudence, if anything, seems designed precisely to shore up the dynamics of interbranch discussion Tulis defends. Instead, the legalization problem
is an example of how the Juridic Constitution undermines a culture of civic
deliberation.

   In brief, then, under the Juridic Constitution, the concept of constitutional failure is conceptualized in terms of legality and manifests chiefly as
a failure of institutions and/or of rights. In contrast, the Civic Constitution
asks us to consider a type of constitutional failure that is different from and
that transcends the failure of constitutional institutions and the protection of
constitutional liberties. Indeed, as I shall argue below, there is a specific kind
of constitutional failure that can occur even and only when constitutional
institutions appear to be in good repair.[56] Under the Civic Constitution,

the problem of failure thus requires an inquiry that reaches well beyond questions of legality. It asks us to consider whether there are failures that cannot be measured by the metrics of constitutional doctrine and case law, or whether there are kinds of failure that go instead to the desirability, or even the possibility, of securing and achieving a constitutional way of life. They include failures of design, and failures of maintenance. Implicit in these conceptions of failure are assumptions about the meaning of constitutional success.

CIVIC SUCCESS

What constitutes success under the Civic Constitution? Although we can properly dismiss longevity as the principal component of constitutional success, the ability of a constitutional regime to maintain itself over time is an element of a comprehensive definition of constitutional success. A regime that cannot persist through time is unlikely to achieve a constitutional way of life. Whatever its other successes (such as the Great Land Ordinances) and failures (among them, its inability to create a central government sufficient to establish a prosperous economic order), the Articles of Confederation and Perpetual Union were a constitutional failure for this reason alone. Our first constitution failed to meet its own improbably ambitious claim to perpetuity, or to resist time itself. But the Articles failed not only to persist through time—they failed more fundamentally to constitute a collective We and to secure the ambitions and purposes of the collective We. Constitutional success must be measured not only temporally but also in terms of ends realized or lost. The durability of a constitutional order provides some evidence that our constitutional ends have been or may yet be achieved, but some kinds of constitutional failure can exist alongside, or independent of, temporal success. Indeed, in some cases, resilience obscures other and more important markers of constitutional achievement.

Under the Civic Constitution, we should define constitutional success as palpable progress toward achieving a constitutional way of life.[57] A constitutional way of life is comprised of two obligations—a commitment to the principles and norms of constitutionalism proper, and a commitment to a conception of civic life in which citizens possess civic agency and assume responsibility for the constitutional project.[58] Constitutional success means maintaining respect for and realizing these commitments, or some measure of both fidelity and civility. Success in one does not guarantee or necessarily result in success in the other: we might maintain and respect fundamental constitutional norms and yet fail, as a people, to assume collective responsibility for them. Similarly, robust civic engagement is no assurance that We the People will elect to honor constitutional values or to pursue constitutional ends as our highest or first ambition.

CIVIC FAILURE

Our definition of success as progress toward achieving a constitutional way of life prompts us to ask: How might the Civic Constitution fail? Is there a connection between a failure of constitutional ends and the means or mechanisms of constitutional failure? Are there specifically civic modes of failure?

If the meaning of constitutional failure takes its cue from constitutional ends (or purposes), then failure under the Civic Constitution would be the defalcation of its citizens to live a constitutional way of life. This means failure can take two forms under the Civic Constitution. We might fail to honor our commitment to constitutional norms (failures of fidelity), and we might fail our civic obligations to shoulder responsibility for sustaining the Constitution (failures of civility). And as with our treatment of the meaning of constitutional success, a failure of fidelity does not presuppose a failure of civility, just as a failure of civility does not necessarily signify a failure of fidelity.

Distinguishing between failures of fidelity and of civility reminds us that in most cases constitutional failure is not obvious or easy to establish. Success and failure are not absolute states, but are instead matters of judgment, in part because success does not require perfection and in part because the terms are political constructs, not bright-line legal tests.[59] A related difficulty goes directly to the meaning and measurement of failure: How do we distinguish between constitutional inadequacies, defects, imperfections, deficiencies, flaws, blemishes, shortcomings—and constitutional failures? What would constitute evidence of failure? Where would we find evidence of it? How much evidence is necessary to substantiate the proposition? Except in truly rare instances, whether we have succeeded or failed in achieving a constitutional way of life will involve crude and tentative assessments based on ambiguous evidence. Just as important, under the Civic Constitution the success or failure of the constitutional enterprise is not simply a matter of judgment. It is also and no less a question about *who* bears responsibility for making the judgment about whether we have made discernible progress toward achieving a constitutional way of life.

Failures of Fidelity

Failures of fidelity implicate our commitment to constitutionalism as a way of organizing political community or our commitment to the constitutive principles that define constitutional governance. They are *not* unique to the Civic Constitution. Any constitutional order that neglects to make and to secure these fundamental commitments can be said to have suffered a failure of fidelity.[60] I have said "neglects to make and to secure" to suggest questions about what fidelity means and how we should define it as a proposition about the Civic Constitution.[61]

The concept of fidelity comprehends a number of different meanings. The term traces to the Latin *fides*, for faith, and there is still a significant sense in which most uses of fidelity incorporate a component of faithfulness. Fidelity's most common denotation—as a requirement of married or committed partners to refrain from sexual relationships with others—is predicated both conceptually and linguistically on this notion of faithfulness; when a partner breaks the link of fidelity, we typically say he or she has been unfaithful.

An accusation of infidelity, Luban argues, is both narrower than and different from an accusation of disloyalty or a lack of devotion. It is narrower because it does not extend to claims that might seem similar, such as accusations that a partner has treated us badly or disrespectfully. Infidelity covers less territory than disloyalty or untrustworthiness; it refers instead to a specific kind of duplicity, one that includes elements of intimacy and loyalty.[62] It is also different from these other accusations because it implies a "three-party relationship involving two spouses and a rival, not a two-party relationship involving spouses alone."[63] Fidelity in marriage speaks to an exceptionally strong bond between persons who have freely chosen to make a voluntary and temporally sustained (perpetual?) commitment to each other. Less common, although still within ordinary usage, we may speak of fidelity between friends and in other kinds of personal relationships, or fidelity with respect to one's religious faith and duties. These other uses of the concept of personal fidelity are also predicated on notions of obligation, faithfulness, and betrayal as between ourselves and another. In neither context, however, do we use the term habitually.

In friendships, the bonds are typically (although not always) less intense and less permanent, and the language of fidelity is correspondingly less common. Instead, we are more likely to describe friendships, and failures thereof, in terms such as trust, constancy, and loyalty, not in terms of fidelity. Similarly, although the usage is hardly unknown in many religious traditions, speaking in terms of fidelity is less frequent, especially as regards abstract propositions of faith and belief, than terms such as "devout, pious, observant, or practicing."[64] Granted, there are similarities between marital fidelity, fraternal fidelity, and religious fidelity. Religious fidelity, depending upon the particulars of one's religious belief and theology, may seem similar to marital fidelity by involving an element of personal commitment (to a spouse; to a deity). But in general, marital fidelity connotes an exceptionally intense and personal commitment to another person and less to a set of abstract propositions of faith or belief.

In Luban's view, law is "not the kind of thing that deserves fidelity,"[65] not because it is unworthy of our attachment (though he thinks it is deeply flawed), but rather because the law is an abstraction. Luban distinguishes between personal fidelity and interpretive fidelity. Personal fidelity involves obligations to others "unmediated by a relationship with an impersonal or abstract entity" like the law.[66] Interpretive fidelity speaks to "being faithful to an original,"[67] as in being faithful to a text, or to a work of art, or, as Lessig has famously observed, to an original text in a work of translation.[68] (Interpretive fidelity thus incorporates an element of mimetic accuracy in the act of interpretation. In Essay Two I described juridic citizenship as essentially mimetic in nature, not unlike how Luban describes the practice of interpretive fidelity.) Fidelity in law is closer to the concept of interpretive fidelity than to that of personal fidelity. Luban concedes that interpretive fidelity in some legal relationships has "moral significance" and involves "moral relationships of trust," but nonetheless concludes "they are different from relationships of personal fidelity."[69] Moreover, "interpretive fidelity is not a sufficient condition of obedience or respect for the law,"[70] whereas, by contrast, personal fidelity is sufficient to create an obligation.

I suspect Luban thinks interpretive fidelity in law is a weaker form of fidelity, of less consequence and moral significance than the stronger form of personal fidelity. The distinction is, however, a useful way of determining what fidelity means as an attribute of the Civic Constitution. The form of fidelity contemplated by the Civic Constitution encompasses interpretive fidelity (We the People should seek the authentic meaning of the Constitution, while recognizing that questions of interpretive authenticity are multifaceted, contestable, and a temporal project entrusted to a We that has a past, present, and future), but is closer to the strong-form fidelity we associate with personal fidelity. This is because civic fidelity is not to an abstraction like the law, or even to the Constitution (equally an abstraction, especially conceived in juridic terms), but to a constitutional way of life as a civic and communal enterprise. Civic fidelity, in other words, is not about interpretive fidelity to the law or to legality, or dependent in any significant way on "faithful interpretation" of a legal text. It is about fidelity to a mutual intertemporal project, to a conception of ourselves that has a past, present, and future.

Both the Juridic and the Civic Constitutions can suffer failures of fidelity. But because they presuppose different answers to the question of *who* bears responsibility for protecting and maintaining the Constitution, as well as a unique understanding about *what* must be maintained and protected, they address the problem of constitutional fidelity in different ways. Broadly speaking, the Juridic Constitution relies upon the reverential or *Miracle at Philadelphia*[71] approach, or a type of filiopiety.[72] Its solution to the attachment problem is to inculcate in citizens a deep reverence for all things constitutional—to teach citizens to love the Constitution superficially and from afar, but not to engage it critically, lest their passion overwhelm their limited capacity for reason in public affairs. As Hannah Arendt has noted, this has resulted in a citizenry that worships the Constitution.[73] And with the advent of Constitution worship, we have precisely the citizens Jefferson feared: "Some men look at constitutions with sanctimonious reverence, and deem them like the ark of the Covenant, too sacred to be touched. They ascribe to the men of the preceding age a wisdom more than human, and suppose what they did to be beyond amendment."[74] Attachment to the Juridic Constitution is less a matter of fidelity than fideism.

Fidelity to the Civic Constitution is grounded in the stronger notions of community and fellowship that attend the practices of civility and tending. Both civility and tending involve a significant element of interpersonal exchange, or a kind of civic intimacy that characterizes a political community located in notions of reciprocity and shared responsibility for a common project.[75] Fidelity to the Civic Constitution demands fidelity to a way of life and to the creation and maintenance of a political community constituted in and defined by a commitment to values and principles whose meaning transcends their application and enforcement as legal commands.

What does it mean to speak of constitutional failure under the Civic Constitution in terms of a failure of fidelity? In constitutional terms, a failure of fidelity might occur, as Whittington has proposed, "when important political actors threaten to become no longer willing to abide by existing constitutional arrangements or systematically contradict constitutional proscriptions."[76] The concept bears some resemblance to Tushnet's description of "constitutional hardball," a key characteristic of which "is that at least one of the participants in the struggle [over the basic features of the extant constitutional order] makes claims or engages in practices that the other side believes violate 'previous constitutional understandings.'"[77] One difference between Whittington's definition of failure and Tushnet's conception of hardball, however, is that in cases of hardball, "[b]ecause the parties fight over pre-constitutional understandings, claims and practices of constitutional hardball have a curious feature. They are at least plausible or 'within the bounds of existing constitutional doctrine'"[78] and so seem not to implicate questions of fidelity to the Constitution itself, though they might involve arguments among the contestants about whether and to what extent their various understandings can or cannot be defended against constitutional commitments.

From the perspective of the Civic Constitution, there are two difficulties with Whittington's definition. First, it is too confined in its assignment of fault and responsibility. Fidelity is an obligation of, and infidelity may be ascribed only to (or at least primarily to), a select number of governmental officials (i.e., "of important political actors"[79]), presumably because the obligation to maintain the Constitution is theirs (and theirs first, if not alone). This is unsatisfactory under the Civic Constitution because it gives no weight to the concept of a genuinely civic obligation to maintain the Constitution, and thus comprehends no significant concept of civic infidelity.

Second, the definition assumes that a decision not "to abide by existing constitutional arrangements" is an act of infidelity. This assumption is unwarranted for several reasons. A decision not to abide by constitutional arrangements might be a decision to respect other, higher-order constitutional commands.[80] In such cases, we might speak, in a limited sense, of infidelity to a constitutional text, but there is no infidelity to the larger constitutional universe in which the text resides.[81] We must distinguish between fidelity to constitutional texts and fidelity to constitutional principles. This is precisely the point I argued in *Constitutions in Crisis*, where I insisted that constitutional norms must govern how we respond to crises even if that crisis warrants a release from textually established constitutional rules and provisions.[82] In addition, even a decision to disregard basic principles of constitutionalism (in addition to textual commands) might be something other than an act of infidelity if it represents a reasoned, deliberate decision to renounce our commitment to constitutional precepts writ large. So, we must ask: is a reasoned decision to reject constitutionalism as a way of life a failure of fidelity? Infidelity presupposes a betrayal of an obligation whose obligatory character is not in question. It *assumes* obligation. Just as failure assumes an account of success, infidelity assumes an obligation or an attachment to which we should be faithful. The relationship is complicated further if we consider that in such cases the betrayal is not of principles, but of ourselves, or as We the People present betraying We the People past and future. In Essay Two I said I would defer a fundamental inquiry concerning constitutional maintenance—*why* should we maintain the Constitution?—to Essay Three. I turn to it now to illuminate the relationship between constitutional infidelity and failure.

A deliberative decision to reject commitments previously embraced is not necessarily an instance of constitutional failure, though it may well represent a failure of a specific constitution.[83] We can imagine two sorts of cases. In the first case, we might imagine a decision to reject a specific constitution as an inferior instantiation of fundamental constitutional values, or as an inadequate manifestation of how to realize them. In such a case, a specific iteration of a constitutional text has failed in the sense that it is inadequate to, or has failed to facilitate, the achievement of a (more perfect) constitutional way of life. We must distinguish constitutional texts, always and necessarily contingent and particular, from universal principles of constitutionalism itself.[84] The constitution(al) text has failed, but there is no failure of fidelity to constitutional principles more broadly.

The more difficult case is where the rejection is of the desirability of constitutional commitments proper. In this second iteration, we might reject constitutional values and principles in favor of some other way of organizing political life.[85] Is this constitutional failure?[86] One argument that it might not be relies on the presence of collective deliberation in making the decision to forswear constitutional commitments. The argument is that insofar as a decision to abandon constitutional principles is itself an exercise of reasoned deliberation, or is civically informed, it should not be decried as constitutional failure, though it may result in a polity constituted in some other, nonconstitutional fashion.

In considering the question, we must remember that reason and deliberation are themselves a constitutive principle of constitutionalism.[87] Reason and deliberation are constitutional ends in themselves, not simply instrumentalities to other constitutional ends. So there is no failure in such an instance, in the qualified sense that one of the two primary components of the Civic Constitution (the requirement that citizens take responsibility for and exercise constituent power) has been satisfied. But deliberation does not comprise the whole of our constitutional commitments; employing reason and deliberation to reject other constitutional commitments, therefore, is not enough in itself to warrant a claim of fidelity to a constitutional way of life because that way of life encompasses more than just its civic or deliberative component—it encompasses as well a commitment to the fundamental precepts that make up liberal constitutionalism. This tells us there may be profound tension between the constitutional and the civic elements of the

Civic Constitution. Strong and robust civic engagement might yield a reasoned, deliberative decision by We the People to renounce constitutionalism itself as a way of organizing political community.[88] This is more than a failure of a constitutional text or of a constitutional order. It is a failure to act constitutionally, in the largest, most comprehensive meaning of the term. But it is also a deliberate and conscious act—less a failure of neglect or omission than an act of volition, a knowing, deliberate, and informed choice to pursue another way of life. Moreover, these new/other prescriptions are not better or "more perfect" understandings of a constitutional way of life, but rather are *different* understandings of how to organize political community.

A measure of success in achieving the civic purposes of the Civic Constitution might therefore yield a larger failure if it results in repudiation of other foundational constitutional principles. (Similarly, fidelity to those principles does not guarantee civic success, and indeed may endure even as we suffer a failure of civic engagement.[89]) Hence, in my hypothetical the principle of civility has been utilized to reject an equally weighty commitment to the normative principles that comprise constitutionalism itself. (The civility principle has occasioned a failure of fidelity.) The failure is the failure of constitutional norms to constitute and govern political community—a failure of fidelity. So, we have constitutional failure in the sense that we have chosen not to govern ourselves in constitutional terms or with regard to constitutional norms, those having been supplanted with some other set of nonconstitutional prescriptions.

There is constitutional failure of another sort in my hypothetical. Recall Murphy's insistence that "democracy cannot mean, one person, one vote, *one time*."[90] In a case where we have rejected our commitment to constitutionalism in favor of some other way of organizing politics, the failure is of the Civic Constitution to maintain itself as a project of the people conceived in intertemporal terms. The failure is to maintain a commitment to constitutional values that govern not only We the People now, but We the People in the future. Our infidelity is not simply to abstract constitutional principles but also and just as significantly to ourselves, or to a future iteration of We the People. We have failed our future selves.[91] (Recalling Luban's argument that fidelity runs to persons [who], more than to principles [what].[92])

Is (a failure of) constitutional fidelity the same thing as (a failure of) constitutional faith? Balkin's description of faith "involves an attachment to the constitutional project," or "putting ourselves on the side of the Constitution," notwithstanding its imperfections and injustices, but believing that they may still be overcome and that the tools necessary to overcome them can be found in the Constitution itself—hence, we can *redeem* the

Constitution. (Contrast this with Levinson, whose sense of the importance of the Constitution's imperfections is that they are so weighty that they cannot be redeemed.[93]) Our attachment to that project must be complicated by the recognition that the constitutional project is not only imperfect, but is in many ways unjust. As Balkin observes, "the Constitution-in-practice still has elements that maintain, preserve, or actively promote injustices."[94] Why, then, should we affirm our fidelity to this project? Redemption means "to have faith in a people and in the development of the institutions of constitutional democracy through which popular will is expressed. Therefore, what is redeemed is not simply a set of promises in a document, but a transgenerational project and a people."[95] Hence, *we* can redeem the Constitution, and in so doing, we redeem *ourselves*.

Constitutional faith, especially when coupled with Balkin's discussion of living originalism, relies heavily on a constitutional culture in which We the People must assume responsibility for redeeming the Constitution; this redemptive project, necessarily intergenerational, requires the political and social mobilization of citizens who, partly as a consequence of their own faith in the Constitution, actively work to correct its imperfections and injustices.[96] As Linda McClain remarks, "for Balkin's approach, faith alone is not enough: constitutional redemption requires that constitutional actors work to realize their constitutional vision."[97] Redemption is impossible, however, if We the People reject constitutionalism as an inferior or less desirable way of imagining political community, or as a granfalloon.[98] Is a rejection of constitutional principles in favor of other (nonconstitutional) commitments a loss of faith, as Balkin might write, in the constitutional project defined in transgenerational terms? The answer must be yes, and in the largest possible sense, for the rejection/loss is not in our (in)ability to attain a constitutional state of affairs under this particular constitution, but under any and all constitutional forms.

I want to underscore that this failure of fidelity, or to order ourselves constitutionally or by constitutional norms, might not be a bad thing, or even represent a failure in some larger moral sense. Indeed, it might yield a community with a more muscular commitment to principles of moral justice and human flourishing. Constitutional failure is not always the worst option or result, or even necessarily a bad outcome. We might conclude that to fail constitutionally is the preferable course, especially if the new order appears more likely to achieve justice or is a morally superior way of organizing political life. As Adrian Vermeule has observed, "the whole enterprise of constitutional fidelity, construed as constitutional faith, reflects a misplaced set of priorities, an overestimation of the role of constitutionalism in political and social life, and a tendency to bow down before a set of idols created by, of all people, politicians and lawyers."[99] Our highest obligation to our (future) selves may not be to live *constitutionally*, but to live *justly*.

Failures of Civility

Civility is the civic virtue that asks us to reflect upon and to examine "what can philosophically be proposed" as the good society as constrained by our commitment to constitutionalism.[100] Constitutional civility, in other words, requires that what we propose as reasons for public action must comport with or at least reference our constitutional commitments. Incivility, therefore, is decidedly not the absence of courtesy or manners or the failure to act politely. Instead, it is the failure to take up the primary responsibilities of good citizenship, to reflect upon, to deliberate, and to act upon the public good.

Incivility is thus a failure to abide by the basic predicates of constitutional life.[101] Its occasional manifestation might be described as a constitutional imperfection, and not all constitutional defects amount to constitutional failure.[102] Epidemic incivility, however, represents a unique kind of constitutional failure—a failure not only of the fundamental constitutional norms of human dignity and equal moral worth (norms that both require civility and depend upon it for their realization), but of the civic life necessary to sustain the Civic Constitution.

It is not easy to determine when incivility amounts to constitutional failure, or even to find much agreement about how pervasive or significant it is. Susan Herbst, for instance, catalogues several notable examples of rudeness and incivility associated with the 2008 presidential campaign and health care in 2009, but concludes that incivility is not substantially more common now than it was in earlier periods of American history.[103] Herbst observes that concerns about incivility are part of "far larger, longitudinal conundrums of political culture,"[104] and that there is no definitive answer to the question of whether "incivility is destructive and blocks proper democratic debate."[105] In contrast, Sandy Maisel, conceding that a precise definition of civility is elusive, thinks "something is different today."[106]

Robert Putnam, to take another prominent example, maintains that for many years the social capital necessary to sustain civic life has been in substantial decline: "In America, at least, there is reason to suspect that this democratic disarray may be linked to a broad and continuing erosion of civic engagement that began a quarter-century ago."[107] Stephen Carter likewise argues the United States suffered a precipitous decline in public civility beginning in the 1960s, a decline both caused by and represented by the loss of "commonality," or the absence of widely shared meanings and commitments that bind us as "social glue."[108] What is lost in this constricted public space, these critics assert, is the rich fabric of community and a commitment to civil discourse and dialogue.

Assuming there is merit in these critiques, they raise an important question: is evidence of *cultural* incivility also evidence of *constitutional* incivility? The question tracks my earlier discussion of constitutional failure as distinct from the failure of constitutional regimes in general. There are two points we must address to resolve this question. First, what is the difference, if any, between incivility as a cultural proposition and incivility as a constitutional trait? Second, can constitutional civility flourish amidst cultural incivility?

Part of the answer to these inquiries may hinge on definition: if cultural civility is shorthand for polite behavior and mannerisms,[109] then we might think its absence does not diminish civic deliberation. Indeed, we might even suggest, as have many critics, that civility suffocates genuine deliberation.[110] There are, however, reasons to resist connecting up the two types of civility. First, constitutional incivility represents a specific sort of shortcoming, a defect in the capacity or willingness of citizens to reflect upon the demands of a constitutional way of life or to deliberate about matters of public or common interest in a universe of reason constrained by constitutional commitments. Constitutional incivility is less a matter of manners than a failure to own up to and practice one's civic responsibilities and obligations. So cultural incivility is not quite the same thing as constitutional incivility. Second, the recent work on popular constitutionalism suggests strongly that even in the midst of epidemic cultural incivility, there remains a live tradition of civic constitutional engagement.[111] Hence, we should not rush to conclude that complaints about incivility in political life in general, no matter how persuasive, are the same thing as critiques about incivility as a *constitutional* failure.

On the other hand, some argue that cultural civility is an important structural precondition for the very possibility of deliberation.[112] Constitutional civility is both a disposition to engage with others and a way of approaching deliberation and conflict. Civility is a prerequisite for conversation and reasoned exchange, and in this sense "democracy rest[s] on a foundation of civil society."[113] Calhoun similarly concludes that civility is a virtue "that fits citizens for life in a participatory democracy, civility thus gets equated with respectful dialogue—keeping a civil tongue."[114] Cultural civility is also a reflection of constitutionalism's commitment to the basic norm of human dignity and equal moral worth.[115] Constitutional and cultural civilities are therefore mutually reinforcing.

My discussion in Essay Two about the relationship between the constitution of the state and the constitution of civil society also suggests there is an important relationship between constitutional and cultural incivility. I argued that constitutional maintenance requires a measure of integration and correspondence between the constitution of the state and the constitution of civil society: "the Civic Constitution envisions a civil society infused with concern for the transmission and flourishing of its commitments."[116] Consequently, the Civic Constitution authorizes the state to "pursue a formative project to foster the capabilities for self-government, both in the sense of democratic self-government and personal self-government."[117] Barber appears to reach a similar conclusion about the relationship between state and society when he concludes that a successful constitution is one that produces a "healthy politics,"[118] especially if our understanding of politics extends beyond institutions and elections. Following this argument, there cannot be a sharp distinction between the cultural and constitutional forms of incivility; widespread cultural incivility is very likely to promote constitutional incivility.[119]

How would we remedy a failure of constitutional civility? As we saw in Essays One and Two, there are several mechanisms of constitutional design that can help to increase civic agency. These include structural and architectural elements that promote interpretive pluralism, as well as comprehensive civic education and expanded opportunities for civic participation.[120] In addition to developing civic virtue through an expansive program of civic education, an effort to remedy incivility will demand that we find ways to encourage and promote the development of civic spaces (both metaphorical and physical). Opening up civic spaces will require public investment to protect and promote civic space, as well as some rethinking about how we nourish or constrict such spaces through constitutional doctrine. In particular, we will need to recalibrate a number of doctrinal approaches to current First Amendment law, including our current understandings of free speech zones and the extent of speech and associational rights in public forums, in limited public forums, and on private property,[121] which work individually and in tandem to constrict civic space.

Is there a relationship between fidelity and civility? A failure of civility, unlike a failure of fidelity, *is* exclusive to the Civic Constitution. Failures of civility may or may not result in failures of fidelity. As a community, we might fail to be civically minded without being unfaithful to the full complement of constitutional principles; we might, without engaging or caring for constitutional norms, nevertheless continue to profess our devotion and commitment to them, trusting in their enforcement by courts and other institutional actors. In this case, the constitutional order might continue to respect (some) constitutional precepts, even as its citizens fail to live a constitutional way of life. So there is no necessary connection between failures of civility and failures of fidelity. But this analysis misses an important point: as I shall argue below in my discussion of constitutional rot, failures of civility, although logically severable from failures of fidelity, make failures of fidelity more probable.

We must remember also that constitutional incivility does not threaten the filiopietistic sort of attachment the Juridic Constitution favors. Indeed, the Juridic Constitution welcomes citizens who act incivilly, in the sense that they do not ordinarily engage in the self-reflective manner described above. The kind of attachment valued by the Civic Constitution might disrupt the juridic concept of maintenance, because under the Juridic Constitution strong civic engagement is thought to be potentially subversive of constitutionality and the rule of law more generally.

To conclude: failure can occur at two points in the life cycle of constitutional regimes and can take two forms. First, we might fail to abide by the constitutive principles that make up constitutionalism proper, thus occasioning a failure of fidelity. Second, we might fail to create or might neglect to nourish the conditions and mechanisms necessary to sustain civic maintenance, resulting in a failure of civility. Infidelity and incivility do not always amount to constitutional failure; sometimes they are simply constitutional imperfections. The difference between faults and failures is necessarily a question of judgment; it cannot be measured by a bright-line test. But no less importantly, it is also a question of to whom that judgment should be entrusted. The Civic Constitution puts that responsibility in the people themselves, while recognizing they might fail to exercise it.

CONSTITUTIONAL ROT AS A VARIETY OF CONSTITUTIONAL FAILURE

Behold an ugly picture:[122] a citizenry unwilling to hold its representatives or itself accountable to basic, fundamental constitutional norms, either because our attachment to them is outweighed by some other end (such as security) or impulse (such as fear), or perhaps because it does not *know* what those norms and values are or why or even if they are at risk. I have in mind a constitutional order that does not formally repeal or repudiate elemental constitutional values, and in which all of the forms and appearances of constitutional legality are maintained, but one that systematically violates or ignores basic constitutional commitments. I do not mean what Murphy called "constitutionism,"[123] or what Loewenstein earlier called "fictive constitutions,"[124] where the Constitution exists on paper only and makes no serious claim on political practice or the hearts of citizens. I mean, instead, a circumstance where the Constitution inspires reverence and heartfelt devotion (where we all profess true allegiance), but does not constrain political practice and where the people take no responsibility for that consequence.

To take an acute hypothetical, envision a functioning constitutional order, with separation of powers, strong-form judicial review,[125] and a bill of rights, all of which appear to be fully functional and in good repair. (Recalling our discussion about how to distinguish flaws from failures, in every working constitutional democracy there will be deviations from constitutional ideals and all manner of everyday infirmities. That does not mean we cannot distinguish between flawed constitutional orders and fictive constitutional orders.) Now, imagine the same constitutional order being in service of ends (such as slavery or pervasive racism) and/or employing means (such as torture and other violations of the principles of human dignity and equal moral worth) that are fundamentally incompatible with the constitutive premises of liberal constitutionalism. Moreover, in my hypothetical, no institutional actor entrusted with responsibility to maintain the Constitution, nor the people themselves, holds us to account for compromising our constitutional commitments—indeed, we may not recognize them as compromises at all. I have in mind, in other words, simultaneous failures of fidelity and civility. In such a case, we have constitutional rot.

Constitutional rot is a specific kind of constitutional default. Rot sets in when all of the formal guarantees and institutions of the regime appear to be in full working order, but when their meaning and significance "has been evacuated,"[126] or when they wait upon programs and policies that are fundamentally incompatible and cannot be reconciled with the normative premises of constitutional government.[127] In this case, the Constitution has failed, but its forms linger; it exists as mere text.[128] Constitutional rot can occur, in other words, only in cases where we calculate constitutional success in terms of legality and where our understanding of success and failure embraces no criteria other than legality.

Constitutional rot is a state of constitutional being in which the exterior forms of constitutional legality appear functional, but are indifferent to or in service of ends or pursued through means that cannot be squared with the normative presuppositions of constitutionalism. It is a kind of failure where the neglect or subversion of constitutional precepts is of those precepts understood not in terms of legality or the violation of legal rules, but in terms of aspirations and commitments. Rot occurs when questions of legality obscure questions of constitutionality *and* where the people are unwilling or unable to take up those questions as their own. It is made possible where the people abjure responsibility for those commitments to judges and hence is facilitated by the Juridic Constitution. Put simply, rot lies at the confluence of failures of fidelity and failures of civility.

This kind of failure cannot be identified in the way most scholars of constitutional crisis insist. It is not marked by the formal suspension of particular textual constitutional commands or by suspension or repeal of constitutional texts. Such moments assume that crises and failures are clearly demarcated, or, as Schmitt might have said, that there is a clear distinction between the normal and the exceptional. The concept of rot muddies this distinction by undermining the categories themselves, and by doing so silently.[129] Instead, rot occurs precisely and only when there are no apparent or obvious markers of these kind. Part of the reason I call it rot is because the failure is neither loud nor obvious, but rather is quiet, insidious, and subtle.[130]

I take up the concept of constitutional rot for two reasons. First, I hope to demonstrate that the Juridic Constitution does not enable us to recognize rot. Constitutional rot is invisible, or incomprehensible, to the Juridic Constitution, because the failure is not legal in character, or of legal forms, but rather of the normative principles and premises of the constitutional order.[131] We cannot see this failure through the lens of the Juridic Constitution precisely because the regime maintains both the forms and appearances of constitutional legality. The Juridic Constitution therefore significantly narrows the sorts of questions we can bring to the study of constitutional failure. Under the Juridic Constitution we ask a single question: do our policy choices comport with the judicially enforceable (thin) constitution? Once the relevant legal actors have addressed this question it is, for all practical purposes, constitutionally settled. (I argued in Essay Two that settlement is a primary purpose and a chief virtue of the Juridic Constitution.)

In other words, arguments that such policies, even if legal, are incompatible with or a betrayal of our constitutional commitments are out of bounds under the juridical constitution. I say "out of bounds" precisely because they are *not* arguments about legality. And the participants in the legal forums to which such discussions are limited will lack both the skills and the incentives (and the perceived authority, insofar as such questions are nonjusticiable) to consider them. The answers to these questions require an exercise of judgment and are grounded in politics, not in law. The issues are *political* in character—they require an exercise of civic judgment and not the formal(istic) application of specialized legal rules. What has failed in cases of constitutional rot is not the law, but the larger order in which the law resides. Constitutional rot is a political construct, not a legal one.[132]

The Civic Constitution opens up a conception of constitutional failure defined in terms of fidelity and faithfulness to larger constitutional norms whose meaning transcends the meaning of law or legal principles. It is these questions, of identity, fidelity, and fealty that Schmitt insisted are at the center of constitutional inquiry and analysis. And as Schmitt observed, such questions are irreducibly political in their meaning; their application cannot be reduced to legal formulas and formalisms. Constitutional rot is a failure of the Constitution in its larger, more elevated identity, of the principles that give it weight, dignity, and transcendence.

Earlier in this essay, I indicated that the success or failure of the constitutional enterprise is a question of judgment. The concept of constitutional rot tells us it is also a question about *who* bears responsibility for making that judgment. Because juridic accounts of the Constitution begin with the proposition that maintenance is fundamentally an activity grounded in law, they likewise conclude that failure is a legal construct. These two assumptions lead easily to the conclusion that the responsibility for diagnosing and preventing failure is primarily a task for courts. Under the Civic Constitution, however, the determination of our fidelity to constitutional commitments cannot be confined to or entrusted to courts because to do so is itself to abjure one of those constitutional commitments, as well as to transform an inquiry into fidelity into a narrower analysis of legality. In this way, the Juridic Constitution contributes to constitutional rot by fashioning a constitutional order in which citizens do not comprehend their own responsibility for preventing it.

How will We the People know if rot has set in, especially in the absence of judicial findings of constitutional illegality? Because our constitutional commitments are a source of intense and rich disagreement, there will always be questions about whether any particular public policy choice can be reconciled with what they permit. These sorts of disagreements, however unwelcome they may be as regards questions of legality (recall Moore's observation about dichotomous results and the differences between legal disputes and political disputes),[133] are at the heart of civic deliberation about the meaning of the Constitution. Moreover, I want to emphasize that these sorts of disagreements are not evidence of constitutional rot but are instead signs of constitutional vitality and well-being. Rather, it is their *absence* that speaks to rot and that should lead us to think in terms of constitutional failure. Their absence is a sign of a citizenry that has abandoned its responsibility to tend for the Constitution.

My second reason for taking up the topic of constitutional rot is to consider whether we are in a state of rot now, or to think about whether the Constitution has failed. As I have indicated, the possibility of failure is a precondition of constitutional success. Or to put the matter in another form: Fidelity to the Civic Constitution requires that we consider the possibility that rot has set in.

Recognizing Rot:
Constitutional Change after 9/11

In considering the constitutional implications of the antiterrorism security regime adopted after 9/11, we must explore not only what that regime means for constitutional institutions and for constitutional liberties, but just as importantly, what it means for civic life more broadly.[134] Among the challenges to constitutional government linked to the 9/11 era are the rise of the surveillance state, data mining, indefinite detention and the suspension of habeas corpus, harsh interrogations and torture, extraordinary renditions, military commissions, armed drones, and targeted killings.[135] Although there were statutory and administrative precursors to some of these policies,[136] most of them have their immediate incitation in the attacks on 9/11. For instance, soon after 9/11 President Bush sought and received statutory authority under the Authorization to Use Military Force (AUMF) to use "all necessary and appropriate force" against those that had perpetrated or supported the 9/11 attacks "in order to prevent any future acts of international terrorism against the United States by such nations, organizations, or persons." Relying in part on the AUMF and in part on his authority as commander-in-chief,[137] President Bush then issued a military order authorizing the use of military commissions for trying certain classes of individuals for terrorism-related activities.

In addition, the Bush administration secured expedited congressional passage of the USA Patriot Act, under which the federal government may exercise an extensive assortment of powers that threaten a wide variety of constitutional principles and liberties, including the presumption of liberty, the right to counsel and to confront witnesses, access to the courts and habeas corpus, as well as rights to privacy, freedom of speech, and associational liberties.[138] In general, the Patriot Act broadens the definition of "terrorism" to include domestic terrorism, thus increasing the number of activities to which the act's expanded law enforcement powers can be applied. More specifically, the act does three things.[139] First, it expands the authority of law enforcement agencies to search telephone and e-mail communications, as well as medical, financial, and other records.[140] Second, it relaxes restrictions on foreign intelligence gathering within the United States, in part by authorizing government agencies to gather foreign intelligence information from both U.S. and non-U.S. citizens and by altering the Foreign Intelligence Surveillance Act (FISA) to ease the gathering of foreign intelligence information.[141] Third, the Patriot Act expands the secretary of the treasury's authority to regulate financial transactions, particularly those involving foreign individuals and entities.[142]

Especially noteworthy are secret intelligence-gathering programs that authorize the wiretapping of overseas calls to and from residents of the United States without a warrant and outside the statutory framework established by FISA. FISA requires a warrant from special courts for any communications surveillance that concerns foreign intelligence, and permits surveillance of American citizens only if they can be shown to be agents of a foreign power. (The proceedings of these courts are secret, but it is widely known that they nearly always issue requested warrants.[143]) As reported by the *New York Times* in 2005 (the *Times* sat on the story for nearly a year before reporting it), most of the major telecommunications companies allowed "the government to install surveillance equipment in their switching stations, agreed to route overseas calls through domestic switching stations, and helped the NSA pore through the vast communications flowing between the United States and certain countries in the Middle East."[144] The new program, adopted by the president in secret and without consultation with Congress, was "an end run around FISA,"[145] and the Obama administration, until very recently, has likewise sought to insulate surveillance programs from congressional and public oversight.[146]

In addition to the AUMF, the Patriot Act, and various surveillance programs, the security regime established by the Bush administration and expanded by the Obama administration includes the use of drones to assassinate individuals whose names are on "kill lists" prepared by the Central Intelligence Agency and the Pentagon, without congressional or judicial oversight. Under this program, the United States avers authority to kill suspected terrorists, including United States citizens, overseas.[147] Some news accounts reveal that, in addition to targeting individuals, the program has expanded to include "signature strikes" in which the government does not know the identity of individuals, but targets them based on patterns of behavior that have not been made public. The *New York Times* recently reported that the government counts all military-age males in a strike zone as combatants unless there is explicit intelligence posthumously proving them innocent.[148] Other news reports indicate that a "disposition matrix" is used to augment the "separate but overlapping kill lists" maintained by the CIA and the Pentagon. Overseen by the National Counterterrorism Center (NCTC), the matrix has two primary functions. The first is data mining: it collects and aggregates surveillance data about American citizens without warrant or judicial review. Second, it oversees a matrix that determines the disposition (including the execution) of suspected terrorists, including American citizens, without judicial due process or administrative oversight; "the matrix is a centralized clearinghouse for determining who will be executed without due process based upon how one fits into the matrix."[149]

Another fundamental feature of the post-9/11 security regime is the use of torture to interrogate detainees in United States' custody. The Bush administration's decision to utilize what it called "harsh interrogation" is well documented.[150] The techniques of interrogation included prolonged exposure to white noise, sleep deprivation (often by shackling detainees while standing), humiliation (some shackled detainees were forced to wear diapers), stress positions, exposure to extreme heat and cold, exposure to menacing dogs, forced nudity, waterboarding, walling (slamming detainees against false walls constructed of plywood, often as many as twenty to thirty times in close succession), confinement in extremely close spaces, and threats to sexually assault detainees and their families.

The Bush administration made the decision to torture almost immediately after 9/11. The decision was rationalized in a series of legal memoranda prepared by lawyers for Secretary of Defense Donald Rumsfeld and Vice President Cheney, and by certain staffers in the Office of Legal Counsel in the Department of Justice. The best-known of these memos, the first Bybee memo (so named after its author, Jay S. Bybee, then assistant attorney general), was written in 2002 and became public in 2004, and several others were released by the Obama administration in 2009.[151] In general, these memos sought to evade well-established legal strictures prohibiting torture by defining key concepts, such as torture, pain, and custody, in exceptionally narrow and almost certainly indefensible ways. There is an extensive academic literature that discusses several aspects of these memoranda.[152]

In sum, under the post-9/11 security regime, the government claims authority to arrest suspects without judicial review, to detain suspects without trial, to torture them while in custody and restrict their right to habeas corpus, to investigate political groups without evidence of criminal wrongdoing, and to engage in racial profiling. Under the Patriot Act, the executive branch may track an individual's credit information and library usage, monitor mail and electronic communications, and search private homes without a warrant.[153] Further, the government maintains that it may lawfully use drones to kill American citizens abroad on grounds that they are hostile enemies, a decision that is not subject to independent judicial or administrative review.

Implications for Constitutional Governance

My purpose in this section is to consider the implications of the security regime for constitutional governance. In particular, I address three aspects of the security regime. First, many of the policies embraced by the Bush and Obama administrations compromise several of our most basic of constitutional commitments, including the precepts of human dignity and equal moral worth. The authorization and use of harsh interrogations and torture are the most odious and perhaps the most troubling of these departures from constitutional principle,[154] but there others that are equally significant, including the use of drones for targeted killings, preventive and indefinite detention, and extraordinary rendition. Second, I consider how the rise of the preclusive presidency undermines the separation of powers doctrine and constitutional principles of accountability and transparency; the evolution of the preclusive presidency, in particular, is a danger to an understanding of the separation of powers doctrine that advances and contributes to civic deliberation. Third, I consider how key elements of the security regime have become permanent features of the legal order and in so doing corrode our understanding of what constitutional government means. Most of these policies and programs will migrate, if they have not already, to the routine administration of justice; they have evolved or will evolve into more or less permanent features of the constitutional state. They will not, in other words, exist alongside or in exception to the contemporary constitutional state, hermetically sealed and apart, but will instead become an ordinary and integral part of our entire constitutional identity. Together, these developments contribute to a state of constitutional rot by subverting basic constitutional values (a failure of fidelity) and by disabling a civic culture of deliberation and engagement (a failure of civility). They constitute, as Luban has written of torture, "a liberal ideology"[155] of the national security state.

Torture

In a constitutional democracy, the use of torture invokes, or should invoke, moral revulsion. Torture is an affront to the most elemental of constitutional values. It degrades the human person and offends the notions of human dignity that inform our understanding of and commitment to constitutionalism itself. Torture denies our common humanity, as well as the constitutional principle of equal human worth. Perhaps less obviously, the use of torture fundamentally subverts constitutional norms of transparency, accountability, and reason[156] by authorizing governments to do whatever they want, in secret, without having to justify it or explain it (i.e., without reason), and without limitation or review by other constitutional actors.

It should be equally obvious that torture violates international and domestic law. The International Convention against Torture and Other Cruel, Inhuman, or Degrading Treatment or Punishment states that torture violates "the inherent dignity of the human person" and provides plainly in Article 2 that no claim of extraordinary or special circumstances can authorize a derogation from its prohibitions; Article 4 requires that the convention must be incorporated into domestic law, which the United States has done,[157] and Article 8 provides for universal jurisdiction. Finally, the prohibition against torture is categorical, or *jus cogens*,[158] which means it binds nation states whether or not they have ratified the international legal conventions that prohibit it. Torture is also prohibited by the Universal Declaration of Human Rights, the International Covenant on Civil and Human Rights, the American Convention on Human Rights, the Rome Statute, and the Third and Fourth Geneva Conventions, as well as by the U.S. Army's Field Manual. In addition, "every . . . U.S. circuit court that has considered the issue has held that torture violates well-established customary international law,"[159] consistent with the Second Circuit's holding in *Filartiga v. Pena-Irala*[160] that the prohibition is universal.

Several attorneys in the Bush administration crafted arguments designed to demonstrate that harsh interrogations do not violate these restrictions.[161] The near universal consensus is that they are shoddy and shallow in terms of legal craftsmanship. It is widely argued that their chief purpose was to excuse a decision already taken and to provide a shield of protection against any subsequent liability on the part of CIA interrogators and administration officials. But the legality or illegality of torture under the Juridic Constitution is largely insignificant as a matter of constitutional inquiry under the Civic Constitution. The question the Civic Constitution requires us to consider is not torture's legality, but rather whether we can reconcile our decision to use it with our commitment to a constitutional way of life. This inquiry has two dimensions. First, as I have suggested, we must ask if torture comports with the normative premises of human dignity and equal moral worth that underlie constitutionalism. Second, we must ask if our decision to torture is a result of civic deliberation, or of decisions made and embraced in a culture of civic deliberation. As we shall see more fully below, the decision to torture, like many of the most significant decisions taken by the Bush administration, was done in secret, without consulting Congress, with a purpose to avoid judicial scrutiny, and with little or no public deliberation. These efforts violate constitutional norms of reason and transparency, as well as undermine the very possibility of civic deliberation required by the Civic Constitution. Perhaps even more damaging to the principle of deliberation and engagement, however, than the decision to operate in secrecy was the decision to supplant a culture of civic deliberation with a culture of fear, a point I develop more fully below.

The Preclusive Presidency and the Separation of Power

The war on terrorism has precipitated a constitutional jurisprudence in which the executive branch, under a concept of the unitary or preclusive presidency,[162] has putative authority to wage war against enemy belligerents, citizens or not, without regard for basic constitutional norms or without account or review by other constitutional actors. The most visible, if not the most significant, manifestation of this authority is the practice of targeted killings. Consider the case of Anwar Awlaki, an American citizen and a Yemeni imam and, according to the United States government, a prominent publicist for and a regional commander in al-Qaeda. Awlaki maintained an extensive Internet presence, including a blog, a Facebook page, and several YouTube videos, in which he repeatedly called for jihad against the United States. The Yemeni government tried him in absentia in November 2010, for plotting to kill foreigners and being a member of al-Qaeda. A Yemeni judge ordered him captured dead or alive.

In April 2010, President Obama placed Awlaki on the kill list. In response, Awlaki's father filed for an injunction against President Obama in a federal district court, arguing the president had no constitutional authority to assassinate his son without due process of law. The administration asked the court to dismiss the lawsuit without hearing the merits. In December 2010, the district court dismissed the suit on two grounds. First, the court concluded that Awlaki's father had no standing to sue. Second, the court concluded that the case presented a nonjusticiable political question. Of greater consequence for the Civic Constitution, however, are Judge Bates's remarks about the underlying claim. Bates wrote that the case raised "stark, and perplexing, questions," including whether the president could "order the assassination of a U.S. citizen without first affording him any form of judicial process whatsoever, based on the mere assertion that he is a dangerous member of a terrorist organization." But while the "legal and policy questions posed by this case are controversial and of great public interest," Bates wrote, "they would have to be resolved on another day and, probably, outside a courtroom."[163] The United States killed Awlaki by armed drones in Yemen in 2011; the same attack also resulted in the death of Samir Kahn, an American citizen born in Pakistan. In July 2012, Awlaki's family and the family members of two other Americans killed in drone strikes filed a wrongful death suit in a federal court, alleging that the Obama administration's targeted killings program violates due process guarantees and international law.[164]

The targeted killing program poses a substantial challenge to several constitutional principles and practices, but more important for the Civic Constitution is the underlying understanding of the office of the presidency it rests upon and its implications for how we understand the possibility of constitutional failure. The targeted killing program is illustrative of a larger element of the post-9/11 security regime: many of the decisions to adopt key elements of the security regime were taken unilaterally, without the counsel of Congress, the federal courts, or other agencies and actors in the executive branch.[165]

Administration officials have defended the targeted killings program as authorized by the nation's right of self-defense, as well as on the basis of the AUMF and the president's authority as commander-in-chief.[166] Part of the argument is that the government owes no obligation of due process to American citizens who have joined the enemy to take up arms against the state.[167] In a speech at the Northwestern University School of Law in March 2012, however, Attorney General Holder made a somewhat different claim. Holder insisted that the program undergoes robust oversight within the administration, and maintained that due process of law does not require judicial review: "Due process and judicial process are not one and the same, particularly when it comes to national security. The Constitution guarantees due process; it does not guarantee judicial process."[168]

Insofar as it concedes presidential decision making must satisfy due process, Holder's speech may seem a significant concession to constitutional principles. But Holder's speech tells us little about how the process due actually works, including who has the authority to issue or to deny kill orders, or on what evidence a decision may be predicated. A recently released Department of Justice White Paper provides a marginally fuller discussion of these questions, but also raises new ones.[169] The Obama administration's policy effectively means that the government may execute American citizens without judicial process and on the basis of evidence that it need not share with any other official or any other branch of government.[170]

There is some merit to the distinction between due process and judicial process, but Holder's remarks elide most of the difficult questions. First, although constitutional due process need not always be judicial due process, the presumption must be in favor of judicial process, and claims about the necessity of departures from it require authorities to advance reasons in support of that variance. Additionally, any scheme of due process, judicial or otherwise, demands that governmental officials offer reasons in support of their action and further, those reasons must be subject to review by a neutral third party. This is also a necessary precondition for the sort of civic deliberation Judge Bates suggested will have to occur outside a courtroom; no meaningful discussion of those issues can occur in any forum, judicial or otherwise, if the executive need not explain or advance reasons for his decisions.

In a previous work, I differentiated sharply between a decision to suspend or set aside a particular constitution and its attendant legal rules and the larger decision to set aside a commitment to the constitutive principles of constitutionalism itself.[171] One of those principles is that governments must produce, in public and transparently, reasons that justify a departure from textually ordained commitments.[172] What the Constitution requires in an emergency is not invariance from legal rules but public justification for such departures.[173] Some critics who objected to this formulation complained about the putative authority for such a requirement—the conditions that overwhelm textual commands, some suggested, will similarly overwhelm extratextual constitutional norms. This objection, juridic in character, fundamentally misunderstands the argument because it mistakenly considers that all constitutional questions are questions of law or legality, and fails to appreciate their inescapably political character. The Civic Constitution seeks to establish a civic culture of deliberation, a political context, in which the exercise of extraordinary, extralegal powers must be supported by reasons that are made public and subject to civic deliberation and debate. "[W]hen we view the Constitution as the creation of a civic culture of constitutionalism, we can see that, when exercised, extralegal discretionary power takes place in a political context that still has to justify its extralegal quality."[174] The Civic Constitution thus requires, at a minimum, that we find ways to fortify a civic culture of deliberation. One possibility would be to impose public disclosure requirements to assist public oversight, perhaps by requiring as a matter of law that the administration periodically provide information about drone strikes to an impartial review panel. Another would be to pass legislation that requires the administration to consult with Congress (or the National Security Council, or some other group), or seek their approval, before undertaking extraordinary actions like drone attacks.[175] The Obama administration's insistence that it need not produce specific reasons in support of a targeted killing order, to other constitutional actors or in public, is a direct challenge to the Civic Constitution's regard for principles of reason and deliberation, as well as of public civility. It is a strategy of governance that seeks to evade and disable the culture of civic deliberation itself.

Indeed, Jack Goldsmith's account of a Bush administration determined to go it alone in the war on terrorism describes an administration whose larger purpose was to evade the constitutional principles of transparency, reason giving, and accountability in pursuit of its security policies.[176] Denvir describes this larger strategy as comprised of three elements: (1) making a conscious and deliberate effort to forestall informed public discussion of security policy issues by crafting "sophisticated tools of mass persuasion to mobilize public support for his national security policies"; (2) limiting access by Congress and the courts to important national security information; and (3) limiting the public's access to information, and hence speech and public discussion, in public spaces.[177] In other words, the Bush administration's plan was designed in toto to constrict civic space, both by limiting the information available in that space, thus diminishing its importance, and by literally constricting the physical dimensions of that space.[178] Preserved and extended at its core by the Obama administration,[179] the plan is designed to evade the principles and mechanisms of civic deliberation that are the heart of the Civic Constitution.

The Preclusive Presidency

Stephen Griffin observes that the most constitutionally significant aspects of the Bush administration's security regime "shared a common characteristic: they could not have happened unless it was assumed that the President had the unilateral power under the Constitution to authorize the violation of federal law and judicial doctrine, even in the absence of a prior finding that the law in question was unconstitutional."[180] This conception of unilateral presidential power was strongly championed by Vice President Cheney and his legal counsel, David Addington, and both inside and outside the administration by John Yoo.[181] In the infamous August 1, 2002, torture memo signed by Jay Bybee and drafted by John Yoo, the Office of Legal Counsel opined that "Congress lacks authority under Article I to set the terms and conditions under which the President may exercise his authority as Commander-in-Chief to control the conduct of operations during a war."[182] Further, "[a]ny effort by Congress to regulate the interrogation of battlefield combatants would violate the Constitution's sole vesting of the Commander-in-Chief authority in the President."[183] Following this logic, the Bush administration could and did argue that a 2005 congressional statute prohibiting torture "interferes with the President's discretion of such core war matters as the detention and interrogation of enemy combatants" and is unconstitutional as a result.[184] Similarly, the president could and did justify the surveillance activities of the NSA as an exercise of inherent presidential power. The claim was that the president possesses "inherent constitutional authority to conduct warrantless searches and surveillance within the United States for foreign intelligence purposes."[185] This conception of presidential power cuts deeply into the separation of powers and the authority of Congress and courts to discipline presidential power.[186] It undermines a civic culture of deliberation by disabling other constitutional institutions from participating in the formulation and oversight of public policy.

There are three arguments ordinarily advanced to support this expansive conception of executive power. First, proponents argue that the institutional design of the executive branch better suits it to gather information about and to assess risk.[187] This is partly an argument based on institutional design, but it is also premised upon deference to policy expertise.[188] Second, arguments in favor of the expansion of executive power sometimes make the related claim that the executive is more accountable to and more likely to maintain the trust of the population.[189] Third, arguments in favor of executive power sometimes are based on history and political theory, and in particular on the claim that in the Western tradition, at least, the executive is invested with the power of prerogative, or that the president possesses an inherent authority to use whatever force is necessary to conduct the war on terrorism.[190]

As Peter Margulies argues, however, the preclusive presidency, far from an argument derived from earlier justifications for extraordinary presidential power, such as those claimed by President Lincoln, is an argument against the separation of power and public accountability. Margulies argues that "there are three crucial differences" between Lincoln's suspension of the writ of habeas corpus and the Bush administration's understanding of presidential power. Lincoln "arguably had authorization from Congress . . . , promptly went public with his decision, and asked Congress for its consent at the earliest possible opportunity."[191] As Tulis has observed, "Lincoln's and Hamilton's understanding of the separation of powers captures the Lockean idea that executives could be an important instrument of prospective judgment and energetic action, while the people through a Congress might provide superior retrospective evaluation."[192] There are, then, important differences between Lincoln's approach to crisis and the Bush approach. The Bush argument envisions little if any role for Congress (or for courts) to play in the conduct of foreign affairs generally or in the war on terrorism specifically.

The accumulation of presidential power in the aftermath of 9/11 represents the rise (return?) of the imperial,[193] unitary,[194] or national security presidency,[195] an executive with extraordinary obligations and equally enormous powers. On this rationale, extraordinary powers are essential to prevent the starkest and most existential of potential constitutional failures—our survival and physical integrity as a nation-state. Barron and Lederman have called this the theory of "preclusive Commander in Chief powers."[196] It asserts "the President's constitutional authority as Commander in Chief to override existing legislative constraints on his conduct of military operations"; it is an executive unconstrained by congressional or judicial counterweights. This is, to put it mildly, a robust theory of the presidency, in which the president's duty to protect us supersedes every other obligation of the office, including the oath to support the Constitution, statutory law, congressional resolutions, and principles of international law (sometimes derided as "lawfare"[197]).

As we saw, some of the scholarly arguments on behalf of the unitary presidency (closely related to the concept of the preclusive presidency, but not identical to it) claim that it focuses responsibility in a single, identifiable public office and thereby promotes democratic accountability.[198] Ironically, however, Goldsmith's description of the terror presidency suggests that the centralizing of public accountability in the single location of the executive branch has had precisely the opposite effect. Fear of being held to public account has not only skewed policy decisions and the policy-making process, it has also led the presidency to isolate itself.[199]

Behind this isolation is a rejection of the value of accountability that animates the separation of powers doctrine. Insofar as counterterrorism legislation eliminates institutional and structural mechanisms designed to make regimes accountable, it is incompatible with the separation of powers. Indeed, appeals for antiterrorism legislation are ordinarily predicated upon a claim that is profoundly antithetical to the separation of powers—that there is an urgent need for extraordinary powers to deal with extraordinary or unusual threats. Such claims see the separation of power doctrine as an impediment to the efficient and rapid response that governments need when they face unconventional threats.

Mariah Zeisberg has astutely observed that models of constitutional decision making in foreign affairs typically invoke, if only silently, some form of the settlement thesis, or the claim that "resolving foundational political questions is precisely the function of a constitution."[200] One might respond that in times of crisis, decision and settlement must be our first objective, even if it does some harm to a culture of deliberation. Posner and Vermeule go further, arguing that there is little evidence that such episodes have undermined constitutional governance over the long run (i.e., that they distort or disrupt the project of constitutional maintenance). Posner and Vermeule argue that many putative episodes of constitutional failure in the United States (they identify six—the Quasi-War with France accompanied by the Sedition Act; the Civil War; World Wars I and II; the early Cold War; and the post-9/11 period) should be regarded as constitutional successes. In each of these campaigns, they observe, the executive branch properly exercised expansive if not extraordinary powers to resolve the emergency at hand, and did so in ways that did not cause long-lasting or permanent interferences with civil liberties or ratchet-up presidential power, or contribute to democratic deficit, or significantly erode any other substantive constitutional value. I think Posner and Vermeule are profoundly mistaken in their assessment of the effects of emergencies on the growth of presidential power and constitutional governance generally, but my point here is somewhat different and twofold. First, Posner and Vermeule are right to observe that claims of constitutional failure must be established, not assumed. Second, success, like failure, requires a standard or benchmark—it must, in other words, be defined against a set of ends that may or may not be realized.[201] We need some account of what success itself means. In Posner and Vermeule's account, constitutional success amounts to little more than endurance; it is an understanding of constitutional success that obscures the possibility of constitutional rot from the inside out.

More broadly, however, the position Posner and Vermeule adopt is fundamentally in tension with the basic precepts of the Civic Constitution. In their view, both Congress and the Court should defer to the executive branch (chiefly due to institutional architecture, which affords to executives several well-known institutional advantages, such as energy and dispatch). Posner and Vermeule counsel the other branches to afford a strong presumption of rationality to executive decision making in times of crisis: judges deciding constitutional claims during times of emergency "should defer to government action so long as there is any rational basis for the government's position." Judicial review in times of emergency "cannot improve matters, because there is no reason to think that courts possessing limited information and limited expertise will choose better security policies than does the government."[202]

In contrast, Zeisberg argues that the settlement thesis is "strikingly inadequate for understanding the Constitution's allocation of war authority" and instead proposes a "relational account of war authority."[203] A relational account is "premised on the value of maintaining the branches in relationships of mutual review" even when that review may lead to interbranch conflict. Rather than assuming that interpretive conflict is a constitutional problem, it assumes that such conflict is or can be a marker of constitutional success, especially insofar as it "can lead the branches to develop governance and interpretive capacities that are useful for broader constitutional aims."[204] Among those aims, I would argue, would be the cultivation of a civic constitutional culture. Dialogic or relational models of the separations of powers require the executive to advance reasons that support policy decisions; the public process of reason giving introduces an important element of accountability into the decision-making process and also opens up the process to additional information and to additional ways of assessing and evaluating information. (It may also improve the quality of executive decision making by requiring the president to advance reasons and to justify policy choices to others. As Stephen Holmes notes, "an executive branch that never has to give reasons for its actions soon stops having plausible reasons for its actions."[205]) The Civic Constitution requires an approach to the separation of powers that encourages the development of these institutional centers, chiefly the Congress and the presidency, to address constitutional concerns as a routine and significant part of their institutional responsibilities. This is a conception of the separation of powers doctrine in which Congress, rather than issuing blanket authorizations to the executive to protect our national security (authorizations that expansive understandings of the Bush doctrine would regard as unnecessary and inappropriate as a matter of law), should instead "concern itself with demarcating the legitimate range of the executive's independent powers." Such a conception "allows Congress and the people to remain constitutionally vigilant."[206]

It should be evident that Congress is not often inclined to vigilance. The growth of presidential power in foreign affairs, and especially concerning military conflict, has been greatly facilitated by Congress and the Court.[207] Every presidential initiative—Libya is a very recent example—provokes some measure of limited objection by individual congressional representatives (in the case of President Obama's Libya policy, such objections were voiced by Senator Richard Lugar and by Representative Roscoe Bartlett).[208] But the general drift of constitutional authority to make war to the executive has been as much facilitated by Congress as resisted by it.[209] The reasons for congressional acquiescence in the growth of presidential power have been well charted; they include several adumbrated by the founders themselves, especially the structural and institutional advantages of efficiency, dispatch, and secrecy that attach to the presidential office;[210] the nature of contemporary military conflict; and an incentive structure that induces congressional representatives to transfer blame to other constitutional offices.

Deference to executive authority by the other branches contributes substantially to the erosion of a civic culture of deliberation. As Louis Fisher has observed, "[i]n time of emergency, national security is weakened when all sectors of government and the public passively and uncritically accept executive actions and justifications."[211] A Congress unwilling to assert its constitutional war powers by holding the presidency to public account undermines the Civic Constitution by teaching citizens that determinations of constitutionality, if they are relevant at all to such momentous policy decisions, are the responsibility not of their representatives, and by extension not of citizens, but are instead best left to the executive branch, better equipped to address them (or perhaps secondarily to courts, best suited to considering their legality after the fact). The result is that questions about the constitutional propriety of these decisions, as distinct from questions about their constitutional legality, will be heard in no forum—Congress will not hear them because it regards them as policy decisions, the wisdom of which is best left to the presidency. As in Awlaki's case, courts in turn describe such decisions as nonjusticiable, precisely because they turn on reasons that transcend legal reasoning.

In sum, the preclusive presidency cannot be reconciled with the Civic Constitution. Its understanding of presidential authority is deeply antagonistic to a civic conception of the separation of powers doctrine, which is premised on the utility of dialogue and exchange between the branches to promote both prudent governmental decision making and civic responsibility.

The Security Regime and Civic Deliberation

Three additional elements of the post-9/11 security regime pose problems for a civic culture of deliberation and tending. First, many of the most significant components of this regime were adopted in a political environment characterized by fear and a prevailing sense that something had to be done immediately. Second, the apparent need for secrecy concerning many of the central components of the security regime also undermines a culture of civic deliberation by denying to citizens the information necessary to deliberate. Third, the erosion of the distinctions between temporary and permanent, and between normal and exceptional, inhibit civic deliberation by obscuring the extent and the importance of the changes to constitutional practice we have countenanced.

URGENCY AND DELIBERATION

The United States responded to 9/11 with remarkable dispatch. Congress passed a joint resolution for "The Authorization for Use of Military Force (AUMF)" on September 18, just a week after the attack, and President Bush signed it the same day.[212] The Patriot Act was introduced on October 2 and signed into law by President Bush on October 26, just forty-five days after the September attacks. Given the contracted time frame, the bill (352 pages) was enacted with few hearings and limited opportunity for congressional or public debate. "The bill passed the Senate on October 11 by a vote of 98 to 1, following a brief debate that made it clear that even supporters of the bill had not read it and did not understand its provisions."[213]

It is important to identify why the demand for immediate legislation threatens constitutional values, and to be clear about what those values are. First, the urgency to enact new legislation implicates a basic constitutional norm and perhaps the ultimate constitutional value—transparency in government. Urgency privileges the desire for some law, any law, over the kind of dispassionate and sober inquiry that produces wise and effective laws.[214] Secondly, and related, there is the risk that impressing emergency statutes in the immediate aftermath of crisis will lead to legislation that is disproportionate to the actual threat. Similarly, the sense of exigency means legislators are unlikely to have the time or resources to consider whether such laws are necessary correctives to existing law or likely to have any practical effect on the war on terrorism. There was little or no legislative discussion about whether the provisions of the Patriot Act would have been necessary to prevent the 9/11 attacks.[215] Urgency helps to create an environment in which such questions either are not asked or are secondary to other considerations.[216]

Urgency compromises our commitment to civic deliberation, in part because it forecloses opportunities for sober deliberation, but also, and no less importantly, because in times of urgency deliberation itself is said to be an impediment to our well-being. As Griffin has noted, deliberation

> is precisely what was missing from post-9/11 America. President Bush thoroughly short-circuited the public sphere by immediately describing the conflict as a "war," and, indeed, a new world war; a meaningful public debate over the nature of 9/11 and whether it should be handled as a war or as a colossal crime against the United States thus never occurred. Groups of bewildered citizens wondering why it was not treated as a crime were left well behind as the Administration moved ahead. [217]

The lack of time required to consider the full ramifications of our public policy choices goes a long way toward debilitating civic deliberation by limiting opportunities for careful consideration of the larger implications of those choices for constitutional values. Just as significantly, urgency helps to replace a culture of deliberation with a culture of fear. Following 9/11, this culture of fear was actively encouraged and promoted by the executive and other governmental officials, as exemplified by Attorney General Ashcroft's comment that "the blood of the victims of future terrorist attacks would be on" Congress's hands "if it did not swiftly adopt the administration's proposals."[218] A culture of fear is deeply antagonistic to a constitutional culture of civility.

SECRECY AND DELIBERATION

A culture of civic deliberation is also difficult to sustain when much of the information necessary for informed policy making cannot or should not be made public. Deliberation flourishes only in political contexts where there is comprehensive access to relevant information. This is sometimes not the case in decisional environments, like the period immediately following a terrorist attack, characterized by low and poor or incomplete information. A related problem is the claim of secrecy that often surrounds the executive's control of information. Proponents of antiterrorism legislation often argue that enforceable mechanisms of accountability may endanger us by requiring the government to disclose information and intelligence that it should keep secret.[219]

The secrecy state, of course, predates the 2001 attacks, but 9/11 has greatly facilitated its rise. Thus, as Griffin notes:

> Secrecy, not public deliberation, was essential to the creation of this new constitutional order. The "War on Terror" featured secret decisions, secret executive orders, and secret programs, not unusual in wartime. However, these initiatives also had secret constitutional rationales, something that was critical to getting them off the ground by shielding them from the normal processes of interagency review. . . . After 9/11 . . . top officials in the administration dealt with FISA the way they dealt with other laws they didn't like: they blew through them in secret based on flimsy legal opinions that they guarded closely so no one could question the legal basis for the operations.[220]

Similarly, Denvir observes, "the Bush administration claimed the right to withhold any information it chose on the ground that information that appears innocent to a layperson might have national security relevance as part of a larger 'mosaic' of information."[221] As a consequence, "Many of the most important initiatives of the Bush Administration did not come to light until early 2004. Even after those controversies, what the Bush Administration did remained so blacked out of the historical record that its opponents were calling for a full accounting as Bush left office."[222]

Secrecy is a threat to the constitutive principle of reason and deliberation, as well as fundamentally in tension with both the principle and the possibility of civic agency, because it denies citizens and Congress the information requisite to engagement. Secrecy incapacitates civic conversation and debate. Where it does not shutter debate completely, it privileges in conversation those who have or can claim access to information that is not accessible to everyone.[223]

There is undoubtedly an authentic and substantial interest in maintaining the secrecy of certain information, but there can be equally little doubt that the power to control public access to information represents a significant challenge to creating a culture of deliberation.[224] What the Civic Constitution requires is some assurance that information withheld from civic space is withheld for need and not simply to influence or dismantle the process of deliberation itself. What is required, in other words, is something akin to the relational or dialogic model we discussed of presidential power earlier. One mechanism might be a requirement that courts interrogate claims of state secrets more rigorously than they do now, perhaps by insisting upon *in camera* demonstrations and presentation of the relevant information in lieu of the current practice of accepting affidavits proffered by relevant executive branch officials.[225] This remedy will not go far to restoring a culture of civic deliberation, however, in part because it relies centrally on courts to interrogate executive decision making, and in part because *in camera* proceedings themselves occur outside public purview. Other possibilities include mandatory public disclosure requirements, and requirements that the executive branch consult with Congress or other actors, but both are limited in scope and rely on the executive branch to supply others with relevant information—they do not, in other words, offset a dynamic that greatly advantages the executive branch.

A complicating element is the power of the executive to "mold public opinion as a part of his job"[226] and thus to set both the terms and the occasions for civic deliberation. As Denvir notes, the power of the national security presidency to dominate and to set the terms of public discourse is a function of the president's unequaled access to the media, his control over most of the information pertinent to that discussion, his (increased) ability to control and to limit access to civic space, and his symbolic status as national leader: "All these factors combine to allow him to drown out competing voices."[227]

From Exceptional to Ordinary,
Temporary to Permanent

Although many of the policies adopted in the immediate aftermath of 9/11 were said to be temporary, most have become a sturdy if not permanent part of a larger and durable security regime.[228] The Obama administration has taken some small steps to curtail the worst excesses of the war on terrorism, but it has also maintained most of the central features of the security regime and has defended an equally if nor more ambitious understanding of presidential power. The Obama administration, for example, has "revived military commission trials and continued the indefinite detention of suspected terrorists without charge, two centerpieces of the Bush administration's war on terror."[229] In addition, the Obama administration continues to defend presidential authority to hold prisoners outside of Guantanamo without judicial review, and it has sought to limit the access of torture victims to federal courts. [230]

The point is well illustrated by the Obama administration's decision to institutionalize "the highly classified practice of targeted killing, transforming ad-hoc elements into a counterterrorism infrastructure capable of sustaining a seemingly permanent war."[231] The policy change highlights two larger features of the security regime that I and other scholars have identified on several occasions. The first feature, or danger, is the undoubted tendency of temporary policies to become permanent parts of the administration of criminal justice. Although "[i]t is true that in most jurisdictions . . . antiterrorism laws are usually introduced on a temporary basis,"[232] it is frequently the case that these temporary changes become permanent.[233] In practice, the temporary counterterrorism regimes put in place after 9/11 are a permanent fixture of the constitutional order.

Consider the USA Patriot Act. Proposals to include sunset clauses in the Patriot Act surfaced early in the drafting process, partly in response to concerns about the potential for abuse of the new powers, and partly in response to concerns about the expansion of presidential power. When the House Judiciary Committee reported the act, it included a two-year sunset. This was replaced by a provision, negotiated with the White House, which provided for a five-year sunset, thus delaying reconsideration of the act from 2003 to 2006. The Bush administration was concerned that the United States would still be fighting the war on terror when the clause came into effect.

The Senate's version of the act did not include a sunset clause. During the reconciliation of the two bills in committee, House and Senate leaders agreed to a four-year sunset provision for several provisions in the act.[234] Nevertheless, President Bush called for the renewal of these provisions in his State of the Union address in January 2003, well in advance of the scheduled expiration. On July 21, 2005, the House of Representatives voted to extend these provisions indefinitely, and the Senate followed on July 29, 2005. On March 2, 2006, after weeks of dispute, the Senate voted 89–10 to renew and make permanent all but two of the provisions, thus rejecting efforts to extend the sunset by four more years. (The House followed five days later, by a vote of 280–138.)

There was always good reason to think that most of the sunsetted provisions of the Patriot Act would become permanent.[235] We can predict that antiterrorism measures will be extended when there are ongoing violent attacks or substantial agreement that the threat is live; in these instances the potential political liability of recriminations following another attack may be too overwhelming for most political actors to resist. Second, renewal of sunsetted provisions is more likely when the party in power needs to establish or polish its security credentials, perhaps because its status as a majority is fragile or subject to an imminent election. Third, provisions that can be shown to have "worked" (admittedly, there will be issues of measurement and assessment) are likely to be extended. Similarly, provisions will be renewed where there is little or no evidence that they have been abused. Fourth, and less obviously, sunsetted provisions will be renewed or made permanent when they have become normalized, or when they have begun to migrate into nonemergency legislation (sometimes called the "spillover effect"). Indeed, proponents of sunsets sometimes argue they are necessary for precisely this reason—to guard against the dangers of normalization by resetting the start point.[236]

The same considerations tell us why the 9/11 security regime will be perdurable. First, if the security legislation is a response to an authentic threat, then the duration of the legislation is directly related to the lifespan of the threat. (If the need is genuine, then the extension of antiterrorism legislation is not only predictable but arguably desirable.) Second, and related, there will always be a case to be made that the war on terrorism, unlike conventional conflicts, has no foreseeable end.[237] As a consequence, the changes such policies work in the administration of criminal justice are likely permanent because the war on terrorism is unending (we are told), and so long as the perceived need persists, so must the response. This suggests a breakdown in the dichotomy between ordinary and emergency legislation at the level of both constitutional theory and practice. As Oren Gross has observed, "The advent of the 'war on terrorism' has . . . led to questions about the relationship between normalcy and exception in the face of a 'war' that may well be endless."[238]

A third and related danger is often called the problem of normalization, or the process by which changes made in counterterrorism policies begin to corrupt the administration of justice in ordinary criminal cases.[239] As one critic has observed of the Patriot Act, "the government is using its expanded authority . . . to investigate suspected drug traffickers, white-collar criminals, blackmailers, child pornographers, money launderers, spies, and even corrupt foreign officials."[240] Inroads on civil liberties and rules of criminal procedure made in cases involving terrorism invariably begin to apply to ordinary criminal processes, in part because they make it easier for the state to secure convictions.[241] Such changes are likely to become permanent because governments find them advantageous in the prosecution of criminal conduct more generally. I made this observation some twenty years ago in my study of antiterrorism legislation in Europe, concluding that "effective emergency legislation threatens constitutional values even when it succeeds, for then the temptation to make such powers permanent increases."[242]

There is another normalization problem as well: each extension of emergency powers, after a time, becomes accepted as the new norm(al). Additional crises justify yet another departure from the norm, both domestically, as states draw upon their own experience, and internationally, as they cite to the experiences of other states.[243] The process of normalization, like the progression of temporary to permanent, muddies the distinction between normalcy and emergency.[244] In so doing it advances the condition of constitutional rot by depressing the public's sense that antiterrorism policies work significant and substantial changes in our constitutional practice and thus require our attention as citizens. An example of this is the Obama administration's reluctance to hold officials in the Bush administration, and especially those who authorized, oversaw, and implemented the use of torture, to account. President Obama refused to appoint a special prosecutor or a commission of inquiry, arguing that such inquiries would be politically divisive, and the Senate has adopted the same posture.[245] One consequence of our unwillingness to confront our decisions is to deny their extraordinary character, or their status as departures from constitutional normalcy, and hence to consider whether there are good reasons for them or whether they compromise constitutional principles.

What is ordinary and unexceptional is unlikely to provoke or require extensive public deliberation. As the security regime matures and endures, the apparent need to consider its ramifications for a constitutional way of life diminishes incrementally. Furthermore, the transition deadens the public's sensitivity to the severity and magnitude of these changes by understating their import and by blurring the distinction between the exceptional and the ordinary, thus undercutting the whole Schmittian notion of crisis as exception. [246] Indeed, where Schmitt wrote that the sovereign is he who decides on the exception, we might now conclude instead that the sovereign is he who decides what is not exceptional.

The war on terrorism is no longer a state of constitutional exception, or a temporary response to a discrete but confined problem. It is instead an ordinary, normal, and typical state of being. It exists not independently of superordinate constitutional norms and values, or in a state of exception to them, but rather as an integral and normal part of the constitutional order itself. This makes it difficult for citizens to see such changes for what they are—as stark departures from an authentically constitutional way of life, one committed to the fundamental moral precepts of constitutional governance and to our collective responsibility as citizens to care for them. Instead, we have come to regard these diversions as a routine and ordinary incident of constitutional survival in a threatening world, and so we rationalize their discordance with basic constitutional ideals.

Civic Deliberation and Judicial Review of the Antiterrorism Regime

There is one additional impediment to a civic culture of deliberation. The Juridic Constitution encourages citizens to forfeit their responsibility to tend for the Constitution to others, presumably more expert than themselves, and notably to judges expert in the law. But for many years, it has been a staple of constitutional law scholarship that judges are both unsuited to and unlikely to hold the political branches to constitutional account in times of perceived crisis or emergency.[247] It is likewise conventional wisdom that antiterrorism legislation, insofar as it tends to concentrate power in the executive branch, undermines judicial power by reducing opportunities for constitutional review.[248] This concentration of executive power in turn has resulted in the weakening of judicial oversight over key parts of the administration of criminal justice and civil liberties more generally. The reasons advanced for relaxing judicial control over antiterrorism policies typically mirror those advanced for concentrating power in the executive. First among them is the claim, often advanced by judges themselves, that they lack institutional competence and expertise in areas of national security and foreign policy.[249]

To the extent this understanding of the role of courts in emergencies is accurate (at best, it is a half-truth[250]), it presents a significant problem for the prospect of meaningful civic deliberation of antiterrorism regimes. It means citizens will have little incentive to take up such issues, trusting (mistakenly) in courts to do so and thinking (mistakenly) that the constitutional questions they raise are preeminently questions of legality. And insofar as courts decline to take up the charge, such issues will be left to the executive branch to determine. The *Awlaki* case illustrates the point well: recall Judge Bates's remark that the case raised "stark, and perplexing, questions." But while the "legal and policy questions posed by this case are controversial and of great public interest," he wrote, "they would have to be resolved on another day and, probably, outside a courtroom."[251] The Juridic Constitution, in concert with the three difficulties I just described, makes it unlikely that citizens will be able to assume that responsibility.

Notwithstanding conventional wisdom about the limited role of courts in times of crisis, there is an argument to make that the Supreme Court, in a line of decisions trimming some of the more obvious recent excesses of presidential power, has vindicated important constitutional values, and in particular the separation of powers. In *Rasul v. Bush* (2004), for example, the Supreme Court held that detainees at Guantanamo may file habeas petitions in a federal court. Justice Stevens wrote that what is "at stake in this case is nothing less than the essence of a free society. Even more important than the method of selecting the people's rulers and their successors is the character of the constraints imposed on the Executive by the rule of law." Congress responded with the Detainee Treatment Act of 2005, which in effect restored the status quo.

Similarly, in *Hamdi v. Rumsfeld* (2004) and *Rumsfeld v. Padilla* (2004), the Court ordered a lower federal court to begin new proceedings in the cases of Yaser Hamdi and Jose Padilla, two American citizens labeled as enemy combatants and held without charge or access to legal counsel. In Justice O'Connor's opinion for the plurality in *Hamdi*, Hamdi's detention was authorized by the Use of Force Resolution passed in 2001, but she also found that certain conditions surrounding Hamdi's detention violated the due process clause of the Fifth Amendment. In particular, the plurality held that Hamdi must be given the factual basis for his detention and an opportunity to rebut that evidence before "a neutral decision maker." In response, the Pentagon announced the creation of "Combatant Status Review Tribunals," which allow detainees to challenge their status in front of a commission staffed by military officers. In *Hamdan v. Rumsfeld* (2006), the Supreme Court ruled that the military commissions created to try detainees at Guantanamo did not have "the power to proceed because its structures and procedures violate both the Uniform Code of Military Justice and the Geneva Conventions signed in 1949." In response, Congress passed the Military Commissions Act of 2006, "to authorize trial by military commission for violations of the law of war." The MCA also stripped federal courts of jurisdiction to hear habeas appeals by aliens detained by the United States government.

The Supreme Court took up the constitutionality of the MCA in *Boumediene v. Bush* (2008). Writing for the majority, Justice Kennedy held that the MCA's suspension of the writ of habeas corpus for detainees at Guantanamo was unconstitutional. In reaching this conclusion, the Court first determined that the writ of habeas corpus does apply to Guantanamo, thus rejecting the Government's argument, following the earlier case of *Johnson v. Eisentrager* (1950), that the writ does not run to areas outside the formal sovereignty of the United States. The second component of the Court's opinion concerned the constitutionality of those provisions in the Detainee Treatment Act and the Military Commissions Act that provided alternatives for ordinary judicial review of the detainee's status. The Court concluded that these alternatives were not an adequate substitute for habeas proceedings.

We might read these decisions to suggest there is a limited role for courts to play in the oversight of some counterterrorism polices. Some observers have lauded the Supreme Court's work, especially in *Boumediene*, calling it a "great victory."[252] But as Hafetz has noted, although these cases established some important principles, including the right of detainees to seek habeas review, they "also left open important questions."[253] What some critics wrote of *Hamdan* might apply with equal force to *Boumediene*: "[T]he 'balance' struck by the plurality imposes little additional burden on the Government. . . . In the last analysis, whereas the plurality rejected Executive unilateralism, when one considers where the balance was struck, the departure from unilateralism was limited."[254] Griffin similarly concludes that "[t]he Supreme Court's decisions have made little difference to the situation of the detainees and did not address issues of interrogation or surveillance."[255] Although the Court appears to have insisted upon some measure of judicial accountability, it has also authorized important and far-reaching departures from what the rule of law requires in ordinary criminal cases. None of these decisions support the president's claim that he has inherent authority to create special courts or military commissions, but neither do they establish clear and unambiguous prohibitions on their use based on constitutional principles. Instead, the overall import of the decisions is to authorize a separate system of jurisprudence and court procedures for offenders designated by the executive branch as enemy combatants. Moreover, even this limited judicial role has provoked sharp criticism. In a sharply worded dissent in *Boumediene*, Justice Scalia asked: "What competence does the Court have to second-guess the judgment of Congress and the president . . . ? None whatsoever." In response, Justice Kennedy argued that judicial involvement "does not undermine the Executive's power. . . . On the contrary, the exercise of those powers is vindicated, not eroded, when confirmed by the Judicial Branch."

In the majority's view, cases such as *Hamdan* and *Boumediene* are part of an ongoing dialogue with the political branches and not simply unwarranted judicial second-guessing. This exchange tells us that the larger value of these decisions might reside in a different, but significant, principle—that of insisting that the president must work within a statutory and regulatory frame-work authorized by Congress. On this more tempered reading of the case law, we might argue that the Court's work, far from undermining the possibility of civic deliberation, has instead encouraged it by requiring the branches to deliberate with each other. This in turn advances a culture of civic deliberation because, as I noted in Essay Two, dialogue among the political branches teaches citizens that determinations of constitutional propriety are not consigned to judges alone or exclusively questions of legality. I indicated there that judicial decisions can sometimes contribute to a conversational model of constitutional discourse by prompting exchange and conversation among coordinate actors, whereas claims of supremacy shut down dialogue. But we must note that the Court's insistence that the president consult with Congress, ostensibly a nod to the separation of powers doctrine and by extension to the constitutional dialogue envisioned by the Civic Constitution, faces an uphill battle in a constitutional order that is essentially juridic in practice.

This partly explains why civic deliberation, whether among the branches or in civil society more broadly, has not followed upon the Court's decisions. In almost every instance (and in particular with respect to the Detainee Treatment Act and the Military Commissions Act), Congress simply acquiesced to presidential demands, even after prompting by the Court to enter into interbranch dialogue. I want to be careful here: my argument that deliberation did not occur after the Court's decisions does not depend simply on the fact that the policies themselves did not change in any material respect. The same result could well follow a full and robust debate between the two branches and the people themselves. Congress might conclude, after fully airing the merits, that the president's initial policy choices were defensible and should be ratified or reinstalled. My claim, instead, is that there is little evidence that deliberation about the merits of these policy decisions took place and good reason to predict that it will not occur.[256] The Court can counsel but it cannot make the branches deliberate with each other, and the structural impediments I identified above—the sense of urgency, the apparent need for secrecy, and the nearly irresistible tendency for political actors to insulate themselves from political accountability—make it unlikely that such deliberation will occur.

In sum, the line of cases from *Rasul* to *Hamdan* to *Boumediene* may have vindicated some measure of constitutional principle, both by trimming the substantive policies in question somewhat and by insisting upon some measure of consultation with Congress.[257] I think this argument overreaches,[258] but my discussion here is designed to sidestep otherwise contentious questions about the constitutional legality of these policies, though an important part of my argument assumes that courts have decided largely in favor of their constitutionality. Their unconstitutionality under the Civic Constitution (if they are unconstitutional—an open question under the Civic Constitution, and not fully settled under the Juridic either) is a function not of infidelity in law, but rather of their infidelity as a matter of political obligation, as a violation, first, of what those values and commitments mean as political and moral proscriptions and, second, in the unwillingness or inability of the people to demand their realization.

I do not hold that judicial inquiries into the legality of security policies are entirely irrelevant to an inquiry into constitutional failure. As I suggested above, their utility depends upon the form they assume and how they contribute to or suppress the civic agency of citizens. Consequently, an assessment of the Court's antiterrorism jurisprudence is required as a part of an inquiry into the possibility of constitutional rot. A second inquiry requires us to consider whether and to what extent the civic sphere has taken up these constitutional questions.

Assessing Rot

Constitutional failure is typically a question of degree, rather than an absolute state. As a consequence, the question of whether the changes to the constitutional order adopted following 9/11 amount to constitutional failure in general, or to constitutional rot in particular, must be a matter of estimation. These judgments cannot reduce to and cannot be exhausted by judicial (or academic) inquiries into the constitutional legality of the security architecture. They implicate questions substantially broader than determinations of legality, and they must be resolved not by judges but by the people and their representatives collectively.

My contention that the security regime has resulted in a state of constitutional rot, one in which we have suffered failures of fidelity and civility alike, might strike some observers as unduly pessimistic.[259] Where I see a civic culture largely unconcerned with and untroubled by the constitutional dimensions of the war on terrorism, others may be encouraged by the efforts of some citizens' groups to put such questions on the public agenda. Susan Herman, for example, has concluded that "the Constitution's multiple interlocking layers of self-protection have worked to limit the extent of the damage done."[260] Among those interlocking layers of protection, she concludes, are juries, judges, and freedom of the press—all of which, she argues, have contributed to efforts to limit the insult done to the Constitution by the war on terrorism. As Herman observes, "Even the structures of federalism got into the act. Over 400 cities, towns, and villages, and eight states signed on to variations on a Bill of Rights Defense Committee resolution, fighting back against the USA PATRIOT Act. The Bill of Rights Defense Committee maintains a website and coordinates a 'People's Campaign for the Constitution' to protest the rise of the surveillance state and to campaign for constitutional liberties."[261]

We should not dismiss as inconsequential the state and local political activity Herman describes. Indeed, it is precisely the sort of civic engagement that the Civic Constitution prizes, and it should be encouraged and applauded. It is some sign that the Civic Constitution remains a part of our constitutional identity. My contrary sense, however, is that most Americans are not troubled by the security policies we have adopted or much interested in whether they comport with constitutional ideals. Consider, for example, the remarks of Glenn Greenwald, who argues: "What's most amazing is that its citizens will not merely refrain from objecting, but will stand and cheer the U.S. Government's new power to assassinate their fellow citizens, far from any battlefield, literally without a shred of due process from the U.S. Government. Many will celebrate the strong, decisive, Tough President's ability to eradicate the life of Anwar al-Awlaki."[262] I think Greenwald is correct, but let's assume that the foregoing evidence of civic engagement is sufficient to conclude that we have not experienced a failure of civility and tending. Or consider the possibility that we could at least imagine the requisite degree of civic engagement. Would that engagement yield a "better" result, or a sturdier commitment to constitutional principles?

Constitutional dialogue of the sort required by the Civic Constitution does not guarantee superior or better constitutional settlements. It may be that vibrant and robust civic deliberation about the "war" on terrorism would yield a security regime that looks more or less like the one we have now, or one even less attentive to basic constitutional precepts and values. An engaged and responsible citizenry, dedicated to tending and equipped with the civic virtue of civility, might through the exercise of reason and deliberation, conclude that other ends (security, safety, prosperity) are more valuable than our aspiration to live a constitutional way of life. A civically engaged people might also make "bad" choices while nonetheless intending to act in ways we imagine are in fact consistent with our constitutional aspirations. In other words, there is no assurance that a deliberative civic culture will produce results markedly more attentive to constitutional precepts. Success in promoting the Civic Constitution's end of civic deliberation does not guarantee that we will succeed in achieving its other ends. In both of these cases, the resolution reached by civic engagement might be constitutionally worse than those that might be reached by other constitutional actors (such as courts). So I want to stress also that attending to constitutional maintenance in this way is not the same thing, necessarily, as preserving the Constitution or the extant constitutional order. Civic dialogue is not a hedge against constitutional failure.

On the other hand, it is not obvious that civic constitutionalism will yield results that are unpalatable to constitutionalists. A citizenry with knowledge of and a responsibility for preserving constitutional values might well be up to the charge. To the extent we have not yet been inclined to tend to constitutional ideals, we must ask also if we have had the opportunity or incentive to do so. As Mansbridge has noted, "Power produces ownership, with its attendant responsibility. . . . Uninvolved in deciding about these matters, [the citizen] will not develop 'the spirit of ownership nor any ideas about improvement.'" The Civic Constitution assumes citizens will develop a taste for and attend to what Villa calls "public liberty," and public liberty contemplates a citizenry that both understands and participates in the articulation and application of constitutional principles. The Civic Constitution thus needs citizens to acknowledge and to engage in constitutional debate—and it likewise requires citizens who understand and are comfortable with a considerable degree of constitutional uncertainty about what fidelity to the Constitution demands. Constitutional dialogue, independent of outcome, contributes to constitutional ends because it advances the project of constitutional maintenance more generally.[263]

It is a mistake to assume the Civic Constitution guarantees respect for constitutional principles or liberties in times of crisis. But *if* such principles are to be respected, their best chance of doing so depends upon citizens invested with a robust sense of civic responsibility for tending to the Constitution.[264] As Justice Jackson warned in *Korematsu v. United States* (1944),

"The chief restraint upon those who command the physical forces of the country, in the future as in the past, must be their responsibility to the political judgments of their contemporaries and to the moral judgments of history."[265]

CONCLUSION

A security regime that has broken faith with the normative premises of constitutional governance but that has not resulted in the formal suspension or repeal of constitutional rules and commands may fairly be described as constitutional in strictly legal terms. Hence, some will respond to my assessments of failure by noting that no provision of the constitutional text has been suspended or repealed, that elections continue to take place as scheduled, and that the formal institutional and structural components of separation of powers, federalism, and constitutional/judicial review remain largely undisturbed.

Why then should we conclude that the Constitution has failed? What I call rot might be a pressing and perhaps even a desirable accommodation of utopian constitutional ideals to a harsh and terrifying reality. Maybe these compromises represent "a successful failure" of the Constitution.[266] And if the accommodation of principle to exigency still offends our sensibilities, then maybe we should call it some other kind of failure—a moral failure, or a failure of will. How does it help to describe it as a *constitutional* failure, much less the kind of pernicious failure suggested by calling it constitutional rot?

Rot is constitutional failure because it describes a state of affairs in which we are governed by our fear instead of our reason. The threat to our civic life lies in how public institutions, rather than developing a culture of reason and deliberation, have instead promoted a culture of fear. Fear prefers subjects to citizens. Fear withers civic space and constricts public liberty; it silences public conversation and debate.[267] Moreover, fear so incapacitates that we cannot admit our compromise of constitutional principle. The constitution persists, but only as text and as symbol; it does not govern in any meaningful sense.

Rot is constitutional failure because it is a state of being incompatible with the normative commitments that comprise our Constitution *and* because there is no evidence of significant civic discourse about that dissonance.[268] To be more precise, the failure is in the (odious) policy choices we have made *and* in our collective indifference to the constitutional questions those choices raise. In terms of the Civic Constitution, the failure is the failure of citizens to take up our civic responsibilities to care for and to conserve the Constitution. The failure is not of regimes or of institutions—not the unwillingness or inability of Congress or courts to resist such encroachments—but rather of our collective public aspiration "to be rational."[269] The failure must be attributed to us all.

How do we prevent or combat constitutional rot? Although there is no guarantee that civic-minded citizens will safeguard constitutional norms and values, the best remedy for rot is to find ways to promote the constitutional virtues of civility and tending. This requires us to recalibrate constitutional institutions in ways that facilitate civility, that is, by adopting dialogic or relational understandings of the separation of powers doctrine, reinvigorating federalism, and embracing allocations and methods of constitutional interpretation that are inclusive rather than exclusive. It likewise requires that the Court interpret or reinterpret long-held doctrinal positions—concerning freedom of speech, to take one example—that open the possibility of vibrant and robust public discourse, rather than doctrines that depress or marginalize civic space.[270] These last are especially important to what must be the primary method of combating constitutional rot: creating and maintaining a vibrant civic culture of deliberation and tending.

CONCLUSION

What is the point of an inquiry into the Civic Constitution? Behind the question is the intimation that its vision of a constitutional way of life is either demoded or dystopian. The first suggestion holds that whatever the desirability of the Civic Constitution, its time is long past. The second rejects the Civic Constitution as an objectionable way of organizing political life.

The argument from obsolescence holds that even if the Civic Constitution's vision of a constitutional way of life is appealing, it is a way of life we can no longer realize. We might think that the kind of civic culture necessary to sustain the Civic Constitution, as well as the kind of citizens it enjoins, is improbable in our time—it may envision citizens who not only are ideal, to borrow Murphy's formulation,[1] but are indefectible. Put directly, the Civic Constitution simply asks too much of citizens. By "asks too much," I mean it exacts too much in terms of the resources citizens will be willing to commit to civic life. Moreover, the ethics of civility and tending are impractical (and forgotten) in liberal states, where civic space is restricted to mimetic rituals of citizenship.[2] But it might mean also that the Civic Constitution requires a degree of civic knowledge and sophistication well beyond what most citizens can be expected to possess in modern liberal states, which both encourage and reward private rather than public virtue. "Like it or not, the world we inhabit as citizens is irreducibly pluralist, fragmented, and elusive."[3] Civic reengagement may not be possible in contemporary liberal states, where what we call political liberty and public space is "less an arena for the exercise of a distinctive (nonprivate) form of freedom than it is an all-purpose container or scrim for . . . endless lobbying, bogus 'citizen initiatives,' and staged political events."[4] What the Civic Constitution portrays as shortcomings of the Juridic Constitution, in other words, are characteristics of the modern nation-state more broadly; if they can or should be ameliorated, the cure will not be located in arguments about how to revitalize a particular, and likely obsolete, constitutional culture.[5]

This objection might further note that the Juridic Constitution has evolved in ways that make restoration of the Civic unlikely. We might conclude, for instance, that strong-form judicial review and the preclusive presidency are cemented, as I intimated in my discussion of constitutional rot, or that they

have permanently altered our understanding of what constitutional governance means. But however robust or anemic we think our civic life is, its
health is in some measure a consequence of constitutional design and maintenance. The institutions we have are the ones we think the Juridic Constitution requires. They arrange incentives and disincentives for civic life in ways
that are neither inevitable nor inescapable; we can reimagine those same
institutions in ways that facilitate rather than discourage civic engagement.
Recovering the Civic Constitution does not require a new constitutional
architectonics; it is a work of restoration rather than replacement.

The dystopian objection rejects the Civic Constitution not as impractical but rather as an undesirable way of organizing political life. It is better
or more productive or more efficient, it argues, for citizens to devote their
energies to private life or to pursuits both grander and smaller than constitutional politics. A related version of this objection finds virtue in permitting
citizens to choose for themselves which commitments and values are worth
pursuing. The energy and effort expended by citizens on constitutional maintenance is an intrusion upon the autonomy of citizens who might otherwise
choose to devote their resources and energies to some other pursuit. The
burdens of civic citizenship intrude too far on the private lives and choices of
citizens, many of whom might prefer to organize their lives in other ways, or
to make commitments that prioritize other values and choices. Citizens must
be free "to waste their lives."[6] In asking so little of us as citizens, the Juridic
Constitution frees us to be persons. On this approach, the Civic Constitution is an objectionable, or at least a less attractive, way of organizing and
constituting political life, than is the Juridic Constitution.

The complaint is grounded in a particular understanding of liberalism,
one that places a very high value on the private pursuit of the good.[7] From
this premise, the Juridic Constitution is superior to the Civic not in spite of
its thin approach to citizenship, but precisely because of it. By now my disagreement with both iterations of this objection should be clear, but I want
to emphasize that the liberal objection is premised on and reflects a choice
about how to organize political community—it is not hardwired into the
Constitution or beyond our command.

There are other reasons why we might resist the Civic Constitution. One
might be that it offers insufficient protection for civil liberties or for constitutional values and principles more generally. This fear assumes the people are
ignorant of and insufficiently committed to constitutional principles. A related objection insists that the sorts of constitutional settlements we will find
under the Civic Constitution are demonstrably inferior to those that will be
secured if we entrust them instead to courts or some similar forum of princi-

ple.[8] These and comparable objections often rest on an empirical claim,[9] that citizens have little regard for fundamental constitutional norms and values, and are especially inhospitable to the rights and liberties of the unpopular or marginalized. So the Civic Constitution "may simply permit the political processes to proceed, such as they are," write Fleming and McClain, "and to trample on or neglect basic principles of liberty and equality."[10] As a consequence, justice-seeking accounts of constitutional life, in which the Constitution is committed to the preservation and maintenance of constitutional norms and principles (whether entrenched or not), are likely to see in the Civic Constitution an insufficient commitment to these principles at the expense of popular participation in constitutional maintenance. If our ultimate purpose is to achieve the best constitutional way of life, and if that way of life requires fidelity to fundamental constitutional precepts, the argument runs, then the Juridic Constitution is a more promising vehicle. I suspect most of us, even those who otherwise champion a significant constitutional role for citizens, assume too easily that the people will be unreliable guardians of constitutional norms. But the available evidence here is thin,[11] and we make too much of what evidence there is. American history is rich with instances of deliberation and civic engagement concerning the meaning and vitality of our commitment to constitutional norms and principles.[12] It is not obvious that a robust conception of civic constitutionalism will consistently yield results that are unpalatable to constitutionalists, rights-theorists, or civil libertarians. A citizenry with responsibility for preserving constitutional values might be up to the task. Additionally, some concerns raised by critics about constitutional populism of the sort advanced by Kramer, Tushnet, and myself, such as complaints that citizens lack the knowledge or competence required to maintain the Constitution, are premised on specific and contestable claims about what kind of knowledge the project demands.[13]

More importantly, to the extent public incapacity to honor our constitutional commitments is a social fact, we mistake cause for effect. If citizens are uncongenial to constitutional rights, then we have precisely the kind of citizens the juridic monopoly helped to create. If We the People have not shown much inclination to tend to the Constitution, then it is also true that we have had little opportunity or incentive to do so. Deprived of significant opportunity or reason to tend to constitutional norms, should we wonder that most citizens fail to embrace them as fully as we might like? As Jefferson counseled, "if we think [the people] not enlightened enough to exercise their control with a wholesome discretion, the remedy is not to take it from them, but to inform their discretion by education."[14] Constitutional maturity can be won only through the chance to exercise and learn responsibility.[15]

I think we should admit, though, that the Civic Constitution will not always showcase our best constitutional selves. (I should not have to add that we can criticize the Juridic Constitution on the same ground.) Sometimes we will act based on interests rather than principles, on passion rather than reason.[16] Indeed, sometimes we will act without deliberating or considering what our constitutional commitments require of us. Worse, these results may well violate some understandings of justice, the good life, or even principles and commitments that are meant to be foundational or entrenched. The Civic Constitution, no less than the Juridic, must acknowledge our imperfections and our failures, a point I tried to make in Essay Three.

Finally, we might think the Civic Constitution is an unwelcome understanding of the Constitution because it undermines the constitutional enterprise as a whole. On this view, intimate knowledge of the Constitution's imperfections and our own failures threatens our attachment to the Constitution. If this Madisonian objection is correct, then the Civic Constitution reminds us tranquility is purchased at a very high cost. No doubt, some measure of veneration and affection is a useful, and perhaps a necessary, part of securing both the Constitution's authority and our fidelity to it.[17] On the other hand, most of whom and what we come to love in life are flawed; our affection is made deeper, more profound, more mature, when we look at the things of the world and see them for what they are.[18]

What is the point of an inquiry into the Civic Constitution? The Civic Constitution, no less than the Juridic, is who We are, a part of the constitutional imagination invoked by the Preamble to the Constitution. Indeed, the Preamble makes clear that although We the People exist in the present, we are also "caught between the possibilities of looking backward or looking forward."[19] To ask after the Civic Constitution, then, is simply to ask who We are, or to inquire into who We were and who We might be, simultaneously a work of remembrance and of imagination.

NOTES

Introduction

1. I outlined a preliminary approach to the Civic Constitution and coined the term in "The Civic Constitution: Some Preliminaries," in *Constitutional Politics: Essays on Constitution Making, Maintenance, and Change,* ed. Sotirios A. Barber and Robert P. George (Princeton, N.J.: Princeton University Press, 2001), 41–69.

2. As Elkin has observed, "The Constitution is not a law just like any other, only more important. It is, instead, the outline of a political regime to which we as Americans are committed. . . . It designates the purposes and constitutes features of that regime." Stephen L. Elkin, *Reconstructing the Commercial Republic: Constitutional Design after Madison* (Chicago: University of Chicago Press, 2006), 99.

3. For a general discussion of the concept of constitutional identity, see Gary J. Jacobsohn, *Constitutional Identity* (Cambridge, Mass.: Harvard University Press, 2010).

4. See Sotirios A. Barber, *On What the Constitution Means* (Baltimore: Johns Hopkins University Press, 1984).

5. Elizabeth Beaumont, *The Civic Constitution: Civic Visions and Struggles in the Path toward Constitutional Democracy* (New York: Oxford University Press, 2014).

6. For a more extensive discussion of the Juridic Constitution, see Finn, "Civic," 42.

7. Ibid. See Edward S. Corwin, *Court over Constitution: A Study of Judicial Review as an Instrument of Popular Government* (Princeton, N.J.: Princeton University Press, 1938); Robert F. Nagel, *Constitutional Cultures: The Mentality and Consequences of Judicial Review* (Berkeley: University of California Press, 1989).

8. This reference overlooks important questions about the meaning of "law." For example, we might distinguish between a conception of law as rules and law "as reasoning of a certain form." See Judge Easterbrook, *Politics and the Constitution: The Nature and Extent of Interpretation* (Washington, D.C.: National Legal Center for the Public Interest, 1990), 23. I take up some of these questions in Essay One.

9. See, e.g., John Brigham, *The Cult of the Court* (Philadelphia: Temple University Press, 1987), 35; David Ray Papke, *Heretics in the Temple: Americans Who Reject the Nation's Legal Faith* (New York: New York University Press, 1998), 3–13. I discuss the logic of the "Constitution is law" claim, and the origins of the Juridic Constitution, more fully in "Civic," 45–47.

10. A point illustrated by much of the recent academic work on popular constitutionalism. See, for example, Larry D. Kramer, *The People Themselves: Popular Constitutionalism and Judicial Review* (New York: Oxford University Press, 2004); Syl-

via Snowiss, *Judicial Review and the Law of the Constitution* (New Haven, Conn.: Yale University Press, 1990).

11. Marshall's opinion in *Marbury* was not the first (nor the last) effort to tie the legal nature of the text to questions about who possesses institutional responsibility for discerning its meaning, but it is the most familiar version. Marshall wrote, for example, "Certainly all those who have framed written constitutions contemplate them as forming the fundamental and paramount law of the nation," *Marbury v. Madison* (1803). For a different take on *Marbury*'s understanding of the Constitution and its relationship to claims of legal expertise, see Paul W. Kahn, *The Reign of Law: Marbury v. Madison and the Construction of America* (New Haven, Conn.: Yale University Press, 1997), especially 212–229.

12. Sheldon S. Wolin, *Politics and Vision: Continuity and Innovation in Western Political Thought* (Boston: Little, Brown, 1960), 66.

13. See Michael P. Zuckert, "Legality and Legitimacy in *Dred Scott*: The Crisis of the Incomplete Constitution," *Chicago-Kent Law Review* 82 (2007): 291. For a rather different treatment of the concept of constitutional incompleteness, see Jean-Michel Josselin and Alain Marciano, "Constitutional Incompleteness: Theoretical Assessment and Case Studies," paper presented to European Public Choice Society, 2005, http://www.dur.ac.uk/john.ashworth/EPCS/Papers/Josselin_Marciano.pdf.

14. As a point of clarification, I do not think *Marbury* itself makes this claim, although the idea that *Marbury* establishes strong-form judicial review is widely held. See generally Sylvia Snowiss, "The *Marbury* of 1803 and the Modern *Marbury*," *Constitutional Commentary* 20 (2003): 231.

15. See Nagel, *Constitutional Cultures*, 6–26.

16. See *Federalist* #1; see generally, Sotirios A. Barber and Robert P. George, eds., *Constitutional Politics: Essays on Constitution Making, Maintenance, and Change* (Princeton, N.J.: Princeton University Press, 2001).

17. For a general discussion of constitutional fidelity, albeit one that treats the concept as related centrally to questions of interpretation, see Pamela S. Karlan, Goodwin Liu, and Christopher H. Schroeder, *Keeping Faith with the Constitution* (New York: Oxford University Press, 2010). For an extended discussion of the meaning and uses of fidelity, see *Fidelity in Constitutional Theory*: "Editors' Foreword," 1247 (1997), http://ir.lawnet.fordham.edu/flr/vol65/iss4/1. See also Jack M. Balkin, "Fidelity to Text and Principle," in *The Constitution in 2020*, ed. Jack M. Balkin and Reva B. Siegel (New York: Oxford University Press, 2009), 20.

18. See generally Jacobsohn, *Constitutional Identity*, Introduction, especially xiv–xv, 135.

19. Ibid., 88.

20. Kahn, *Reign of Law*, 3.

21. George Thomas, *The Madisonian Constitution* (Baltimore: Johns Hopkins University Press, 2008).

22. Colleen A. Sheehan, *James Madison and the Spirit of Republican Self-Government* (New York: Cambridge University Press, 2009).

23. Elkin, *Commercial Republic.*

24. Jacobsohn, *Constitutional Identity*, 134.

25. Finn, "Civic," 50.

26. Hanna F. Pitkin, "The Idea of a Constitution." *Journal of Legal Education* 37 (1987): 167, 168.

27. See Walter F. Murphy, *Constitutional Democracy: Creating and Maintaining a Just Political Order* (Baltimore: Johns Hopkins University Press, 2007), 13; Aristotle, *The Politics*, ed. and trans. Ernest Barker (London: Oxford University Press, 1948), ch. II, 1295a.

28. Aristotle, *Politics, Book Three* (Mineola, N.Y.: Dover Publications, 2000).

29. For a discussion about the difference between commitment and consent, see Jeb Rubenfeld, "Legitimacy and Interpretation," in *Constitutionalism: Philosophical Foundations*, ed. Larry Alexander (Cambridge: Cambridge University Press, 1998), 216–219.

30. One might say that every constitution commits its citizens to a constitutional way of life. Every constitution, we might conclude, commits us to its own unique vision of how we ought to constitute and order the polity. In this way, we could fairly conclude that the Juridic Constitution equally commits us to a constitutional way of life, but one that looks very different from some others. I do not think this objection is sound in any sense other than nominally. To speak of a constitutional way of life as simply a specific manifestation of a specific constitution, no matter the character or substance of that constitution, is to ignore a rich intellectual history that conceptualizes constitutions as manifestations of constitutionalism. See generally, Murphy, *Constitutional Democracy*, esp. 6–7; Charles H. McIlwain, *Constitutionalism: Ancient and Modern* (Ithaca, N.Y.: Cornell University Press, 1947).

31. Thus conceding the inevitability of imperfection, as well as opening up difficult questions about the meaning of "perfect." For a discussion of some of the various meanings of perfect, see John E. Finn, "The Perfect Recipe: Taste and Tyranny, Cooks and Citizens," *Food, Culture, and Society* 14 (2011): 503.

32. As Barber has observed, "The aspirational tone of the Constitution is unmistakable in the Preamble" as well as "present in the Constitution's logic." Barber, *On What the Constitution Means*, 34.

33. John Finn, *Constitutions in Crisis: Political Violence and the Rule of Law* (New York: Oxford University Press, 1991), 34.

34. When I use the word "commitments," I typically mean it in the way Rubenfeld does. *Freedom and Time: A Theory of Constitutional Self-Government* (New Haven, Conn.: Yale University Press, 2001); see also *Revolution by Judiciary: The Structure of American Constitutional Law* (Cambridge, Mass.: Harvard University Press, 2005).

35. In some ways, the distinction tracks Tushnet's distinction between justice-talk and constitution-talk, but not precisely. I distinguish between universal and particular commitments, but both are expressions of constitutionalism. Mark V. Tushnet, "Constitution-Talk and Justice-Talk," *Fordham Law Review* 69 (2001): 1999.

36. See my work on "constitutive principles" in *Constitutions in Crisis: Political Violence and the Rule of Law* (New York: Oxford University Press, 1991), ch. 1. For a slightly different treatment, see Jacobsohn, *Constitutional Identity*, 5–7.

37. Why these documents and not some others? I discuss this question more fully below and again in Essay One. Additional candidates might include, for instance, the Mayflower Compact, the Kentucky and Virginia Resolutions, the Northwest Ordinances, Calhoun's *Discourses*, John Brown's "Provisional Constitution and Ordinances for the People of the United States," and many others. Under the Civic Constitution, a determination of which documents contribute substantially to our constitutional identity cannot be established conclusively, but is instead itself a part of the ongoing process of constitutional conversation that makes up the project of constitutional maintenance. For a general discussion of how these texts might contribute to our constitutional understanding, but one that does not fully engage the problem of whether these texts should be understood as part of the Constitution or simply as aids to meaning, see Akhil Reed Amar, *America's Unwritten Constitution: The Precedents and Principles We Live By* (New York: Basic Books, 2012). For a fascinating discussion of John Brown's Constitution as an example of fringe constitutionalism, see Robert L. Tsai, "John Brown's Constitution," *Boston College Law Review* 51 (2010): 151.

38. Kramer, *People Themselves*.

39. Bruce Ackerman, *We the People*, vol. 1: *Foundations* (Cambridge, Mass.: Belknap Press of Harvard University Press, 1993).

40. One might object that the term "civic" is so broad that it simply references all forms of political conversation and activity. As Fleming has noted of Kramer's work, "it is not clear that the Constitution, or constitutionalism, is doing much work in popular constitutionalism." James E. Fleming, "Judicial Review without Judicial Supremacy: Taking the Constitution Seriously Outside the Courts," *Fordham Law Review* 73 (2005): 1378, 1379. Elsewhere, making a similar point, Fleming observes that popular constitutionalism has been more directed to the *who* of interpretation than the *what*, 1390: "For another, it is not clear that the people themselves . . . are ultimately interpreting the Constitution, as distinguished from it simply being the case that public opinion about wants, interests, or justice has prevailed as a fact of political power over judicial interpretations of the Constitution." Fleming, "Judicial Review," 1390. These are important concerns, and I shall attempt to address them throughout. But in brief, I do not think every form of civic activity is constitutionally directed or relevant, or that the categories overlap perfectly, but neither can we draw a sharp distinction between political and constitutional, especially (1) once we conceptualize constitutional commitments as including more than prescriptions of law, and (2) once we also recognize that citizens must actively assume the responsibility to conserve a constitutional way of life. In addition, the constitutionalist components of the Civic Constitution require efforts at civic engagement to respect fundamental constitutional precepts. Hence, the Constitution does "some of the work," I will argue, by putting

constraints on what the people may do. I discuss this more fully below. Nor do I think it is difficult to find many instances of the people's civic engagement that expressly engage the Constitution or make explicit reference to constitutional norms and ideals. To take just one example, see the work of David C. Williams, *The Mythic Meanings of the Second Amendment: Taming Political Violence in a Constitutional Republic* (New Haven, Conn.: Yale University Press, 2003), where he writes of the pronounced tendency of "the way people take their deepest fears and hopes and render them into constitutional stories, so that others will have to take notice." Williams, "Civic Constitutionalism, the Second Amendment, and the Right of Revolution," *Indiana Law Journal* 79 (2004): 379, 389. Finally, as I discuss below (see p. 24), civic conversation and civic practice must include the work of those whom Papke calls "legal heretics," or individuals and social movements that advance direct challenges to constitutional government as insufficiently committed to the pursuit of justice or some other, superordinate human purpose, which further complicates the distinction between constitutional and political. Papke, *Heretics in the Temple*, 2–4.

41. Kramer, *People Themselves*.

42. Les Swanson, review of *The People Themselves: Popular Constitutionalism and Judicial Review* by Larry D. Kramer, http://www.osbar.org/_docs/sections/constitu /july05/SwansonReview.pdf. My earlier work on the Civic Constitution, and especially those parts of it that address departmentalism and judicial supremacy, may have contributed to this in a small way. See Finn, "Civic," 57–60.

43. According to one definition, "the essence of popular constitutionalism is the supremacy of 'the people' over the meaning of constitutional law." Richard Stith, "Securing the Rule of Law through Interpretive Pluralism: An Argument from Comparative Law," *Hastings Law Quarterly* 35 (2008): 401, 404n7. As I indicate below, if this is a correct understanding, then the Civic Constitution is not a kind of popular constitutionalism, because the Civic Constitution includes foundational elements that are beyond the authority of any actor, the people included, to alter at will. See Essay Two, pp. 146–149. For two general treatments, see Kramer, *People Themselves;* for a critical response, see Lawrence B. Solum, "Popular? Constitutionalism?" *Harvard Law Review* 118 (2005): 1594. For a brief but interesting discussion of where accounts of departmentalism and popular constitutionalism converge and diverge, see Stith, "Securing the Rule of Law," 404n7.

44. Jeremy Waldron, *Law and Disagreement* (New York: Oxford University Press, 2001); Mark V. Tushnet, *Taking the Constitution Away from the Courts* (Princeton, N.J.: Princeton University Press, 2000).

45. Lawrence G. Sager, *Justice in Plainclothes: A Theory of American Constitutional Practice* (New Haven, Conn.: Yale University Press, 2004). For a discussion of five different types of popular constitutionalism, see Fleming, "Judicial Review," 1379.

46. See Harry C. Boyte, "Beyond Deliberation: Citizenship as Public Work," *Political Economy of the Good Society* 5 (1995): 15.

47. For a fuller discussion of civic life as civic work, and not just as deliberation, see pp. 53–54.

48. See, for example, Kramer, *People Themselves;* and Mark V. Tushnet, "Popular Constitutionalism as Political Law," *Chicago-Kent Law Review* 81 (2006): 991–1006.

49. This concern relates directly to the civic dimension of the constitutional order: insofar as the Civic Constitution depends upon citizens for its conservation, we might wonder how secure its constitutional elements will be. I consider this objection in Essays Two and Three.

50. Jacobsohn, *Constitutional Identity*, 348–349. See generally Erik H. Erikson, *Identity and the Life Cycle*, vol. 1 (New York: W. W. Norton, 1994).

51. Tushnet, "Constitution-Talk and Justice-Talk."

52. Christopher Eisgruber, *Constitutional Self-Government* (Cambridge, Mass.: Harvard University Press, 2007).

53. Lawrence Sager, in Larry Alexander, ed., *Constitutionalism: Philosophical Foundations* (Cambridge: Cambridge University Press, 2001), 238. See also Sager, *Justice in Plainclothes.*

54. Alexander, *Constitutionalism*, 238.

55. Ibid., 239.

56. Ibid., 86.

57. Ibid., 240.

58. Ibid., 242.

59. Fleming, "Judicial Review," 1383. There are also, Sager notes, "trace elements" of these unenforceable principles in "the ore of otherwise anomalous judicial doctrine," *Justice in Plainclothes*, 189.

60. James E. Fleming, "The Balkinization of Originalism," *University of Illinois Law Review* 2012 (2012): 669, 678: "In any case, a moral reading is not necessarily a court-centered, antipopular reading. In fact, I daresay that constitutional Protestantism and popular constitutionalism are most obviously expressed in the form of moral readings."

61. Fleming, "Judicial Review," 1380.

62. See Tushnet, *Taking the Constitution Away from the Courts* (1999), 95–128; Fleming, "Judicial Review," 1396.

63. Cass Sunstein, *Legal Reasoning and Political Conflict* (New York: Oxford University Press, 1996).

64. On deliberative democracy generally, see James S. Fishkin, *Democracy and Deliberation* (New Haven, Conn.: Yale University Press, 1993); Amy Gutmann and Dennis Thompson, *Democracy and Disagreement* (Cambridge, Mass.: Harvard University Press, 1998); Seyla Benhabib, "Toward a Deliberative Model of Democratic Legitimacy," in *Democracy and Difference: Contesting the Boundaries of the Political*, ed. Seyla Benhabib (Princeton, N.J.: Princeton University Press, 1996). On deliberative constitutionalism, see Jürgen Habermas, *Between Facts and Norms: Contributions to a Discourse Theory of Law and Democracy* (Cambridge, Mass.:

MIT Press, 1998); Carlos Santiago Nino, *The Constitution of Deliberative Democracy* (New Haven, Conn.: Yale University Press, 1996); Cass Sunstein, *The Partial Constitution* (Cambridge, Mass.: Harvard University Press, 1993). For an overview, see John J. Worley, "Deliberative Constitutionalism," *Brigham Young University Law Review* 2009 (2009) 431.

65. Richard S. Kay, "American Constitutionalism," in Alexander, *Constitutionalism*, 6–57.

66. As described by Habermas, the "concept of the public sphere . . . includes several requirements for authenticity. These include open access, voluntary participation outside institutional roles, the generation of public judgment through assemblies of citizens who engage in political deliberation, the freedom to express opinions, and the freedom to discuss matters of the state and to criticize the way state power is organized." http://www.scottlondon.com/reports/tele.html. In *A Theory of Justice*, "John Rawls delineates a number of other conditions as well: adequate information; a norm of political equality in which 'the force of the argument' takes precedence over power and authority; an absence of strategic manipulation of information, perspective, processes, or outcomes in general; and a broad public orientation toward reaching right answers rather than serving narrow self-interest." http://www.scottlondon.com/reports/tele.html.

67. Finn, *Crisis*, ch. one.

68. Kahn, *Reign*, 53. And it occurs in public space.

69. Or, as Brandeis noted, "Those who won our independence believed . . . that in its government the deliberative forces should prevail over the arbitrary," *Whitney v. California* (1927).

70. For the important argument that democratic deliberation must find room for moral sentiment, and that such arguments are not inherently incompatible with claims of reason, see Sharon Krause, *Civil Passions: Moral Sentiment and Democratic Deliberation* (Princeton, N.J.: Princeton University Press, 2008). For additional arguments about the proper place of emotion, passion, and even prejudice in civic discourse, see Russell Muirhead, "Can Deliberative Democracy be Partisan?" *Critical Review* 22, no. 2–3 (2010): 129–157; Bryan Garsten, *Saving Persuasion: A Defense of Rhetoric and Judgment* (Cambridge, Mass.: Harvard University Press, 2009); Nancy Rosenblum, *Membership and Morals: The Personal Uses of Pluralism in America* (Princeton, N.J.: Princeton University Press, 1998).

71. Finn, *Crisis*, 31–34.

72. Amy Gutmann and Dennis Thompson, *Why Deliberative Democracy?* (Princeton, N.J.: Princeton University Press, 2004), 3.

73. John Rawls, "The Idea of Public Reason Revisited," *University of Chicago Law Review* 64 (1997): 765; see also Joshua Cohen, "Deliberation and Democratic Legitimacy," 1, http://philosophyfaculty.ucsd.edu/faculty/rarneson/JCOHENDELIBERATIVE%20DEM.pdf.

74. There is an important objection here: In short form, the complaint is that my conception of civic reason disqualifies from civic conversation arguments grounded

in religious faith and that such arguments have a long and noble heritage in our constitutional history. Moreover, one might observe that some of the precepts I describe as constitutive of constitutionalism itself—such as equal moral worth and human dignity—are grounded in such forms of argument. I will take up these points in more detail in Essays One and Three, but first I would concede that many if not most of the fundamental precepts of Western constitutional thought cannot be understood independent of their religious pedigree. See, for example, Carl J. Friedrich, *Transcendent Justice: The Religious Dimension of Constitutionalism* (Indianapolis: Lilly Endowment Research Program in Christianity and Politics, 1964); Edward S. Corwin, "The Higher Law Background of American Constitutional Law," *Harvard Law Review* 42 (1928): 149. Partly for that reason, some arguments about the public good, grounded in claims of faith, will be deeply consonant with principles, reasons, and arguments that are demonstrably constitutional in character, or that others can recognize as advancing constitutional ends. I take up a related point below (see note 174 and accompanying text), when I discuss criticisms of reason as hostile to forms of human knowledge grounded in emotion and alternative ways of knowing; see, for example, Krause, *Civil Passions*. It is partly for this reason that I have tried to indicate that the Civic Constitution must be located not only in deliberation but also in civic practice/work, in which citizens, through the necessity of practical engagement with others, learn the virtues of empathy and "the capacity to feel with the widest range of others." Krause, *Civil Passions*, 135. Finally, Robert Nagel reminds me that much of our constitutional practice and meaning has "been established by warfare, demonstrations, myth making, and sloganeering." See also Rogers M. Smith, *Civic Ideals: Conflicting Visions of Citizenship in U.S. History* (New Haven, Conn.: Yale University Press, 1997). I am not fully persuaded that these practices are evidence of "unreason," or of passion and will, to the exclusion of reason and deliberation. When we look for the Civic Constitution as practice, and not simply as a theoretical prospect, we must look for it not only in civic practices that celebrate or conform to constitutional norms and ideals, but also where civic practices challenge or reject those same norms. But surely Professor Nagel's larger point—that the Constitution writ large is not simply a product of reason and deliberation—is a fair one. Like all constitutions, the Civic Constitution is a product of design and chance, ideal and practice, reason and passion. Its authority, in the words of Nathan Tarcov, "must rest both on the aspiration of the people to be rational and on its habitual reverence for a Constitution that has stood the test of time." Nathan Tarcov, "Ideas of Constitutionalism Ancient and Modern," in *The Supreme Court and the Idea of Constitutionalism*, ed. Steven Kautz, Arthur Melzer, Jerry Weinberger, and M. Richard Zinman (Philadelphia: University of Pennsylvania Press, 2009), 28. See also *Federalist* #49.

75. Finn, *Crisis*, 35.

76. Id.

77. Worley, "Deliberative Constitutionalism."

78. For this reason alone, the Civic Constitution cannot be simply a deliberative constitution. As Gutmann and Thompson note, a deliberative account of public

life "does not seek a foundational principle or set of principles that, in advance of actual political activity, determines whether a procedure or law is justified. Instead, it adopts a dynamic conception of political justification, in which change over time is an essential feature of justifiable principles." *Why Deliberative Democracy*, 132.

79. See Mary P. Ryan, "Gender and Public Access," in Craig Calhoun, ed., *Habermas and the Public Sphere* (Cambridge, Mass.: MIT Press, 1992).

80. "None of this should be romanticized—such ideas and practices often had strong personal and parochial dimensions." Boyte, "Beyond Deliberation," 18. See generally, Harry C. Boyte, *Everyday Politics: Reconnecting Citizens and Public Life* (Philadelphia: University of Pennsylvania Press, 2005); *Building America: The Democratic Promise of Public Work*, with Nancy N. Kari (Philadelphia: Temple University Press, 1996).

81. Our best constitutional selves, although centered on concepts of deliberation and reason-giving, are also, under the Civic Constitution, committed to practicing the virtues of civility and tending, located in civic engagement as well as in reason and deliberation. The concept of deliberation under the Civic Constitution, in other words, is more attentive to difference than the depictions of public deliberation associated with theorists like Habermas and Rawls, and less susceptible to charges that deliberation is an inadequate account of public life. See Krause, *Civil Passions*, Introduction and ch. 5.

82. Boyte, "Beyond Deliberation," 13.

83. Ibid., 17.

84. Ibid., 18.

85. Ibid., 17.

86. Civic work, because it requires citizens to engage with difference, augments the capacity of citizens to "feel with the widest range of others." Krause, *Civil Passions*, 135.

87. This is not to say that the activity of maintenance is restricted to debates over the meanings of seminal texts. See also Brett Marston, "Citizen Constitutional Knowledge, Civic Capacities, and Constitutional Meaning: The Civic Constitution Meets Interest Groups and Social Movements," paper delivered at MPSA, April 2003, 13.

88. Pierre Hadot, *Philosophy as a Way of Life: Spiritual Exercises from Socrates to Foucault*, ed. Arnold Davidson (New York: Wiley-Blackwell, 1995).

89. Robert Dahl, *Democracy and Its Critics* (New Haven, Conn.: Yale University Press, 1980), 15.

90. See especially William Wiecek, *Sources of Antislavery Constitutionalism in America* (Ithaca, N.Y.: Cornell University Press, 1977). On popular resistance to the Alien and Sedition Acts, see Michael Kent Curtis, *Free Speech, The People's Darling Privilege: Struggles for Freedom of Expression in American History* (Durham, N.C.: Duke University Press, 2000). See also Beaumont, *Civic Constitution* (reviewing the efforts of citizens to reinvent constitutional democracy during four crucial eras: the revolutionaries of the 1770s and 1780s; the civic founders of state republics and the

national Constitution in the early national period; abolitionists during the antebellum and Civil War eras; and suffragists of the late nineteenth and early twentieth centuries).

91. Kramer, *People Themselves.*

92. William E. Forbath, "Constitutional Welfare Rights: A History, Critique and Reconstruction," *Fordham Law Review* 69 (2001): 1821, 1829.

93. Ibid., 1829–1832; see also William E. Forbath, *Law and the Shaping of the American Labor Movement* (Cambridge, Mass.: Harvard University Press, 1991).

94. See the important article by L.A. Powe Jr., "Are the 'People' Missing in Action (and Should Anyone Care?)," *Texas Law Review* 83 (2005): 855.

95. The obvious objection is that voting rights movements are democratic practices, but not constitutional ones, and thus that public involvement in such controversies is not actually an example of constitutional maintenance. But the distinction is too easy and cannot be maintained. Part of what's relevant here is precisely the distinction between constitutional aspirations and the judicially enforceable constitution, in part because so much of the voting rights movement was centered upon the enlisting the courts in that movement. This is not an argument against the Civic Constitution, but instead reminds us that the Civic and Juridic Constitution sometimes work in tandem.

96. For an insightful discussion, see James E. Fleming and Linda C. McClain, *Ordered Liberty: Rights, Responsibilities, and Virtues* (Cambridge, Mass.: Harvard University Press, 2013).

97. Toni Marie Massaro, *Constitutional Literacy: A Core Curriculum for a Multicultural Nation* (Durham, N.C.: Duke University Press, 1993), 128–153. See also Linda C. McClain, "The Domain of Civic Virtue in a Good Society: Families, Schools, and Sex Equality," *Fordham Law Review* 69 (2001): 1635.

98. Dana Villa, *Public Freedom* (Princeton, N.J.: Princeton University Press, 2008), 26.

99. Although there are obvious points of comparison, I do not think of the Civic Constitution in terms of combining aspects of deliberative democracy with constitutional democracy to yield a "deliberative constitutionalism." For an insightful treatment of the prospects for deliberative constitutionalism, see Worley, "Deliberative Constitutionalism."

100. The concept of experiential space has different meanings in different academic disciplines, but is most prominently associated with geography. I use it in a somewhat different sense, partly influenced by the work of Yi-Fu Tuan, *Space and Place: The Perspective of Experience* (Minneapolis: University of Minnesota Press, 1977).

101. For a discussion of the civic importance of local juries—and by implication why its mention in the constitutional document of 1789 is further evidence of the text's civic and juridical dimensions—see Suzette Hemberger, "What Did They Think," in Barber and George, *Constitutional Politics*, 144–147.

102. On the historic importance of farmer's markets as centers of civility and

political intercourse in American public life, see Janet Flammang, *The Taste for Civil Society: Food, Politics, and Civil Society* (Urbana: University of Illinois Press, 2009), 255; 258–259.

103. Ray Oldenburg, *The Great Good Place: Cafes, Coffee Shops, Bookstores, Bars, Hair Salons, and Other Hangouts at the Heart of a Community* (Cambridge, Mass.: Da Capo Press, 1999).

104. See also Michael Walzer, *What It Means to be an American: Essays on the American Experience* (New York: Marsilo Publishers, 1996), 99: "What is necessary is the expansion of the public sphere."

105. Benjamin R. Barber, "An American Civic Forum," *Political Economy of the Good Society* 5 (1995): 10, 11.

106. Ibid., 11.

107. Ibid., 12.

108. Ibid., 13.

109. Flammang, *Taste*, 86.

110. Ibid., 86.

111. Ibid., 85.

112. Ibid., 87.

113. Boyte, "Beyond Deliberation," 15.

114. See Hadot, *Philosophy as a Way of Life*.

115. See, for example, Jürgen Habermas, *The Theory of Communicative Action* (Boston: Beacon Press, 1981) and *Between Facts and Norms*; Michael Sandel, *Democracy's Discontent: America in Search of a Public Philosophy* (Cambridge, Mass.: Harvard University Press, 1997); Cornell West, *Democracy Matters: Winning the Fight against Imperialism* (New York: Penguin Press, 2004).

116. Boyte, "Beyond Deliberation," 16.

117. Jürgen Habermas, *Knowledge and Human Interests* (Boston: Beacon Press, 1962), 58.

118. Barber, "Civic Forum," at 13.

119. Ibid., 11.

120. Ibid.

121. Sanford L. Levinson, *Constitutional Faith* (Princeton, N.J.: Princeton University Press, 1988), 35. Papke, *Heretics in the Temple*, 12–13: Law is the "official discourse" and "the principal medium" of the Republic. Quoting Christopher L. Tomlins, *Law, Labor, and Ideology in the Early American Republic* (Cambridge: Cambridge University Press, 1993), 16.

122. See, for example, Laurence Tribe and Michael C. Dorf, *On Reading the Constitution* (Cambridge, Mass.: Harvard University Press, 1991); if necessary, we could offer many examples of scholars who want to insist upon the "dialogic" or conversational character of constitutional interpretation. This list would include Levinson, Dworkin, Powell, Fiss, Perry, Wellington, and several others. There is, however, very little that is public about these conversations. For a fuller discussion, see Finn, "Civic," 48–49; see also Ira Strauber, "The Supreme Court, Constitutional

Interpretation, and Civic Education," paper delivered at the Annual Meeting of the Midwest Political Science Association, Chicago, Ill., April 9–11, 1992; Roger Cotterrell, *The Politics of Jurisprudence: A Critical Introduction to Legal Philosophy* (Philadelphia: University of Pennsylvania Press, 1989), 177.

123. For a discussion of civility as a public virtue, or as resting at the intersection of public and private, see Richard Boyd, "The Value of Civility," *Urban Studies* 50 (October 1, 2013): 863–878. Flammang similarly argues that the civic virtue, defined historically as the pursuit of the common good in the public sphere, was relegated to private life. Hence, "virtue came to be associated with middle-class propriety rather than civic life, and selflessness applied to motherhood, not the citizen's pursuit of a common good." *Taste*, 42. For general citations, see: Michael Walzer, "Civility and Civic Virtue," *Social Research* 41 (1974): 593–611; Burton Zwiebach, *Civility and Disobedience* (New York: Cambridge University Press, 1975); Clifford Orwin, "Civility," *American Scholar* 60 (1991): 553–564; Mark Kingwell, *A Civil Tongue: Justice, Dialogue and the Politics of Pluralism* (University Park: Pennsylvania State University Press, 1995); John Rawls, *A Theory of Justice* (Cambridge, Mass.: Harvard University Press, 1971), and *Political Liberalism* (New York Columbia University Press, 1993); Richard C. Sinopoli, "Thick-Skinned Liberalism: Redefining Civility," *American Political Science Review* 89 (1995): 612–620.

124. Flammang, *Taste*, 92. In describing civility as a civic virtue, I resist Herbst's suggestion that we should instead treat civility as a tool, or as "a strategic asset" in "the rhetorical and behavioral arsenals of politics." Susan Herbst, *Rude Democracy: Civility and Incivility in American Politics* (Philadelphia: Temple University Press, 2010), 6.

125. Cheshire Calhoun, "The Virtue of Civility," *Philosophy and Public Affairs* 29 (2000): 252.

126. Ibid., 251–252.

127. Finn, *Crisis*, 221.

128. Benjamin R. Barber, "The Discourse of Civility," in *Citizen Competence and Democratic Institutions*, ed. Stephen L. Elkin and Karol Edward Soltan (State College: Pennsylvania State University Press, 1999), 40.

129. Joanne Finkelstein, *Dining Out: A Sociology of Modern Manners* (New York: New York University Press, 1989), 9.

130. Barber, "Discourse," 42. He adds the public voice has nine characteristics; among them, it must also be common, inclusive, and provisional.

131. I borrow heavily from Joanne Finkelstein's definition of civility as "continual reflection on and examination of what constitutes the good life" and as "what can philosophically be proposed as the good society." Finkelstein, *Dining Out*, 174.

132. John Rawls, *Political Liberalism* (New York: Columbia University Press, 1993), 224.

133. Ibid., 217.

134. As I noted earlier, the virtues of civility and tending also soften the hard edge of a Rawlsian conception of reason that is inattentive to or dismissive of emotion and passion in the public sphere. See Krause, *Civil Passions*, ch. 1.

135. As described by Herbst, *Rude Democracy*, 19. Herbst cites "Considering Political Civility: A Case Study of the United States," paper presented at the Annual Meeting of the International Society for Political Psychology, 1999, http: //www.sam .kau.se/stv/ksspa/papers/sapiro_considering_political_civility_historically.pdf.

136. See Agnes Heller, *The Power of Shame* (London: Routledge and Kegan Paul, 1986), 71–230; see also the discussion in Finkelstein, *Dining Out*, 174.

137. Flammang, *Taste*, 2.

138. Calhoun, *Redefining Civility*, 256.

139. As Barber notes, "The public voice of civility is deliberative." Barber, "Discourse," 42. As Barber has noted, "Giving a civic and public voice legitimate civic articulation is a priority for all who want to invest that once sublime title citizen with renewed meaning." Ibid., 40.

140. Flammang, *Taste*, 14.

141. For an argument that reciprocity is a key component of civility, see Heinz Eulau, "Technology and the Fear of the Politics of Civility," *Journal of Politics* 35 (1973): 369.

142. Herbst, *Rude Democracy*, 19.

143. Finn, *Crisis*, 30–35.

144. Flammang, *Taste*, 82.

145. The reasons we advance must reference or relate to the overarching constitutional values and principles that we have determined constitute the good polity, or that we have determined make up our collective commitment to a constitutional way of life. I noted above that reasons must not reduce to claims of authority or of faith. This claim is not as hostile to communities of faith as some readers might fear. Some arguments grounded in religious faith have a long and noble heritage in our constitutional history. Indeed, some of the precepts I describe as constitutive of constitutionalism itself—such as equal moral worth and human dignity—are grounded in such forms of argument: many if not most of the fundamental precepts of western constitutional thought cannot be understood independent of their religious pedigree. See, for example, Friedrich, *Transcendent Justice*. Partly for that reason, some arguments about the public good, grounded in claims of faith, will be deeply consonant with principles, reasons, and arguments that are demonstrably constitutional in character, or that others can recognize as advancing constitutional ends. Arguments from faith that cannot be so reconciled, as I discuss below, must still be admitted into public conversation, chiefly because constitutionalists must be willing to hear challenges to constitutionalism itself as a condition of their acceptance of constitutionalism. Nevertheless, we should recognize such challenges for what they are—as rejections of constitutionalism as a preferred form of human community.

146. For a discussion of public reasonableness and transformative liberalism in the context of marginalizing some conservative religious viewpoints, see Stephen Macedo, "Transformative Constitutionalism," in Barber and George, *Constitutional Politics*, 167–192.

147. Boyd, *Civility*, 863–878.

148. Edward Shils, *The Virtue Of Civility* (Indianapolis: Liberty Fund, 1997), 338.

149. Boyd, *Civility*, 865.

150. Flammang, *Taste*, 80.

151. Ibid., 83.

152. Michael Schudson, "Why Conversation Is Not the Soul of Democracy," *Critical Studies in Mass Communication* 14 (1997): 297, 301.

153. Id.

154. Amy Gutmann and Dennis Thompson, *Democracy and Disagreement* (Cambridge, Mass.: Harvard University Press, 1996). See also Stephen Macedo, ed., *Deliberative Politics: Essays on Democracy and Disagreement* (New York: Oxford University Press, 1999). To insist that the Civic Conversation prizes constitutional conversation (or dialogue) is to suggest that conversation ranks higher than some other constitutional necessities and functions, and specifically to intimate that this dialogic function holds a preferred position over the settlement function. I take up this point in Essays Two and Three.

155. Calhoun, *Civility*, 252 passim.

156. Alexis de Tocqueville, *Democracy in America,* ed. J. P. Mayer (Garden City, N.Y.: Anchor Books, 2006), 606.

157. Boyd, *Civility*, 864. For a somewhat different account that nonetheless suggests that we distinguish between different approaches to the concept of civility, see Richard C. Sinopoli, "Thick-Skinned Liberalism: Redefining Civility," *American Political Science Review* 89 (1995): 612, who connects these different conceptions up to different approaches to liberalism more generally, or to differences between "interest and status-based" liberalisms.

158. Recalling Carl Schmitt's claim that the first act of politics is to distinguish us from them. See *The Concept of the Political*, trans. by George Schwab (1932) (Chicago: University of Chicago Press, 2007).

159. Rosenblum, *Membership and Morals*, 351.

160. Calhoun, *Civility*, 254.

161. John Kasson, *Rudeness and Civility: Manners in Nineteenth-Century Urban America* (New York: Wang and Hill, 1991), 59–62.

162. Boyd, *Civility*, 872.

163. Jean-Jacques Rousseau, *Discourse on Inequality* (1755) (Indianapolis: Hackett Publishing, 1992).

164. Boyd, *Civility*, 873. Boyd relies heavily here on the work of Holloway Sparks, "Dissident Citizenship: Democratic Theory, Political Courage, and Activist Women," *Hypatia: A Journal of Feminist Philosophy* 12 (1997): 74–110.

165. Indeed, claims of professional expertise, whether by Hamilton, or John Marshall in the celebrated case of *Marbury v. Madison* (1803), or Dean Wellington in *Interpreting the Constitution*, typically rest upon the assumption—sometimes admitted, sometimes not, but rarely defended—that the constitution is primarily a legal instrument. Elkin argues, "Some legalists might shy away from the brutal clar-

ity of this progression, but it is fair to say that it captures the implications of their position." Elkin, *Commercial Republic*, 98. The Juridic Constitution configures a constitutional culture that approaches constitutional questions as chiefly the prerogative and responsibility of experts (judges) tasked with institutional responsibility for constitutional interpretation.

166. Flammang, *Taste*, 12.

167. Boyd, *Civility*, 863.

168. See Flammang, *Taste*, 85–89.

169. Ibid., 14. Flammang adds, "Conversations require courtesy, a respect and willingness to consider things from another conversant's position."

170. Ibid., 3.

171. Boyd, *Civility*, 870.

172. Flammang, *Taste*, 12. See also Krause, *Civil Passions*, 10: "Since judgment and deliberation cannot do without passions, the best hope for impartiality lies not in trying to transcend the passions but in reforming the political context that helps shape them."

173. Flammang, *Taste*, 14. For arguments about the proper place of emotion, passion, and even prejudice in civic discourse, see Russell Muirhead, "Can Deliberative Democracy be Partisan?" *Critical Review* 22, no. 2–3 (2010): 129–157; Bryan Garsten, *Saving Persuasion: A Defense of Rhetoric and Judgment* (Cambridge, Mass.: Harvard University Press, 2009); Rosenblum, *Membership and Morals*; Krause, *Civil Passions*.

174. Catherine Soanes and Angus Stevenson, eds., *The Oxford Dictionary of English* (rev. ed.) (New York: Oxford University Press).

175. "If the ability to articulate reasons for actions is a good basis from which to judge the development of an individual's consciousness, then it becomes reasonable to see inarticulateness . . . as an equally good indication of the absence of full consciousness." Finkelstein, *Dining Out*, 183.

176. Shils, *Virtue of Civility*, 338–340.

177. Boyd, *Civility*, 867.

178. Ibid., 865.

179. I addressed a specific version of this problem, concerning the proscription of antidemocratic political parties, in "Electoral Regimes and the Proscription of Anti-Democratic Parties," *Journal of Terrorism and Political Violence* 12 (2000): 51–77; see also Walter F. Murphy, "May Constitutional Democracies 'Outlaw' a Political Party?" in *Politicians and Party Politics*, ed. John Gray Geer (Baltimore: Johns Hopkins University Press, 1998).

180. Sotirios A. Barber, "Notes on Constitutional Maintenance," in Barber and George, *Constitutional Politics*, 162. See also Barber, *On What the Constitution Means*, 9–62.

181. Finn, *Crisis*, 30.

182. Jeffrey Tulis, "Constitution and Revolution," in Barber and George, *Constitutional Politics*, 121.

183. Papke, *Heretics in the Temple*, 23.

184. On constitutional faith, see Levinson, *Constitutional Faith*; Jack M. Balkin, *Constitutional Redemption: Political Faith in an Unjust World* (Cambridge, Mass.: Harvard University Press, 2011).

185. See especially Marston, "Citizen Constitutional Knowledge," 14–17. Marston writes: "Papke's legal heretics share an important similarity with Finn in that all reject the pieties that surround the juridical constitution."

186. Finn, *Crisis*, 23–24.

187. Robert D. Putnam, "Bowling Alone: America's Declining Social Capital," *Journal of Democracy* 6 (1995): 65–78, at 77.

188. See the discussion in Murphy, *Constitutional Democracy*, 15–16. The term "acquisitive society" traces to R. H. Tawney, *The Acquisitive Society* (New York: Harcourt, Brace, and Howe, 1920).

189. Mary Ann Glendon, *Rights Talk: The Impoverishment of Political Discourse* (New York: Free Press, 1991). See also Sonu Bedi, *Rejecting Rights* (Cambridge: Cambridge University Press, 2009).

190. For example, Michael J. Sandel, *Democracy's Discontent* (Cambridge, Mass.: Harvard University Press, 1996); see also Murphy, "Alternative Political Systems," in Barber and George, *Constitutional Politics*, 16.

191. Finkelstein, *Dining Out*, 172.

192. Michael Marsh, "Second-Order Elections," in *International Encyclopedia of Elections*, ed. Richard Rose (London: Macmillan, 2000).

193. Murphy, *Constitutional Democracy*, 3.

194. See Sheldon Wolin's distinction between "politics" and "the political," in "Fugitive Democracy," *Constellations* 1 (1994): 11–25. See also Murphy, *Constitutional Democracy*, 3n5.

195. Lim observes, for instance, that "If the Federalists trusted in virtue, it was not the virtue inherently possessed by men or emanating from communities but a virtue reconfigured when funneled through the interplay of institutions." Elvin T. Lim, *The Lovers' Quarrel: The Two Foundings and American Political Development* (forthcoming), 271.

196. Sheldon Wolin, *The Presence of the Past: Essays on the State and the Constitution* (Baltimore: Johns Hopkins University Press, 1990), 89.

197. I can't resist: John le Carré, *The Constant Gardener: A Novel* (New York: Pocketstar, 2005).

198. Jason Peters, ed., *Wendell Berry: Life and Work* (Lexington: University of Kentucky Press, 2010).

199. Finn, *Crisis;* Murphy, *Constitutional Democracy.*

200. See Jacobsohn, *Constitutional Identity*, 324. See also George Thomas, "What Is Political Development? A Constitutional Perspective," *Review of Politics* 73 (2011): 275.

201. James Joyce, *Finnegan's Wake* (London: Faber and Faber, 1939).

202. Christy Wampole, "The Essayification of Everything," *New York Times,*

May 26, 201), http://opinionator.blogs.nytimes.com/2013/05/26/the-essayification-of-everything/.

203. Phillip Lopate, "The Essay, an Exercise in Doubt," *New York Times*, February 16, 2013, http://opinionator.blogs.nytimes.com/2013/02/16/the-essay-an-exercise-in-doubt/. I noted earlier that what we ought to count as evidence of the Civic Constitution in practice ought also extend to the hereticals who reject our constitutional faith. See Papke, *Heretics in the Temple.*

204. One might plausibly argue that this creative act is simultaneously destructive insofar as it necessitates the elimination, or possibly the assimilation, of a preexisting political order. Breslin makes just this point, observing that "foundings play a dual theoretical role. . . . The adoption of a new constitutional charter represents the *destruction* of an existing political design." Beau Breslin, *From Words to Worlds: Exploring Constitutional Functionality* (Baltimore: Johns Hopkins University Press, 2008), 31 (emphasis in original).

205. This is more an empirical claim than a theoretical one. As a live matter, contemporary constitutional states announce themselves to citizens and the world at large through the creation of a constitutional document or, at times, by pointing to several texts (England and Israel, for example). See Breslin, *Words to Worlds*, 4–8.

206. Jacobsohn: "The constitutional text is usually a critical component of constitutional identity but not coterminous with it." *Constitutional Identity*, 78; see also 26–27.

207. William F. Harris, "Bonding Word and Polity," *American Political Science Review* 76 (1982): 34.

208. As Elkin notes, "The idea of legal reasoning as a guide to constitutional thinking is attractive for at least two reasons. First, in pointing to the rule of law, legalists reinforce the idea that even the rule of the people must be limited in a principled way. Second . . . legalists emphasize that a politics dominated by self-interest and political calculation is something we should resist." Elkin, *Commercial Republic*, 99.

209. *See Federalist* #1, for example, on the necessity of "national discussion" and public deliberation.

210. For a similar analytical rubric, see Murphy, *Constitutional Democracy.*

211. Keith Whittington, *Political Foundations of Judicial Supremacy: The Presidency, the Supreme Court, and Constitutional Leadership in U.S. History* (Princeton, N.J.: Princeton University Press, 2007).

212. Murphy, *Constitutional Democracy*, 367.

213. Maria Zeisberg, "The Constitution of Conflict." (PhD dissertation, Princeton University, 2005); see also Mariah Zeisberg, "Constitutional Fidelity and Interbranch Conflict," Good Society 13 (2004): 24–30. See also Finn, "Civic," 61; Donald G. Morgan, *Congress and the Constitution: A Study of Responsibility* (Cambridge, Mass.: Harvard University Press, 1966), 16–42. See Larry Alexander, "Constitutional Rules, Constitutional Standards, and Constitutional Settlement: Marbury v. Madison and the Case for Judicial Supremacy," *Constitutional Commentary* 20 (2003–2004): 369.

214. Finn, "Civic," 57–60. See also Christine Bateup (NYU Law School), "The Dialogic Promise: Assessing the Normative Potential of Theories of Constitutional Dialogue," NYU Public Law Working Paper no. 05–24, *Brooklyn Law Review* 71 (2006); Miguel Schor, "Constitutional Dialogue and Judicial Supremacy," December 23, 2010, Suffolk University Law School Research Paper 10–66.

215. Mark Tushnet, "The Supreme Court and Contemporary Constitutionalism: The Implications of the Development of Alternative Forms of Judicial Review," in Kautz, *Constitutionalism*, 128.

216. Sheehan, *James Madison*, 13.

217. Keith Whittington, "Yet Another Constitutional Crisis," *William and Mary Law Review* 43 (2002): 2093, 2111.

218. Barber argues that "formal institutional failure" is not "sufficient grounds for declaring constitutional failure, or at least unequivocal constitutional failure." Barber, "Constitutional Failure: Ultimately Attitudinal," in *The Limits of Constitutional Democracy*, ed. Jeffrey K. Tulis and Stephen Macedo (Princeton, N.J.: Princeton University Press, 2012), 19. I would add that the absence of formal institutional failure is likewise not sufficient ground for determining that we have *not* failed.

219. Finn, "Civic," 54.

220. Daniel B. Rodriguez, "State Constitutional Failure," *University of Illinois Law Review* 2011 (2011): 1243, 1278.

Essay One: Constituting

1. F. A. Hayek, *The Fatal Conceit: The Errors of Socialism* (Chicago: University of Chicago Press, 1991). Like the distinctions between constituting/maintaining/failing, the neat analytical distinction between constituted and spontaneous orders breaks down in practice.

2. Adam Ferguson, *Essay on the History of Civil Society* (1767), ed. Fania Oz-Salzberger (Cambridge: Cambridge University Press, 1996); Friedrich Hayek, *Law and Liberty* (Chicago: University of Chicago Press, 1978).

3. Clinton Rossiter, ed., *The Federalist Papers* (New York: New American Library, 1961), #1.

4. John E. Finn, *Constitutions in Crisis: Political Violence and the Rule of Law* (New York: Oxford University Press, 1991), ch. 1.

5. Ibid. at 29–36.

6. See *Crisis*, ch. 1. In brief, I argued that there are rules that govern the enterprise, much as there are rules that govern games. See also some of Walter F. Murphy's work (distinguishing between constitutionalism and constitutionism, *Constitutional Democracy: Creating and Maintaining a Just Political Order* [Baltimore: Johns Hopkins University Press, 2007], 15–16) and Gary J. Jacobsohn's table analogy in *Constitutional Identity* (Cambridge, Mass.: Harvard University Press, 2010), 6–7.

7. Finn, *Crisis*, 23; see also Murphy, *Constitutional Democracy*, 15–16.

8. Donald P. Kommers, John E. Finn, and Gary J. Jacobsohn, eds., *American*

Constitutional Law: Essays, Cases and Comparative Materials, 3rd ed. (Lanham, Md.: Rowman and Littlefield, 2009), 121.

9. Ibid., 106.

10. See Bruce Ackerman, "Obama's Unconstitutional War," http://www.foreign-policy.com/articles/2011/03/24/obama_s_unconstitutional_war.

11. For example, consider the questions of constitutionality raised by Congress's decision to create the United States Sentencing Commission in 1984. Some of these questions were addressed in *Mistretta v. United States* (1989).

12. See generally Murphy, *Constitutional Democracy*, esp. pt. 1, as well as Beau Breslin, *From Words to Worlds: Exploring Constitutional Functionality* (Baltimore: Johns Hopkins University Press, 2009), esp. ch. 4, and Cass Sunstein, *Designing Democracy: What Constitutions Do* (New York: Oxford University Press, 2001).

13. Finn, *Crisis*, ch. 1.

14. Jacobsohn, *Constitutional Identity*, 112–117.

15. See Charles Howard McIlwain, *Constitutionalism: Ancient and Modern*, rev. ed. (Ithaca, N.Y.: Cornell University Press, 1947).

16. William N. Eskridge Jr., "The California Proposition 8 Case: What Is a Constitution For?" *California Law Review*, http://www.californialawreview.org/assets/pdfs/98–4/Eskridge.FINAL.pdf.

17. Ibid.

18. Ibid.

19. John Finn, "The Civic Constitution: Some Preliminaries," in *Constitutional Politics: Essays on Constitution Making, Maintenance, and Change*, ed. Sotirios A. Barber and Robert P. George (Princeton, N.J.: Princeton University Press, 2001), 50.

20. Sheldon S. Wolin, *The Presence of the Past: Essays on the State and the Constitution* (Baltimore: Johns Hopkins University Press, 1990). Sharon Krause rightly reminds us that creating a sense of obligation and attachment to the laws requires sentiment as well as reason. Sharon R. Krause, *Civil Passions: Moral Sentiment and Democratic Deliberation* (Princeton, N.J.: Princeton University Press, 2008), ch. 6.

21. Breslin, *Words to Worlds*, 10.

22. Jacobsohn, "The constitutional text is usually a critical component of constitutional identity but not coterminous with it." *Constitutional Identity*, 78; see also 26–27.

23. See Jacobsohn, *Constitutional Identity*, 348, 349, quoting Hanna Pitkin.

24. As Murphy has noted, "typically a constitutional document becomes a palimpsest: the original words are soon overwritten by customs, usages, and interpretations." Murphy, *Constitutional Democracy*, 15. See also: "no constitutional document or set of documents long remains coextensive with the constitutional order," 14, quoting the well-known work of Edward S. Corwin, "Constitution v. Constitutional Theory," *American Political Science Review* 19 (1920): 290.

25. Jacobsohn, *Constitutional Identity*, 22–27, 213–270.

26. For a discussion of constitutional textuality, see Breslin, *Words to Worlds*, 172–173. Much of the current literature on textuality discusses the concept in light

of originalist approaches to constitutional interpretation. For an example, see Dennis J. Goldford, *The American Constitution and the Debate over Originalism* (London: Cambridge, 2005).

27. Umberto Eco, *Interpretation and Overinterpretation* (New York: Cambridge University Press, 1992).

28. Andrea K. Newlyn, "Redefining 'Rudimentary' Narrative: Women's Nine-teenth-Century Manuscript Cookbooks," in Janet Floyd and Laurel Forster Floyd, *The Recipe Reader: Narratives, Contexts, Traditions* (Burlington, Vt.: Ashgate, 2003), 31.

29. For a general treatment, see John R. Vile, *The Constitutional Amending Process in American Political Thought* (New York: Praeger, 1992). For a discussion of amendment outside the parameters of Article 5, see Akhil Reed Amar, "Philadelphia Revisited: Amending the Constitution Outside Article V," *University of Chicago Law Review* 55 (1988): 1043.

30. But see Breslin, *Words to Worlds*, 9–11.

31. Thus, Noah Webster wrote that "the very attempt to make *perpetual* constitutions, is the assumption of a right to control the opinions of future generations." Quoted in Gordon S. Wood, *The Creation of the American Republic, 1776–1787* (New York: W. W. Norton, 1972), 379 (emphasis in original). For the well-known Jefferson quote, see Letter of Thomas Jefferson to James Madison, September 6, 1789, reprinted in Alpheus T. Mason, *Free Government in the Making*, 3rd ed. (New York: Oxford University Press, 1965), 374.

32. For a discussion, see Murphy, *Constitutional Democracy*, 510–518. Obviously the literature on consent, even when limited to the role of consent in constituting and legitimating constitutional democracies, is voluminous. An especially good treatment is in Joseph Raz, "Government by Consent," in *Authority Revisited*, ed. J. Roland Pennock and John W. Chapman (New York: New York University Press, 1987). On tacit consent, see A. John Simmons, "Tacit Consent and Political Obligation," *Philosophy and Public Affairs* 5 (1976): 274, and the classic work by Hanna Pitkin, "Obligation and Consent," *American Political Science Review* 59 (1965): 990.

33. Donald P. Kommers, "Constitutions and National Identity," *Review of Politics* 74 (2012): 127.

34. "Interpreting the *Variorum*," in *The Book History Reader*, ed. David Finkel-stein and Alistair McCleery (New York: Routledge, 2002), 351.

35. Many "have argued that discursive practices, including narrative, contribute to the very constitution of self and community." Carolyn Korsmeyer, *Making Sense of Taste: Food and Philosophy* (Ithaca, N.Y.: Cornell University Press, 1999), 186n2.

36. See Justice Baldwin, dissenting in *Cherokee Nation*, on "plain meaning" of the Constitution. *Cherokee Nation v. Georgia*, 30 U.S. 1 (1831).

37. Breslin notes that beginning in the eighteenth century, "constitutions took on a new appearance. . . . These new constitutions were very public documents. They were shared by a population that, at least in a limited sense, experienced a sense of ownership in the documents themselves." *Words to Worlds*, 19.

38. For a discussion of the concept of racial identity and "linked fate," see Michael C. Dawson, *Behind the Mule: Race and Class in African American Politics* (Princeton, N.J.: Princeton University Press, 1995).

39. Brian Weinstein, *The Civic Tongue: Political Consequences of Language Choices* (New York: Longman, 1983).

40. See generally, Joseph Goldstein, *The Intelligible Constitution: The Supreme Court's Obligation to Maintain the Constitution as Something We the People Can Understand* (New York: Oxford University Press, 1992). This is an admirable effort, but it does not do enough because in the end, it is not the Court's obligation to make the Constitution intelligible. The fault traces not to the Court, but to our understanding of what the Constitution is and the nature of its authority.

41. Defined as the "the interaction of two or more national languages within a given culture." http://postcolonial.net/backfile/view?id=78: "Heteroglossia is perhaps one of Bakhtin's most misunderstood and misinterpreted ideas, often being confused with 'polyphony' as meaning the multi-voiced nature of dialogic discourse. But this is not exactly what Bakhtin means. In his Essay 'From the Prehistory of Novelistic Discourse,' Bakhtin defines heteroglossia as the inherent diversity of unofficial forms of a particular national language — similar in nature to dialect. Bakhtin contrasts heteroglossia with 'polyglossia.'"

42. Weinstein, *Civic Tongue*.

43. Robert Parks, Review, *American Political Science Review* 78 (1984): 294.

44. "As an impenetrable discourse it ranks second to none: at least sociology does not use Latin." Colin Sumner, *Reading Ideologies: An Investigation into the Marxist Theory of Ideology and Law* (New York: Academic Press, 1979), 271.

45. For a fascinating discussion of rabbinical interpretation of the Talmud and some comparisons with constitutional interpretation, see Joseph Lupinsky's discussion of Robert Cover's *Nomos and Narrative* (1983), "Law in Education: A Reminiscence with Some Footnotes to Robert Cover's *Nomos and Narrative*," *Yale Law Journal* 96 (1987): 1836. See also David Luban, "The Coiled Serpent of Argument: Reason, Authority, and Law in a Talmudic Tale," *Chicago-Kent Law Review* 79 (2004): 1253; Thomas C. Grey, "The Constitution as Scripture," *Stanford Law Review* 37 (1984): 1. On parallels between biblical and constitutional interpretation, see Jaroslav Pelikan, *Interpreting the Bible and the Constitution* (New Haven, Conn.: Yale University Press, 2004).

46. Robert F. Nagel, *Constitutional Cultures: The Mentality and Consequences of Judicial Review* (Berkeley: University of California Press, 1989).

47. I use these terms in their nontechnical sense here. For a more sophisticated version, see Keith Whittington on the differences between constitutional construction and constitutional interpretation. Keith E. Whittington, *Constitutional Construction: Divided Powers and Constitutional Meaning* (Cambridge, Mass.: Harvard University Press, 2001).

48. Obviously the literature on the uses of appeals to purpose in constitutional interpretation is large and unwieldy. For a treatment on appeals to purpose in con-

stitutional and legal interpretation generally, see Aharon Barak, *Purposive Interpretation in Law*, trans. Sari Bashi (Princeton, N.J.: Princeton University Press, 2005).

49. See Sylvia Snowiss, *Judicial Review and the Law of the Constitution* (New Haven, Conn.: Yale University Press, 1990); Finn, *Civic*, 44–50.

50. For a full elaboration of this approach to Article 6, see Sotirios A. Barber, *On What the Constitution Means* (Baltimore: Johns Hopkins University Press, 1984).

51. The Juridic Constitution did not emerge fully developed from Article 6. It evolved, receiving partial expression in *Federalist* #78 and of course in *Marbury v. Madison* (1803), where Marshall wrote, "Certainly all those who have framed written constitutions contemplated them as forming the fundamental and paramount law." Snowiss thus argues that there are two *Marburys*, the *Marbury* of 1803 and the "modern *Marbury*." "The modern *Marbury*, and the Constitution's status as supreme, ordinary law, are the products of an evolutionary process whose most significant dimension is that it took place in the absence of discussion and conscious recognition of the transformations taking place." Sylvia Snowiss, "The *Marbury* of 1803 and the Modern *Marbury*," *Constitutional Commentary* 20 (2003): 231. It continues to evolve as well, as evidenced by the assertions of judicial supremacy in cases such as *Cooper v. Aaron* (1958) and *Boerne v. Flores* (1997), and as advocated by proponents of strong-form judicial review; see also Larry Alexander, "Constitutional Rules, Constitutional Standards, and Constitutional Settlement: Marbury v. Madison and the Case for Judicial Supremacy," *Constitutional Commentary* 20 (2003): 369.

52. Nagel, *Constitutional Cultures*, 7. See also Christopher L. Eisgruber, "Judicial Supremacy and Constitutional Distortion," in Barber and George, *Constitutional Politics*, 77.

53. On originalism generally, see Jack N. Rakove, *Original Meanings: Politics and Ideas in the Making of the Constitution* (New York: Alfred A. Knopf, 1996); Keith E. Whittington, *Constitutional Interpretation: Textual Meaning, Original Intent, and Judicial Review* (Lawrence: University Press of Kansas, 1999). For a provocative recent treatment, see Jack M. Balkin, *Living Originalism* (Cambridge, Mass.: Harvard University Press, 2011).

54. Just to be clear, I think cases in which the Court has labored to find justiciable rules implicit in the Tenth Amendment, such as *National League of Cities v. Usery* (1976), are fundamentally mistaken, but eminently predictable once we characterize the Constitution as essentially juridic in character. See Jesse H. Choper, *Judicial Review and the National Political Process: A Functional Reconsideration of the Role of the Supreme Court* (Chicago: University of Chicago Press, 1980).

55. We might describe this as a kind of constitutional distortion. For a discussion of the concept of constitutional distortion, see Christopher L. Eisgruber, "Judicial Supremacy and Constitutional Distortion," in Barber and George, *Constitutional Politics*, 70–90.

56. See Mark V. Tushnet, *Weak Courts, Strong Rights: Judicial Review and Social Welfare Rights in Comparative Constitutional Law* (Princeton, N.J.: Princeton University Press, 2009), 81.

57. Barber, *On What the Constitution Means*, 34.

58. Scott Douglas Gerber, *To Secure These Rights: The Declaration of Independence and Constitutional Interpretation* (New York: New York University Press, 1995), 60.

59. Finn, *Crisis*, ch. 1.

60. There are similar provisions in the Thirteenth and Fifteenth Amendments.

61. A more expansive congressional power of interpretation does not mean, of course, that congressional interpretations of the Fourteenth Amendment will always be "better" or more capacious readings of constitutional liberties and rights. Congress may well use its power of interpretation under Section 5 to constrict constitutional liberty—and indeed, the fear that Congress might do so undergirds the ratchet theory. But any significant measure of responsibility invites the possibility of abuse (or of making poor or unwise choices). Two points are worth stressing here. First, it is hardly clear that poor choices are a more likely result in a system of shared power than if left to courts alone. Some evidence for this is revealed when we recall that the RFRA sought to expand religious freedom, contra *Employment Division*. Second, the objection seems to assume there will be general agreement about what the best result is, or what a poor result is, when in fact, both the congressional approach and the *Smith* approach to free exercise can plausibly be justified as "good" or as the "best" understanding of the free exercise clause.

62. The familiar criticisms of Justice Douglas's "expansive" readings of the Bill of Rights in *Griswold v. Connecticut* (1965) sometimes reflect this fundamentally juridic way of reading the text. For a discussion of how Douglas read the Bill of Rights in *Griswold*, see Bruce Ackerman, *We the People*, vol. 1: *Foundations* (Cambridge, Mass.: Belknap Press of Harvard University Press, 1993), 150–158.

63. See generally Tushnet, *Weak Courts*.

64. George Thomas, "The National University and Sustaining the American Constitutional Order" (unpublished ms.; 2010), 27.

65. Ronald Dworkin, *Freedom's Law: The Moral Reading of the American Constitution* (Cambridge, Mass.: Harvard University Press, 1997); see also James Boyd White, *When Words Lose Their Meaning: Constitutions and Reconstitutions of Language, Character, and Community* (Chicago: University of Chicago Press, 1985).

66. James Madison to Thomas Jefferson, October 17, 1788, http://www.constitution.org/jm/17881017_bor.htm. In his response of March 15, 1789, Jefferson wrote: "In the arguments in favor of a declaration of rights, you omit one which has great weight with me, the legal check which it puts into the hands of the judiciary. This is a body, which if rendered independent, and kept strictly to their own department merits great confidence for their learning and integrity." http://www.gwu.edu/~ffcp/exhibit/p7/p7_1text.html. Too many scholars, emphasizing Jefferson's reference to the judiciary, have failed to note the departmentalist limitation implied by the words "kept strictly to their own department."

67. Stephen L. Elkin, *Reconstructing the Commercial Republic: Constitutional Design after Madison* (Chicago: University of Chicago Press, 2006), 99.

68. Colleen A. Sheehan, *James Madison and the Spirit of Republican Self-Government* (New York: Cambridge University Press, 2009), 108.

69. *Ryan v. Attorney General. I.R.* 294 (Ir. S. C. 1965). See Jacobsohn, *Constitutional Identity*, 147–148.

70. The classic study is by Herbert McCloskey and Alida Brill, *Dimensions of Tolerance: What Americans Believe about Civil Liberties* (New York: Russell Sage, 1983). For a critical review of the McCloskey and Brill study, see Jennifer Hochschild, "Dimensions of Liberal Self-Satisfaction: Civil Liberties, Liberal Theory, and Elite-Mass Differences," *Ethics* 96 (1986): 396. See also Gary Schmitt and Cheryl Miller, "Why Is U.S. History High-Schoolers' Worst Subject?" June 16, 2011, http://www.nationalreview.com/corner/269809/why-us-history-high-schoolers-worst-subject-gary-schmitt. For a contrary view, see Delli Carpini and Michael and Scott Keeter, *What Americans Know about Politics and Why It Matters* (New Haven, Conn.: Yale University Press, 1996) (arguing for a "pragmatic view" of democracy and that enough people know enough of politics to make informed policy choices). I take up this objection more fully in the Conclusion.

71. Trey Parker, Matt Stone, and Pam Brady, *Team America: World Police*, Paramount Pictures, 2004.

72. Thus, "discursive authority . . . the intellectual credibility, ideological validity, and aesthetic value claimed by or conferred upon a work, author, narrator, character, or textual practice—is produced interactively." Susan Sniader Lanser, *Fictions of Authority: Women Writers and Narrative Voice* (Ithaca, N.Y.: Cornell University Press, 1992), 6.

73. As Elizabeth J. McDougall notes, "The reader's creative impulses bring endless plurality to texts, a plurality derived from the multiple meanings inherent in words and language." Elizabeth J. McDougall, "Voices, Stories, and Recipes in Selected Canadian Community Cookbooks," in *Recipes for Reading: Community Cookbooks, Stories, Histories*, ed. Anne L. Bower (Amherst, Mass.: University of Massachusetts Press, 1997), 114–115.

74. Finn, *Crisis*, ch. 1.

75. Walter F. Murphy, "Who Shall Interpret? The Quest for the Ultimate Constitutional Interpreter," *Review of Politics* 48 (1986): 401; see also H. Jefferson Powell, "Constitutional Law as Though the Constitution Mattered," review of *American Constitutional Interpretation* by Walter F. Murphy, James E. Fleming, William F. Harris, *Duke Law Journal* 5 (1986): 915.

76. Breslin, *Words to Worlds*, 10.

77. It is important to recognize that a civic identity is both contested and an ongoing object of contest. See, for example, Samuel Huntington, *Who are We? The Challenges of America's National Identity* (New York: Simon and Schuster, 2004); Rogers M. Smith, *Civic Ideals: Conflicting Visions of Citizenship in U.S. History* (New Haven, Conn.: Yale University Press, 1999).

78. Finn, *Civic*, 54–55.

79. See, for example, Justice Scalia's opinion for the Court in *District of Columbia*

v. Heller (2008); see also Mortimer J. Adler, *We Hold These Truths: Understanding the Ideas and Ideals of the Constitution* (New York: Macmillan, 1987), 7.

80. William Lee Miller, *Lincoln's Virtues: An Ethical Biography* (New York: Alfred A. Knopf, 2002); see also James Tackach, *Lincoln's Moral Vision: The Second Inaugural Address* (Jackson: University Press of Mississippi, 2002).

81. See Gerald Garvey, *Constitutional Bricolage* (Princeton, N.J.: Princeton University Press, 1971).

82. Amar's discussion of the Northwest Ordinances is relevant here. In Amar's view, the Ordinances warrant "inclusion in the constitutional canon" because the symbolic constitution "encompasses texts that *'at some point in American history'* won the hearts and minds of a wide swath of the American people, thereby helping to bind citizens together as a legal and political entity." Akhil Reed Amar, *America's Unwritten Constitution: The Precedents and Principles We Live By* (New York: Basic Books, 2012), 558n11. For a discussion of John Brown and the concept of fringe constitutionalism, see Robert L. Tsai, "John Brown's Constitution," *Boston College Law Review* 51 (2010): 151.

83. Much of this discussion is taken from my review of the book, published in *Law and Politics Book Review* 26 (2013): 172–174, http://www.lpbr.net/2013/04/americas-unwritten-constitution.html.

84. Amar, *America's Unwritten Constitution*, 19.

85. Ibid., 20.

86. Ibid.

87. Ibid., 74.

88. This position seems necessitated also by Amar's well-known commitment to textualism.

89. Ibid., 199.

90. See Akhil Reed Amar, "The Consent of the Governed: Constitutional Amendment Outside Article V," *Columbia Law Review* 94 (1994): 457; Ackerman, *We the People*.

91. Amar, "The Consent of the Governed," 258.

92. Finn, review of Amar, *America's Unwritten Constitution*.

93. For a discussion of constitutional canons, see John E. Finn and Donald P. Kommers, "A Comparative Constitutional Law Canon?" *Constitutional Commentary* 17 (2000): 219.

94. I say "self-evidently canonical," but that presses a little too far insofar as it assumes that the text is ipso facto part of the Constitution. As I have argued in other forums, I reject this proposition—parts of the text that do not correspond with the constitutive principles of constitutionalism itself are "unconstitutional." See Finn, *Crisis*, ch. 1. For similar arguments, see Walter F. Murphy, "Merlin's Memory: The Past and Future Imperfect of the Once and Future Polity," in *Responding to Imperfection: The Theory and Practice of Constitutional Amendment*, ed. Sanford Levinson (Princeton, N.J.: Princeton University Press, 1995) 163–190; Jacobsohn, *Constitutional Identity*, 34–83.

95. Some readers have expressed astonishment at my insistence that the Constitution's boundaries are unknown, in the sense that there will always be contest and uncertainty about which additional texts do or do not qualify as part of the Constitution. First, I want to clarify that this is indeed my meaning. Second, I do not think the proposition is as outlandish as it might seem: even devotees of the Juridic Constitution typically concede that the Constitution admits more than the four corners of the "canonical" text. Moreover, we tolerate a certain amount of ambiguity even about the four corners. See, for example, Sanford Levinson, "Authorizing Constitutional Text: On the Purported Twenty-Seventh Amendment," *Constitutional Commentary* 11 (1994): 101. Perhaps ironically, the amendment's resurface could be attributed partially to the kind of civic engagement the Civic Constitution prizes: http://old .post-gazette.com/nation/20021127amendment_27p9.asp.

96. Jeffrey K. Tulis, "Constitution and Revolution," in Barber and George, *Constitutional Politics*, 120–121.

97. Brett Marston, "Citizen Constitutional Knowledge, Civic Capacities, and Constitutional Meaning: the Civic Constitution Meets Interest Groups and Social Movements," paper delivered at MPSA, April 2003, 12.

98. See, for example, Carl L. Becker, *The Declaration of Independence: A Study in the History of Political Ideas* (New York: Vintage, 1958); Gerber, *To Secure These Rights*.

99. "Fragment on the Constitution and the Union," published in *Collected Works of Abraham Lincoln*, ed. Roy P. Basler, 8 vols. (New Brunswick, N.J.: Rutgers University Press, 1953), 4:168–169.

100. Gary Wills, *Lincoln at Gettysburg: The Words That Remade America* (New York: Simon and Shuster, 1993); see also Harry Jaffa, *Crisis of the House Divided: An Interpretation of the Issues in the Lincoln-Douglas Debates* (Chicago: University of Chicago Press, 1999).

101. Adler, *We Hold These Truths*, 7.

102. See Justice Scalia's discussion in *District of Columbia v. Heller* (2008). I do not think we need here to examine the relationship between prefatory clauses, absolute or otherwise, and operative clauses, or their specific use in Scalia's *Heller* opinion.

103. Quoted in Gerber, *To Secure These Rights*, 3.

104. See, for example, Lysander Spooner, *The Unconstitutionality of Slavery* (1845), in *The Collected Works of Lysander Spooner* (1834–1886), 5 vols. (Indianapolis: Liberty Fund, 2013). Spooner discusses the Declaration of Independence at length in chapter 5. http://www.lysanderspooner.org/UnconstitutionalityOfSlavery5 .htm#P1CHAPV.

105. See, for example, the work of M. E. Bradford, "Lincoln, the Declaration, And Secular Puritanism: A Rhetoric for Continuing Revolution," http://www.thesouthernpar tisan.com/wp-content/uploads/2011/02/01.1-ARCHIVEBradfordSecularPuritanism-37p.pdf; and Willmoore Kendall, "Equality: Commitment or Ideal," http://www.the imaginativeconservative.org/category/willmoore-kendall/#.UT3lrTfD63Y.

106. See Calhoun's *Oregon Bill Speech* (1848), http://teachingamericanhistory .org/library/document/oregon-bill-speech/.

107. Pauline Maier, *American Scripture: Making the Declaration of Independence* (New York: Vintage Books, 1998), 200.

108. In *Cotting v. Godard*, 183 U.S. 79 (1901), the Court stated:

"The first official action of this nation declared the foundation of government in these words: 'We hold these truths to be self evident, that all men are created equal, that they are endowed by their Creator with certain unalienable rights, that among these are life, liberty, and the pursuit of happiness.' While such declaration of principles may not have the force of organic law, or be made the basis of judicial decision as to the limits of right and duty, and while in all cases reference must be had to the organic law of the nation for such limits, yet the latter is but the body and the letter of which the former is the thought and the spirit, and it is always safe to read the letter of the Constitution in the spirit of the Declaration of Independence. No duty rests more imperatively upon the courts than the enforcement of those constitutional provisions intended to secure that equality of rights which is the foundation of free government." See also Clarence Thomas, "Toward a Plain Reading of the Constitution—The Declaration of Independence in Constitutional Interpretation," *Howard Law Journal* 30 (1987): 983.

109. Jim Allison, "The United States Supreme Court and the Declaration of Independence," http://candst.tripod.com/doi-pream.htm.

110. For a clear exception, see Gerber, *To Secure These Rights*, 96. I should add that many, if not most, of the self-identified members of the so-called Princeton School would readily agree that the Declaration has and should have substantive significance for the meaning of the Constitution, though some would disagree with Gerber's more particular claim that it is the natural rights philosophy of the Declaration that has interpretive significance. Gerber likewise concludes that the primary institutional responsibility for "identifying and applying the natural rights philosophy of the Declaration of Independence in constitutional interpretation" vests in the Supreme Court. It might be possible to defend this claim under the Juridic Constitution, but it cannot be justified under the Civic Constitution.

111. "Elena Kagan on Declaration of Independence at Supreme Court confirmation hearings," July 2, 2010, http://www.examiner.com/nonpartisan-in-san-diego/elena-kagan-on-declaration-of-independence-at-supreme-court-confirmation-hearings.

112. On the concept of easy cases generally, see Frederick Schauer, "Easy Cases," *Southern California Law Review* 58 (1985): 399.

113. For an insightful discussion, see Wayne D. Moore, "Reconceiving Interpretive Autonomy: Insights from the Virginia and Kentucky Resolutions," *Constitutional Commentary* 11 (1994): 315. See also Larry D. Kramer, *The People Themselves: Popular Constitutionalism and Judicial Review* (New York: Oxford University Press, 2004), 136.

114. See Moore, *Interpretive Autonomy*; see also my discussion of federalism and civic dialogue in Essay Two. The literature on nonjudicial interpretation of the

Constitution is now quite large. For a general overview, see Bruce G. Peabody, "Nonjudicial Constitutional Interpretation, Authoritative Settlement, and a New Agenda for Research," *Constitutional Commentary* 16 (1999): 63.

115. See, for example, the reaction of several southern states to *Brown v. Board of Education* (1954), and the Court's response in *Cooper v. Aaron* (1958).

116. Marc Lacey, "Arizona Lawmakers Push New Round of Immigration Restrictions," *New York Times*, February 23, 2011, http://www.nytimes.com/2011/02/24/us/24arizona.html?_r=1andscp=1andsq=nullification%20immigrationandst=cse.

117. Emily Ramshaw, "Health Law Response Goes 2 Ways," *New York Times*, January 29, 2011, http://www.nytimes.com/2011/01/30/us/30ttreform.html?scp=1andsq=nullification%20obamacareandst=cse.

118. Ian Millhiser, "Texas Nullificationists Secede From Federal Light Bulb Standards," *Think Progress*, June 13, 2011, http://thinkprogress.org/justice/2011/06/13/243539/texas-nullification-light-bulb/.

119. Indeed, I argued in *Constitutions in Crisis* that the Articles' claim to perpetuity has continuing significance for how we understand the Constitution's claim to authority. See Finn, *Crisis*, 4–5. This might also be a good place to expand on the point by Breslin that founding moments are not simply about creating—they are also about destroying. *Words to Worlds*, 7; 36. If the "moment" of creation, like one of the seven days of creation, is actually of extended duration, or is always incomplete in the sense that it is unfinished ("to form a more perfect union"), then the act of creation looks backward as well as forward. Thus the Constitution looked forward, to form a more perfect union for ourselves and our posterity, and backward, insofar as it replaced the Articles. For a recent discussion about the enduring significance of the Articles in contemporary public discourse, see Gary Faraci, "Government's Role Debate Was Settled Back in 1788," August 18, 2011, http://www.app.com/article/20110818/NJOPINION02/308180050/Government-s-role-debate-settled-back-1788?odyssey=nav|head.

120. As Marston observes, "The civic constitution . . . exists in practice in a variety of garbs that can be obscured if we focus too intently on how these claims link up with more traditionally recognizable arguments inspired by seminal public texts." Marston, "Citizen Constitutional Knowledge," 13.

121. Ibid., 12.

122. Such as the Bill of Rights Defense Committees, formed in response to the Patriot Act. See ibid., and Susan Herman, *Taking Liberties: The War on Terror and the Erosion of American Democracy* (New York: Oxford University Press, 2011).

123. Jacobsohn, *Constitutional Identity*, 348–349; Murphy, *Constitutional Democracy*, 14–15.

124. See Breslin, *Words to Worlds*, 9–11.

125. Contra Ackerman, *We the People*.

126. Elizabeth Beaumont, *The Civic Constitution: Civic Visions and Struggles in the Path toward Constitutional Democracy* (New York: Oxford, 2013).

127. Kramer covers some of these episodes in *The People Themselves*—see 215–

218. For a fascinating discussion, see David Ray Papke, *Heretics in the Temple: Americans Who Reject the Nation's Legal Faith* (New York: New York University Press, 1998).

128. As Marston has observed, "The civic constitution should be understood less as a unitary attachment to broad principles and more as a wide spectrum of particular causes and claims that have constitutional principles as their partial focus." Marston, "Citizen Constitutional Knowledge," 13.

129. Giovanni Sartori, *Comparative Constitutional Engineering: An Inquiry into Structures, Incentives and Outcomes,* 2d ed. (New York: New York University Press, 1997). See also Carl J. Friedrich, *Constitutional Government and Democracy; Theory and Practice in Europe and America* (New York: Ginn, 1950), especially but not only part 2.

130. The stakes are even higher when we reflect that bad choices may sow the seeds of constitutional failure—Article 48 of the Weimar Constitution comes to mind, even if unfairly (see Essay Three)—and early failure, not long-term success, is the fate of most constitutions. In Essay Three, we shall see that constitutional failure comes in a variety of guises. Making design decisions without due consideration of the ends we want to advance, and careful consideration of how or whether the constitution's institutional architecture serves those ends, is a failure not just of the constitutional document, but of the constitutional enterprise generally.

131. Michael G. Kammen, *A Machine that Would Go of Itself: The Constitution in American Culture* (New York: Alfred A. Knopf, 1986). The phrase originates with James Russell Lowell, "The Place of the Independent in Politics," *Literary and Political Addresses* (Boston: Houghton, Mifflin, and Co., 104), 252. For an insightful discussion of its meaning for constitutional education, see George Thomas, *The Constitution of Mind* (ms.), 1.

132. Breslin, *Words to Worlds*, 71.

133. Ibid., 72.

134. Murphy, *Constitutional Democracy*, 367.

135. Center for Civic Education, "National Standards for Civics and Government," http://www.civiced.org/index.php?page=stds.

136. For an argument that the terms of this debate were themselves restricted primarily to questions about the scope of national power, see Suzette Hemberger, "What Did They Think They Were Doing When They Wrote the U.S. Constitution, and Why Should We Care?" in Barber and George, *Constitutional Politics*, 128–129.

137. James D. Savage, "Corruption and Virtue at the Constitutional Convention," *Journal of Politics* 56 (1994): 174.

138. Bernard Grofman and Donald Wittman, *The Federalist Papers and the New Institutionalism*, vol. 2 (Flemington: Agathon Press, 1989), 11.

139. Roger Pilon, "Madison's Constitutional Vision: The Legacy of Enumerated Powers," http://www.acslaw.org/files/Madison%20Constitutional%20Vision.pdf. He continues: "Madison's moral vision was taken from the Declaration of Independence."

140. Stephen Macedo, "Transformative Constitutionalism and the Case of Religion: Defending the Moderate Hegemony of Liberalism," in Barber and George, *Constitutional Politics*, 169.

141. Ibid., 168–170.

142. James A. Marone, *The Democratic Wish: Popular Participation and the Limits of American Government* (New York: Basic Books, 1999), 63–64; Wolin, *Presence of the Past*, 189. For a somewhat different perspective, see Thomas Pangle, "The Federalist Papers' Vision of Civic Health and the Tradition out of which That Vision Emerges," *Western Political Quarterly* 39 (1986): 577.

143. See, for example, Michael Parenti, "A Constitution for the Few: Looking Back to the Beginning," http://www.iefd.org/articles/constitution_for_the_few.php.

144. See Finn, *Civic*, 52–53.

145. For an interesting if somewhat dated discussion, see Peter S. Onuf, "Reflections on the Founding: Constitutional Historiography in Bicentennial Perspective," *William and Mary Quarterly* 46 (1989): 341.

146. See, for example, George Thomas, *The Madisonian Constitution* (Baltimore: Johns Hopkins University Press, 2008); Sheehan, *James Madison*; Elkin, *Commercial Republic*.

147. See Elkin, *Commercial Republic*, 77. Elkin notes, "Institutions cannot be understood simply as a collection of rules that those who operate them will follow. They are, instead, ongoing forms of relation among those who operate and are affected by them—and, as such, they are complex political entities."

148. These two questions trade on the earlier distinction between *writing* the text and *reading* the text.

149. As I indicated in the Introduction, and should be readily apparent here, the distinctions between constituting, maintaining, and failing break down in practice and are not strictly linear.

150. Yi-Fu Tuan, *Space and Place: The Perspective of Experience* (Minneapolis: University of Minnesota Press, 1977).

151. Constitutionalism's insistence upon the protection of human dignity, the production of reasons in support of the exercise of public power, and its concern for civil liberty, all necessitate some set of limitations upon governmental power. The separation of power is not only a bulwark for liberty. It is also a chief architectural component of regimes committed to deliberation and reason in public affairs. As I wrote in *Constitutions in Crisis*, "We value this institutional arrangement for limiting power . . . because we think it instrumental to constructing a political community based on reason and choice. . . . The separation of powers is thus an instrumental mechanism through which constitutionalism's commitment to a public life conducted on the basis of articulated reason is secured." Finn, *Crisis*, 32–33.

152. Ibid.

153. Murphy, *Constitutional Democracy*, 193.

154. Ibid., 366; Brandeis, dissenting in *Olmstead v. United States* (1928).

155. As I discuss later in this essay (see pp. 63–69) and again in Essay Two, the Civic Constitution therefore favors institutional arrangements that disperse interpretive authority for constitutional review across institutions instead of centralizing it or channeling it a single institution. A judicial monopoly (or any institutional monopoly, for that matter) decreases the number of arenas in which constitutional dialogue occurs; it is corrosive of constitutional literacy and consequently ill suited to the Civic Constitution. The extent to which such corrosion will occur is plainly related to the circumstances and occasions of institutional interpretation—judicial minimalization of the sort proposed by Cass Sunstein, for example, will be less corrosive than more aggressive or virulent forms of judicial supremacy. Cass R. Sunstein, *One Case at a Time: Judicial Minimalism on the Supreme Court* (Cambridge, Mass.: Harvard University Press, 1999.)

156. Elkin, *Commercial Republic*, 35.

157. Richard E. Neustadt, *Presidential Power and the Modern Presidents: The Politics of Leadership From Roosevelt to Reagan* (New York: Free Press, 1991), x.

158. *Federalist #51*.

159. Edward S. Corwin, *The President, Office and Powers, 1787–1984* (Washington, D.C.: Congressional Quarterly Press, 1992), ix.

160. See Choper, *Judicial Review*.

161. Wills, *Lincoln at Gettysburg*.

162. See Mike Ludwig, "Fifty Activist Groups Call for Congressional Hearings on Citizens United," *TruthOut*, February 15, 2012, http://www.truth-out.org/news/item/6703:fifty-activist-groups-call-for-congressional-hearings-on-citizens-united. For a general discussion of congressional interpretation of the Constitution, see Louis Fisher, "Constitutional Interpretation by Members of Congress," *North Carolina Law Review* 63 (1984–1985): 707; Neal Kumar Katyal, "Legislative Constitutional Interpretation," *Duke Law Journal* 50 (2001): 1335; Scott E. Gant, "Judicial Supremacy and Nonjudicial Interpretation of the Constitution," *Hastings Constitutional Law Quarterly* 24 (1996–1997): 359; Bruce G. Peabody, "Congressional Constitutional Interpretation and the Courts: A Preliminary Inquiry into Legislative Attitudes, 1959–2001," *Law and Social Inquiry* 20 (2004): 127.

163. Legal language is "the product of a society in which only a very limited class of 'legally competent' people can read the texts of that language." Finn, *Civic*, 50. As Weinstein notes, language is overtly political, especially when language skills are used to control access to resources or participation in certain activities or practices, as evidenced, for example, by the licensing requirements of state bar associations. Weinstein, *Civic Tongue*, 83.

164. For an insightful discussion, see Ira L. Strauber, *Neglected Policies: Constitutional Law and Legal Commentary as Civic Education* (Durham, N.C.: Duke University Press, 2002).

165. Finn, *Civic*, 48, 50. Even within the interpretive community, there are identifiable inequalities in status, inequalities that raise important issues about the allocation or distribution of political power.

166. Roger Cotterrell, *The Politics of Jurisprudence: A Critical Introduction to Legal Philosophy* (Philadelphia: University of Pennsylvania Press, 1989), 177.

167. For a discussion of "demosprudence," or the idea that courts, especially speaking through dissents, can contribute to or galvanize legal movement and social change, see Lani Guinier, "Foreword: Demosprudence Through Dissent," *Harvard Law Review* 122 (2008): 4. For a general critique, see Gerald N. Rosenberg, "Romancing the Court," *Boston University Law Review* 89 (2009): 563. For a discussion in the specific context of same-sex marriage, see Michael J. Klarman, *From the Closet to the Altar: Courts, Backlash, and the Struggle for Same-Sex Marriage* (New York: Oxford University Press, 2012). Klarman argues, contrary to the so-called backlash thesis, that litigation played a significant part in advancing same-sex marriage rights.

168. Eugene W. Rostow, "The Democratic Character of Judicial Review," *Harvard Law Review* 66 (1952): 193, 208.

169. Christopher L. Eisgruber, "Is the Supreme Court an Educative Institution"? *New York University Law Review* 67 (1992): 962, 963n2.

170. Ibid., 968.

171. Ibid., 974. Consider, as possible candidates, *Minersville v. Gobitis* (1940), or *Dred Scott*, or *Korematsu*.

172. Ibid., 968.

173. See Introduction, pp. 21–22, distinguishing between homogeneous and heterogeneous models of conversation.

174. The same hierarchy is modeled in the juridic reading of Article 6. Recall in the Introduction that we contrasted this juridic reading with a civic reading of the same Article.

175. Eisgruber, *Educative Institution*, 1002. Eisgruber's reference to the need for "conclusive" adjudication suggests that one of the virtues that might be "corrupted" is the Court's settlement function. In Essay Two I will argue that the Juridic Constitution prioritizes the settlement function over the educative or dialogic functions that form the core of the Civic Constitution. One might think, then, that the Civic Constitution, having loosened the Court from strict demands of the settlement function, might give the Court more opportunities to engage in civic education. This shift is unlikely. As I indicated above, the Constitution is neither strictly juridic nor civic—it is a curious and uneasy mixture of the two conceptions, and the juridic function of constitutional settlement in the Civic Constitution, although reduced in importance or priority, is still significant.

176. Ibid.

177. Ibid., 1031.

178. This approach to federalism recalls Brandeis's familiar reference to the states as "laboratories of experimentation," except in this instance the states serve as laboratories for civic engagement. See Brandeis: "It is one of the happy incidents of the federal system that a single courageous State may, if its citizens choose, serve as a laboratory; and try novel social and economic experiments without risk to the rest of the country" (dissenting in *New State Ice Co. v. Liebmann* [1932]).

179. See generally Jean M. Yarbrough, *American Virtues: Thomas Jefferson on the Character of a Free People* (Lawrence: University Press of Kansas, 2009).

180. Bradley Hays, *Federal Constitutionalism* (unpublished ms.).

181. See, for instance, the work of Larry Kramer on popular constitutionalism, or treatments by Tushnet, Waldron, Balkin, and Finn, or even Bruce Ackerman (though he is certainly not a popular constitutionalist, his argument about constitutional moments does try to carve out a significant role for citizens in constitutional politics).

182. See p. 125, Essay Two.

183. Sotirios A. Barber, *The Fallacies of States' Rights* (Cambridge, Mass.: Harvard University Press, 2013), 18.

184. To put it more simply, arguments in favor of states' rights are not the same thing as arguments in favor of federalism.

185. Barber, *States' Rights*, 3–4.

186. Civic or strong-form federalism, insofar as it must respect the constitutional commitments that comprise the Civic Constitution itself, thus comes closer to Barber's Marshallian conception of federalism than does states' rights or process federalism. But as I shall argue in Essay Two, and as Barber appears to argue as well, our understanding of Article 6 as committing us to a constitutional order in which reason and deliberation may persuade us to reject the Constitution must mean also that "the nation must be open to a states' rights argument. I mean the nation must be open to its own dissolution." Barber, *States' Rights*, 13.

187. Elkin, *Commercial Republic*, 151.

188. Finn, *Crisis*, ch. 1.

189. For an overview, see Murphy, *Constitutional Democracy*, ch. 7.

190. For a discussion, see Mark Tushnet, "Two Versions of Judicial Supremacy," *William and Mary Law Review* 39 (1998) 945.

191. This is a long-standing issue in democratic theory. For a recent treatment, see Frank Fischer, *Democracy and Expertise: Reorienting Policy Inquiry* (New York: Oxford University Press, 2009).

192. The classic text is Charles Grove Haines, *The American Doctrine of Judicial Supremacy* (New York: Macmillan, 1914). The contemporary literature is too voluminous to cite; for especially useful accounts, see Larry Alexander and Frederick Schauer, "On Extrajudicial Constitutional Interpretation," *Harvard Law Review* 110 (1997): 1359, and "Defending Judicial Supremacy: A Reply" (with Frederick Schauer), *Constitutional Commentary* 17 (2000): 455.

193. See the discussion of judicial overhang in Essay Two; Tushnet, *Weak Courts*, 81.

194. Tushnet argues, for example, that strong-form judicial review "can threaten democratic self-governance." "The Implications of the Development of Alternative Forms of Judicial Review," in *The Supreme Court and the Idea of Constitutionalism*, ed. Steven Kautz, Arthur Melzer, Jerry Weinberger, and M. Richard Zinman (Philadelphia: University of Pennsylvania Press, 2009), 117.

195. Nagel, *Constitutional Cultures*, 1. Elkin makes the same point: "We rely too

heavily on the Supreme Court to carry the deliberative burden of the regime." Elkin, *Commercial Republic*, 147.

196. I have argued elsewhere, however, that efforts to democratize judicial review and constitutional interpretation are complicated because they assume the touchstone of legitimacy is conformity to principles of democratic self-government. In other words, their "rightness" resides chiefly in the fact that they represent our choice. Foundationalists locate the touchstone of legitimacy not in self-governance but in conformity with the basic presuppositions or constitutive principles of constitutionalism, i.e., with a principle of "rightness" that does not depend upon their election by the people themselves. Finn, *Crisis*, ch. 1; see also Essay Two, pp. 146–149.

197. Richard Stith, "Securing the Rule of Law through Interpretive Pluralism," *Hastings Law Quarterly* 35 (2008): 401.

198. Or, in other words, by giving them "ambition." See *Federalist* #51.

199. Stith, *Pluralism*, 402.

200. See Essay Two, pp. 134–136.

201. Benjamin A. Kleinerman, "'The Court Will Clean It Up': Executive Power, Constitutional Contestation, and War Powers," in Kautz et al., *The Supreme Court and the Idea of Constitutionalism* (Philadelphia: University of Pennsylvania Press, 2009), 233.

202. Mark Tushnet, "*Marbury v. Madison* around the World," *Tennessee Law Review* 71 (2004): 251, 262–263.

203. Bradley Hays, *Federal Constitutionalism* (unpublished ms.); see also Robert A. Schapiro, *Polyphonic Federalism: Toward the Protection of Fundamental Rights* (Chicago: University of Chicago Press, 2009).

204. Sanford Levinson, *Constitutional Faith* (Princeton, N.J.: Princeton University Press, 1988), 43–49.

205. Ibid., 53. For something similar, see Article 20(4) of the German Basic Law, which provides "[A]ll Germans have the right to resist any person or persons seeking to abolish [the] constitutional order, should no other remedy be possible."

206. See Robert F. Nagel, "Judicial Supremacy and the Settlement Function," *William and Mary Law Review* 39 (1998): 849. See also Kramer, *People Themselves*, 234–235.

207. The phrase is from Ronald Dworkin, "Forum of Principle," *New York University Law Review* 56 (1981): 469; see additionally Larry Alexander and Frederick Schauer, "Defending Judicial Supremacy: A Reply," *Constitutional Commentary* 17 (2000): 455, contra Louis Michael Seidman, *Our Unsettled Constitution: A New Defense of Constitutionalism and Judicial Review* (New Haven, Conn.: Yale University Press, 2001); Neal Devins and Louis Fisher, "Judicial Exclusivity and Political Instability," *Virginia Law Review* 84 (1998): 83. For a different treatment of extrajudicial settlements, see Keith Whittington, "Extrajudicial Constitutional Interpretation: Three Objections and Responses," *North Carolina Law Review* 80 (2002): 773.

208. Exactly which settlements would be worse and why is itself an important point of civic dialogue. So, for example, public disagreement about the wisdom and

constitutionality of the Court's decision in *Roe v. Wade* (1973), or in *Lawrence v. Texas* (2003), would itself constitute civic dialogue.

209. See pp. 107–116 for a discussion; see also Sanford Levinson, "What Should Citizens (As Participants in a Republican Form of Government) Know about the Constitution," *William and Mary Law Review* 50 (2008): 1239.

210. In *Boerne*, the Court's assertion of judicial supremacy had the practical effect of reinstalling a doctrinal standard that results in significantly less protection for free exercise than the congressional standard in the RFRA. See also Schapiro, *Polyphonic Federalism*. Schapiro argues "a multifaceted government can best realize the potential of federalism to protect fundamental rights."

211. Jeremy Waldron, *Law and Disagreement* (New York: Oxford University Press, 2001); Mark V. Tushnet, *Taking the Constitution Away from the Courts* (Princeton, N.J.: Princeton University Press, 2000).

212. Jeremy Waldron, "A Right-Based Critique of Constitutional Rights," *Oxford Journal of Legal Studies* 13 (1993): 18; see also Waldron's review of Ackerman's *We the People*, vol. 1: *Foundations, Journal of Philosophy* 90 (1993): 149, 153.

213. This recalls the many warnings by Felix Frankfurter, as well as other justices, that the Court cannot save the people from themselves.

214. Jack M. Balkin and Reva B. Siegel, eds., *The Constitution in 2020* (New York: Oxford University Press, 2009), 6. See also Robert A. Dahl, "Decision-Making in a Democracy: The Supreme Court as a National Policy-Maker," *Journal of Public Law* 6 (1957): 291; Richard Funston, "The Supreme Court and Critical Elections," *American Political Science Review* 69 (1975): 796.

215. For an example, see Lincoln's response to *Dred Scott*. First Inaugural Address, Washington, D.C. (March 4, 1861).

216. Adler, *We Hold These Truths*, 86.

217. Peter Riesenberg, *Citizenship in the Western Tradition: Plato to Rousseau* (Chapel Hill: University of North Carolina Press, 1994), 270.

218. Carl Schmitt, *The Concept of the Political*, trans. by George Schwab (1927) (Chicago: University of Chicago Press, 2007). Schmitt's conception speaks to a distinction grounded in violence.

219. Chantal Mouffe, "Carl Schmitt and the Paradox of Liberal Democracy," in *The Challenge of Carl Schmitt*, ed. Chantal Mouffe (London: Verso, 1999), 43.

220. Riesenberg, *Citizenship*, 25.

221. Bruce Ackerman, "The Citizenship Agenda," in Balkin and Siegel, *The Constitution in 2020*, 109.

222. See Brandon, note 235. To be precise, and to illustrate once again that the act of constituting both is an ongoing affair and includes more than just the formal document, the effort to create national citizenship for African Americans predates the Fourteenth Amendment by virtue of the Civil Rights Act of 1866.

223. For a discussion of some of these proposals, see Nacha Cattan, "Rights Groups Denounce Proposed Bills to Remove 'Birthright Citizenship,'" *Christian Science Monitor*, January 5, 2011, http://www.csmonitor.com/World/Americas

/2011/0105/Rights-groups-denounce-proposed-bills-to-remove-birthright-citizen ship.

224. One obvious example of how the qualification for citizenship affects one's eligibility for the blessings of liberty is *Plyler v. Doe* (1982).

225. I refer back to the distinction I drew between the universalistic, or foundational, components of the Civic Constitution and the particularistic or contingent elements. The liberties that we assign to personhood—equality and due process— might be said to be universalistic, and so do not depend for their protection on the status of citizenship.

226. Wayne D. Moore, "Constitutional Citizenship," in Barber and George, *Constitutional Politics*, 253.

227. Ibid., 245. As Moore describes it, Douglass thus came to a position of "advocating fundamental continuity through radical change."

228. Ibid., 238.

229. For an overview, see Feifei Sun, "Behind the Cover: America's Undocumented Immigrants," *Time*, June 14, 2012, http://lightbox.time.com/2012/06/14/ behind-the-cover-americas-undocumented-immigrants/#1.

230. Moore, *Citizenship*, 253.

231. See Lewis A. Kornhauser, "Modeling Collegial Courts. II. Legal Doctrine," *Journal of Law, Economics, and Organization* 8 (1992): 441.

232. For a general discussion, see Søren Kierkegaard, *Either/Or* (1843). See also Robert Bolton, "Plato's Distinction between Being and Becoming," *Review of Metaphysics* 29 (1975): 66.

233. Contrast this silence with the language of the Declaration of Independence, where the We in "We hold these truths to be self-evident" is arguably created out of whole cloth, and then later, at the end, defined as "We, Therefore, the Representatives of the United States of America." As Tulis notes, "In fact, the people cannot be easily identified before the Declaration." Barber and George, *Constitutional Politics*, 120. It is also useful to consider the opening to the Articles of Confederation, which begins by referencing the several states.

234. Or "compromise," in the words of Justice Thurgood Marshall, who wrote: "No doubt it will be said, when the unpleasant truth of the history of slavery in America is mentioned during this bicentennial year, that the Constitution was a product of its times, and embodied a compromise which, under other circumstances, would not have been made. But the effects of the Framers' compromise have remained for generations. They arose from the contradiction between guaranteeing liberty and justice to all, and denying both to Negroes." Remarks of Thurgood Marshall at the Annual Seminar of the San Francisco Patent and Trademark Law Association in Maui, Hawaii, May 6, 1987, http://www.thurgoodmarshall.com/speeches/ constitutional_speech.htm.

235. See the moving speech by Frederick Douglass, Oration, delivered in Corinthian Hall, Rochester, by Frederick Douglass, July 5th, 1852, http://www.lib .rochester.edu/index.cfm?page=2945; William Lloyd Garrison, "a covenant with

hell." Quoted in Walter M. Merrill, *Against Wind and Tide: A Biography of Wm. Lloyd Garrison* (Cambridge, Mass.: Harvard University Press, 1973), 205. For a general discussion, see Jack M. Balkin, "Agreements with Hell and Other Objects of Our Faith," *Fordham Law Review* 65 (1997): 1703. For a general discussion of slavery and constitutional failure, see Mark E. Brandon, *Free in the World: American Slavery and Constitutional Failure* (Princeton, N.J.: Princeton University Press, 1998).

236. See Sanford Levinson, "Compromise and Constitutionalism," *Pepperdine Law Review* 38 (2011): 5.

237. James Madison, *Notes of Debates in the Federal Convention of 1787* (New York: W. W. Norton and Co.), 530. Later, however, in *Federalist* #42, he wrote "It ought to be considered as a great point gained in favor of humanity, that a period of twenty years may terminate forever, within these States, a traffic which has long and so loudly upbraided the barbarism of modern policy; that within that period it will receive considerable discouragement from the Federal government and be totally abolished, by a concurrence of the few States which continue the unnatural traffic in the prohibitory example which has been given by so great a majority of the Union."

238. A subject is related to power in a position of subservience. The relationship is an empirical fact. In contrast, the relationship between citizen and authority is not simply an empirical fact—it is a prescriptive relationship as well, in which the related concepts of consent and legitimacy transform subject into citizen, and power into authority. For a general discussion of this transformation, see Dana Villa, *Public Freedom* (Princeton, N.J.: Princeton University Press, 2008), 260–269. See also Riesenberg, *Citizenship*, who argues that "[s]ince the Renaissance, Bodin's kind of citizenship, which is a form of subjectship that places the individual in direct subordinate relationship to the prince, has prevailed. Stripped of the institution of the monarchy, it survives as the basis of the relationship between the individual and the government in every modern country," xi.

239. Attributed to Alexander Hamilton. For a discussion, see Stephen F. Knott. *Alexander Hamilton and the Persistence of Myth* (Lawrence: University Press of Kansas, 2002), 74.

240. Wolin, *Presence of the Past*, 189.

241. Ibid.

242. But note that not even Machiavelli provided an account of citizenship that completely elevates self-interest at the expense of community. Riesenberg, *Citizenship*, xi.

243. Rossiter, *The Federalist Papers*, #49.

244. Sheehan, *James Madison*, 172.

245. Ibid., 83.

246. Ibid., 12–13.

247. Ibid., 164.

248. Elkin, *Commercial Republic*, esp. chaps 2 and 3.

249. Ibid., 66–67.

250. Recalling my point earlier in this essay that the Civic Constitution influences both how we write the Constitution and how we read it. This also recalls Justice Frankfurter's comments on reading congressional silence in *Helvering v. Hallock* (1940): http://newdeal.feri.org/court/frankfurter.htm. See also Lawrence H. Tribe, "Toward a Syntax of the Unsaid: Construing the Sounds of Congressional and Constitutional Silence," *Indiana Law Journal* 57 (1982): 515, http://www.repository.law.indiana.edu/ilj/vol57/iss4/1.

251. Alexander Hamilton, *The Papers of Alexander Hamilton*, ed. Harold C. Syrett (New York, Columbia University Press, 1962), 3:544–545.

252. Villa, *Public Freedom*, 18, 348.

253. Samuel Adams, *The Writings of Samuel Adams*, ed. Harry Alonzo Cushing (New York: G. P. Putnam's Sons, 1907), 4:256, in the *Boston Gazette* on April 16, 1781.

254. John Jay, *The Correspondence and Public Papers of John Jay*, ed. Henry P. Johnston (New York: G. P. Putnam Sons, 1890), 4:365.

255. Examples include Australia and, until recently, Chile. See Central Intelligence Agency, *The World Factbook*, https://www.cia.gov/library/publications/the-world-factbook/fields/2123.html#le.

256. See also Richard Rose and Harve Mossawir, "Voting and Elections: A Functional Analysis," *Political Studies* 15 (1996): 173.

257. For an overview, see Arend Lijphart, "Unequal Participation: Democracy's Unresolved Dilemma," *American Political Science Review* 91 (1997): 1; Bernard Berelson et al., *Voting* (Chicago: University of Chicago Press, 1954).

258. See Joanne Finkelstein, *Dining Out: A Sociology of Modern Manners* (New York: New York University Press, 1989), 172: "Mimetic events . . . are not imitations of real-life events, rather they are devices employed to induce the individual to feel in certain circumstances and at certain times, in accordance with the conventions and manners of the epoch."

259. Hemberger, *What Did They Think*, 142.

260. Ibid., 145.

261. A third duty of citizenship is the payment of taxes. Also, naturalized citizens must take an oath of loyalty, and all citizens may be tried for treason, within the confines of Article 3, Section 3. For a discussion of treason, see *Federalist* #43. On loyalty oaths, see Sanford Levinson, "Taking Oaths Seriously: A Comment on Carter and Sunstein," *Yale Journal of Law and the Humanities* 2, no. 1, article 8, http://digitalcommons.law.yale.edu/yjlh/vol2/iss1/8.

262. Kramer discusses juries as instruments of popular constitutionalism in *The People Themselves*, 157.

263. See, for example, *Batson v. Kentucky* (1986); see also *Strauder v. West Virginia* (1880) and *Virginia v. Rives* (1879).

264. For an argument that juries remain a significant instrument of civic participation, see Andrew Guthrie Ferguson, *Why Jury Duty Matters: A Citizen's Guide to Constitutional Action* (New York: New York University Press, 2013); Albert W.

Dzur, *Punishment, Participatory Democracy, and the Jury* (New York: Oxford University Press, 2012).

265. See Nancy L. Schwartz, *The Blue Guitar: Political Representation and Community* (Chicago: University of Chicago Press, 1988), 10.

266. Riesenberg, *Citizenship*, xvi–xvii.

267. Ibid.

268. See also Judith N. Shklar, *American Citizenship: The Quest for Inclusion* (Cambridge, Mass.: Harvard University Press, 1991).

269. See, for example, *Federalists* #49 and #55.

270. See Barber, *On What the Constitution Means*, 104.

271. Riesenberg, *Citizenship*, xi. See Schwartz, *Blue Guitar*, 10.

272. Public also references the sense of public spaces described by Arendt, as "predicated upon the equality of citizens. Such civic equality was an equality of peers, and—as such—stood in the sharpest possible contrast to the (seemingly natural) hierarchy that pervaded the private . . . realm." Villa, *Public Freedom*, 339.

273. In sharp contrast, say, with Ackerman's view. John E. Finn, "Transformation or Transmogrification? Ackerman, Hobbes (as in Calvin and Hobbes), and the Puzzle of Changing Constitutional Identity," *Constitutional Political Economy* 10 (1999): 355.

274. Villa, *Public Freedom*, 347.

275. Riesenberg, *Citizenship*, 45.

276. As Larry Kramer writes, "Politics today has thus become a remote, passive activity for most of us. We read newspapers or watch TV; we discuss the issues with friends; we vote and maybe give some money to a party or other organization. But apart from that, we leave the management of our political affairs to others." "Political Organization and the Future of Democracy," in Balkin and Siegel, *The Constitution in 2020*, 176.

277. Wolin, *Presence of the Past*; Michael Parenti, "A Constitution for the Few," http://www.iefd.org/articles/constitution_for_the_few.php; Parenti, *Democracy for the Few*, 9th ed. (Boston: Wadsworth, 2010), ch. two.

278. Murphy, *Constitutional Democracy*, 346.

279. Ibid., 349.

280. The state has an important role to play in constituting the citizens of the Civic Constitution. Stephen Macedo, "Transformative Constitutionalism and the Case of Religion: Defending the Moderate Hegemony of Liberalism," in Barber and George, *Constitutional Politics*, 169.

281. Murphy, *Constitutional Democracy*, 367.

282. Riesenberg, *Citizenship*, 262.

283. Thomas, "National University," 26.

284. For a notable exception, see Linda C. McClain, "The Domain of Civic Virtue in a Good Society: Families, Schools, and Sex Equality," *Fordham Law Review* 69 (2001): 1617, 1619.

285. See Finn, *Crisis*; see also Jon Elster, *Ulysses Unbound: Studies in Rationality,*

Precommitment, and Constraints (Cambridge: Cambridge University Press, 2000). For a criticism, see Waldron, *Law and Disagreement.*

286. See Thomas C. Schelling, "The Intimate Contest for Self-Command," *Public Interest*, no. 60 (1980): 94–118, http://www.nationalaffairs.com/public_interest/detail/the-intimate-contest-for-self-command.

287. In Rubenfeld's evocative terminology. Jeb Rubenfeld, *Freedom and Time: A Theory of Constitutional Self-Government* (New Haven, Conn.: Yale University Press, 2001). See also Schelling, "Intimate Contest."

288. McClain, "Domain of Civic Virtue," 1617, 1619.

289. Although I will not explore the topic here, revitalization of the Civic Constitution, and of civic space in particular as a public good, should lead us also consider the extent to which civic participation in the constitutional life of the polity can be promoted by governments through the design and implementation of public policy. Suzanne Mettler, "Bringing the State Back in to Civic Engagement: Policy Feedback Effects of the G.I. Bill for World War II Veterans," *American Political Science Review* 96 (2002): 351–365; see also Helen Ingram and Anne Schneider, "Constructing Citizenship: The Subtle Messages of Policy Design," in *Public Policy for Democracy*, ed. Helen Ingram and Steven Rathgeb Smith (Washington, D.C.: Brookings, 1993), 68. As Suzanne Mettler has demonstrated, "Despite contemporary concern over the decline of social capital and participation, we have not developed a systematic way of investigating the role that governments play in shaping citizens' involvement." Mettler, "Bringing the State Back," 351. Mettler's pioneering work on civic engagement as shaped by the G.I. Bill of Rights suggests strongly that the G.I. Bill "promoted civic participation among groups that were somewhat less advantaged in the typical prerequisites for participation." Ibid., 362. Mettler concludes, much in line with the earlier work of Schattschneider and Lowi, that "policies function as institutions" and institutions teach by "reshaping politics itself." Ibid., 352.

290. Nathan Tarcov, "Ideas of Constitutionalism Ancient and Modern," in Kautz et al., *Idea of Constitutionalism*, 28.

291. See my earlier reference to functional nonvoting literature of 1950s, supra note 257.

292. Riesenberg, *Citizenship*, 262: recalling Rousseau, "Emotion is a desideratum of good citizenship. . . . Such an education must start 'the first moment of life.'" For a sense of just how expansive and intensive such training for citizenship can be, see generally J. J. Rousseau, *The Government of Poland* (Indianapolis: Hackett Publishing, 1985).

293. For a fascinating and provocative discussion of the role of myth and narrative in the construction of national identity, see Rogers Smith, *Civic Ideals.*

294. Madison wrote, "[A]s every appeal to the people would carry an implication of some defect in the government, frequent appeals would, in a great measure, deprive the government of that veneration which time bestows on every thing, and without which perhaps the wisest and freest governments would not possess the requisite stability. . . . In a nation of philosophers, this consideration ought to be

disregarded. A reverence for the laws would be sufficiently inculcated by the voice of an enlightened reason. But a nation of philosophers is as little to be expected as the philosophical race of kings wished for by Plato. And in every other nation, the most rational government will not find it a superfluous advantage to have the prejudices of the community on its side." *Federalist* #49.

295. Ackerman, *We the People*, 3–4.

296. Finn, *Civic*, 57.

297. Contrast Hemberger on political knowledge: *What Did They Think*, 138.

298. Thomas, "National University," 26; *The Constitution of the Mind* (forthcoming).

299. Thomas, "National University," 16–21.

300. Ibid., 2.

301. We do ask such citizens, unlike citizens by birth, to take an oath of allegiance that explicitly references fidelity: "I hereby declare, on oath, that I absolutely and entirely renounce and abjure all allegiance and fidelity to any foreign prince, potentate, state, or sovereignty of whom or which I have heretofore been a subject or citizen; that I will support and defend the Constitution and laws of the United States of America against all enemies, foreign and domestic; that I will bear true faith and allegiance to the same; that I will bear arms on behalf of the United States when required by the law; that I will perform noncombatant service in the Armed Forces of the United States when required by the law; that I will perform work of national importance under civilian direction when required by the law; and that I take this obligation freely without any mental reservation or purpose of evasion; so help me God."

302. Such as *Mozert v. Hawkins*, 827 F. 2d 1058 (1987). I discuss *Mozert* in Essay Two, pp. 113–114.

303. American Civil Liberties Union, *The Persecution of Jehovah's Witnesses* (New York: ACLU, 1941). For a recent discussion, see David Thomas Smith, "Essays on the Persecution of Religious Minorities" (PhD thesis, University of Michigan, 2011), http://deepblue.lib.umich.edu/bitstream/2027.42/84555/1/davidsth_1.pdf.

304. For a history, see Richard J. Ellis, *To the Flag: The Unlikely History of the Pledge of Allegiance* (Lawrence: University Press of Kansas, 2005).

305. Alexis de Tocqueville, *Democracy in America*, vol. 2 (1840).

306. For a full elaboration of this logic, see Sotirios A. Barber, *The Constitution of Judicial Power* (Baltimore: Johns Hopkins University Press, 1993), 64–65. See also Murphy, *Constitutional Democracy*, 376–377.

307. Finkelstein, *Dining Out*, 174.

308. "Of course, in order for the constitutional framework to have any long term impact, its values had to become internalized in the thinking processes and emotional attachments of a large part of the American elite (particularly lawyers, journalists and publishers) and take root among a significant portion of the population at large." Rodney Jay Blackham, *Foreign Fanaticism and American Constitutional Values* (Durham, N.C.: Carolina Academic Press, 2010), 61; Dahl quote in Finn, *Crisis*, 221.

309. I agree with Thomas that insofar as the Civic Constitution embraces the Aristotelian understanding of constitutionalism as "a way of life," it thus shapes civil society "giving us more than a 'negative' charter of liberties." "National University," 27. See discussion below at pp. 105–106.

310. Stephen Macedo, "Liberal Hegemony," in Barber and George, *Constitutional Politics*, 176. Macedo develops this point in a discussion that addresses the important question about the relationship of liberal democracy and the constitution, and regulation, of religious communities, especially those that are uncomfortably illiberal.

311. See Rossiter, *The Federalist Papers*, #26: "Schemes to subvert the liberties of a great community *require time* to mature them for execution."

312. See Harry Eckstein, "Congruence Theory Explained," CSD Working Papers, Center for the Study of Democracy, UC Irvine, 1997, http://repositories.cdlib.org/cgi/viewcontent.cgi?article=1120andcontext=csd. Eckstein argues that congruence is of greater importance in social units and aspects of civic culture that are "more adjacent" to "governmental performance," while simultaneously suggesting—probably incorrectly—that "family life probably is less important for congruence in advanced industrial societies than in others." Ibid., 7. Still, "it is inconceivable that a democracy could be highly stable and effective if authority relations in families . . . are despotic." This does not mean that the Civic Constitution is necessarily militant, to use Jacobsohn's terms, but for all practical purposes, we live in a thin political culture, a consequence in part of the regnancy of the Juridic Constitution. Any displacement in favor of the Civic Constitution will require that we understand the Civic Constitution, at least initially, as militant in character and object. *Constitutional Identity*, 217.

313. Stephen Macedo, "Transformative Constitutionalism and the Case of Religion: Defending the Moderate Hegemony of Liberalism," in Barber and George, *Constitutional Politics*, 169; see also 170 for a reference to thriving. Macedo, we should note, subscribes to an understanding of constitutional democracy very much similar to the one proposed by Murphy, which I discussed above. One of the advantages to Macedo's formulation is that it reveals how inadequacies of design are likely to subvert constitutional maintenance.

314. Of the many examples one could cite here, especially instructive is Rousseau, *The Government of Poland*.

315. See, for instance, Stephen Macedo, *Liberal Virtues: Citizenship, Virtue, and Community in Liberal Constitutionalism* (Oxford: Clarendon Press, 1990); *Diversity and Distrust: Civic Education in a Multicultural Democracy* (Cambridge, Mass.: Harvard University Press, 2000).

316. Stephen Macedo, "The Constitution, Civic Virtue, and Civil Society: Social Capital as Substantive Morality," *Fordham Law Review* 69 (2001): 1573, 1574.

317. Ibid., 1575, 1582–1583, 1591.

318. McClain, "Domain of Civic Virtue," 1619.

319. Robert D. Putnam, *Bowling Alone: The Collapse and Revival of American Community* (New York: Simon and Schuster, 2000), 22–23. The distinction recalls

my discussion in the Introduction of two conversational models—the homogeneous and the heterogeneous. I argued there that the Civic Constitution must make room for both, but places a higher value on the heterogeneous model.

320. See Eckstein, "Congruence Theory Explained."

321. Rousseau wrote, "It is education that must give souls the national form" and every citizen must be indoctrinated into "love of fatherland, that is to say love of law and love of freedom" from the very beginning. *Government of Poland*, 189.

322. As Villa notes, the citizen "must be given something to do for the public" that "transcends the (occasionally meaningless) ritual of electoral participation." Villa, *Public Freedom*, 17–18.

323. Ibid., 16. Villa cites Wolin for this proposition; presumably Stephen Elkin's work on the commercial republic would fit into this category as well, though Wolin's treatment is considerably more hostile to the general proposition than is Elkin's. Elkin, *Commercial Republic*.

324. Villa, *Public Freedom*, 18.

325. Michael Marsh, "Second-Order Elections," in *International Encyclopedia of Elections*, ed. Richard Rose (London: Macmillan, 2000).

326. Murphy, *Constitutional Democracy*, 3.

327. See Wolin's distinction between "politics" and "the political," in "Fugitive Democracy," *Constellations* 1 (1994): 11–25. See also Murphy, *Constitutional Democracy*, 3n5.

328. On the radical character of the revolution, see, for example, Gordon S. Wood, *The Creation of the American Republic 1776–1787* (Chapel Hill: University of North Carolina Press, 1998), and *The Radicalism of the American Revolution* (New York: Vintage, 1993); see also Stanley Elkins and Eric McKitrick, "The Founding Fathers: Young Men of the Revolution," *Political Science Quarterly* 76 (1961): 181. For a discussion of "demophobia," see Jeremy Engels, "Demophilia: A Discursive Counter to Demophobia in the Early Republic," *Quarterly Journal of Speech* 97 (2011): 131.

329. See Norbert Elias, *The Civilizing Process: Sociogenetic and Psychogenetic Investigations*, rev. ed. (New York: Blackwell Publishing, 2000). See also Norbert Elias and Eric Dunning, *The Quest for Excitement* (Oxford: Basil Blackwell, 1986), 66–90; Finkelstein, *Dining Out*, 42.

330. See Essay Three.

331. Catherine Drinker Bowen, *Miracle at Philadelphia: The Story of the Constitutional Convention* (Boston: Back Bay Books, 1986).

Essay Two: Maintaining

1. Gary J. Jacobsohn, *Constitutional Identity* (Cambridge, Mass.: Harvard University Press, 2010), 348–349.

2. See ibid., 59–60, for a discussion of the temporal dimension of revolution, "as discontinuity" and as distinct from "reform."

3. Indeed, we might describe some subsequent political contests as crises of identity. See, for example, Paul W. Kahn, *The Reign of Law: Marbury v. Madison and the Construction of America* (New Haven, Conn.: Yale University Press, 1997), 10. I do not, however, mean to suggest that civic identity is simply a function of constitutional design. For insightful treatments, see Jacobsohn, *Constitutional Identity*, and Rogers M. Smith, *Civic Ideals: Conflicting Visions of Citizenship in U.S. History* (New Haven, Conn.: Yale University Press, 1997), ch. 1.

4. See Elvin T. Lim, *The Lovers' Quarrel* (New York: Oxford University Press, forthcoming), for an argument that such disputes are the chief explanatory variable in accounting for American political development; ch. 1, passim. Consider this quotation from John C. Calhoun: "[T]he very idea of an *American People*, as constituting a single community, is a mere chimera. Such a community never for a single moment existed—neither before nor since the Declaration of Independence." As quoted in Paul C. Nagel, *One Nation Indivisible: The Union in American Thought, 1776–1861* (New York: Oxford University Press, 1964), 47.

5. Kahn, *Reign of Law*, 3.

6. I think this is a fair description of most of Dworkin's constitutional theory; see, for example, *Freedom's Law: The Moral Reading of the American Constitution* (Cambridge, Mass.: Harvard University Press, 1997). Joseph Raz has made the same claim. See Joseph Raz, "On the Authority and Interpretation of Constitutions," in *Constitutionalism: Philosophical Foundations,* ed. Larry Alexander (Cambridge: Cambridge University Press, 1998), 157. For a contrary perspective, see Walter F. Murphy, *Constitutional Democracy: Creating and Maintaining a Just Political Order* (Baltimore: Johns Hopkins University Press, 2007), and Sotirios A. Barber, *On What the Constitution Means* (Baltimore: Johns Hopkins University Press, 1983).

7. Francis Gerald Downing, *Cynics and Christian Origins,* vol. 1 (Edinburgh: T & T Clark, 1992), 167.

8. Neither our juridic nor our civic identity emerged full-blown from the founding. Instead, both developed over time. *Marbury* may be emblematic of the Juridic Constitution, for example, but it started rather than completed the Juridic Constitution. See Sylvia Snowiss, *Judicial Review and the Law of the Constitution* (New Haven, Conn.: Yale University Press, 1990); "The *Marbury* of 1803 and the Modern *Marbury*," *Constitutional Commentary* 20 (2003): 231; see also Finn, *Civic,* 54–56; Stephen L. Elkin, *Reconstructing the Commercial Republic: Constitutional Design after Madison* (Chicago: University of Chicago Press, 2006), 1–5; David Ray Papke, *Heretics in the Temple: Americans Who Reject the Nation's Legal Faith* (New York: New York University Press, 2010).

9. For a discussion of the concept of constitutional distortion, see Christopher L. Eisgruber, "Judicial Supremacy and Constitutional Distortion," in *Constitutional Politics: Essays on Constitution Making, Maintenance, and Change,* ed. Sotirios A. Barber and Robert P. George (Princeton, N.J.: Princeton University Press, 2001), 70–90.

10. See Murphy, *Constitutional Democracy.*

11. I use this phrase, rather than the neater "constitutional litigation," because litigation itself might be a kind of civic engagement or activity initiated by citizens, interest groups, or social movements; to be precise we ought to distinguish it from the interpretive work of judges as a form of constitutional maintenance. For a discussion of "demosprudence," or the idea that courts, especially speaking through dissents, can contribute to or galvanize social change, see Lani Guinier, "Foreword: Demosprudence through Dissent," *Harvard Law Review* 122 (2008): 4. For a general critique, see Gerald N. Rosenberg, "Romancing the Court," *Boston University Law Review* 89 (2009): 563.

12. Hanna Fenichel Pitkin, "The Idea of a Constitution," *Journal of Legal Education* 37 (1987): 167–168.

13. See *Federalist* #51. Madison also rejected "periodic appeals" to a formal institutionalized body. His rejection was premised upon his reading of Pennsylvania's experience with the Council of Censors. Richard Burt has concluded, I think correctly, that Madison's comments on the Council of Censors suggest that he foresaw similar difficulties "[w]ith entrusting constitutional enforcement to the Supreme Court." We should be careful, therefore, to distinguish Madison's approach to the constitutional enterprise from Hamilton's. Richard Burt, *The Constitution in Conflict* (Cambridge, Mass.: Harvard University Press, 1992), 59.

14. H. Mark Roelofs, *The Poverty of American Politics: A Theoretical Interpretation* (Philadelphia: Temple University Press, 1992), 48.

15. See *Federalist* #49: "A reverence for the laws would be sufficiently inculcated by the voice of an enlightened reason. But a nation of philosophers is as little to be expected as the philosophical race of kings wished for by Plato. And in every other nation, the most rational government will not find it a superfluous advantage to have the prejudices of the community on its side."

16. Keith Whittington, *Political Foundations of Judicial Supremacy: The Presidency, the Supreme Court, and Constitutional Leadership in U.S. History* (Princeton, N.J.: Princeton University Press, 2007).

17. And to believe in the Juridic Constitution is to accept, at least implicitly, somewhat dubious claims about the integrity and autonomy of legal knowledge. Indeed, insofar as the Juridic Constitution seeks to insulate law from politics, it rests upon a claim either that law and politics are distinct or that law is a distinctive kind of politics.

18. Ernest Barker, ed., *The Politics of Aristotle* (New York: Oxford University Press, 1968), 1275a2w3, 93–94.

19. For an especially useful discussion of the doctrinal implications of citizenship conceived in a similar way, see William N. Eskridge Jr., "The Relationship between Obligations and Rights of Citizens," *Fordham Law Review* 69 (2001): 1721.

20. Quoted in Finn, *Civic*, 53.

21. James A. Morone, *The Democratic Wish: Popular Participation and the Limits of American Government* (New York: Basic Books, 1990), 65.

22. In Eisgruber's formulation, the word "citizen" means "voter" and "taxpayer"

and little else. See Christopher Eisgruber, "Civic Virtue and the Limits of Constitutionalism," *Fordham Law Review* 69 (2001): 2131–2132.

23. On the role of loyalty oaths in making this transformation, see Sanford Levinson, *Constitutional Faith* (Princeton, N.J.: Princeton University Press, 1988), 112.

24. Aristotle, *Ethics*, ed. and trans. Martin Ostwald (Indianapolis: Library of Liberal Arts, 1962) , 1099b30.

25. Eisgruber, *Civic Virtue*, 2144.

26. Ibid., 2137.

27. See Benjamin Barber, "Neither Leaders Nor Followers: Citizenship under Strong Democracy," in *A Passion for Democracy: American Essays* (Princeton, N.J.: Princeton University Press 2000), 98.

28. Jürgen Habermas, *Knowledge and Human Interests* (Boston: Beacon Press, 1962), 58. See also Introduction, 12–16.

29. For an example, see Christopher L. Eisgruber; see especially, *Civic Virtue*, 2131, 2132. Eisgruber describes the "inevitable tendency of democratic constitutions to reduce citizens to voters and taxpayers." What Eisgruber describes as an "inevitable tendency" is simply one account—the juridic—of the Constitution.

30. There are dozens of works I could cite here. In addition to Roelofs, *Poverty of American Politics*, see Kenneth L. Karst, "Foreword: Equal Citizenship under the Fourteenth Amendment," *Harvard Law Review* 91 (1997): 1; Frederick Schauer, "Community, Citizenship, and the Search for National Identity," *Michigan Law Review* 84 (1986): 1504; Jack M. Balkin and Reva B. Siegel, eds., *The Constitution in 2020* (New York: Oxford University Press, 2009), esp. pt. 3.

31. T. Alexander Aleinikoff, "Citizenship Talk: A Revisionist Narrative," *Fordham Law Review* 69 (2001): 1690. Part of the narrative, he notes, is concerned with equality claims, and hence with discrimination (especially racial), but Aleinikoff suggests this narrative is wrong in both its object of analysis and its teleology.

32. Bruce Ackerman, *We the People*, vol. 1: *Foundations* (Cambridge, Mass.: Belknap Press of Harvard University Press, 1993), 5.

33. As one observer has concluded, "Absent are the voices of ordinary citizens." Robert W. Scheef, "Public Citizens and the Constitution: Bridging the Gap between Popular Sovereignty and Original Intent," *Fordham Law Review* 69 (2001): 2205.

34. See ibid., note 16; see also Jennifer Nedelsky, "The Puzzle and Demands of Modern Constitutionalism," *Ethics* 104 (1994): 503–504.

35. Scheef, "Public Citizens," 2233.

36. Ackerman, *We the People*: *Foundations*, 243; again, note Ackerman's description of public citizens as "high-minded men and women who disdain high salaries to work eighty-hour weeks in crummy offices in Washington and many other places across the nation," 232.

37. See Ackerman, *We the People*: *Foundations*, 230–231, 233–234.

38. James E. Fleming, "The Missing Selves in Constitutional Self-Government," *Fordham Law Review* 71 (2003): 1790.

39. For a notable exception, see Paul Brest, "Constitutional Citizenship," *Cleveland State Law Review* 34 (1986): 6.

40. See our discussion of self-commands, note 309, and accompanying text.

41. Benjamin R. Barber, "An American Civic Forum," *Political Economy of the Good Society* 5 (1995): 12.

42. Janet A. Flammang, *The Taste for Civil Society: Food, Politics, and Civil Society* (Urbana: University of Illinois Press, 2009), 173. The phrase "third places" is a reference to Ray Oldenburg, *The Great Good Place: Cafes, Coffee Shops, Bookstores, Bars, Hair Salons, and Other Hangouts at the Heart of a Community* (Cambridge, Mass.: Da Capo Press, 1999).

43. Note, however, that Rawls's conception of civility is rather different from the one I advocate. John Rawls, *Political Liberalism* (New York: Columbia University Press, 1993), 194–195.

44. Ibid., 14.

45. John Rawls, "The Idea of Public Reason Revisited," *University of Chicago Law Review* 64 (1997): 788.

46. Linda C. McClain, "The Domain of Civic Virtue in a Good Society: Families, Schools, and Sex Equality," *Fordham Law Review* 69 (2001): 1617, 1625.

47. *Federalist* #55: "republican government presupposes the existence" of certain civic virtues "in a higher degree than any other form." *Federalist* #55 is quoted in Council on Civil Society, *A Call to Civil Society: Why Democracy Needs Moral Truths* (New York: Council on Civil Society, 1998).

48. McClain, "Domain," 1627, quoting *A Call to Civil Society*.

49. *A Call to Civil Society*, 7; see also McClain, "Domain," 1627.

50. *A Call to Civil Society*, 10; McClain, "Domain," 1628.

51. *A Call to Civil Society*, 6; McClain, "Domain," 1627.

52. McClain, "Domain," 1629.

53. Stephen Macedo, *Diversity and Distrust: Civic Education in a Multicultural Democracy* (Cambridge, Mass.: Harvard University Press, 2000), 239.

54. McClain, "Domain," 1628. McClain rightly observes that much of the literature associated with this second perspective, and especially *A Call to Civil Society*, embraces a "thick account" of civic virtue based on a set of moral truths that "is in large part biblical and religious." Ibid., 1627n33. McClain wants to argue instead for "an approach more akin to political liberalism [that is] better suited to a constitutional democracy characterized by reasonable moral pluralism." Ibid. I concur with her qualification, but would add that there is sufficient room within "political liberalism" to accommodate something similar to this second perspective, and to accommodate the third perspective she describes.

55. For a very insightful discussion of how and where formal civic education might interfere with parental authority, see McClain, "Domain," 1653–1661.

56. Flammang, *Taste*, 173; Oldenburg, *Great Good Place*. We should resist the temptation to think third spaces are always and necessarily hospitable to civil virtue. First, as I shall discuss below, some of them will be organized along principles that

are antithetical to constitutional values. Second, most if not all of them will suffer from the same sorts of inequalities and incivilities, such as racism, sexism, classism, and other significant inequalities and injustices, that characterize the polity in which they reside. Consider, for example, the civic space of farmer's markets. Rachel Slocum argues that "[w]hiteness in alternative food efforts rests, as well, on inequalities of wealth that serve both to enable different food economies and to separate people by their ability to consume. . . . These well-intentioned food practices reveal both the transformative potential of progressive whiteness and its capacity to become exclusionary in spite of itself." See Rachel Slocum, "Whiteness, Space and Alternative Food Practice," *Geoforum* 38 (2007): 520–533.

57. Flammang, *Taste*, 14.

58. James H. S. Bossard, "Family Table Talk: An Area for Sociological Study," *American Sociological Review* 8 (1943): 298.

59. The scholarly literature here is voluminous. In addition to Bossard, "Family Table Talk," see, for example, Anne Murcott, "Family Meals: A Thing of the Past?" in *Food, Health, and Identity*, ed. Pat Caplan (New York: Psychology Press, 1997). Especially interesting is Caron F. Bove and Jeffery Sobal, "Foodwork in Newly Married Couples: Making Family Meals," *Food, Culture, and Society* 9 (2006): 69. For an excellent treatment grounded in political theory, see Flammang, *Taste*, esp. chs. 1–6.

60. McClain, "Domain," 1618.

61. Flammang, *Taste*, 11.

62. Ibid., 20.

63. Flammang does not, however, address the question of congruence.

64. See, for example, *Troxel v. Granville* (2000); *Prince v. Massachusetts* (1944); *Pierce v. Society of Sisters* (1925); *Meyer v. Nebraska* (1923).

65. McClain, "Domain," 1619.

66. Nancy Rosenblum, *Membership and Morals: The Personal Uses of Pluralism in America* (Princeton, N.J.: Princeton University Press, 1998). See in particular Rosenblum's discussion of "liberal anxiety," 10–15.

67. See my discussion on pp. 126–139 and in Essay Three. See also Jane Mansbridge on "counterpublics," "Using Power/Fighting Power: The Polity," in *Democracy and Difference: Contesting the Boundaries of the Political*, ed. Seyla Benhabid (Princeton, N.J.: Princeton University Press, 1996).

68. See Harry Eckstein, "Congruence Theory Explained," CSD Working Papers, Center for the Study of Democracy, UC Irvine, 1997, http://repositories.cdlib.org/cgi/viewcontent.cgi?article=1120&context=csd.

69. Indeed, the distinction between private and public, and the terms of their interaction, is questionable. Foucault's concept of governmentality, for example, emphasizes how power is exercised by "disciplining people's bodily practices at a micro-level. Here politics is seen as sets of processes taking place on all levels of society, including those operating in the everyday lives of citizens." Bente Halkier, "Handling Food-related Risks: Political Agency and Governmentality," in *The Poli-*

tics of Food, eds. Marianne E. Lien and Brigitte Nerlich (New York: Bloomsbury Academic, 2004), 24, 33.

70. George Thomas, "The National University and Sustaining the American Constitutional Order" (unpublished ms., 2010), 26.

71. Herbert J. Storing and Murray Dry, eds., *The Complete Anti-Federalist* (Chicago: University of Chicago Press, 1981), 1:21.

72. *Federal Farmer* 16, 1/20/1788, in Storing and Dry, *Complete Anti-Federalist*, 2:324–325 (2.8.196).

73. Finn, *Civic*, 43.

74. Suzette Hemberger, "What Did They Think They Were Doing When They Wrote the U.S. Constitution, and Why Should We Care?" in Barber and George, *Constitutional Politics*, 148.

75. For a discussion of the meaning of the Second Amendment and civic constitutionalism, see David C. Williams, "Civic Constitutionalism, the Second Amendment, and the Right of Revolution," *Indiana Law Review* 79 (2004): 379.

76. See generally, Andrew Guthrie Ferguson, *Why Jury Duty Matters: A Citizen's Guide to Constitutional Action* (New York: New York University Press, 2013); Albert W. Dzur, *Punishment, Participatory Democracy, and the Jury* (New York: Oxford University Press, 2012).

77. Alexis de Toqueville, *Democracy in America*, ed. J. P. Mayer and Max Lerner (New York: Anchor, 1966), 254.

78. For a discussion of the civic importance of local juries—and by implication why its mention in the constitutional document of 1789 is further evidence of the text's civic and juridical dimensions—see Hemberger, *What Did They Think*, 144–147.

79. John Gastil and Phillip J. Weiser, "Jury Service as an Invitation to Citizenship: Assessing the Civic Value of Institutionalized Deliberation," *Policy Studies Journal* 34 (2007): 606. Gastil and Weiser conclude that jury service has a measurable impact on civic engagement beyond voting. They find in a large-sample survey of persons reporting for jury service that "a rewarding jury experience was associated with increases in a wide range of civic and political behaviors," 614. For a less sanguine view, see Lynn M. Sander, "Against Deliberation," *Political Theory* 25 (1997): 347. See also, Ferguson, *Why Jury Duty Matters*.

80. Gastil and Weiser, "Jury Service."

81. The Juridic Constitution educates as well. A judicial monopoly on the Constitution's meaning encourages us to retreat into our private lives and to delegate our public responsibilities to others. See Finn, *Civic*, 49–50.

82. McClain, "Domain," 1624–1625.

83. Rousseau, *On the Social Contract*, bk. 1, ch. 8: "On the Civil State," para. 1. http://etext.lib.virginia.edu/etcbin/toccer-new2?id=RouSoci.xml&images=images/modeng&data=/texts/english/modeng/parsed&tag=public&part=8&division=div2.

84. Jane Mansbridge, "Does Participation Make Better Citizens?" *Political Economy of the Good Society* 5 (1995): 1, 4.

85. Tocqueville, *Democracy in America*, 1:63.

86. Carole Pateman, *Participation and Democratic Theory* (Cambridge: Cambridge University Press, 1970), 42.

87. Center for Civic Education, "The Role of Civic Education: A Report of the Task Force on Civic Education," prepared for Second Annual White House Conference on Character Building for a Democratic, Civil Society, May 19–20 [1995]; quoted in McClain, "Domain," 1625.

88. Nor does it shed much light on the meaning of "responsible" citizenship. *Irresponsible* citizenship surely consists of inattention to our most basic civic obligations—to vote, to pay taxes, to serve on juries. See Howard Schweber, http://digitalcommons.law.umaryland.edu/cgi/viewcontent.cgi?article=1087&context=schmooze_papers. If failing to vote is a notable or significant dereliction of our civic duty, even if a sometimes rational one, should we not penalize it? See Andrew Sullivan, "Democracy's Odds," *The Dish*, September 22, 2012, http://andrewsullivan.thedailybeast.com/2012/09/democracys-odds.html. It is not unusual for states to couple civic obligations with penalties. Unexcused absences from jury service can be a criminal offense, as is refusal to make one's self available for the draft by failing to register. And voting itself is obligatory in several other constitutional democracies, often punishable at law. Nothing in the Juridic Constitution encourages citizens to view such actions as irresponsible or as failures of citizenship.

89. Papke, *Heretics in the Temple*, 6.

90. For a slightly different definition, see Linda McClain, who quotes approvingly from the Task Force on Civic Education: "developing the knowledge, understandings, and intellectual and participatory skills necessary for competent and responsible citizenship in our constitutional democracy." "Domain," 1625. There is much to commend in this definition, in particular its insistence upon understanding and participatory skills, in addition to rote facts, but it ignores the extent to which the determination of those skills and understandings is itself dependent upon how we conceptualize the term "constitutional democracy." The Juridic understanding would lead to a much narrower conclusion about what kinds of understandings and skills are necessary to sustain constitutional democracy than does the Civic.

91. Macedo, *Diversity*, 239.

92. Elizabeth Hollander, John Saltmarsh, Edward Zlotwoski, "The Civic Responsibility of Higher Education: Linking Legal Studies and Civic Engagement," *FOCUS* 18 (2002): 1.

93. See generally Brian Weinstein, *The Civic Tongue: Political Consequences of Language Choices* (New York: Longman, 1983).

94. See Harry C. Boyte, "Beyond Deliberation: Citizenship as Public Work," *Political Economy of the Good Society* 5 (1995): 17.

95. Morris Janowitz, *The Reconstruction of Patriotism: Education for Civic Consciousness* (Chicago: University of Chicago Press, 1983), 13.

96. See, for example, Amy Gutmann, who argues that children must acquire

"the capacity for rational deliberation to make hard choices in situations where authorities do not supply clear or consistent guidance," *Democratic Education*, rev. ed (Princeton, N.J.: Princeton University Press, 1999), 50–52; and Sherry, who argues similarly that critical thinking is a core element of citizenship education. Suzanne Sherry, "Responsible Republicanism: Educating for Citizenship," *University of Chicago Law Review* 62 (1995): 131.

97. Murphy, *Constitutional Democracy*, 376–377.

98. Alexander Stille, "Textbook Publishers Learn: Avoid Messing With Texas," *New York Times,* June 29, 2002, http://www.nytimes.com/2002/06/29/arts/text book-publishers-learn-avoid-messing-with-texas.html.

99. *Minersville v. Gobitis* (1940); *West Virginia v. Barnette* (1943).

100. Peter Riesenberg, *Citizenship in the Western Tradition: Plato to Rousseau* (Chapel Hill: University of North Carolina Press, 1994), 25.

101. I do not mean to imply that these decisions are uncomplicated or non-controversial. See James C. McKinley Jr., "Texas Conservatives Win Curriculum Change," *New York Times,* March 12, 2010, discussing a decision by the Texas Board of Education to "put a conservative stamp on history and economics textbooks, stressing the superiority of American capitalism, questioning the Founding Fathers' commitment to a purely secular government and presenting Republican political philosophies in a more positive light." http://www.nytimes.com/2010/03/13/education/13texas.html?_r=0.

102. Center for Civic Education, "National Standards for Civics and Government," http://www.civiced.org/index.php?page=stds_preface. For an analysis, see Murray Dry, "Review of National Standards for Civics and Government," *PS: Political Science and Politics* 29 (1996): 49–53.

103. Center for Civic Education, "National Standards for Civics and Government."

104. For an example, see Linda McClain, who argues that civic education ought to include teaching citizens about the history of not only racial discrimination, but also gender discrimination. Similarly, Toni Massaro has argued that "constitutional literacy" must include teaching about the history of "excluding people on the basis of race, religion, ethnicity, and gender," as well as instruction concerning contemporary conflicts about what constitutional concepts mean for us. See McClain, "Domain," 1635. For a general discussion of constitutional curricula in the founding era and immediately thereafter, see George Thomas, *The Constitution of Mind* (unpublished ms.).

105. See generally, Elizabeth Beaumont, *The Civic Constitution* (New York: Oxford University Press, 2014).

106. Another approach would deny that the internment orders were racist. This is apparently the approach favored in Texas. Consider this report from the *New York Times,* discussing a decision by the Texas Board of Education regarding public textbooks: "Mr. Bradley won approval for an amendment saying students should study 'the unintended consequences' of the Great Society legislation, affirmative action and

Title IX legislation. He also won approval for an amendment stressing that Germans and Italians as well as Japanese were interned in the United States during World War II, to counter the idea that the internment of Japanese was motivated by racism." See McKinley, "Texas Conservatives Win."

107. In the academy, see Mark V. Tushnet, "Defending Korematsu? Reflections on Civil Liberties in Wartime," *Wisconsin Law Review* 2003 (2003): 273; Eric A. Posner and Adrian Vermeule, *Terror in the Balance: Security, Liberty, and the Courts* (New York: Oxford University Press, 2007), ch. 3; Page Smith, *Democracy on Trial: The Japanese American Evacuation and Relocation in World War II* (New York: Simon and Schuster, 1995). Outside the academy, see Michelle Malkin, *In Defense of Internment: The Case for "Racial Profiling" in World War II and the War on Terror* (Washington, D.C.: Regnery Publishing, 2004).

108. See, for example, Alice Yang Murray, *What Did the Internment of Japanese Americans Mean?* (Bedford: St. Martins, 2000); Robert Sadamu Shimabukuro, *Born in Seattle: The Campaign for Japanese American Redress* (Seattle: University of Washington Press, 2001); Charles J. McClain, ed., *The Mass Internment of Japanese Americans and the Quest for Legal Redress* (New York: Routledge, 1994).

109. "Did the Court Err in Korematsu?" *Landmark Cases of the U.S. Supreme Court,* http://www.streetlaw.org/en/Page/313/Did_the_Court_Err_in_Korematsu.

110. Ibid.

111. Holloway Sparks, "Dissident Citizenship: Democratic Theory, Political Courage, and Activist Women," *Hypatia* 12 (1997): 75.

112. For a further discussion of the concept, see McClain, "Domain," 1625, discussing dissident citizenship in the context of campaigns for sex equality. See also Wayne D. Moore's important discussion of Frederick Douglass, "Constitutional Citizenship," in Barber and George, *Constitutional Politics,* 239–260.

113. Papke, *Heretics in the Temple.*

114. Several surveys seem to testify to this. For just one example, see Mark Hansen, "Flunking Civics: Why America's Kids Know So Little," *American Bar Association Journal,* May 1, 2011, located at: http://www.abajournal.com/magazine/article/civics/. The classic study is by Herbert McCloskey and Alida Brill, *Dimensions of Tolerance: What Americans Believe about Civil Liberties* (New York: Russell Sage, 1983).

115. APSA Task Force on Civic Education, Washington, D.C., "Civic Education," 2002, http://www.apsanet.org/content_4899.cfm?navID=568.

116. 647 F. Supp. 1194 (E.D. Tenn. 1986).

117. William A. Galston, *Liberal Purposes: Goods, Virtue, and Diversity in the Liberal State* (Cambridge: Cambridge University Press, 1991), 254.

118. See, for example, Nomi Maya Stolzenberg, "He Drew a Circle That Shut Me Out: Assimilation: Indoctrination, and the Paradox of a Liberal Education," *Harvard Law Review* 106 (1993): 609–611. See also Shelley Burt, "Religious Parents, Secular Schools: A Liberal Defense of an Illiberal Education," *Review of Politics* 56 (1994): 51.

119. Stephen Macedo, "Transformative Constitutionalism and the Case of Religion: Defending the Moderate Hegemony of Liberalism," in Barber and George, *Constitutional Politics*, 169; see also 170 for a reference to thriving. Macedo, we should note, subscribes to an understanding of constitutional democracy similar to the one proposed by Murphy, which I discussed above. I suspect Macedo's conception of citizenship is closer to Murphy's ideal citizen than to his adequate citizen.

120. For a very different treatment, see Stephen Arons, *Compelling Belief: The Culture of American Schooling* (New York: McGraw Hill, 1983).

121. Both *Pierce* and *Meyer* began in efforts in various states to require all students to attend public schools. Often these campaigns were virulently anti-Catholic and "patriotic," in some instances (Oregon is a notable example) sponsored by Masons and the KKK.

122. Jane Mansbridge on counterpublics, "Using Power/Fighting Power," note 67.

123. See Macedo, *Diversity*, 181–186.

124. National Constitution Center, http://constitutioncenter.org/ncc_edu_Land ing.aspx. The Center describes civic education as "the civic knowledge, skills, and dispositions necessary to participate in, preserve, and strengthen our republic. By promoting high-quality civic learning, America can live up to the ideal of a government of the people, by the people, and for the people."

125. Bill of Rights Institute, http://www.billofrightsinstitute.org/.

126. For a discussion of Constitution Day, see Alan E. Garfield, "What Should We Celebrate on Constitution Day," *Georgia Law Review* 41 (2006): 453. See also Linda Greenhouse, "Happy (Un)constitution(al) Day," *New York Times*, September 19, 2012, http://opinionator.blogs.nytimes.com/2012/09/19/happy-unconstitutional-day/.

127. See pp. 82–83.

128. Contrast with Bruce Ackerman's call for a national holiday called "Deliberation Day," in Balkin and Siegel, *Constitution in 2020*, 111–117.

129. Murphy, *Constitutional Democracy*, 193.

130. Stephen Elkin, "The Constitutional Theory of the Commercial Republic," *Fordham Law Review* 69 (2001): 1966.

131. Ibid.

132. Ibid.

133. Ibid., 195.

134. Ibid.

135. Ibid., 196.

136. For an overview, see Patrick M. Condon, *Design Charrettes for Sustainable Communities* (Washington, D.C.: Island Press, 2007).

137. *Clinton v. Cedar Rapids and the Missouri River Railroad*, 24 Iowa 455 (1868): "Municipal corporations owe their origin to, and derive their powers and rights wholly from, the legislature. It breathes into them the breath of life, without which they cannot exist. As it creates, so may it destroy. If it may destroy, it may abridge and control." See also John Forest Dillon, *The Law of Municipal Corporations* (New York: J. Cockcroft, 1873).

138. See *People v. Hurlbut,* 24 Mich. 44, 108 (1871): "[L]ocal government is a matter of absolute right; and the state cannot take it away." (Cooley, J., concurring.) Elkin, *Commercial Republic,* 197.

139. *Focus on Law Studies,* 1.

140. Dana Villa, *Public Freedom* (Princeton, N.J.: Princeton University Press, 2008), 9.

141. Murphy, *Constitutional Democracy,* 20. Or it draws too sharp a distinction between the concept of private interest and the civic life. Under the Civic Constitution, the state may properly assume that there is a public interest in private life, and the state may act to inculcate and reinforce public and civic virtues in the private sphere.

142. One might think this result is not so obvious as regards the children. See Justice Douglas, dissenting, in *Wisconsin v. Yoder* (1972). But this overlooks the Court's determination that the state did have an interest in requiring education through middle school, and its further observation that the Amish made provision for additional education, albeit oriented to competency as members of Amish communities.

143. See the majority opinion in *Pierce:* "No question is raised concerning the power of the State reasonably to regulate all schools, to inspect, supervise and examine them, their teachers and pupils; to require that all children of proper age attend some school, that teachers shall be of good moral character and patriotic disposition, *that certain studies plainly essential to good citizenship must be taught,* and that nothing be taught which is manifestly inimical to the public welfare" (emphasis added).

144. A response might be grounded in Justice Scalia's observation that religious minorities disadvantaged by the ruling should avail themselves of the political process, and note likewise that passage of the Religious Freedom Restoration Act is itself some evidence that the remedy is viable. Moreover, such a remedy might be said to be a paradigmatic instance of civic constitutionalism, insofar as it is an example of popular reaction to an unpopular judicial decision. To the extent this is so, the civic impulse is short-circuited by the Court in *Boerne.*

145. Consider Justice Stevens's concurring opinion in *Kiryas Joel v. Grumet* (1994): "New York created a special school district for the members of the Satmar religious sect in response to parental concern that children suffered 'panic, fear and trauma' when 'leaving their own community and being with people whose ways were so different.' To meet those concerns, the State could have taken steps to alleviate the children's fear by teaching their schoolmates to be tolerant and respectful of Satmar customs. Action of that kind would raise no constitutional concerns and would further the strong public . . . interest in promoting diversity and understanding in the public schools. Instead, the State responded with a solution that affirmatively supports a religious sect's interest in segregating itself and preventing its children from associating with their neighbors. The isolation of these children, while it may protect them from 'panic, fear and trauma,' also unquestionably increased the likelihood that they would remain within the fold, faithful adherents of their parents' religious

faith. By creating a school district that is specifically intended to shield children from contact with others who have 'different ways,' the State provided official support to cement the attachment of young adherents to a particular faith."

146. Sparks, "Dissident Citizenship." This is precisely the kind of activity the Civic Constitution embraces.

147. As Elkin notes, "there is far too little discussion of whether the working constitution contemplated in the written Constitution is one to which we ought to give our allegiance." Elkin, "The Constitutional Theory of the Commercial Republic," 1934. Elkin distinguishes between what he calls the written Constitution and the working Constitution. The distinction rests implicitly on the distinction between founding and maintaining, and reminds us that questions of allegiance are not and cannot be settled at the founding—they must be a continuing element of the constitutional enterprise. See also Levinson, *Constitutional Faith*; Barber, *On What the Constitution Means*.

148. Jack M. Balkin, *Constitutional Redemption: Political Faith in an Unjust World* (Cambridge, Mass.: Harvard University Press, 2011).

149. Levinson, *Constitutional Faith*. On the other hand, as Thomas observes in his discussion of proposals for a national university, the logic of the constitutional "mindset" was "not neutral." Hence, a curriculum (such as that proposed at the University of Virginia) could "embrace a sort of orthodoxy. There was room for wide spread disagreement within the contours of the American constitutional order, but the teaching of political principles unfolded from, and conformed to, the essential character of that order." *National University*, 31.

150. Barber, *On What the Constitution Means*, 127.

151. For a more extensive discussion, see John E. Finn, "Electoral Regimes and the Proscription of Anti-Democratic Parties," *Terrorism and Political Violence* 12 (2000): 51–77.

152. Stephen L. Elkin, "Constitutional Collapse," *Political Economy of the Good Society* 18 (2009): 7. Elkin argues that an enlightened citizenry is central to strengthening the "deliberative core" of the polity, and "It is important to recognize that it is through *experience* . . . that men and women can learn to judge political character" (emphasis in original).

153. Edward S. Corwin, *The President, Office and Powers, 1787–1984* (New York: New York University Press, 1984).

154. Kleinerman makes just this point in arguing against judicial supremacy in the arena of war powers. I explore this more fully in Essay Three. Benjamin Kleinerman, "'The Court Will Clean It Up': Executive Power, Constitutional Contestation, and War Powers," in Kautz et al., *The Supreme Court and the Idea of Constitutionalism* (Philadelphia: University of Pennsylvania Press, 2009), 235.

155. Eckstein's argument about vertical congruence, which we consider at pp. 104–105, also has relevance to vertical separations of power.

156. See generally Jean M. Yarbrough, *American Virtues: Thomas Jefferson on the Character of a Free People* (Lawrence: University Press of Kansas, 2009).

157. Mark V. Tushnet, *Taking the Constitution Away from the Courts* (Princeton, N.J.: Princeton University Press, 2000).

158. Robert F. Nagel, "Nationalized Political Discourse," *Fordham Law Review* 69 (2001): 2057.

159. Ibid., 2057. For exceptions, see 2058n7.

160. Ibid., 2058.

161. Ibid.

162. Ibid., 2059.

163. Ibid., 2072.

164. Ibid.

165. Bradley Hays, *Federal Constitutionalism* (unpublished ms.).

166. For a general overview of different approaches, see Akhil Reed Amar, "Five Views of Federalism: Converse-1983 in Context," *Vanderbilt Law Review* 47 (1994): 1229. For an argument that the Supreme Court ought to relax its supervisory role over state governments, see Nelson Lund, "Federalism and Civil Liberties," *University of Kansas Law Review* 45 (1996–1997): 1045.

167. See also our discussion of states' rights arguments in Essay One. Sotirios A. Barber, *The Fallacies of States' Rights* (Cambridge, Mass.: Harvard University Press, 2013), 3–4.

168. Bradley D. Hays, "A Place for Interposition? What John Taylor of Caroline and the Embargo Crisis Have to Offer Regarding Resistance to the Bush Constitution," *Maryland Law Review* 67 (2007): 200. Hays notes that many early uses of interposition involved challenges to executive authority.

169. Ibid.

170. Ibid., 219.

171. Robert A. Schapiro, *Polyphonic Federalism: Toward the Protection of Fundamental Rights* (Chicago: University of Chicago Press, 2009), see especially ch. 4.

172. Barber, *On What the Constitution Means*, ch. 3; 127.

173. Barber, *The Fallacies of States' Rights*.

174. Raz, "Authority and Interpretation," 178: "To secure continuity, the interpretation should be backward-looking."

175. Kahn, *Reign of Law*, 185. The perpetuity claim is underexplored in constitutional theory. See Finn, *Crisis*, ch. 1; Kenneth M. Stampp, "The Concept of a Perpetual Union," *Journal of American History* 65 (1978): 5–33.

176. Sotirios A. Barber, "Fidelity and Constitutional Aspirations," *Fordham Law Review* 65 (1997): 1757.

177. On veneration, see Sanford Levinson, *Our Undemocratic Constitution: Where the Constitution Goes Wrong* (New York: Oxford University Press, 2008), 16–17.

178. For two subtle and nuanced, but very different, discussions of faith, see Balkin, *Constitutional Redemption*, and Levinson, *Constitutional Faith*.

179. See Kahn, *Reign of Law*, 185.

180. Thus, in the words of Nathan Tarcov, "the authority of the Constitution must rest both on the aspiration of the people to be rational and on its habitual

reverence for a Constitution that has stood the test of time." Nathan Tarcov, "Ideas of Constitutionalism Ancient and Modern," in Kautz et al., *Constitutionalism*, 28.

181. See James Madison, *Federalist* #37: "When the Almighty himself condescends to address mankind in their own language, his meaning, luminous as it must be, is rendered dim and doubtful, by the cloudy medium through which it is communicated. Here then are three sources of vague and incorrect definitions; indistinctness of the object, imperfection of the organ of conception, inadequateness of the vehicle of ideas. Any one of these must produce a certain degree of obscurity. The Convention, in delineating the boundary between the Federal and State jurisdictions, must have experienced the full effect of them all."

182. Some of these compromises may, in turn, facilitate constitutional failure; see Essay Three.

183. For a comprehensive overview of the necessity of constitutional interpretation and its relationship to constitutional maintenance, see Murphy, *Constitutional Democracy*, 461–496.

184. Some constitutional theorists think constitutional interpretation is an essential part of constitutional theory. Joseph Raz, for instance, has argued that "[c]onstitutional theory comprises two major parts, an account of the authority of constitutions and an account of the way constitutions should be interpreted." Raz, "Authority and Interpretation," 157. Raz is correct that constitutional authority and constitutional interpretation are joined inquiries. He is also correct if we understand him to say that a comprehensive constitutional theory must account for the practice of constitutional interpretation. The stronger claim he appears to make, however, that two inquiries are equal in explanatory function and weight, or equal as explanatory objects in constitutional theory, is mistaken. This equality might be a fair description of the weight constitutional interpretation holds under the Juridic Constitution, but it is a mistake to equate interpretation and maintenance under the Civic Constitution. The Civic Constitution requires interpretation, but unlike the Juridic Constitution, which requires only interpretation, interpretation of the Civic Constitution is only a part of the project of constitutional maintenance.

185. Again, following Murphy's well-known framework of what, who, and how as setting the analytical framework for understanding constitutional interpretation. See *Constitutional Democracy*, chapter 14.

186. Lawrence G. Sager, *Justice in Plainclothes: A Theory of American Constitutional Practice* (New Haven, Conn.: Yale University Press, 2006); Tushnet, *Taking the Constitution*.

187. I use "interpretation" in the more restricted sense Whittington proposes, to distinguish it from "construction."

188. Sager, *Justice in Plainclothes*; Tushnet, *Taking the Constitution*; Finn, *Civic* (2001).

189. Sager, *Justice in Plainclothes*; Tushnet, *Taking the Constitution*.

190. Alexander M. Bickel, *The Least Dangerous Branch: The Supreme Court at the Bar of Politics* (New Haven, Conn.: Yale University Press, 1986).

191. James Bradley Thayer, "The Origin and Scope of the American Doctrine of Constitutional Law," *Harvard Law Review* 7 (1893): 129.

192. The term originates with Bickel. Bickel, *Least Dangerous Branch*. See also Barry Friedman, "The Birth of an Academic Obsession: The History of the Counter-majoritarian Difficulty," *Yale Law Journal* 112 (2002): 153.

193. For one recent example, but there are dozens of others, see Sager, *Justice in Plainclothes*.

194. Lawrence G. Sager, "Thin Constitutions and the Good Society," *Fordham Law Review* 69 (2001): 1989. See generally, Sager, *Justice in Plainclothes*.

195. Sager, "Thin Constitutions."

196. Ibid.

197. Ibid., 1991.

198. Tushnet, *Taking the Constitution*.

199. Sager, "Thin Constitutions," 1992.

200. Sager, "Thin Constitutions," 1995.

201. Ibid.

202. James E. Fleming, "Judicial Review without Judicial Supremacy," *Fordham Law Review* 73 (2005): 1380.

203. Sager, "Thin Constitutions," 1994.

204. Ibid.

205. Here it would be wise to recognize, as Fleming has observed, that there are a number of different types of popular constitutionalism and that there are important differences between them. Fleming identifies at least five distinct varieties—they differ chiefly, but not entirely, in the role they envision for judicial review. Fleming's third category—"popular constitutionalism that accepts constitutional limits on self-government and accepts judicial review, but rejects judicial supremacy" partially describes the conception of constitutional review imagined in the Civic Constitution, but the Civic Constitution also includes elements of Fleming's fifth variety, or "social movement constitutionalism . . . that focuses on how popular social movements outside the courts transform the norms that ultimately are accepted by the courts." Fleming, "Judicial Review," 1380–1381.

206. Ibid., 1390.

207. Ibid.

208. Ibid.

209. Sager, "Thin Constitutions," 1994.

210. As some have noted, "there are features basic to any democratic constitution that are likely to provide citizens with incentives of exactly the wrong kind—incentives that lead them to be selfish and lazy rather than public-spirited and active." Eisgruber, "Civic Virtue," 2137. Among these features are the electoral institutions often associated with large-scale democracies. According to some critics, elections themselves reduce citizens "to alienated spectators," and voting reduces to the pursuit of self-interest or partisanship. Benjamin Barber, "Neither Leaders Nor Followers: Citizenship under Strong Democracy," in *A Passion for Democracy:*

American Essays (Princeton, N.J.: Princeton University Press, 2000), 98. Moreover, as Eisgruber notes, some particular voting rules—such as the guarantee of anonymity—create an "incentive to act on the basis of self-interest" precisely because voters need not defend or account for their decision as an exercise of deliberation about the public good.

211. See generally Mark Tushnet, "Some Notes on Congressional Capacity to Interpret the Constitution," *Boston University Law Review* 89 (2009): 499.

212. In the sense that limits of jurisdiction and justiciability are self-imposed. There are obvious additional limitations that derive from Article 3 proper, including, for example, but not limited to Congress's authority to alter the appellate jurisdiction of Article 3 courts.

213. Martin S. Flaherty, "The Better Angels of Self-Government," *Fordham Law Review* 71 (2003): 1777. See also Christopher L. Eisgruber, *Constitutional Self-Government* (Cambridge, Mass.: Harvard University Press, 2007), 96–99.

214. Sager, "Thin Constitutions," 1994. Dean Rostow made a similar point over fifty years ago, arguing that judicial review helps to initiate and structure "a vital national seminar" on the meaning of the Constitution. Eugene V. Rostow, "The Democratic Character of Judicial Review," *Harvard Law Review* 66 (1952): 193. For a more recent argument about the Court's obligation, see Paul R. Dimond, *The Supreme Court and Judicial Choice: The Role of Provisional Review in a Democracy* (Ann Arbor: University of Michigan Press, 1989). See also the work on "demo-sprudence." Lani Guinier, "Forward: Demosprudence through Dissent," *Harvard Law Review* 22 (2008): 4. For a critical treatment, see Rosenberg, "Romancing the Court."

215. In this respect, it is worth consulting Joseph Goldstein's *The Intelligible Constitution: The Supreme Court's Obligation to Maintain the Constitution as Something We the People Can Understand* (New York: Oxford University Press, 1992).

216. For a similar argument, see Mary Ann Glendon, *Rights Talk: The Impoverishment of Political Discourse* (New York: Free Press, 1991). See also the exchange between Justices O'Connor and Scalia in *Planned Parenthood v. Casey*, 505 U.S. 833 (1992).

217. For an interesting examination of how litigation can influence the rhetorical strategies of popular constitutional argumentation, see Mary Ziegler, "Originalism Talk: A Legal History," FSU College of Law, Public Law Research Paper No. 638 (2013), http://papers.ssrn.com/sol3/papers.cfm?abstract_id=2274787. For a discussion in the specific context of same-sex marriage, see Michael J. Klarman, *From the Closet to the Altar: Courts, Backlash, and the Struggle for Same-Sex Marriage* (New York: Oxford University Press, 2012).

218. See Essay One, pp. 63–69, and accompanying text; see also Finn, *Crisis*, ch. 1.

219. Mark Tushnet, "The Supreme Court and Contemporary Constitutionalism: The Implications of the Development of Alternative Forms of Judicial Review," in Kautz et al., *Constitutionalism*, 128.

220. See Essay One, pp. 59–61.

221. See Mauro Cappelletti, *Judicial Review in the Contemporary World* (Indianapolis: Bobbs-Merrill, 1971).

222. First Inaugural Address of Abraham Lincoln, March 4, 1861, http://avalon.law.yale.edu/19th_century/lincoln1.asp.

223. Justice Kennedy also observed, "Shifting legislative majorities could change the Constitution and effectively circumvent the difficult and detailed amendment process contained in Article V." I take up Article 5 below, pp. 144–161.

224. On interpretive communities, see Harry H. Wellington, *Interpreting the Constitution* (New Haven, Conn.: Yale University Press, 1991); Ira L. Strauber, "The Supreme Court, Constitutional Interpretation, and Civic Education," paper delivered at the Annual Meeting of the Midwest Political Science Association, April 9–11, 1992, Chicago, Ill., 5; Ira L. Strauber, *Neglected Policies: Constitutional Law and Legal Commentary as Civic Education* (Durham, N.C.: Duke University Press, 2002).

225. Jeb Rubenfeld, "Legitimacy," in Alexander, *Constitutionalism*, 197.

226. Unless we are all originalists. See James E. Fleming, "The Balkinization of Originalism," *Maryland Law Review* 67 (2007): 10.

227. Richard A. Posner, "The People's Court" (Review of Kramer), *New Republic,* July 19, 2004, http://www.newrepublic.com/article/the-peoples-court#.

228. Jack M. Balkin, "Fidelity to Text and Principle," in Balkin and Siegel, *Constitution in 2020*, 20.

229. Jack M. Balkin, "The Distribution of Political Faith," *Maryland Law Review* 71 (2012): 1146.

230. A fuller discussion would require some attention to a related issue: if other constitutional actors are to interpret the Constitution, in what form will those practices occur and develop? One might find presidential interpretation in vetoes, signing statements, the opinions of the attorney general, the Office of Legal Counsel (OLC), and in public speeches. For a discussion, see Fleming, "Judicial Review," 1396. Just as judicial interpretation must account for institutional constraints, we would want to consider whether and how the institutional constraints of the executive branch (or of Congress) would affect its practice of constitutional interpretation.

231. See Raz, "Authority and Interpretation," 183–186; Murphy, *Constitutional Democracy*, ch. 14, passim.

232. Raz, "Authority and Interpretation," 178.

233. Ibid.

234. See Barber, "Fidelity and Constitutional Aspirations," 1758: "The ends of constitutional interpretation require that we view the constitutional text as adumbrating an ideal way of life that defines the nation's aspirations." Barber points to Lincoln's First Inaugural as an example of this approach.

235. Consider this observation by Wayne Moore on the meaning of the Fourteenth Amendment: "My premise is not that the Fourteenth Amendment's authority was perfected and its meaning locked in place at the time it was added to the text of the U.S. Constitution. Nor is the analysis oriented toward rediscovering or defending a univocal or singular conception of original meaning." Moore, "The Fourteenth

Amendment's Initial Authority: Problems of Constitutional Coherence," *Temple Political and Civil Rights Law Review* 13 (2004): 518.

236. Balkin, "Text and Principle," 35–36.

237. Barber, "Fidelity and Constitutional Aspirations," 1758. Barber also notes that we must take the prospect of its failure seriously; see Essay Three.

238. Keith Whittington, "It's Alive! The Persistence of the Constitution," *Political Economy of the Good Society* 11 (2002): 8, 10. See also Whittington, *Political Foundations of Judicial Supremacy*. Whittington has observed, "We should take heed of what James Madison and John Marshall, James Iredell and James Wilson said about written constitutions and judicial review not because they have special authority to tell us how the Constitution should be interpreted but because they thoughtfully grappled with making sense of the bold constitutional experiment that the former colonies were making and, in this case, their words hold wisdom for those of us seeking to continue and preserve their experiment in constitutional self-government." Keith E. Whittington, "How to Read the Constitution: Self-Government and the Jurisprudence of Originalism," *Heritage Foundation*, May 1, 2006, http://www.heritage.org/research/reports/2006/05/how-to-read-the-constitution-self-government-and-the-jurisprudence-of-originalism.

239. Fleming, "Judicial Review," 1394. There is a considerable literature on the principal-agent relationship in constitutional law. Among the more interesting pieces is Jonathon T. Molot, "Ambivalence about Formalism," *Virginia Law Review* 93 (2007): 2, 42–44. See also David S. Law, "A Theory of Judicial Power and Judicial Review," *Georgia Law Journal* 97 (2009): 723.

240. Antonin Scalia, *A Matter of Interpretation: Federal Courts and the Law* (Princeton, N.J.: Princeton University Press, 1997), 40–41.

241. See Murphy's response to Whittington's distinction between interpretation (originalist) and construction (political), *Constitutional Democracy*, 461n3.

242. Lee J. Strang, "Originalism as Popular Constitutionalism? Theoretical Possibilities and Practical Differences," *Notre Dame Law Review* 87 (2011): 253.

243. Saul Cornell, "*Heller*, New Originalism, and Law Office History: Meet the New Boss, Same as the Old Boss," *UCLA Law Review* 56 (2009): 1103.

244. Mitchell N. Berman, "Originalism Is Bunk," *Social Science Research Network,* December 30, 2007, http://papers.ssrn.com/sol3/papers.cfm?abstract_id=1078933. Berman concludes that are seventy-two varieties of originalism. Fleming identifies five different kinds of originalist arguments. Fleming, "Balkinization of Originalism."

245. Strang, "Originalism as Popular Constitutionalism," 262.

246. As Strang correctly perceives, "Whether originalism converges with popular constitutionalism is contingent on the form of originalism in question." Ibid., 254.

247. Balkin, *Constitution in 2020*, 6.

248. Jack M. Balkin, *Living Originalism* (Cambridge, Mass.: Belknap Press of Harvard University Press, 2011), 278.

249. Berman, "Originalism Is Bunk."

250. See James E. Fleming, making a plausible claim about both Balkin and Dworkin, in "The Balkinization of Originalism."

251. "Kagan: 'We Are All Originalists,'" *BLT: The Blog of Legal Times*, June 29, 2010, http://legaltimes.typepad.com/blt/2010/06/kagan-we-are-all-originalists.html.

252. Rubenfeld, "Legitimacy," 220.

253. Ibid.

254. Ibid., 222.

255. Ibid., 223.

256. Raz, *Authority and Interpretation*, 179.

257. Ibid., 180.

258. Later in the same discussion, Raz argues against the immediate objection that his discussion pays no mind to institutional considerations. Ibid., 183–186.

259. Ibid., 191.

260. For an argument that the historical inquiry demanded by originalism makes it incompatible with popular constitutionalism, see Ethan J. Leib, "The Perpetual Anxiety of Living Constitutionalism," *Constitutional Commentary* 24 (2007): 356–357.

261. For a fascinating argument that "originalism talk—the use of arguments, terms, and objectives associated with conservative originalism" had a substantial constraining effect upon public anti-abortion arguments in the 1970s and beyond, and in particular upon its "longstanding constitutional commitments involving the right to life, the personhood of the fetus, and the existence of rights based in natural law or human-rights principles," see Ziegler, "Originalism Talk."

262. Pitkin, "Idea of a Constitution."

263. For an insightful discussion of constitutional theory and American political development, see George Thomas, "What Is Political Development? A Constitutional Perspective" and "A Reply to Orren and Skowronek," *Review of Politics* 72 (2011): 275–294, 301–304.

264. Or consider Paul Kahn: "The opposition of revolution and reform creates the inevitable conundrums of constitutional amendment." *Reign of Law*, 63.

265. For a slightly different formulation, see Jacobsohn, *Constitutional Identity*, "A constitutional amendment may thus be considered problematic in one of two ways: (1) The change it portends could subvert the essentials of constitutional government . . . and (2) The change it portends could substantially transform or negate a fundamental political commitment of the constitutional order . . . central to the nation's self-understanding," 70.

266. John C. Calhoun, *A Discourse on the Constitution and Government of the United States* (1851 posthumous) (Cambridge, Mass.: Hackett, 1993).

267. James E. Fleming, "We the Exceptional American People," in Barber and George, *Constitutional Politics*, note 29.

268. Frederick Douglass, "The Constitution of the United States: Is It Pro-Slavery or Anti-Slavery?" a speech delivered in Glasgow, Scotland, March 26, 1860; Lysander Spooner, *The Unconstitutionality of Slavery* (1845), in *The Collected Works of Lysander Spooner* (1834–1886), 5 vols. (Indianapolis: Liberty Fund, 2013).

269. The claim that the Civil War Amendments amount to reconstitution is hardly novel. See, for example, Eric Foner, *Reconstruction: America's Unfinished Revolution, 1863–1877* (New York: Harper Collins, 1988), and Eric Foner, "The Strange Career of the Reconstruction Amendments," *Yale Law Journal* 108 (2009): 2003; Albert Bergesen, "Nation Building and Constitutional Amendments: The Role of the Thirteenth, Fourteenth, and Fifteenth Amendments in the Legal Reconstitution of the American Polity Following the Civil War," *Pacific Sociological Review* 24 (1981): 3–15; Mark E. Brandon, *Free in the World: American Slavery and Constitutional Failure* (Princeton, N.J.: Princeton University Press, 1998), 200–203. For a slightly different version of the claim, see Peggy Cooper Davis, "Introducing Robert Smalls," *Fordham Law Review* 69 (2001): 1695. See also Jacobsohn, *Constitutional Identity*, 60.

270. For contrasting accounts of the Reconstruction Amendments and what they say about the coherence of the constitutional order (as well as the possibility of its failure), see Walter F. Murphy, who argues broadly that the Fourteenth Amendment was fundamentally compatible with the larger commitments of the constitutional order, and Mark E. Brandon, who argues instead that the Fourteenth Amendment, because it "supplanted dominant conventional understandings of the meaning of the original Constitution," should be regarded as rendering the original Constitution "incoherent." Walter F. Murphy, "Slaughter-House, Civil Rights, and Limits on Constitutional Change," *American Journal of Jurisprudence* 12 (1987): 1, 6–7; Brandon, *Free in the World*, 201, 207. For an especially useful discussion, see Moore, "Fourteenth Amendment's Initial Authority," 522–524. Ackerman's discussion of the Reconstruction Amendments is also very useful. Ackerman, *We the People*, vol. 2: *Transformations* (Cambridge, Mass.: Belknap Press of Harvard University Press, 2000), esp. 99–124.

271. The most intriguing version of this question concerns whether there are some kinds of changes or amendments that must be ruled out altogether. In Murphy's formulation, the question is: "Would this amendment so violate the principles of constitutional democracy as to destroy the nature of the polity?" Murphy, *Constitutional Democracy*, 504. On "unconstitutional constitutional amendments," see Jacobsohn, *Constitutional Identity*, 35–83, and Walter F. Murphy, "Merlin's Memory: The Past and Future Imperfect of the Once and Future Polity," in *Responding to Imperfection: The Theory and Practice of Constitutional Amendment*, ed. Sanford Levinson (Princeton, N.J.: Princeton University Press, 1995), 163, 179 (1995); Richard Albert, "Nonconstitutional Amendments," *Canadian Journal of Law and Jurisprudence* 22 (2009): 5; Jason Mazzone, "Unamendments," *Iowa Law Review* 90 (2005): 1747.

There is now a sophisticated literature on this question. I raise the issue here simply to underscore how questions of change and amendment are caught up with the question of constitutional identity more broadly.

272. Frank I. Michelman, "Constitutional Authorship," in Alexander, *Constitutionalism*, 80.

273. Kahn, *Reign of Law*, 63.

274. Ackerman, *We the People: Foundations,* 6–16.

275. The term "foundational" has a contested meaning, or is used in different ways by different scholars. I take it to represent the position that there are certain foundational or constitutive principles that constitute the meaning of constitutions or constitutional government, and that these principles do not ground their authority in a democratic act of will, but instead in some other source. For a somewhat different use of the term, see Daniel A. Farber and Suzanna Sherry, *Desperately Seeking Certainty: The Misguided Quest for Constitutional Foundations* (Chicago: University of Chicago Press, 2004).

276. Ackerman appears to use the terms interchangeably. See Fleming, "We the Exceptional American People"; Finn, "Transformation or Transmogrification? Ackerman, Hobbes (as in Calvin and Hobbes), and the Puzzle of Changing Constitutional Identity," *Constitutional Political Economy* 10 (1999): 355.

277. In contrast, most constitutional theorists identify our constitutional commitments based on the constitutional text (though how we define "text" is a source of much dispute), and their authority traces to the political decision to be bound by that text. The constitutional commitments of the American people are self-selected, in the sense that we are bound only by the commitments that can fairly be traced to a collective decision to be so bound.

278. Finn, *Crisis,* ch. 1.

279. They are, in other words, constraints on constitutional populism, defined by Michelman as "the proposition that among the requirements of rightness in political arrangements the most basic is the entitlement of the people of a country . . . to decide the country's fundamental laws." Frank I. Michelman, "Populism," in Alexander, *Constitutionalism,* 76.

280. See Article 79(3) of the Basic Law: "Amendments to this Basic Law affecting the division of the Federation into Länder, their participation on principle in the legislative process, or the principles laid down in Articles 1 and 20 shall be inadmissible."

281. See Aaron-Andrew P. Bruhl, "Using Statutes to Set Legislative Rules: Entrenchment, Separation of Powers, and the Rules of Proceedings Clause," *Journal of Law and Politics* 198 (2003): 345, 375.

282. Fleming, "We the Exceptional American People," 107n29, referencing Finn.

283. See Walter F. Murphy, James E. Fleming, Sotirios A. Barber, and Stephen Macedo, *American Constitutional Interpretation* (Mineloa, N.Y.: Foundation Press, 2008), ch. 3.

284. On the other hand, see Michael Walzer, "Philosophy and Democracy," *Political Theory* 9 (1981): 379, 383.

285. Ackerman, *We the People: Foundations,* 11, 13, 388. For a fuller discussion, see Finn, "Transformation or Transmogrification?"

286. Additionally, he is unclear about what foundationalism means and whether there is a difference between foundationalism and rights-foundationalism. I incline to the view that the distinction has little merit.

287. Jeb Rubenfeld, *Freedom and Time* (New Haven, Conn.: Yale University Press, 2001), 174.

288. Ibid., 175.

289. Ibid., 174.

290. Ibid., 175.

291. To the extent Article 5 helps to establish federalism in the American constitutional order, it advances the separation of powers principle on a vertical plane. I have argued elsewhere that horizontal iterations of the separation of powers are a constitutive, or a foundational principle of constitutionalism itself, because they are instrumentally necessary to advance the principles of reason and deliberation in public affairs. Vertical separations of power, or federalism provisions, may also further that purpose, but unlike horizontal separations of power, they are not a constituent component of constitutionalism itself. Understanding the Constitution as civic in character gives us yet another reason why we might want to entrench a federalism provision (because it multiplies the number of arenas in which citizens can engage constitutional questions), but federalism proper is not itself a foundationalist imperative. On the other hand, Article 5 is entrenched in the American constitutional order, and it is so because the people have said so. Although I use the terms interchangeably, largely for convenience, there is a potentially significant difference between foundational or constitutive principles and entrenched provisions. Foundational principles inhere in the constitutional enterprise, and they govern that enterprise whether or not the people have elected to entrench them in a constitution.

292. Ackerman, *We the People: Foundations,* 92. But he admits that it repudiates "some of the fundamental principles." As we shall see, this is a mishmash. Which ones are fundamental but can be repudiated? May they all be repudiated? See discussion above on pp. 144–161.

293. Recall here my earlier reference to the Reconstruction Amendments in the United States.

294. In other words, another political order, perhaps one that is constitutional in character, perhaps not. See Finn, *Crisis,* ch. 1. Such changes are not transformations, but transmogrifications. See Finn, "Transformation or Transmogrification?"

295. Michelman, "Populism," 76.

296. But note also that there are many versions of popular constitutionalism. See Fleming, "Judicial Review," 1380–1381.

297. Finn, *Crisis,* ch. 1.

298. Michelman, "Populism," 76.

299. Nor is the Civic Constitution simply a liberal constitutional alternative to a populist constitutional order. In Michelman's formulation, a liberal constitutional order has as its primary concern "the rightness of the fundamental-legal regime" itself. Because the (constitutional) regime is, like any other, fundamentally coercive, we are entitled to ask why we should consent to be governed by it. We are entitled to a justification, or "a showing that the legal order's constitutive or fundamental laws

are substantively right, or at least that there is something about them giving reason for confidence in their tendency toward rightness." "Populism," 85.

300. "The question whether one generation of men has a right to bind another, seems never to have been stated. . . . Yet it is a question of such consequence not only to merit discussion, but place also among the fundamental principles of every government."

301. Note the formal title of "Articles of Confederation and Perpetual Union" too. See Stampp, "Perpetual Union," 5.

302. See, for example, the general discussion of precommitment in Jeremy Waldron, *Law and Disagreement* (New York: Oxford University Press, 2001), ch. 12, and a slightly different version of the same topic in Waldron, "Precommitment and Disagreement," in Alexander, *Constitutionalism*, 271–299; John Elster, *Ulysses and the Sirens: Studies in Rationality and Irrationality* (Cambridge: Cambridge University Press, 1984); Stephen Holmes, *Passions and Constraint: On the Theory of Liberal Democracy* (Chicago: University of Chicago Press, 1995).

303. Michael Perry has characterized provisions like Article 5 as "disestablishment" provisions, or as efforts to "make it difficult to disestablish" a directive. Michael J. Perry, "What Is the Constitution," in Alexander, *Constitutionalism*, 103.

304. For a discussion of how sunsets shift agendas and consequently affect the distribution of power on a temporal plane, see my article, "Sunset Clauses and Democratic Deliberation: Assessing the Significance of Sunset Provisions in Antiterrorism Legislation," *Columbia Journal of Transnational Law* 48 (2010): 442.

305. Rubenfeld, "Legitimacy," 195.

306. Ibid.

307. Consider Kahn: "The political order exists in the present, caught between the possibilities of looking backward or forward." *Reign of Law*, 180.

308. This is also true of Habermas, who concludes it "is not possible for the citizens to . . . reignite the radical democratic embers of the original position . . . for they find the results of the theory already sedimented in the constitution. . . . [T]he citizens cannot conceive of the constitution as a project." Jürgen Habermas, "Reconciliation through the Public Use of Reason: Remarks on John Rawls' Political Liberalism," *Journal of Philosophy* 92 (1995): 109–131. Habermas's objection to citizens' embracing or conceiving of the constitution as a project is bound temporally to the idea that there is a founding moment (he references the Rawlsian original position argument in particular). Moreover, Habermas implicitly conceptualizes the constitution not only in terms of linear temporality; he assumes too that it is essentially a juridic enterprise.

309. Thomas C. Schelling, "The Intimate Contest for Self-Command," *Public Interest* (Summer 1980): 94–118; also at http://www.nationalaffairs.com/public_interest/detail/the-intimate-contest-for-self-command.

310. Quoted in Gordon S. Wood, *The Creation of the American Republic: 1776–1787* (Chapel Hill: University of North Carolina Press, 1998), 379.

311. Thomas Jefferson, Letter to James Madison, Paris, 1789.

312. I am not suggesting, however, that identity is ahistorical or uninfluenced by the past. Indeed, it must be historical, or, to borrow a word from Rubenfeld, "inherited": "In any particular nation, this *we* will have been the product of a history, a constitutional struggle, usually waged at the cost of considerable blood and fortune." Rubenfeld, *Freedom and Time*, 80.

313. Larry Alexander and Frederick Schauer, "On Extrajudicial Constitutional Interpretation," *Harvard Law Review* 110 (1997): 1359, 1370.

314. Michelman, "Populism," 77.

315. Ibid.

316. Ibid., 85.

317. Ibid., 82.

318. Rubenfeld, "Legitimacy," 218.

319. Jeb Rubenfeld, "Of Constitutional Self-Government," *Fordham Law Review* 71 (2003): 1749, 1759.

320. Rubenfeld, "Legitimacy," 218.

321. Schelling, *Self-Command*, 96.

322. As Schelling has wondered, "Maybe the ordinary man or woman also doesn't behave like a single-minded individual because he or she isn't one," 97. One resulting problem, advanced by Schelling, is the problem of "authenticity," or "which is the authentic I"? 194. As Schelling asks the question, he assumes that "[t]here are two of me, one who was in command" earlier and one in the present. The problem is not fully resolved by supposing that there is a single "I" instead of multiple "I's," for we still must inquire into why one formulation, whether the earlier or the latter expression of preference—ought to govern the other. Schelling, "Self-Command." See also Stephen Holmes, "Precommitment and the Paradox of Democracy," in *Constitutionalism and Democracy*, ed. Jon Elster and Rune Slagstad (Cambridge: Cambridge University Press: 1988), 195–240; Waldron, "Precommitment and Disagreement," in Waldron, *Law and Disagreement* (New York: Oxford University Press, 2001).

323. Rubenfeld, *Time and Freedom*, passim.

324. Murphy, *Constitutional Democracy*, 516.

325. See, for example, Walzer, "Philosophy and Democracy." See also Murphy, *Constitutional Democracy*, 516.

326. Murphy, *Constitutional Democracy*, 515–516.

327. For a similar argumentative heuristic, see John Hart Ely, *Democracy and Distrust: A Theory of Judicial Review* (Cambridge, Mass.: Harvard University Press, 1980).

328. See Finn, *Transmogrification*, 363. For an especially fine treatment of the process-substance distinction, see James E. Fleming, *Securing Constitutional Democracy: The Case of Autonomy* (Chicago: University of Chicago Press, 2006). For a general discussion, see Sotirios A. Barber, *On What the Constitution Means*, chs. 4–5; Laurence H. Tribe, "The Puzzling Persistence of Process-Based Constitutional Theories," *Yale Law Journal* 89 (1980): 1063.

329. This is an argument reminiscent of Sager's under-enforcement thesis, which holds that some principles of political justice, to which the Constitution is committed in abstract, "are wrapped in complex choices of strategy and responsibility that are properly the responsibility of popular political institutions." *Justice in Plainclothes*, 87.

330. Although he does not propose dividing constitutional responsibility on this basis, Michael Perry notes an important distinction between "interpreting a text in the sense of trying to discern what norm a text represents and . . . interpreting a norm in the sense of determining what shape to give the norm in the context of a conflict in which the norm is implicated but in which it is also indeterminate." Perry, "What Is the Constitution," 118.

331. See, for example, Joseph A. Schumpeter, *Capitalism, Socialism, and Democracy*, 2nd ed. (New York: Routledge, 2006); Robert A. Dahl, *On Democracy* (New Haven, Conn.: Yale University Press, 2010).

332. Walzer, "Philosophy and Democracy."

333. For a concise discussion, see Murphy, *Constitutional Democracy*, 4–12.

334. Thomas Ehrlich, ed., *Civic Responsibility and Higher Education* (Westport, Ct.: Greenwood Publishing Group, 2000).

335. See my discussion of fidelity and bonds of fraternity in Essay One.

336. Robert D. Putnam, *Bowling Alone: The Collapse and Revival of American Community* (New York: Simon and Schuster, 2000).

337. See my discussion in Essay One, pp. 85–88, and Essay Two, pp. 103–105.

338. See generally Kenneth Burke, *A Grammar of Motives* (Berkeley: University of California Press, 1945). For a different use, see Jack M. Balkin and Sanford Levinson, "Constitutional Grammar," Yale Faculty Scholarship Series, January 1, 1994, http://digitalcommons.law.yale.edu/cgi/viewcontent.cgi?article=1269&context=fss_papers.

339. Jacobsohn, *Constitutional Identity*, 4–5; 103–117.

340. The classic statement is by Sanford Levinson, *Our Undemocratic Constitution*. For an insightful discussion of Article 5 as support for the living constitution, see David A. Strauss, *The Living Constitution: Inalienable Rights* (New York: Oxford University Press, 2010), 115–116.

341. See *Dillon v. Gloss* (1921) and *Coleman v. Miller* (1939).

342. For a different (and skeptical) treatment of the search for constitutional perfection, see Henry Monaghan, "Our Perfect Constitution," *New York University Law Review* 56 (1981): 353.

343. Levinson, *Our Undemocratic Constitution*, 16–17.

344. Sager, *Justice in Plainclothes*, 217.

345. Fleming, *Judicial Review*, 1385.

346. I want to stress again that civic responsibility for tending to the Constitution encompasses, but is not confined to, the practice of constitutional amendment.

347. Larry D. Kramer, *The People Themselves: Popular Constitutionalism and Judicial Review* (New York: Oxford University Press, 2005).

348. See generally Beaumont, *The Civic Constitution.*

349. See notes 104 and 111 above.

350. At the time I write, sixteen states have formally called for an amendment to overturn the Court's decision in *Citizens' United v. FEC* (2010).

351. Consider just one example: Many progressives embraced an understanding of civic participation and engagement that addressed constitutional principles. As portrayed by William Forbath, for example, Herbert Croley was a critic not only of the laissez-faire Constitution, but of what he thought to be constitutionalism in general and of judge-made constitutionalism in particular: "Thus, in good Deweyan fashion, Croley argued for a more experimental and participatory form of constitutional deliberation and decision." As is well known, Croley (as did some other progressives) in turn argued for a more engaged and responsible citizenry, a citizenry that must "'assume more of the duty of thinking over their political system,' their basic principles, and their 'fundamental political problems.'" Hence, Croley "framed the case for reform within a constitutional narrative and interpretation of the founding." William E. Forbath, "Constitutional Welfare Rights: A History, Critique, and Reconstruction," *Fordham Law Review* 69 (2001): 1821, 1830–1831.

352. In addition to Ackerman, see the important piece by Akhil Reed Amar, "The Consent of the Governed: Constitutional Amendment Outside Article V," *Columbia Law Review* 94 (1994): 457.

353. Ackerman, *We the People: Transformations*, ch. 1 and passim.

354. Ibid., 15–17.

355. Ibid., 88.

356. Ackerman, *We the People: Foundations*, 266.

357. Indeed, Ackerman identifies only three.

Essay Three: Failing

1. John E. Finn, *Constitutions in Crisis: Political Violence and the Rule of Law* (New York: Oxford University Press, 1991), 9.

2. My use of the word "rot" recalls but does not track very closely Justice Scalia's well-known reference to rot: "A society that adopts a bill of rights is skeptical that 'evolving standards of decency' always 'mark progress,' and that societies always 'mature,' as opposed to rot." Antonin Scalia, *A Matter of Interpretation: Federal Courts and the Law* (Princeton, N.J.: Princeton University Press, 1998), 40–41. In particular, I do not embrace the commitment to originalism that seems to some observers to be an implicit part of Scalia's reference. On the other hand, I do think Scalia is correct to suggest that societies do not always mature or progress; this seems inevitable for anyone who takes the possibility of constitutional failure seriously, or who rejects Condorcet's ruminations on perfectibility. Jean-Antoine-Nicolas de Caritat marquis de Condorcet, *Sketch for a Historical Picture of the Progress of the Human Mind* (1795). For an argument about the relative insignificance of constitutional forms, see Jean-Antoine-Nicolas de Caritat marquis de Condorcet, *Condorcet:*

Foundations of Social Choice and Political Theory (Northampton, Mass.: Edward Elgar, 1994).

3. Stephen L. Elkin, *Reconstructing the Commercial Republic: Constitutional Design after Madison* (Chicago: University of Chicago Press, 2006), 95.

4. See generally Juan J. Linz and Alfred Stepan, *The Breakdown of Democratic Regimes* (Baltimore: Johns Hopkins University Press, 1978).

5. Contrary to common belief, even most versions of grand unified theories (GUTS) are incomplete. Compare most of the proposed GUTS, for example, with the "Theory of Everything" (TOE). Even a TOE may not be possible; see Gödel's incompleteness theorems. For an overview, see Francesco Berto, *There's Something about Gödel: The Complete Guide to the Incompleteness Theorem* (Hoboken, N.J.: John Wiley and Sons, 2010).

6. For a similar point, see Sotirios A. Barber, "Constitutional Failure: Ultimately Attitudinal," in *The Limits of Constitutional Democracy*, ed. Jeffrey K. Tulis and Stephen Macedo (Princeton, N.J.: Princeton University Press, 2010), 21: "Distinguished from mere political emergencies . . . *constitutional* emergencies occur when officials believe they have no politically workable option that does not violate some constitutional rule or principle. Lincoln's case is the leading example."

7. James E. Fleming, "Toward a More Democratic Congress," *Boston University Law Review* 89 (2009): 629, 631.

8. Ibid., 640n16.

9. Ellen Kennedy made this point strongly in her excellent study of constitutional failure in the Weimar Republic. See Ellen Kennedy, *Constitutional Failure: Carl Schmitt in Weimar* (Durham. N.C.: Duke University Press, 2004).

10. Mark E. Brandon, "Constitutionalism and Constitutional Failure," in *Constitutional Politics: Essays on Constitution Making, Maintenance, and Change*, ed. Sotirios A. Barber and Robert P. George (Princeton, N.J.: Princeton University Press, 2001), 3. See also Brandon, "Constitutionalism and Constitutional Failure," *Political Economy of the Good Society* 9 (1999): 61, 64–66. I incline to the position that some of them, at least, reside in "constitutive principles" that inhere in our commitment to constitutionalism proper, whereas others will locate them elsewhere; Brandon, for example, locates them not in what he calls "transcendent" principles but instead in a constitutionalism conceived as an enterprise that requires, among things, written expression.

11. Keith E. Whittington, "Constitutional Constraints in Politics," in *The Supreme Court and the Idea of Constitutionalism,* ed. Steven Kautz, Arthur Melzer, Jerry Weinberger, and M. Richard Zinman (Philadelphia: University of Pennsylvania Press, 2009), 223.

12. More importantly, as Whittington has observed, "We cannot expect constitutionalism to operate outside of politics. It has to find a way to make itself felt within and through politics." Ibid. In part this is a way of saying, as have others, that "there is no constitution beyond politics," Steven Kautz et al., "Introduction," in ibid., 4, which I take to be a recognition that constitutions depend for their existence, and

preservation, upon political factors. See generally, Robert Dahl, *A Preface to Democratic Theory* (Chicago: University of Chicago Press, 1956).

13. Brandon makes the same argument about his four categories of failure: "Thus, a constitutional failure at one level may actually suggest or permit success at another, just as success in one may incite failure in another." Brandon, "Constitutionalism and Constitutional Failure," *Political Economy of the Good Society* 9 (1999): 63.

14. See Barber, "Constitutional Failure," 14.

15. Carl Schmitt, *Political Theology: Four Chapters on the Concept of Sovereignty,* trans. George Schwab (Chicago: University of Chicago Press, 2006).

16. Sotirios A. Barber, "Fidelity and Constitutional Aspirations," *Fordham Law Review* 65 (1997): 1757, 1759.

17. Barber, "Constitutional Failure," 18.

18. Ibid., 16. Barber adds to the definition of success as well as "marked by a certain quality of debate." Barber's criteria for constitutional success include "a healthy politics." A measure of the quality of public debate as a criterion of constitutional success is a consequence of the requirement that constitutional ends must be defended as publicly reasonable, which is in turn prompted by Barber's insistence that constitutional authority itself requires citizens who might choose to reject the Constitution through the exercise of reason.

19. Barber, "Constitutional Failure," 15.

20. Randy Barnett, *Restoring the Lost Constitution* (Princeton, N.J.: Princeton University Press, 2003), 33–38.

21. Michael P. Zuckert, "On Constitutional Welfare Liberalism: An Old-Liberal Perspective," in *Liberalism: Old and New,* ed. Ellen Frankel Paul, Fred D. Miller, and Jeffrey Paul (New York: Cambridge University Press, 2007), 313–315.

22. Barber, "Constitutional Failure," at 14. Barber's characterization of these accounts is a little oversimplified. Negative libertarian theorists might be said not to privilege negative rights over certain substantive ends, but instead to imagine an account of ends that includes the protection of negative liberties. Barber appears not to go so far, though he does concede that "some negative rights are functional to the pursuit of real ends." Ibid., 22n43. If I understand him correctly, Barber still denies that an account of ends might include, as ends themselves, the protection of negative liberties.

23. Ibid., 15.

24. For an argument of this sort, see Sheldon Wolin, *Democracy Incorporated: Managed Democracy and the Specter of Inverted Totalitarianism* (Princeton, N.J.: Princeton University Press, 2008).

25. See generally Walter F. Murphy, *Constitutional Democracy: Creating and Maintaining a Just Political Order* (Baltimore: Johns Hopkins University Press, 2007); see also James E. Fleming, "Successful Failures," in Tulis and Macedo, *Limits,* 36–37.

26. Elkin calls these examples of design failure in the Madisonian theory of the constitutional order. Stephen Elkin, "Constitutional Collapse: The Faulty Found-

ing," *Political Economy of the Good Society* 18 (2009): 1; see also Elkin, *Commercial Republic*, 51–83, 88.

27. A failure at the founding to constitute citizens equal to the task of constitutional maintenance might take another, but related, form. In *Free in the World*, Brandon concludes that the founders failed "to supply the means by which slaves could attach themselves and construct their political identities by reference to the Constitution. Simply, the Constitution placed slaves outside the bounds of political membership, of citizenship." *Free in the World: American Slavery and Constitutional Failure* (Princeton, N.J.: Princeton University Press, 1998), x. There is an argument, therefore, that some "constituting decisions of design," although necessary or useful at the founding, (i.e., not failures at the founding moment) nevertheless portend failure in constitutional maintenance. Slavery is the obvious example, but there may be others (some might argue the Second Amendment; other examples might include the electoral college), and some of them may lie fallow until much later in the constitutional enterprise.

28. Elkin, *Commercial Republic*, 36–42, 65–68.

29. John Finn, "The Civic Constitution: Some Preliminaries," in *Constitutional Politics: Essays on Constitution Making, Maintenance, and Change,* ed. Sotirios A. Barber and Robert P. George (Princeton, N.J.: Princeton University Press, 2001), 41–69.

30. Murphy, *Constitutional Democracy.*

31. See generally ibid.; see also Fleming, "Successful Failures," 36–37.

32. Murphy, *Constitutional Democracy*, 460–496; see also Fleming, "Successful Failures," 13. See the discussion of originalism as interpretive methodology in Essay Two. As I noted there, not all forms of originalism are as strictly preservationist as they might seem at first look. For a recent treatment, see Jack M. Balkin, *Living Originalism* (Cambridge, Mass.: Harvard University Press, 2011).

33. Representative of the older, classical literature are works by Clinton Rossiter, *Constitutional Dictatorship: Crisis Government in Modern Democracies* (Princeton, N.J.: Princeton University Press, 1948); Carl J. Friedrich, *Constitutional Reason of State: The Survival of the Constitutional Order* (Providence, R.I.: Brown University Press, 1957); and Carl Schmitt's several works. I think it fair if immodest to say that contemporary inquiry into these problems is marked by the publication in 1991 of my work *Constitutions in Crisis*. Among the many recent entries are Mark V. Tushnet, ed., *The Constitution in Wartime* (Durham, N.C.: Duke University Press, 2005), David Dyzenhaus, "Humpty Dumpty Rules or the Rule of Law: Legal Theory and the Adjudication of National Security," *Australian Journal of Legal Philosophy* 28 (2003): 29; David Dyzenhaus, "The Constitution of Law: Legality in a Time of Emergency," *Canadian Journal of Political Science* 40 (2007): 1072; Benjamin A. Kleinerman, *The Discretionary President: The Promise and Peril of Executive Power* (Lawrence: University Press of Kansas, 2009); Oren Gross and Fionnuala Ní Aoláin, *Law in Times of Crisis: Emergency Powers in Theory and Practice* (New York: Cambridge University Press, 2006); Oren Gross, "The Normless and Exceptionless

Exception: Carl Schmitt's Theory of Emergency Powers and the 'Norm-Exception' Dichotomy," *Cardozo Law Review* 21 (2000): 1835.

34. Rossiter's work should be counted as a part of the so-called Princeton school, not because it was part of Rossiter's dissertation under Corwin, but because its central themes and methods fall squarely within the definition of the Princeton school offered by Stanley C. Brubaker as "concerned . . . with a more fundamental, far-reaching, and interesting set of questions—the meaning and worth of constitutionalism, its preconditions, and the way of life it fosters. The Princeton School has thus reconnected public law with political theory and returned political science to a mode of discourse shared by citizens." Endorsement, *Princeton University Press,* http://press.princeton.edu/titles/7220.html.

35. See note 34 above; in addition, see Frederick Watkins, "The Problem of Constitutional Dictatorship," in *Public Policy*, ed. Carl J. Friedrich and Edwards S. Mason (Cambridge, Mass.: Harvard University Press, 1940), and *The Failure of Constitutional Emergency Powers under the German Republic* (Cambridge, Mass.: Harvard University Press, 1939); Karl Loewenstein, *Political Power and the Governmental Process* (Chicago: University of Chicago Press, 1957); Edward S. Corwin, *Total War and the Constitution* (New York: Alfred A. Knopf, 1947).

36. John Locke, *Two Treatises of Government* [1690], ed. Peter Laslett (Cambridge, Mass.: Harvard University Press, 1960); Second Treatise, sections 159–161, 163, 168.

37. Jeffrey K. Tulis, "The Possibility of Constitutional Statesmanship," in Tulis and Macedo, *Limits*, 115.

38. Arthur M. Schlesinger Jr., *The Imperial Presidency* (Boston: Houghton Mifflin, 1974).

39. Corwin, *Total War and the Constitution*.

40. For an argument that "a prerogative-as-outside-the-Constitution view" does not descend from the Roman model, but rather that it is "actually the American-inside-the-Constitution view of prerogative" that descends from the Roman model, see Tulis, "Constitutional Statesmanship," 119.

41. James Madison to Thomas Jefferson, October 17, 1788, in *The Papers of James Madison*, ed. William T. Hutchinson et al., 11 vols. (Charlottesville: University Press of Virginia, 1977), 11:297–300.

42. I made this point in *Crisis*, 18. For another treatment, see Kleinerman, *Discretionary President*.

43. Tulis, "Constitutional Statesmanship," 115.

44. Ibid., 116.

45. Bruce Ackerman, *Before the Next Attack: Preserving Civil Liberties in an Age of Terrorism* (New Haven, Conn.: Yale University Press, 2007).

46. Carl Schmitt, *Legality and Legitimacy* (1932), ed. Jeffrey Seitzer (Durham, N.C.: Duke University Press, 2004).

47. Ibid., 20.

48. Kennedy, *Constitutional Failure*. See my review of Kennedy, *Law and Politics*

Book Review 15, no. 1 (2005): 64–67, http://www.gvpt.umd.edu/lpbr/subpages/reviews/kennedy105.htm.

49. Kennedy, *Constitutional Failure*, 178. See also Gross, "Normless and Exceptionless Exception."

50. Kennedy, *Constitutional Failure*, 178.

51. Finn, *Crisis*, ch. 1.

52. Ibid.

53. Tulis, "Constitutional Statesmanship," 121.

54. Ibid., 123.

55. Ibid.

56. Barber argues that "formal institutional failure" is not "sufficient grounds for declaring constitutional failure, or at least unequivocal constitutional failure." Barber, "Constitutional Failure," 19. I would add that the absence of formal institutional failure is likewise not sufficient ground for determining that we have *not* failed.

57. See William F. Harris, "Constitution of Failure: The Architechtonics of a Well-Founded Constitutional Order," in Tulis and Macedo, *Limits*, 73: "A Constitution determines the traits of its own potential demise."

58. In Barber's terms, this is a welfarist account of the constitutional order. Barber, "Constitutional Failure," 17.

59. Keith Whittington, "Yet Another Constitutional Crisis," *William and Mary Law Review* 43 (2002): 2093, 2111.

60. What Murphy has called "constitutionism" might be a failure of this sort. Murphy, *Constitutional Democracy,* 6. Constitutionism refers to the practice of what others have called sham constitutionalism—or the decision to adopt a paper constitution without any real purpose to govern constitutionally or to embrace and respect the fundamental principles and ideals of constitutional government. These are failures of fidelity in the sense of failing to commit, but these are not truly cases of failure. Just as Barber and others have argued that failure presupposes a definition of success, failure also presupposes the *possibility* of success—a possibility not imagined in cases of constitutionism.

61. Among the earliest uses I know of is Lawrence Lessig, "Fidelity in Translation," *Texas Law Review* 71 (1993): 1165. Of course, the term has a long history outside its use in constitutional theory.

62. The element of loyalty leads some commentators to compare infidelity to the concept of treason. See David Luban, "Misplaced Fidelity," *Texas Law Review* 90 (2012): 673, 682.

63. Ibid., 681.

64. Ibid.

65. Ibid., 678.

66. Ibid., 684. The two forms of fidelity obviously interact in some ways. Even in questions that seem to implicate only personal fidelity, for example, there remain possible disputes between the parties (lovers, friends) about the terms of their obligation to each other. Disputes of this sort seem to implicate questions closer to interpretive

fidelity. The connection may be even more important when we take up fidelity as a religious concept.

67. Ibid., 685.

68. Lessig, "Fidelity in Translation."

69. Luban, "Misplaced Fidelity," 685.

70. Ibid.

71. Catherine Drinker Bowen, *Miracle at Philadelphia: The Story of the Constitutional Convention, May–September 1787* (Boston: Back Bay Books, 1986). For a general discussion on reverence for the law, see David Ray Papke, *Heretics in the Temple: Americans Who Reject the Nation's Legal Faith* (New York: New York University Press, 1998), 3–13.

72. See also Sotirios A. Barber, *On What the Constitution Means* (Baltimore: Johns Hopkins University Press, 1984), 165, who attributes a similar sentiment to Lincoln.

73. Hannah Arendt, *On Revolution* (New York: Penguin Classics, 1991), 198, 203–204; see also Dana Villa, *Public Freedom* (Princeton, N.J.: Princeton University Press, 2008), 104–105.

74. Thomas Jefferson, on reform of the Virginia Constitution. For a general treatment of this as a problem for constitutional governance, see Sanford Levinson, *Our Undemocratic Constitution: Where the Constitution Goes Wrong (and How We the People Can Correct It)* (New York: Oxford University Press, 2008).

75. Luban, "Misplaced Fidelity," 684: "[R]espect for the law really means respect for the people in one's political community."

76. Whittington, "Yet Another Constitutional Crisis," 2109.

77. Mark V. Tushnet, "Constitutional Hardball," *John Marshall Law Review* 37 (2004): 523.

78. Jack M. Balkin, "Constitutional Hardball and Constitutional Crises," *Quinnipiac Law Review* 26 (2008): 579, 581. A crisis, in contrast, involves substantially more than constitutional disagreement. See Sanford Levinson and Jack M. Balkin, "Constitutional Crises," *University of Pennsylvania Law Review* 157 (2009): 707 (arguing that a "constitutional crisis" refers to a turning point in the health and history of a constitutional order, not a mere constitutional disagreement, and identifying three types of constitutional crises).

79. Whittington, "Yet Another Constitutional Crisis," 2112. But note that generally, Whittington does not regard constitutional maintenance as a task reserved only to courts. See Keith E. Whittington, *Constitutional Construction: Divided Powers and Constitutional Meaning* (Cambridge, Mass.: Harvard University Press, 2001).

80. Finn, *Crisis*, ch. 1.

81. Ibid.; see also Brandon, *Free in the World*.

82. Walter Murphy later reached the same conclusion. See *Constitutional Democracy*, 15–16.

83. See Brandon's fourfold typology of constitutional failure: failures of discourse, of order, of a constitution, and of constitutionalism. *Free in the World*.

84. Finn, *Crisis*, ch. 1.

85. This might have seemed a more probable outcome at the end of the Second World War than it does now, when we speak (too) confidently (if not always approvingly) of the triumph of constitutionalism. See Bruce Ackerman, "The Rise of World Constitutionalism," *Virginia Law Review* 83 (1997): 771; Sujit Choudhry, "Globalization in Search of Justification: Toward a Theory of Comparative Constitutional Interpretation," *Indiana Law Journal* 74 (1999): 819. For a discussion of the related phenomenon of global judicialization, see Ran Hirschl, *Towards Juristocracy: The Origins and Consequences of the New Constitutionalism* (Cambridge, Mass.: Harvard University Press, 2004); C. Neal Tate and Torbjörn Vallinder , eds., *The Global Expansion of Judicial Power* (New York: New York University Press, 1997). For more general criticisms of political voluntarism, see A. John Simmons, *Moral Principles and Political Obligations* (Princeton, N.J.: Princeton University Press, 1979).

86. We might think this sort of failure is remote, especially given the territorial expansion of constitutionalism in the late-twentieth and early-twenty-first centuries; see citations listed in note 85 above. On the other hand, the question is live in the sense that many constitutional democracies continue to struggle with one important version of it: should the state have the constitutional authority to proscribe political parties that denounce constitutional democracy itself? This was one of the jurisprudential difficulties we associate with the Weimar Republic, but it has contemporary manifestations as well. See Walter F. Murphy, "May Constitutional Democracies 'Outlaw' a Political Party," in *Politicians and Party Politics*, ed. John Geer (Baltimore: Johns Hopkins University Press, 1998); John E. Finn, "Electoral Regimes and the Proscription of Anti-Democratic Parties," *Terrorism and Political Violence* 12 (2000): 51–57; Katherine A. Sawyer, "Rejection of Weimarian Politics or Betrayal of Democracy: Spain's Proscription of Batasuna under the European Convention on Human Rights," *American University Law Review* 52 (2003): 1531.

87. Finn, *Crisis*, ch. 1.

88. Or, as Brandon states, "the failure of a constitution may be for reasons compatible with the principles of constitutionalism or for reasons incompatible. Hence, it may or may not represent a simultaneous failure of constitutionalism." Brandon, "Constitutionalism and Constitutional Failure," *Political Economy of the Good Society* 9 (1999): 65.

89. Over time, however, I suspect this is unlikely. See the discussion on constitutional rot, pp. 187–219.

90. Murphy, *Constitutional Democracy*, 516 (emphasis added).

91. In forfeiting our constitutional inheritance, we may also have failed our past selves.

92. Luban, "Misplaced Fidelity," 685.

93. Jack M. Balkin, "The Distribution of Political Faith," *Maryland Law Review* 71 (2012): 1144, 1149.

94. Ibid., 1144.

95. Ibid., 1159.

96. As Linda McClain has observed, this understanding (there are others, as Mc-Clain notes) of the redemptive project requires a certain kind of citizenry, and consequently must imagine a certain kind of civic education. Linda C. McClain, "Constitutional and Religious Redemption: Assessing Jack Balkin's Call for a 'Constitutional Project,'" *Boston University Law Review* 92 (2012): 1187, http://www.bu.edu/law/central/jd/organizations/journals/bulr/documents/MCCLAIN_000.pdf. Putting the point more broadly, redemption is an effort to maintain and to sustain the constitutional order, and all efforts at constitutional maintenance must find ways to construct the citizenry it needs to sustain itself. See Essays One and Two for a discussion.

97. Ibid., 1203.

98. See Kurt Vonnegut, *Cat's Cradle: A Novel* (New York: Dell, 1963).

99. Adrian Vermeule, "Ideals and Idols," review of *Constitutional Redemption*, *National Review*, June 8, 2011, http://www.tnr.com/book/review/constitutional-redemption-jack-balkin#.

100. Joanne Finkelstein, *Dining Out: A Sociology of Modern Manners* (Cambridge: Polity Press, 1989), 174.

101. For a very different treatment of civility and incivility, see Susan Herbst, *Rude Democracy: Civility and Incivility in American Politics* (Philadelphia: Temple University Press, 2010), 6. Herbst argues that we should treat civility and incivility as "strategic assets," or as "a strategic tool or weapon in politics." In contrast, I approach the concept of civility as a constitutional norm and as a civic virtue.

102. Whittington, "Yet Another Constitutional Crisis," 2111; see also Fleming, "Successful Failures."

103. Herbst, *Rude Democracy*.

104. Ibid., 3.

105. Ibid., 9.

106. L. Sandy Meisel, "The Negative Consequences of Uncivil Political Discourse," *PS: Political Science and Politics* (July 2012): 406. For a content analysis that concludes that "American politics is not always characterized by heightened levels of incivility," see ibid., 402; see also Daniel M. Shea and Alex Sproveri, "The Rise and Fall of Nasty Politics in America," *PS: Political Science and Politics* (July 2012): 416–421.

107. Robert D. Putnam, "Bowling Alone: America's Declining Social Capital," *Journal of Democracy* 6 (1995): 77.

108. Stephen Carter, *Civility, Manners, Morals and the Etiquette of Democracy* (New York: Basic Books, 1998), 53.

109. What Calhoun calls "polite civility" as distinct from "political civility." Cheshire Calhoun, "The Virtue of Civility," *Philosophy and Public Affairs* 29 (2000): 251–275. See also Essay One, pp. 16–25.

110. For an insightful and comprehensive discussion of this point, see Richard Boyd, "The Value of Civility?" *Urban Studies* 43 (2006): 863, 872–875.

111. See, for example, Larry D. Kramer, *The People Themselves: Popular Constitutionalism and Judicial Review* (New York: Oxford University Press, 2005); Mark

V. Tushnet, *Taking the Constitution Away from the Courts* (Princeton, N.J.: Princeton University Press, 2000).

112. See, for, example, Amy Gutmann and Dennis Thompson, *Why Deliberative Democracy?* (Princeton, N.J.: Princeton University Press, 2004); Stephen Macedo, *Deliberative Politics: Essays on Democracy and Disagreement* (New York: Oxford University Press, 1999).

113. Janet A. Flammang, *The Taste for Civil Society: Food, Politics, and Civil Society* (Urbana: University of Illinois Press, 2009), 2.

114. Calhoun, *Civility*, 256.

115. Boyd, "Value of Civility?"

116. See Essay Two, pp. 100–105.

117. Linda C. McClain, "The Domain of Civic Virtue in a Good Society: Families, Schools, and Sex Equality," *Fordham Law Review* 69 (2001): 1617, 1619.

118. Barber, "Constitutional Failure," 16.

119. The influence might run in the other direction as well: constitutional incivility might contribute to cultural incivility, a suggestion implicit, I think, in Putnam's argument that there is a link between "democratic disarray" and the "broad and continuing erosion of civic engagement that began a quarter-century ago." Putnam, "Bowling Alone," 77.

120. Herbst argues too that education is a key component of improving civility. She favors "making argumentation central to education during vital years when young people learn to be citizens (middle school and high school.)" "We need to learn skills of 'hard listening'—making the best possible effort to *process* what is said to us. . . . But at the same time we need a national approach to thoughtful listening as well." Herbst, *Rude Democracy*, 126.

121. See, for example, John Denvir, *Freeing Speech: The Constitutional War over National Security* (New York: New York University Press, 2010).

122. Bruce Ackerman, *We the People,* vol. 1: *Foundations* (Cambridge, Mass.: Belknap Press of Harvard University Press, 1991), 5.

123. Murphy, *Constitutional Democracy*, 15.

124. Loewenstein, *Political Power*, 147–148. Sartori called them "façade" constitutions. Giovanni Sartori, "Constitutionalism: A Preliminary Discussion," *American Political Science Review* 56 (1962): 853. See also Beau Breslin, *From Words to Worlds: Exploring Constitutional Functionality* (Baltimore: Johns Hopkins University Press, 2009), 26–29.

125. I do not mean to suggest that strong-form review is a necessary, or a preferable, component of a functioning constitutional state. But it is characteristic of the Juridic Constitution. See Mark V. Tushnet, "The Supreme Court and Contemporary Constitutionalism: The Implications of the Development of Alternative Forms of Judicial Review," in Kautz et al., *Idea of Constitutionalism*, 116–117.

126. Kennedy, *Constitutional Failure*, 178.

127. This presupposes substantive limits of the sort Murphy imagined when he distinguished between efforts to amend the Constitution and those that repudiate it,

and which informed his argument that constitutionalism rests "squarely on substantive values, which inexorably shape the nature and character of the political community." *Constitutional Democracy*, 13–14. See also Fleming, "Successful Failures," 10–11. As I argued in *Constitutions in Crisis*, there are principles that transcend the specific normative commitments that are regime specific and contingent upon inclusion in specific constitutional texts. But even if one denies that there are such superordinate principles, it will still be the case that particular constitutional regimes will (purport to) subscribe to particularistic norms and values that make up its specific identity; rot can infect either form.

128. See Ellen Kennedy, writing of the appointment of Hitler as chancellor in 1933: "Liberal constitutionalism ceased in Germany. It was dead as legal theory, and its forms too would soon cease." *Constitutional Failure*, 169.

129. Although it is not quite the same, especially given the formal markers necessitated by the invocation of Article 48, Ellen Kennedy's discussion of Article 48 and presidential power in Weimar as "a means of governing without regard for parliament" makes a similar point. See Kennedy, *Constitutional Failure*, 159–160.

130. See Alice Ristroph, "Is Law? Constitutional Crisis and Existential Anxiety," 25 *Constitutional Commentary* 431 (2009). In Whittington's terms, rot is closer to a crisis of fidelity than an operational crisis, but neither term fits perfectly well. Whittington, "Yet Another Constitutional Crisis." Nor is constitutional failure the same thing as constitutional hardball, which may be, as Tushnet describes it, "distasteful," but is not a sign of systemic failure. Indeed, hardball seems an ordinary, not an exceptional, part of constitutional practice. Mark V. Tushnet, "Constitutional Hardball."

131. Or a failure of "the inner-most self." Finn, *Crisis*, 44.

132. Some readers might suggest a different approach. In such cases, they might argue, we simply confront an old and well-worn problem in the philosophy of law between natural law and legal positivism. Retracing Hart, Fuller, and Dworkin, we could argue whether a constitutional regime that pursues evil is law(ful), or whether citizens are under a legal (not moral) obligation to comply with regime rules. For a recent treatment, see Peter Kane, ed., *The Hart-Fuller Debate in the Twenty-First Century* (Oxford: Hart Publishing, 2010). In this essay, however, I am not so much concerned with the legality (or with the lawfulness and consequent problems of obligation) of such policies. Instead, I am interested in whether such regimes should be classified, as a matter of constitutional politics, as successful constitutional regimes or as constitutional failures.

133. See Essay One, pp. 71–72, where Moore explains why the law, which requires dichotomous results, is unsuited for asking questions about politics.

134. See Barber on the differences between proceduralist, negative libertarian, and welfarist accounts of failure, pp. 167–168.

135. For a concise overview, see Peter Margulies, *Law's Detour: Justice Displaced in the Bush Administration* (New York: New York University Press, 2010), 7–25; Austin Sarat and Nasser Hussain, eds., *When Governments Break the Law: The*

Rule of Law and the Prosecution of the Bush Administration (New York: New York University Press, 2010), 4–16.

136. See John E. Finn, "Counterterrorism Regimes and the Rule of Law: The Effects of Emergency Legislation on Separation of Powers, Civil Liberties, and Other Fundamental Constitutional Norms," in *The Consequences of Counterterrorism*, ed. Martha Crenshaw (New York: Russell Sage Foundation, 2010), 33–93; David Cole and James X. Dempsey, *Terrorism and the Constitution: Sacrificing Civil Liberties in the Name of National Security*, 1st ed. (Tallahassee: First Amendment Foundation, 2002), pt. 1. In particular, the Anti-Terrorism and Death Penalty Act of 1996, which allows the State Department to designate Foreign Terrorist Organizations and permits prosecutors to bring cases against individuals without proof that they have engaged in terrorism, aided or abetted terrorists, or planned to commit terrorism. Under the 1996 act, the government may freeze the assets of designated terrorist groups and use secret witnesses against those suspected of having links to terrorists. For a discussion on the use of torture prior to 9/11, see Marjorie Cohn, ed., *The United States and Torture: Interrogation, Incarceration, and Abuse* (New York: New York University Press), xiii.

137. See William Eskridge and John Ferejohn, *A Republic of Statutes: The New American Constitution* (New Haven, Conn.: Yale University Press, 2010), who argue that the Bush administration relied on the AUMF to defend itself against critics. In contrast, Stephen Griffin argues that the central point is that although President Bush "participated in the process that led to the September 2001 AUMF, the president made his position clear that he did not need it to prosecute the war." Stephen M. Griffin, "The National Security Constitution and the Bush Administration," *YLJ Online*, March 25, 2011, http://yalelawjournal.org/the-yale-law-journal-pocket-part/executive-power/the-national-security-constitution-and-the-bush-administration/. "In two subsequent letters to Congress, the President ignored the AUMF and apparently invoked his customary power to respond to sudden attacks by stating that he had ordered military action 'pursuant to my constitutional authority to conduct U.S. foreign relations and as Commander in Chief and Chief Executive.' This meant that the President did not intend to be bound even by the broad terms of the AUMF."

138. Cole and Dempsey, *Terrorism and the Constitution*. Cole and Dempsey argue that the federal government has used our fear of terrorism to increase government power at the expense of constitutional liberties, such as the presumption of innocence, the right to counsel, the right to confront witnesses, the right of access to the courts, and privacy rights. For an extended and insightful discussion of the effect of the security regime on speech and association freedoms, see Denvir, *Freeing Speech*.

139. It is important to note that the Patriot Act, although important, is just one part of a much larger counterterrorism regime in the United States. See Finn, "Counterterrorism Regimes," 37.

140. See Uniting and Strengthening America by Providing Appropriate Tools Requited to Intercept and Obstruct Terrorism (USA PATRIOT) Act of 2001, Pub. L. No. 107–56, 115 Stat. 272, Title II, §§ 201–04, 215.

141. See ibid. §§ 206–07, 214–15, 218, 225.

142. See ibid. Title III. Some of the material in this section is from my chapter "Counterterrorism Regimes and the Rule of Law," in Crenshaw, *Counterterrorism*.

143. See Sarat and Hussain, *When Governments Break the Law*, 5. There are two FISA courts—the Foreign Intelligence Surveillance Court and the Foreign Intelligence Surveillance Court of Review. According to the *Hartford Courant*, "Staff for . . . Connecticut senator [Blumenthal, D-Conn.] said that federal agencies have gone to the FISA courts nearly 34,000 times in its 33-year history to seek approval to put people under surveillance. They said the court has only denied 11 requests in that time." Wes Duplantier, "In Wake of Spying Uproar, Blumenthal Seeks Shake-Up In Secret Courts," August 1, 2013. http://www.courant.com/news/politics/hc-blumenthal-fisa-refoms-0802–20130801,0,5825744.story.

144. Howard M. Wasserman, "Constitutional Pathology, the War on Terror, and *United States v. Klein*," June 15, 2011, http://jnslp.com/wp-content/uploads/2011/06 /06_Wasserman.pdf. President Bush acknowledged the existence of the program and defended it as necessary for national security.

145. Margulies, *Law's Detour*, 18. In 2008, Congress passed the FISA Amendment Act, which authorizes the attorney general and the director of national intelligence to authorize special surveillance programs for as long as a year, permits emergency surveillance without a warrant for up to seven days, and retroactively immunizes communication service providers from liability for their participation in the earlier program. In 2013, the Supreme Court dismissed a challenge to the law by attorneys for detainees at Guantanamo and several journalists. Dismissing the suit for lack of standing, the Court's majority opinion by Justice Alito held that the plaintiffs could not demonstrate with sufficient certainty that their conversations had been monitored, or that if they had been monitored, it was under the authority of FISA and not some other federal law. *Clapper v. Amnesty Int'l.* (2013).

146. Several news reports indicate that the Obama administration has maintained the policy of seeking to evade congressional oversight. The *Washington Post*, for example, reported that the Obama administration "showed little interest in subjecting the NSA to meaningful oversight and public debate prior to Snowden's actions. When Sen. Ron Wyden (D-Ore.) asked for a 'ballpark figure' of the number of Americans whose information was being collected by the NSA last year, the agency refused to give the senator any information, arguing that doing so would violate the privacy of those whose information was collected. In March, at a Congressional hearing, Director of National Intelligence James Clapper answered 'no sir' when Wyden asked whether the NSA had collected 'any type of data at all on millions of Americans.' We now know his statement was incorrect. Wyden and Sen. Jay Rockefeller (D-W.V.) had also been pressing for almost four years for access to the Foreign Intelligence Surveillance Court's legal opinions interpreting Section 215 of the Patriot Act. Until Snowden's disclosures, the senators made no headway. Now, the Obama administration has announced it intends to release its legal interpretation of Section 215." Timothy B. Lee, "The President Is Wrong:

The NSA Debate Wouldn't Have Happened without Snowden," *Washington Post*, August 9, 2013, http://www.washingtonpost.com/blogs/the-switch/wp/2013/08/09/the-president-is-wrong-the-nsa-debate-wouldnt-have-happened-without-snowden/. For the administration's defense of the NSA programs, see Administration White Paper, "Bulk Collection of Telephony Metadata under Section 215 of the USA Patriot Act," August 9, 2013, http://s3.documentcloud.org/documents/750223/obama-administrations-legal-rationale-for.pdf. The Obama administration has also announced plans to create an independent advisory board to consider reforms to the current process: Scott Wilson and Zachary A. Goldfarb, "Obama Announces Proposals to Reform NSA Surveillance," *Washington Post*, August 9, 2013, http://articles.washingtonpost.com/2013–08–09/politics/41225487_1_president-obama-news-conference-edward-snowden.

147. In response to Senator Rand Paul's filibuster of President Obama's nominee to direct the CIA, Attorney General Holder disavowed presidential authority to assassinate an American citizen, not engaged in combat, on American soil. See http://www.cbsnews.com/8301–250_162–57573102/pauls-filibuster-provokes-answer-from-holder/. The precise terms of Senator Paul's question, and the administration's response, suggest strongly a number of unanswered questions about the extent of presidential power to use drones in American territory.

148. ACLU, "Al-Aulaqi v. Panetta: Lawsuit Challenging Targeted Killings," December 14, 2012, http://www.aclu.org/national-security/al-aulaqi-v-panetta.

149. Glenn Greenwald, "Obama Moves to Make the War on Terror Permanent," *Guardian*, October 24, 2012, http://www.guardian.co.uk/commentisfree/2012/oct/24/obama-terrorism-kill-list.

150. See Constitution Project, *The Report of the Constitution Project's Task Force on Detainee Treatment* (Washington, D.C.: Constitution Project, 2013), http://s3.documentcloud.org/documents/684407/constitution-project-report-on-detainee-treatment.pdf.

151. For an overview of the tactics and methods of interrogation authorized, see Cohn, *United States and Torture*, 283–284; Margulies, *Law's Detour*, 36–42.

152. The literature here is extensive. See, for example, Philippe Sands, *Torture Team: Rumsfeld's Memo and the Betrayal of American Values* (New York: Palgrave, Macmillan, 2008); Jane Mayer, *The Dark Side: The Inside Story on How the War on Terror Turned into a War on American Ideals* (New York: Doubleday, 2008); Jack Goldsmith, *The Terror Presidency: Law and Judgment Inside the Bush Administration* (New York: W. W. Norton, 2009); Harold H. Bruff, *Bad Advice: Bush's Lawyers in the War on Terror* (Lawrence: University Press of Kansas, 2009); Margulies, *Law's Detour*. I have been especially impressed by David Luban's treatment in "The Torture Lawyers of Washington," in *Legal Ethics and Human Dignity* (New York: Cambridge University Press, 2007), 162–205, and David Cole, *The Torture Memos: Rationalizing the Unthinkable* (New York: New Press, 2009).

153. On March 15, 2013, a federal district court ruled that the "National Security Letters" provision of the Patriot Act is unconstitutional. See *Hartford Courant*,

http://www.slate.com/blogs/future_tense/2013/03/15/susan_illston_district_court_
judge_declares_national_security_letters_unconstitutional.html.

154. Most of the controversy, as I read it, does not challenge the claim that torture
is incompatible with constitutional ideals or any plausible definition of human dignity, but is instead directed to the proposition that the principles of harsh interrogation utilized in the Bush administration were not, in fact, torture—or a variation of
one sort or another of the Bybee-Yoo memoranda. I leave that argument to apologists.

155. David Luban, "Liberalism, Torture, and the Ticking Time Bomb," in *The
Torture Debate in America,* ed. Karen J. Greenberg (New York: Cambridge: Cambridge University Press, 2007), 36. The literature on torture and the Constitution is
voluminous. Recent works include Joseph Margulies, *What Changed When Everything Changed: 9/11 and the Making of National Identity* (New Haven, Conn.: Yale
University Press, 2013); George C. Thomas III and Richard A. Leo, *Confessions of
Guilt: From Torture to Miranda and Beyond* (New York: Oxford University Press,
2012); Dean Reuter and John Yoo, *Confronting Terror: 9/11 and the Future of
American National Security* (Jackson, Tenn.: Encounter Books, 2011); Charles Fried
and Gregory Fried, *Because It Is Wrong: Torture, Privacy and Presidential Power in
the Age of Terror* (New York: W. W. Norton, 2010).

156. See Finn, *Crisis,* ch. 1; Finn, "Counterterrorism Regimes," ch. 1.

157. See 113 USC Sec. 2340.

158. Additionally in the category of *jus cogens* norms are slavery, genocide, and
wars of aggression.

159. Jeanne Mirer, "The Law of Torture and Accountability of Lawyers Who
Sanction It," in Cohn, *United States and Torture,* 244.

160. 630 F.2d 876 (2d Cir. 1980).

161. For an overview, see Constitution Project, "Detainee Treatment."

162. David J. Barron and Martin S. Lederman, "The Commander in Chief at
the Lowest Ebb — Framing the Problem, Doctrine, and Original Understanding,"
Harvard Law Review 121 (2008): 689.

163. Charlie Savage, "Suit over Targeted Killings Is Thrown Out," *New
York Times,* December 7, 2010, http://www.nytimes.com/2010/12/08/world/
middleeast/08killing.html.

164. ACLU, "Al-Aulaqi v. Panetta"; Charlie Savage, "Relatives Sue Officials
over U.S. Citizens Killed by Drone Strikes in Yemen," *New York Times,* July 18,
2012, http://www.nytimes.com/2012/07/19/world/middleeast/us-officials-sued-over-
citizens-killed-in-yemen.html.

165. Goldsmith, *Terror Presidency.*

166. See, for example, the Department of Justice White Paper, "Lawfulness of a
Lethal Operation Directed against a U.S. Citizen Who Is a Senior Operational Leader
of Al Qa'ida or an Associated Force," released on 1/29/2013, http://msnbcmedia
.msn.com/i/msnbc/sections/news/020413_DOJ_White_Paper.pdf.

167. See also Andrew Kent, "Just Don't Ask for Money," *Slate,* http://www
.slate.com/articles/news_and_politics/jurisprudence/2012/07/anwar_al_awlaki_suit_

courts_should_award_damages_in_national_security_cases_.html: "First, here's why there's no winning constitutional claim: Our founding document does not prevent the U.S. government from killing U.S. citizens when they have joined the enemy in an armed conflict, as Anwar al-Awlaki and Khan did, or when they are located in the same place as enemy fighters and killed as collateral damage, as was Abdulrahman al-Awlaki. . . . There were U.S. citizens in the ranks of enemy armies during both World War I and World War II, and no one thought that the U.S. Constitution protected them from being killed. The al-Awlakis and Khan are like them, even though they're not officially serving in a nation's army, because hostilities with terrorist groups can rise to the level of war, and the United States considers itself to be in just such an armed conflict with al-Qaida and its affiliates."

168. Josh Gerstein, "Eric Holder: Targeted Killings Legal, Constitutional," *Politico*, March 5, 2012, http://www.politico.com/news/stories/0312/73634_Page2.html.

169. Department of Justice White Paper, "Lawfulness of a Lethal Operation Directed against a U.S. Citizen," *MSN.com*, http://msnbcmedia.msn.com/i/msnbc/sections/news/020413_DOJ_White_Paper.pdf. Among the questions it leaves unresolved are issues surrounding the Administration's argument that it may target Americans who have "recently" been involved in terrorist "activities." A related question concerns the meaning of the word "imminent."

170. Glenn Greenwald, "Obama Moves to Make the War on Terror Permanent": "The central role played by the NCTC in determining who should be killed —'It is the keeper of the criteria,' says one official to the *Post*—is, by itself, rather odious. As Kade Crockford of the ACLU of Massachusetts noted in response to this story, the ACLU has long warned that the real purpose of the NCTC—despite its nominal focus on terrorism—is the 'massive, secretive data collection and mining of trillions of points of data about most people in the United States.'" Greenwald also observes, "the U.S. Government has seized and exercised exactly the power the Fifth Amendment was designed to bar ('No person shall be deprived of life without due process of law'), and did so in a way that almost certainly violates core First Amendment protections (questions that will now never be decided in a court of law)." Glenn Greenwald, "The Due-Process-Free Assassination of U.S. Citizens Is Now Reality," *Salon*, September 30, 2011, http://www.salon.com/2011/09/30/awlaki_6/. For a fuller discussion of some of the potential First Amendment issues, see Glenn Greenwald, "Criminalizing Free Speech," *Salon*, June 1, 2011, http://www.salon.com/2011/06/01/free_speech_4/.

171. Finn, *Crisis*, 21–28.

172. Ibid., 36–38.

173. Michael Ignatieff, *The Lesser Evil: Political Ethics in an Age of Terror* (Princeton, N.J.: Princeton University Press, 2004), quoting Finn.

174. Benjamin A. Kleinerman, "'The Court Will Clean It Up': Executive Power, Constitutional Contestation, and War Powers," in Kautz et al., *Idea of Constitutionalism*, 246.

175. For a discussion of these and similar proposals, see Gerard N. Magliocca,

"Legal Justifications for Drone Attacks on Citizens," *Balkinization*, February 5, 2013, http://balkin.blogspot.com/2013/02/legal-justification-for-drone-attacks.html.

176. Goldsmith, *Terror Presidency*.

177. Denvir, *Freeing Speech*, 6; 81–104. Although he does not directly make this argument, Denvir's work can be read to support my claim, developed below, that the security regime creates a civic culture of fear in place of reason and deliberation. On the other hand, Denvir is clear that, unlike some popular constitutionalists, he favors an active role for courts and judicial review; see ibid., 144–147.

178. See generally Denvir, *Freeing Speech*, esp. chs. 2, 3, and 4.

179. As evidenced, for example, by the Obama administration's continued reliance on the state secrets defense in federal litigation, and by its continued defense of executive branch employees, such as John Yoo, whom it has defended in lawsuits brought by former enemy combatants attempting to sue government officials who are responsible for their torture. See Bob Egelko, "Obama Lawyers Argue to Drop Yoo Torture Suit," *San Francisco Chronicle*, March 7, 2009, http://www.sfgate.com/news/article/Obama-lawyers-argue-to-drop-Yoo-torture-suit-3169031.php; Thomas Ehrlich Reifer, "Torture, War, and Presidential Power," in Cohn, *United States and Torture*, 313.

180. Griffin, "National Security Constitution."

181. John Yoo, *The Powers of War and Peace: The Constitution and Foreign Affairs after 9/11* (Chicago: University of Chicago Press, 2005).

182. Ibid.

183. Ibid.

184. Jay S. Bybee, "Memorandum for Alberto R. Gonzalez Counsel to the President," August 1, 2002, in Karen J. Greenberg and Joshua L. Dratel, *The Torture Papers: The Road to Abu Ghraib* (Cambridge: Cambridge University Press, 2005), 202.

185. United States Department of Justice, "Legal Authorities Supporting the Activities of the National Security Agency Described by the President," January 19, 2006, http://www.justice.gov/olc/2006/nsa-white-paper.pdf.

186. For a criticism of the concept that disputes the claim of its proponents that the unitary presidency actually facilitates public accountability, see my review of Goldsmith. Finn, http://www.bsos.umd.edu/gvpt/lpbr/subpages/reviews/goldsmith1008.htm.

187. See, for example, the Court in *United States v. Curtiss-Wright Exp. Corp.* (1936): "[The President] has . . . confidential sources of information. He has his agents in the form of diplomatic, consular and other officials. Secrecy in respect of information gathered by them may be highly necessary, and the premature disclosure of it productive of harmful results."

188. Consider the following quotation by Justice Clarence Thomas: "It is crucial to recognize that judicial interference in this domain destroys the purpose of vesting primary responsibility [to protect national security] in a unitary executive." *Hamdi v. Rumsfeld* (2004) (Thomas, J., dissenting). See also Cass Sunstein, "The Laws of Fear," *Harvard Law Review* 115 (2002): 1119; Victor V. Ramraj, "Terrorism, Risk

Perception and Judicial Review," in *Global Anti-Terrorism Law and Policy*, ed. Victor V. Ramraj, Michael Hor, and Kent Roach (New York: Cambridge University Press, 2005), 116.

189. A similar argument sometimes appears in the literature on the unitary presidency. Advocates of the unitary theory of the presidency argue that the president has expansive powers in times of crisis, powers that trump ordinary constitutional or legal constraints on presidential power. One of the arguments in favor of this understanding of the presidency is that it is said to encourage democratic accountability by centering responsibility in a single, identifiable location. See, for example, Steven G. Calabresi and Christopher S. Yoo, *The Unitary Executive: Presidential Power from Washington to Bush* (New Haven, Conn.: Yale University Press, 2008); Yoo, *Powers of War and Peace.*

190. Perhaps the most expansive proponent is John Yoo, *Powers of War and Peace*. For a response, see Helen Duffy, *The War on Terror and the Framework of International Law* (New York: Cambridge University Press, 2005).

191. Margulies, *Law's Detour*, 164.

192. Tulis, "Constitutional Statesmanship," 122–123.

193. See Schlesinger, *Imperial Presidency*; see also Charlie Savage, *Takeover: The Return of the Imperial Presidency and the Subversion of American Democracy* (Boston: Back Bay Books, 2007).

194. Calabresi and Yoo, *Unitary Executive.*

195. Denvir, *Freeing Speech*, 11–32.

196. Barron and Lederman, "Commander in Chief."

197. A term coined by Jack Goldsmith. See *Terror Presidency*. See also Jack Goldsmith and Eric A. Posner, *The Limits of International Law* (New York: Oxford University Press, 2005). Other academic proponents of the unitary presidency include Calabresi and Yoo, *Unitary Executive*. See also Eric A. Posner and Adrian Vermeule, *Terror in the Balance: Security, Liberty, and the Courts* (New York: Oxford University Press, 2007). In his review of Posner and Vermeule, Fisher writes: "They wrote the book 'to restrain other lawyers and their philosophical allies from shackling the government's response to emergencies with intrusive judicial review and amorphous worries' about the consequences of what executive officials do in the face of threats (p. 275). They criticize academic lawyers for being 'reflexively hostile to executive power in matters of national security' without ever having to be responsible for governmental decisions (p. 274)." Louis Fisher, review of Posner and Vermeule, *Law and Politics Book Review* 17 (2007): 696–700, http://www.bsos.umd.edu/gvpt/lpbr/subpages/reviews/posner-vermeule0807.htm.

198. Calabresi and Yoo, *Unitary Executive.*

199. See my review of Goldsmith, http://www.bsos.umd.edu/gvpt/lpbr/subpages/reviews/goldsmith1008.htm.

200. Mariah Zeisberg, "The Relational Conception of War Powers," in Tulis and Macedo, *Limits*, 169. See also Mariah Zeisberg, *War Powers: The Politics of Constitutional Authority* (Princeton, N.J.: Princeton University Press, 2013), 42.

201. See pp. 167–168; see also Barber, "Fidelity and Constitutional Aspirations."

202. Posner and Vermeule, *Terror in the Balance*, 12.

203. Zeisberg, "Relational Conception," 169. See also Zeisberg, *War Powers*.

204. Zeisberg, "Relational Conception," 169.

205. Stephen Holmes, *The Matador's Cape: America's Reckless Response to Terror* (New York: Cambridge University Press, 2007).

206. Benjamin A. Kleinerman, "In the Name of National Security: Executive Discretion and Congressional Legislation in the Civil War and World War I," in Tulis and Macedo, *Limits*, 108.

207. Eric A. Posner and Adrian Vermeule, *The Executive Unbound: After the Madisonian Republic* (New York: Oxford University Press, 2011); Louis Fisher, *Presidential War Power* (Lawrence: University Press of Kansas, 2004).

208. Richard G. Lugar, "The Obama administration's dangerous course on Libya," *Washington Post* (June 5, 2011), located here: http://articles.washington post.com/2011–06–05/opinions/35266502_1_war-powers-resolution-congressional-declaration-military-action.

209. Posner and Vermeule, *Executive Unbound*.

210. *Federalist* #70.

211. Fisher, review of Posner and Vermeule.

212. Some of this discussion appears also in Finn, "Counterterrorism Regimes," ch. 1.

213. John Riley, "Review Essay: Terrorism and the Constitution: Security, Civil Rights, and the War on Terror," *Alaska Justice Forum* 23 (2007): 2–5, http://justice .uaa.alaska.edu/forum/23/4winter2007/b_terrorism.html.

214. There is likely a relationship between the kind of public and legislative debate following terrorist attacks and the underlying nature of the polity, such as whether our conception of democracy is thin/populist or deliberative. In "Terrorism, Risk Perception and Judicial Review," 113–114, Victor V. Ramraj notes that "social forces amplify and distort our judgments about risk. . . . Only on a thin, populist conception, could democracy be seen simply as an aggregating mechanism for mere popular opinion, rather than as a sophisticated system to promote public deliberation. . . ." I would add that the kind of democratic deliberation and public dialogue Ramraj references are subsumed with the constitutional norm of civic deliberation I have described here.

215. Some critics, for example, have argued, "The failure was not in the provisions of the criminal law, but rather with the investigative bureaucracy that enforces those laws." Michael P. O'Connor and Celia M. Rumann, "Into the Fire: How to Avoid Getting Burned by the Same Mistakes Made Fighting Terrorism in Northern Ireland," *Cardozo Law Review* 24 (2003): 1657, 1734.

216. Finn, in "Counterterrorism Regimes," 73–78.

217. Griffin, "National Security Constitution."

218. Riley, "Review Essay."

219. The United States has sometimes been willing to forgo criminal convictions

in favor of keeping certain intelligence information classified, and of course one of the central justifications for extraordinary courts—such as military tribunals—is the necessity of confidentiality and secrecy. Kent Roach, "The Criminal Law and Terrorism," in Ramraj, *Global Anti-Terrorism*, 145.

220. Griffin, "National Security Constitution."

221. Denvir, *Freeing Speech*, 82.

222. Griffin, "National Security Constitution."

223. It is important to note that this superiority does not run simply to governments over citizens, but also is an important part of the dynamic of separation of powers. Thus, as suggested in *Federalist* #70, the presidency has distinct institutional advantages over Congress (and courts) in the conduct of foreign affairs generally. As we have seen, arguments about comparative institutional advantage almost always accompany expansions of presidential power; such arguments form an important part of the rationale for concepts like the unitary or preclusive presidency.

224. See Griffin, commenting on Eskridge and Ferejohn, and Ackerman's work concerning constitutional change: "[T]hese theories depend upon extensive public deliberation to ensure that the constitutional changes that they describe are accepted as authoritative. But this is precisely what was missing from post-9/11 America. President Bush thoroughly short-circuited the public sphere by immediately describing the conflict as a 'war,' and, indeed, a new world war; a meaningful public debate over the nature of 9/11 and whether it should be handled as a war or as a colossal crime against the United States thus never occurred." Griffin, "National Security Constitution."

225. Most suits to challenge the Bush Administration's NSA domestic surveillance programs have been dismissed on grounds of standing. For example, in *NSA v. ACLU*, 493 F.3d 644 (6th Cir. 2007), cert. denied, 178 S.Ct.1334 (2008), the 6th Circuit dismissed a suit challenging the constitutionality of the program because the plaintiffs (lawyers and journalists who alleged that some of their communications had been monitored) lacked standing, chiefly because, in the court's view, they could not prove they had been the targets of such surveillance. (And under the state secrets doctrine, such proof could not be established through discovery.) In his opinion for the majority, Judge Batchelder wrote that a plaintiff could "still assert his views in the political forum or at the polls. Slow, cumbersome, and unresponsive though the traditional electoral process may be thought at times, our system provides for changing members of the political branches when dissatisfied citizens convince a sufficient number of their fellow electors that elected representatives are delinquent in performing duties committed to them." Ibid., 676. As John Denvir has trenchantly pointed out, Judger Batchelder's decision is profoundly flawed. Its reliance on a model of civic or public deliberation to change public policy is misplaced in two ways. First, insofar as it suggests "that the victims could work to elect new members of Congress who would pass laws prohibiting the challenged conduct, that path would appear to be inadequate since Congress had already passed such a law (FISA) that the president had ignored," 142. Second, Judge Batchelder's opinion ignores how the state secrets

doctrine and the secrecy of security initiatives generally undermine the very possibility of the kind of conversation he proposes as a remedy.

226. Denvir, *Freeing Speech*, 33.

227. Ibid., 34.

228. See ibid.; Dempsey and Cole, *Terrorism and the Constitution*.

229. Jonathan Hafetz, *Habeas Corpus after 9/11: Confronting America's New Global Detention System* (New York: New York University Press, 2011), 3.

230. For a more extensive discussion of continuity and change in the Obama administration, see Hafetz, *Habeas Corpus*, ch. 13. On May 23, 2013, President Obama announced his intention to seek "refinement and ultimately repeal" of the AUMF and to continue to seek the closure of U.S. facilities at Guantanamo Bay. Obama stated, "Our systematic effort to dismantle terrorist organizations must continue. But this war, like all wars, must end. That's what history advises. That's what our democracy demands." Peter Baker, "Pivoting from a War Footing, Obama Acts to Curtail Drones," *New York Times*, May 23, 2013, http://www .nytimes.com/2013/05/24/us/politics/pivoting-from-a-war-footing-obama-acts-to-curtail-drones.html?pagewanted=all&_r=0. In the same speech, President Obama "embraced ideas to limit his own authority. He expressed openness to the idea of a secret court to oversee drone strikes, much like the intelligence court that authorizes secret wiretaps, or instead perhaps some sort of independent body within the executive branch. He did not outline a specific proposal, leaving it to Congress to consider something along those lines."

231. Greg Miller, "Plan for Hunting Terrorists Signals U.S. Intends to Keep Adding Names to Kill Lists," *Washington Post*, October 23, 2012, http://www .washingtonpost.com/world/national-security/plan-for-hunting-terrorists-signals-us-intends-to-keep-adding-names-to-kill-lists/2012/10/23/4789b2ae-18b3–11e2-a55c-39408fbe6a4b_story.html.

232. Quoted in Finn, "Counterterrorism Regimes," 88.

233. Louise Richardson, "Britain and the IRA," in *Democracy and Counterterrorism: Lessons from the Past*, ed. Robert J. Art and Louise Richardson (Washington, D.C.: United States Institute of Peace, 2007), 95; see also Finn, *Crisis*, 134.

234. Most of the sunsetted provisions concerned the authority of law enforcement authorities to engage in search and surveillance activities, located in Title II of the act. Under section 224, for example, several of the surveillance portions (200-level sections) in the act were coupled with sunset clauses.

235. This discussion borrows from a more comprehensive account; see John E. Finn, "Sunset Clauses and Democratic Deliberation: Assessing the Significance of Sunset Provisions in Antiterrorism Legislation," *Columbia Journal of Transnational Law* 48 (2010): 442.

236. Adapted from ibid.

237. Consider the following quote from President George W. Bush: "The war on terror we fight today is a generational struggle that will continue long after you and I have turned our duties over to others." State of the Union Address, January 23, 2007.

238. Oren Gross, "What Emergency Regime?" *Constellations* 13 (2006): 74–75.

239. Finn in Crenshaw, *Counterterrorism*, 44–45, 75–78. The pattern is evident in many other constitutional democracies; see ibid.

240. Gross, "What Emergency Regime?" 81–82.

241. O'Connor and Rumann, "Into the Fire," 1706.

242. Finn, *Crisis*, 134.

243. See Finn, in Crenshaw, *Counterterrorism*, ch. 1, passim. See also Art and Richardson, *Democracy and Counterterrorism*; Gross, "What Emergency Regime?" 74, 82.

244. It also undermines the concept of proportionality as a constitutional norm. Finn, in Crenshaw, *Counterterrorism*, 78–81.

245. See Michael Ratner, "From Guantanamo to Berlin: Protecting Human Rights after 9/11," in Cohn, *United States and Torture*, 203. For a general introduction, see Sarat and Hussain, *When Governments Break the Law*, esp. 3–4, 38–42, 104–105.

246. Villa, *Public Freedom*, 25.

247. See Posner and Vermeule, *Terror in the Balance*, for an argument that defends this posture. For another discussion of courts and emergency legislation, see Finn, in Crenshaw, *Consequences*, 61.

248. For a discussion of national security and executive power, see Ramraj, "Terrorism, Risk Perception," 114–118. For a review of the problems engendered in controlling executive power, see Mark Tushnet, "Controlling Executive Power in the War in Terrorism," *Harvard Law Review* 118 (2005): 2673.

249. See the remark by Justice Thomas in *Hamdi v. Rumsfeld* (2004): "It is crucial to recognize that judicial interference in this domain destroys the purpose of vesting primary responsibility [to protect national security] in a unitary executive" (Thomas, J., dissenting). In the United Kingdom, see *Liversidge v. Anderson* (1942). In Israel, see *Ajuri v. IDF Commander in the West Bank* (2002) (regarding the residences of Arabs in the West Bank), where Chief Justice Barak noted, "In exercising judicial review . . . we do not make ourselves into security experts. We do not replace the military commander's security considerations with our own. . . . Our job is to maintain boundaries . . . [and to insist that those decisions] fall into the range of reasonableness."

250. See my discussion of courts and antiterrorism regimes in Crenshaw, *Counterterrorism*, 61–70.

251. Savage, "Suit over Targeted Killings."

252. Ronald Dworkin, "Why It Was a Great Victory," *New York Review of Books* 55 (August 14, 2008): 13.

253. Hafetz, *Habeas Corpus*, 4.

254. See Michael Rosenfeld, "Judicial Balancing in Times of Stress: Comparing the American, British, and Israeli Approaches to the War on Terror," *Cardozo Law Review* 27 (2006): 2079, 2113. Hafetz similarly concludes that the victories are "both limited and incomplete." *Habeas Corpus*, 2.

255. Griffin, "National Security Constitution." See also Jenny S. Martinez, "Process and Substance in the War On Terror," *Columbia Law Review* 108 (2008): 1013.

256. For a similar argument, see Finn, "Sunset Clauses." See also Paul Quirk and William Bendix, "Deliberating Security and Democracy: The Patriot Act and Surveillance Policy, 2001–2008," paper presented at the Annual Meeting of the Midwest Political Science Association, 67th Annual National Conference, on file with the *Columbia Journal of Transnational Law*.

257. See, for example, Dworkin, "Why It Was a Great Victory."

258. But see Finn, in Crenshaw, *Counterterrorism*, 62–64.

259. As an aside: I was voted "Most Pessimistic" in my senior high school class. I was confident the much-coveted award would go to one of my closest friends.

260. Susan N. Herman, "Saving the Constitution from the War on Terror," *ACS Blog*, September 29, 2011, http://www.acslaw.org/acsblog/saving-the-constitution-from-the-war-on-terror. See generally, Herman, *Taking Liberties: The War on Terror and the Erosion of American Democracy* (New York: Oxford University Press, 2011).

261. Herman, "Saving the Constitution." As I indicated in Essay Two, federalism may play an important role in the sustenance of a robust civic culture, chiefly because it might provide civic space in which citizens can tend to their constitutional responsibilities.

262. Greenwald, "Due-Process-Free Assassination."

263. As Kleinerman has observed, "active contestation of constitutional constraints actually contributes to the healthiness of constitutionalism." Kleinerman, "'The Court Will Clean It Up,'" 242.

264. Henry Milner, for example, has argued that high levels of civic literacy are positively correlated with popular support for public policies that promote equality and political participation across all social classes. See Henry Milner in *Focus on Legal Studies: Teaching about Law in the Liberal Arts* 18 (2002): 15, http://www.americanbar.org/content/dam/aba/publishing/focus_on_law_studies/publiced_focus_fall_02.authcheckdam.pdf.

265. *Korematsu v. United States*, 323 U.S. 214 (1944).

266. Fleming, "Successful Failures," 29–46.

267. Villa, *Public Freedom*, 10: Fear is as "disempowering as privatism and economic insecurity."

268. See Finn, *Counterterrorism*, in Crenshaw, *Consequences*, arguing that some post-9/11 antiterrorism policies adopted in the United States violate the constitutional principles of accountability, transparency and deliberation, and proportionality. 57–81. On cognitive dissonance, see Leon Festinger, Henry W. Riecken, and Stanley Schachter, *When Prophecy Fails: A Social and Psychological Study of a Modern Group That Predicted the Destruction of the World* (Minneapolis: University of Minnesota Press, 1956).

269. Nathan Tarcov, "Ideas of Constitutionalism Ancient and Modern," in Kautz et al., *Idea of Constitutionalism*, 28.

270. For an extensive discussion of these specific doctrines, see Denvir, *Freeing Speech*, chs. 4 and 5.

Conclusion

1. Walter F. Murphy, *Constitutional Democracy: Creating and Maintaining a Just Political Order* (Baltimore: Johns Hopkins University Press, 2007), 345.

2. Dana Villa, *Public Freedom* (Princeton, N.J.: Princeton University Press, 2008), 5.

3. Ibid., 107.

4. Ibid., 5.

5. Christopher L. Eisgruber, "Civic Virtue and the Limits of Constitutionalism," 69 *Fordham Law Review* 69 (2001): 2131, 2132; see generally Jürgen Habermas, "Reconciliation through the Public Use of Reason: Remarks on John Rawls' Political Liberalism," *Journal of Philosophy* 92 (1995): 109–131.

6. Eisgruber, "Civic Virtue," 2132. See also Bruce Ackerman, *We the People, Foundations* (Cambridge, Mass.: Belknap Press of Harvard University Press, 1991), 5.

7. See Nancy L. Rosenblum, ed., *Liberalism and the Moral Life* (Cambridge, Mass.: Harvard University Press, 1989); James Meadowcraft, ed., *The Liberal Political Tradition: Contemporary Reappraisals* (Cheltenham: Edward Elgar Press, 1996).

8. Ronald Dworkin, "The Forum of Principle," *New York University Law Review* 56 (1981): 469.

9. Herbert McCloskey and Alida Brill, *Dimensions of Tolerance: What Americans Believe about Civil Liberties* (New York: Russell Sage, 1983). For an argument that most citizens are generally informed about political matters, but are not information "specialists," see Michael Delli Carpini and Scott Keeter, *What Americans Know about Politics and Why It Matters* (New Haven, Conn.: Yale University Press, 1996).

10. James E. Fleming and Linda C. McClain, "In Search of a Substantive Republic," *Texas Law Review* 76 (1997): 547.

11. See note 9 above. Recently, Henry Milner has argued that high levels of civic literacy are positively correlated with popular support for public policies that promote equality and political participation across all social classes. See Henry Milner, *Civic Literacy: How Informed Citizens Make Democracy Work* (Boston: Tufts University Press, 2002), 15.

12. See, for example, the discussion in Essay Two. See generally, Larry D. Kramer, *The People Themselves: Popular Constitutionalism and Judicial Review* (New York: Oxford University Press, 2005).

13. Even when the people have failed to honor constitutional precepts, we are too quick to equate their rejection as instances of public disregard for constitutional ideals instead of reasoned deliberation about whether, when, and why we ought to abide them. In some cases, the latter is not evidence of public incapacity for respecting constitutional norms, but is instead evidence of a deep, profound constitutional maturity—i.e., evidence of the capacity to reason about, to object to, and even sometimes to reject the claims of the Constitution.

14. Thomas Jefferson to William C. Jarvis, Sept. 28, 1820, in *The Writings of*

Thomas Jefferson, collected and ed. Paul Leicester Ford, 10 vols. (New York: G. P. Putnam's Sons, 1892–1899), 10:161.

15. See Robert F. Nagel, *Constitutional Cultures: The Mentality and Consequences of Judicial Review* (Berkeley: University of California Press, 1989), 26.

16. For arguments that seek to carve out a role for passion, emotion, and perhaps even prejudice in public deliberation, see Russell Muirhead, "Can Deliberative Democracy be Partisan?" *Critical Review* 22, no. 2–3 (2010); Bryan Garsten, *Saving Persuasion: A Defense of Rhetoric and Judgment* (Cambridge, Mass.: Harvard University Press, 2009); Sharon Krause, *Civil Passions: Moral Sentiment and Democratic Deliberation* (Princeton, N.J.: Princeton University Press, 2008); Nancy Rosenblum, *Membership and Morals: The Personal Uses of Pluralism in America* (Princeton, N.J.: Princeton University Press, 1998).

17. Thus, in the words of Nathan Tarcov, "the authority of the Constitution must rest both on the aspiration of the people to be rational and on its habitual reverence for a Constitution that has stood the test of time." Nathan Tarcov, "Ideas of Constitutionalism Ancient and Modern," in Steven Kautz, Arthur Melzer, Jerry Weinberger, and M. Richard Zinman, eds., *The Supreme Court and the Idea of Constitutionalism* (Philadelphia: University of Pennsylvania Press, 2009), 28.

18. Robert F. Capon, *The Supper of the Lamb: A Culinary Reflection* (New York: Macmillan, 2002), 19: "Man's real work is to look at the things of the world and to see them for what they are." For a general discussion, see Martha C. Nussbaum, *Love's Knowledge: Essays on Philosophy and Literature* (New York: Oxford University Press, 1992).

19. Paul W. Kahn, *The Reign of Law: Marbury v. Madison and the Construction of America* (New Haven, Conn.: Yale University Press, 1997), 179.

SELECTED BIBLIOGRAPHY

Ackerman, Bruce. *We the People*. Vol. 1: *Foundations*. Cambridge, Mass.: Belknap Press of Harvard University Press, 1993.

———. *We the People*. Vol. 2: *Transformations*. Cambridge, Mass.: Belknap Press of Harvard University Press, 2000.

Alexander, Larry, ed. *Constitutionalism: Philosophical Foundations*. Cambridge: Cambridge University Press, 2001.

Amar, Akhil Reed. *America's Unwritten Constitution: The Precedents and Principles We Live By*. New York: Basic Books, 2012.

Balkin, Jack M. *Constitutional Redemption: Political Faith in an Unjust World*. Cambridge, Mass.: Harvard University Press, 2011.

Balkin, Jack M., and Reva B. Siegel, eds. *The Constitution in 2020*. New York: Oxford University Press, 2009.

Barber, Benjamin R. *Strong Democracy: Participatory Politics for a New Age*. Berkeley: University of California Press, 1984.

Barber. Sotirios A. *The Fallacies of States' Rights*. Cambridge, Mass.: Harvard University Press, 2013.

———. *On What the Constitution Means*. Baltimore: Johns Hopkins University Press, 1984.

———. *Welfare and the Constitution*. Princeton, N.J.: Princeton University Press, 2003.

Barber, Sotirios A., and James E. Fleming. *Constitutional Interpretation: The Basic Questions*. New York: Oxford University Press, 2007.

Barber, Sotirios A., and Robert P. George, eds. *Constitutional Politics: Essays on Constitution Making, Maintenance, and Change*. Princeton, N.J.: Princeton University Press, 2001.

Beaumont, Elizabeth. *The Civic Constitution: Civic Visions and Struggles in the Path toward Constitutional Democracy*. New York: Oxford University Press, 2014.

Bower, Anne L., ed. *Recipes for Reading: Community Cookbooks, Stories, Histories*. Amherst: University of Massachusetts Press, 1997.

Boyte, Harry C. *Everyday Politics: Reconnecting Citizens and Public Life*. Philadelphia: University of Pennsylvania Press, 2005.

Brandon, Mark E. *Free in the World: American Slavery and Constitutional Failure*. Princeton, N.J.: Princeton University Press, 1998.

Breslin, Beau. *From Words to Worlds: Exploring Constitutional Functionality*. Baltimore: Johns Hopkins University Press, 2008.

Burgess, Susan. *Contest for Constitutional Authority*. Lawrence: University Press of Kansas, 1992.

Burt, Richard. *The Constitution in Conflict*. Cambridge, Mass.: Harvard University Press, 1992.

Dahl, Robert. *Democracy and Its Critics*. New Haven, Conn.: Yale University Press, 1980.

Dworkin, Ronald. *Law's Empire*. Cambridge, Mass.: Harvard University Press, 1986.

Dzur, Albert W. *Punishment, Participatory Democracy, and the Jury*. New York: Oxford University Press, 2012.

Eisgruber, Christopher L. *Constitutional Self-Government*. Cambridge, Mass.: Harvard University Press, 2007.

Elkin, Stephen L. *Reconstructing the Commercial Republic: Constitutional Design after Madison*. Chicago: University of Chicago Press, 2006.

Elkin, Stephen L., and Karol Edward Soltan, eds. *Citizen Competence and Democratic Institutions*. State College: Pennsylvania State University Press, 1999.

Eskridge, William N., and John Ferejohn. *A Republic of Statutes: The New American Constitution*. New Haven, Conn.: Yale University Press, 2010.

Ferguson, Andrew Guthrie. *Why Jury Duty Matters: A Citizen's Guide to Constitutional Action*. New York: New York University Press, 2013.

Finkelstein, Joanne. *Dining Out: A Sociology of Modern Manners*. New York: New York University Press, 1989.

Finn, John E. "The Civic Constitution: Some Preliminaries." In *Constitutional Politics: Essays on Constitution Making, Maintenance, and Change*, ed. Sotirios A. Barber and Robert P. George, 41–69. Princeton, N.J.: Princeton University Press, 2001.

———.*Constitutions in Crisis: Political Violence and the Rule of Law*. New York: Oxford University Press, 1991.

Fisher, Louis. *Constitutional Dialogues: Interpretation as Political Process*. Princeton, N.J.: Princeton University Press, 1988.

Fishkin, James S. *Democracy and Deliberation*. New Haven, Conn.: Yale University Press, 1993.

Flammang, Janet A. *The Taste for Civil Society: Food, Politics, and Civil Society*. Urbana: University of Illinois Press, 2009.

Fleming, James E. *Securing Constitutional Democracy: The Case of Autonomy*. Chicago: University of Chicago Press, 2006.

Fordham Law Review. *Symposium: The Constitution and the Good Society*. 69 Ford. L. Rev. 1569–2267 (2001).

Gerber, Scott Douglas. *To Secure These Rights: The Declaration of Independence and Constitutional Interpretation*. New York: New York University Press, 1995.

Goldstein, Joseph. *The Intelligible Constitution: The Supreme Court's Obligation to Maintain the Constitution as Something We the People Can Understand*. New York: Oxford University Press, 1992.

Gutmann, Amy, and Dennis Thompson. *Democracy and Disagreement*. Cambridge, Mass.: Harvard University Press, 1998.

———. *Why Deliberative Democracy?* Princeton, N.J.: Princeton University Press, 2004.

Habermas, Jürgen. *Between Facts and Norms: Contributions to a Discourse Theory of Law and Democracy*. Cambridge, Mass.: MIT University Press, 1998.

———. *The Crisis of the European Union: A Response*. Cambridge: Polity, 2012.

———. *Knowledge and Human Interests*. Boston: Beacon Press, 1962.

———. *The Structural Transformation of the Public Sphere: An Inquiry into a Category of Bourgeois Society*. Cambridge, Mass.: MIT University Press, 1991.

Hafetz, Jonathan. *Habeas Corpus after 9/11: Confronting America's New Global Detention System*. New York: New York University Press, 2011.

Herbst, Susan. *Rude Democracy: Civility and Incivility in American Politics*. Philadelphia: Temple University Press, 2010.

Jacobsohn, Gary J. *Constitutional Identity*. Cambridge, Mass.: Harvard University Press, 2010.

Jaffa, Harry. *Crisis of the House Divided: An Interpretation of the Issues in the Lincoln-Douglas Debates*. Chicago: University of Chicago Press, 1999.

Kahn, Paul W. *The Reign of Law: Marbury v. Madison and the Construction of America*. New Haven, Conn.: Yale University Press, 1997.

Kammen, Michael G. *A Machine That Would Go of Itself: The Constitution in American Culture*. New York: Alfred A. Knopf, 1986.

Kasson, John F. *Rudeness and Civility: Manners in Nineteenth-Century Urban America*. New York: Wang and Hill, 1991.

Kautz, Steven, Arthur Melzer, Jerry Weinberger, and M. Richard Zinman, eds. *The Supreme Court and the Idea of Constitutionalism*. Philadelphia: University of Pennsylvania Press, 2009.

Kingwell, Mark. *A Civil Tongue: Justice, Dialogue and the Politics of Pluralism*. University Park: Pennsylvania State University Press, 1995.

Klarman, Michael J. *From the Closet to the Altar: Courts, Backlash, and the Struggle for Same-Sex Marriage*. New York: Oxford University Press, 2012.

Kramer, Larry D. *The People Themselves: Popular Constitutionalism and Judicial Review*. New York: Oxford University Press, 2004.

Krause, Sharon. *Civil Passions: Moral Sentiment and Democratic Deliberation*. Princeton, N.J.: Princeton University Press, 2008.

Lanser, Susan Sniader. *Fictions of Authority: Women Writers and Narrative Voice*. Ithaca, N.Y.: Cornell University Press, 1992.

Levinson, Sanford. *Constitutional Faith*. Princeton, N.J.: Princeton University Press, 1988.

———. *Our Undemocratic Constitution: Where the Constitution Goes Wrong (and How We the People Can Correct It)*. New York: Oxford University Press, 2008.

——— ed. *Responding to Imperfection: The Theory and Practice of Constitutional Amendment*. Princeton, N.J.: Princeton University Press, 1995.

Macedo, Stephen. *Diversity and Distrust: Civic Education in a Multicultural Democracy*. Cambridge, Mass.: Harvard University Press, 2000.

————. *Liberal Virtues: Citizenship, Virtue, and Community in Liberal Constitutionalism*. New York: Oxford University Press, 1990.

Massaro, Toni Marie. *Constitutional Literacy: A Core Curriculum for a Multicultural Nation*. Durham, N.C.: Duke University Press, 1993.

Miller, William Lee. *Lincoln's Virtues: An Ethical Biography*. New York: Alfred A. Knopf, 2002.

Milner, Henry. *Civic Literacy: How Informed Citizens Make Democracy Work*. Boston: Tufts University Press, 2002.

Moore, Wayne. *Constitutional Rights and Powers of the People*. Princeton, N.J.: Princeton University Press, 1996.

Morone, James. *The Democratic Wish*. New York: Basic Books, 1990.

Murphy, Walter F. *Constitutional Democracy: Creating and Maintaining a Just Political Order*. Baltimore: Johns Hopkins University Press, 2007.

Nagel, Robert F. *Constitutional Cultures: The Mentality and Consequences of Judicial Review*. Berkeley: University of California Press, 1989.

Nino, Carlos Santiago. *The Constitution of Deliberative Democracy*. New Haven, Conn.: Yale University Press, 1996.

Oldenburg, Ray. *The Great Good Place: Cafes, Coffee Shops, Bookstores, Bars, Hair Salons, and Other Hangouts at the Heart of a Community*. Cambridge, Mass.: Da Capo Press, 1999.

Papke, David Ray. *Heretics in the Temple: Americans Who Reject the Nation's Legal Faith*. New York: New York University Press, 1998.

Putnam, Robert D. *Bowling Alone: The Collapse and Revival of American Community*. New York: Simon and Schuster, 2000.

Rawls, John. *Political Liberalism*. New York: Columbia University Press, 1993.

————. *A Theory of Justice*. Cambridge, Mass.: Harvard University Press, 1971.

Riesenberg, Peter. *Citizenship in the Western Tradition: Plato to Rousseau*. Chapel Hill: University of North Carolina Press, 1994.

Roelofs, H. Mark. *The Poverty of American Politics: A Theoretical Interpretation*. Philadelphia: Temple University Press, 1992.

Roman, Ediberto. *Citizenship and Its Exclusions: A Classical, Constitutional, and Critical Race Critique*. New York: New York University Press, 2010.

Rosenblum, Nancy. *Membership and Morals: The Personal Uses of Pluralism in America*. Princeton, N.J.: Princeton University Press, 2000.

Rubenfeld, Jed. *Freedom and Time: A Theory of Constitutional Self-Government*. New Haven, Conn.: Yale University Press, 2001.

Sager, Lawrence G. *Justice in Plainclothes: A Theory of American Constitutional Practice*. New Haven, Conn.: Yale University Press, 2006.

Sandel, Michael. *Democracy's Discontent: America in Search of a Public Philosophy*. Cambridge, Mass.: Harvard University Press, 1997.

Schapiro, Robert. A. *Polyphonic Federalism: Toward the Protection of Fundamental Rights*. Chicago: University of Chicago Press, 2009.

Sheehan, Colleen A. *James Madison and the Spirit of Republican Self-Government*. New York: Cambridge University Press, 2009.

Shils, Edward. *The Virtue of Civility*. Indianapolis: Liberty Fund, 1997.

Smith, Rogers M. *Civic Ideals: Conflicting Visions of Citizenship in U.S. History*. New Haven, Conn.: Yale University Press, 1997.

Snowiss, Sylvia. *Judicial Review and the Law of the Constitution*. New Haven, Conn.: Yale University Press, 1990.

Strauber, Ira L. *Neglected Policies: Constitutional Law and Legal Commentary as Civic Education*. Durham, N.C.: Duke University Press, 2002.

Sumner, Colin. *Reading Ideologies: An Investigation into the Marxist Theory of Ideology and Law*. New York: Academic Press, 1979.

Sunstein, Cass. *The Partial Constitution*. Cambridge, Mass.: Harvard University Press, 1993.

Tackach, James. *Lincoln's Moral Vision: The Second Inaugural Address*. Jackson: University Press of Mississippi, 2002.

Thomas, George. *The Madisonian Constitution*. Baltimore: Johns Hopkins University Press, 2008.

Tulis, Jeffrey K., and Stephen Macedo, eds. *The Limits of Constitutional Democracy*. Princeton, N.J.: Princeton University Press, 2012.

Tushnet, Mark V. *The New Constitutional Order*. Princeton, N.J.: Princeton University Press 2003.

———. *Taking the Constitution Away from the Courts*. Princeton, N.J.: Princeton University Press, 2000.

———. *Why the Constitution Matters*. New Haven, Conn.: Yale University Press, 2010.

Villa, Dana. *Public Freedom*. Princeton, N.J.: Princeton University Press, 2008.

Waldron, Jeremy. *Law and Disagreement*. New York: Oxford University Press, 2001.

Walzer, Michael. *What It Means to Be an American: Essays on the American Experience*. New York: Marsilo Publishers, 1996.

Weinstein, Brian. *The Civic Tongue: Political Consequences of Language Choices*. New York: Longman, 1983.

Wellington, Dean. *Interpreting the Constitution*. New Haven, Conn.: Yale University Press, 1991.

Whittington, Keith. *Constitutional Construction*. Cambridge, Mass.: Harvard University Press, 2001.

———. *Political Foundations of Judicial Supremacy: The Presidency, the Supreme Court, and Constitutional Leadership in U.S. History*. Princeton, N.J.: Princeton University Press, 2007.

Wills, Gary. *Lincoln at Gettysburg: The Words That Remade America*. New York: Simon and Shuster, 1993.

Wolin, Sheldon. *Politics and Vision: Continuity and Innovation in Western Political Thought.* Boston: Little, Brown, 1960.

———. *The Presence of the Past: Essays on the State and the Constitution.* Baltimore: Johns Hopkins University Press, 1990.

Wood, Gordon S. *The Creation of the American Republic 1776–1787.* Chapel Hill: University of North Carolina Press, 1998.

Zeisberg, Mariah. *War Powers: The Politics of Constitutional Authority.* Princeton, N.J.: Princeton University Press, 2013.

INDEX